NONTRADITIONAL FAMILIES:

Parenting and Child Development

NONTRADITIONAL FAMILIES:
Parenting and Child Development

edited by
MICHAEL E. LAMB
University of Utah

LEA LAWRENCE ERLBAUM ASSOCIATES, PUBLISHERS
1982 Hillsdale, New Jersey   London

Lawrence Erlbaum Associates, Inc., Publishers
365 Broadway
Hillsdale, New Jersey 07642

Library of Congress Cataloging in Publication Data
Main entry under title:

Nontraditional families.

   Bibliography: p.
   Includes indexes.
   1. Parenting.   2. Child development.   3. Parent
and child.   4. Family.   5. Broken homes.   6. Socialization.   I. Lamb, Michael E., 1953–
HQ755.8.N66   306.8'5   82-1474
ISBN 0-89859-178-3   AACR2

Printed in the United States of America
10   9   8   7   6   5   4   3   2   1

Contents

Preface   ix

List of Contributors   xi

1. **Parental Behavior and Child Development in
   Nontraditional Families: An Introduction**   1
   Michael E. Lamb
   Origins of the Traditional Family   2
   The Assumed Strengths of Traditional Families   3
   Outline of the Volume   6
   Summary   10

2. **The Two-Provider Family: Problems and Potentials**   13
   Phyllis Moen
   Introduction   13
   Work-Family Linkages   15
   Family Resources   18
   Family Functioning   26
   A Life-Course Perspective   33
   Two-Provider Families in a Societal Context   34
   Conclusions   37

3. **Maternal Employment and Child Development:
   A Review**   45
   Michael E. Lamb
   Why Mothers Seek Employment   47
   Effects of Maternal Employment on Family Dynamics   50
   Effects of Maternal Employment on Children   52
   Effects in Cultural Context   60
   Conclusion   62

v

4. The Ecology of Day Care   **71**
Jay Belsky, Laurence D. Steinberg, and Ann Walker
Day Care Today   77
The Effects of Day Care   85
The Wider Ecology of Day Care   99
Conclusions   108

5. Varying Degrees of Paternal Involvement in
Infant Care: Attitudinal and Behavioral Correlates   **117**
Michael E. Lamb, Ann M. Frodi,
Carl-Philip Hwang, and Majt Frodi
The Swedish Study: Goals and Procedure   119
Parental Attitudes: Prenatal and Postnatal   122
Observational Data: Three and Eight Months   129
Conclusion   134

6. Shared-Caregiving Families: An Australian Study   **139**
Graeme Russell
Introduction   139
Family Life-Styles   141
Adopting a Shared-Caregiving Life-Style   145
Possible Consequences   156
Continuing in a Nontraditional Life-Style:
    A Two-Year Follow-Up   161
Summary and Conclusions   164

7. Primary Caregiving and Role-Sharing Fathers   **173**
Norma Radin
Sample   177
Procedure   178
Data Analysis   181
Results   181
Discussion   196

8. Antecedents and Consequences of Various Degrees
of Paternal Involvement in Child Rearing: The Israeli Project   **205**
Abraham Sagi
Definition of Nontraditional Fathers   206
Descriptions of the Study with Urban Families   208
Components of Paternal Involvement   209
Determinants of Paternal Involvement   211
Consequences for Children   217
Fathers in other Israeli Subcultures   223
Conclusion   228

9. **Effects of Divorce on Parents and Children**   **233**
    E. Mavis Hetherington, Martha Cox, and Roger Cox
    Method   235
    Change, Stress, and Coping in Divorce   244
    Family Functioning   251
    The Child in School   263
    The Relationship of Parent-Child Interactions and
        Cognitive and Social Development in Children   272
    Support Systems   279
    Remarriage and Stepparents   281
    Comments and Cautions   285

10. **Social Development and Parent-Child Interaction
    in Father-Custody and Stepmother Families**   **289**
    *John W. Santrock, Richard A. Warshak,
    and Gary L. Elliott*
    Social Development and Parent-Child Interaction in
        Father-Custody and Mother-Custody Families   290
    Social Development and Parent-Child Interaction
        in Stepmother Families   303
    Summary   312

11. **Comparative Socialization Practices in Traditional
    and Alternative Families**   **315**
    *Bernice T. Eiduson, Madeleine Kornfein,
    Irla Lee Zimmerman, and Thomas S. Weisner*
    Comparisons of Traditional Married and
        Alternative Life-Style Families   319
    Differences Among Alternative Life-Styles:
        Communal Living Groups   325
    Differences Among Alternative Life-Styles:
        Social-Contract Families   330
    Differences Among Alternative Life-Styles:
        Single-Mother Families   332
    Discussion   336
    Development of Children   338

Author Index   347

Subject Index   357

Preface

Social scientists have speculated about and researched parental and family influences on child development for many decades. As sociopolitical philosophies have changed with time, so too have the assumptions and recommendations of social scientists. One assumption has remained consistent, however: the notion that "the ideal family" contains a primary caretaking and housekeeping mother, and a breadwinning father. Consequently, analyses of the family have consistently portrayed this traditional constellation as the most appropriate context in which to raise children. As a result, any and every deviation from "the norm" is usually considered briefly and disparagingly.

Even today, the traditional family is frequently recalled romantically and nostalgically by those who bemoan its demise. Demographers, however, doubt that traditional families were ever as common as these Cassandras imply and social scientists question whether the decline of the nuclear family can legitimately be viewed as the cause of the contemporary social malaise. Certainly, the traditional family is far from being today's norm, but unfortunately, little reliable evidence regarding the effects of 'deviant' family styles was available until recently. The goal of this volume is to review what we know about the effects of nontraditional family styles on parental behavior and child development. The focus is on those deviations that are most common and those whose analysis is most likely to advance our understanding of the socialization process. Thus the volume contains chapters on: families in which both parents are employed outside the home; families in which fathers share child-rearing responsibilities with their wives more equitably than parents in traditional families do; single-parent families headed by both men and women; 'alternative' family styles in which mothers deliberately choose to avoid legal marriage; and the effects of extrafamilial child care on child development. Three of the ten chapters (excluding the introduction) provide reviews of areas that have been explored in some detail; the remaining seven present hitherto unpublished results from various ongoing studies. These studies are being conducted in four different countries (the United States, Sweden, Israel, Australia), and the reader thus gets a broader perspective than if they were all conducted in the United States.

The chapters have been written so as to be valuable to a fairly diverse audience. Detailed results are presented for the use of research scientists and graduate students in developmental and clinical psychology and family sociology. In addition, the authors have elaborated upon their results and place them in a broader perspective so as to clarify their implications for mental health professionals (social workers, clinical and school psychologists, psychiatrists) and those responsible for the development of social policy concerning families and children. We have tried, in other words, to make the volume of interest to and comprehensible by all those who aim to understand or help families and children.

Of the many people who helped in the preparation of this book, I would especially like to thank my assistant, Karen Boswell, who kept track of the production process and prepared the subject index, and Art Lizza, our cheerful production editor at LEA.

Michael E. Lamb
Salt Lake City, Utah

List of Contributors

Jay Belsky, Division of Individual and Family Studies, Pennsylvania State University, University Park, Pennsylvania 16802

Martha Cox, Bush Program in Child Development and Social Policy, University of North Carolina, Chapel Hill, North Carolina 27514

Roger Cox, DIDDL, University of North Carolina, Chapel Hill, North Carolina 27514

Bernice T. Eiduson, Department of Psychiatry, University of California, Los Angeles, California 90024

Gary L. Elliot, Department of Psychology, University of Texas at Dallas, Richardson, Texas 75080

Ann M. Frodi, Department of Psychology, University of Rochester, Rochester, New York 14627

Majt Frodi, Institute of Psychology, University of Göteborg, S-400 20 Göteborg, Sweden

E. Mavis Hetherington, Department of Psychology, University of Virginia, Charlottesville, Virginia 22901

Carl-Philip Hwang, Institute of Psychology, University of Göteborg, S-400 20 Göteborg, Sweden

Madeleine Kornfein, Department of Psychiatry, University of California, Los Angeles, California 90024

Michael E. Lamb, Departments of Psychology, Psychiatry and Pediatrics, University of Utah, Salt Lake City, Utah 84112

Phyllis Moen, Department of Human Development and Family Studies, Cornell University, Ithaca, New York 14853

Norma Radin, School of Social Work, University of Michigan, Ann Arbor, Michigan 48109

Graeme Russell, School of Behavioural Science, Macquarie University, North Ryde, NSW 2113, Australia

Abraham Sagi, School of Social Work, University of Haifa, Mt. Carmel, Haifa, Israel

John W. Santrock, Department of Psychology, University of Texas at Dallas, Richardson, Texas 75080

Laurence D. Steinberg, Program in Social Ecology, University of California, Irvine, California 92717

Ann Walker, Child Development Council of Centre County, Bellefonte, Pennsylvania 19802

Richard A. Warshak, Health Sciences Center, University of Texas at Dallas, Richardson, Texas 75080

Thomas S. Weisner, Departments of Anthropology and Psychiatry, University of California, Los Angeles, California 90024

Irla Lee Zimmerman, Department of Psychiatry, University of California, Los Angeles, California 90024

NONTRADITIONAL FAMILIES:

Parenting and Child Development

1
Parental Behavior and Child Development in Nontraditional Families: An Introduction

Michael E. Lamb
University of Utah

Parental influences on children's development have been the topic of speculation for centuries and the focus of theory and research for decades. Although efforts in this area vary in degree of sophistication, one consistent similarity has been the preoccupation with traditional family styles and traditional parental roles. Thus social scientists have been concerned with family dynamics, parental behavior, and child development in two-parent families in which mothers are full-time homemakers and child tenders while fathers are primary breadwinners with minimal direct involvement in child rearing. The exclusive focus on families of this type has become increasingly anacronistic, however, in the face of demographic changes that have made traditional families less and less characteristic of the home environments in which most children are raised. The goal of this volume is to discuss in depth the ways in which various deviations from traditional family styles affect child-rearing practices and child development. In this introductory chapter, I review the principal issues raised in the study of nontraditional families and their impact on child development.

Many discussions regarding familial influences on early socioemotional development implicitly assume that the traditional family constellation is normative and thus the most adaptive for parents and children. Consequently, most considerations of nontraditional families begin with the assumption that these families are deviant and are likely to have adverse effects—especially on young children growing up in them. Fortunately, some of these deviant forms of family organization have been in evidence long enough for researchers to determine empirically just how valid is the assumption that "nontraditional is necessarily harmful." This is especially true of the concerns expressed about maternal employment and extrafamilial child care. On the other hand, many of the deviant styles and practices are of such recent origin that empirical research has only recently

1

become possible. In fact, several of the chapters in this volume present previously unpublished findings and descriptions of ongoing research projects, because no body of findings other than these exist.

In this introductory chapter, I first explore some myths about the origins and history of the traditional family. I then define the four principal assumptions that appear to form the basis of prevalent beliefs about the inherent superiority of traditional over nontraditional family forms. Finally, I present an outline of the volume, including an indication of the relationship between each chapter or set of chapters and the propositions mentioned in the second section.

ORIGINS OF THE TRADITIONAL FAMILY

The belief that traditional families are more likely to preserve marital harmony and raise psychologically healthy children has achieved widespread and almost unquestioned acceptance, even though this belief reflects an unwarranted equation between what *is* usually the case and what *should be* the case. Ironically, it also involves misunderstanding of both: (1) the origins of the traditional family organization; and (2) the social adaptability of the human species.

Contrary to the claims of its contemporary defenders, the traditional family is of relatively recent origin. Although it is true that women have always and everywhere assumed primary responsibility for the care of very young children, this responsibility has seldom precluded either major involvement in subsistence provision, or a substantial reliance on substitute or supplementary caretakers. Consider, for example, the !Kung Bushmen, whose habitat and hunting and gathering ways constitute a modern representation of the ecological niche for which we probably evolved. Among the !Kung, gathering by women accounts for about 60% of the group's nutritional needs, and toddlers or preschool-aged children are frequently left in the care of older children and siblings (Lee, 1979). The same occurs in a variety of other societies, whether they have hunting, gathering, pastoral, or agricultural economic bases. In most such primitive societies, furthermore, men are expected to assume a role in the socialization of young boys and so are more directly involved in child rearing than are most western fathers.

Shared responsibility for economic provision and (to a lesser extent) child rearing appears to have been common throughout most of our history. It was the industrial revolution that brought it to an end. Instead of working in fields or workshops close to their homes, men now had to travel to mines or factories located some distance away, and instead of perfecting skills they could proudly pass on to their sons, men found that their only salable commodity was unskilled labor. Concomitantly, the subsistence economy gave way to a monetary economy, and thus the fathers' yield in the form of wages increased in importance while the ability of their wives to contribute significantly declined. Nevertheless, most women (only the well-to-do were exempt) entered the paid labor force and remained employed except for a brief interruption for childbearing and child rearing. Only when general increases in wage levels occurred around the turn of the century did it become unnecessary for women to work. It was at this point that the traditional family style emerged—less than a century ago.

On the other hand, certain aspects of traditional family organization that are now being questioned by the proponents of alternative family style have been with us far longer. First of all, as noted previously, women have always and everywhere assumed primary responsibility for early child care. Until the invention of the nursing bottle, only the availability of wet nurses could free mothers of caretaking responsibilities, and this expensive option was available to relatively few. On the other hand, respect for the sanctity of childhood was limited, and so children were forced into paid employment at very young ages (Aries, 1962). Child care simply was not accorded much consideration by either men or women. Similarly, single parenthood has always been considered deviant, although the number of illegitimate children born to unwed mothers appears to have been considerable, especially in medieval cities and towns. Furthermore, the stigma attached to illegitimacy and divorce appears to have developed only in the Victorian era. Curiously, until the middle of the last century, children were customarily placed in the custody of their fathers (not their mothers) when marital dissolution occurred. Under common law, children were viewed as their fathers' possessions, and it was assumed that men could make satisfactory arrangements for their children's care until they remarried or their children reached adulthood. The "traditional" belief that custody should be awarded to mothers can be traced to judicial decisions in the 1830s, which gradually gained acceptance over the succeeding decades. In all, therefore, only the belief that women should assume primary responsibility for child rearing has been with us for more than a few generations.

The preceding paragraphs reveal also that human social behavior is highly adaptable in the face of changing ecological demands. To an extent unequalled in any other species, our behavior is highly flexible; relatively few of our behavior patterns appear to be innately and immutably organized. Indeed, the evolutionary success of our species is attributable to our enormous adaptability. Furthermore, even when biologically based predispositions exists, they are usually tendencies that bias behavior in certain directions subject to environmental demands; seldom do we find humans biologically impelled to behave in one way or another. This realization appears not to have occurred to contemporary guardians of the "natural" family organization.

THE ASSUMED STRENGTHS OF TRADITIONAL FAMILIES

The assumption that the traditional ways of allocating family responsibilities and of raising children are necessarily preferable is itself based on four principal axioms or beliefs, namely: (1) children need two parents, one of each sex; (2) family responsibilities should be divided between the parents, with fathers as economic providers and mothers as homemakers and caretakers, because this distribution of responsibilities mirrors the sex roles prevalent in the society at large; (3) mothers are better suited for child rearing and caretaking than fathers are; (4) primary caretaking for young children should be provided by family members. Each of these assumptions are subject to scrutiny in the chapters that follow.

In the first three chapters, the focus is on two-parent families in which both parents contribute to economic support of the family. There are two sources of concern here. First, the traditional division of parental responsibilities is altered, with fathers sharing the responsibility for breadwinning, and so (it is argued) losing authority and status. Second, some of the responsibility for child care is shifted to persons outside the family. These persons are said to be less reliable and consistent and to lack the commitment that parents manifest. As far as child development is concerned, harm is likely to result both because the developing relationships between parents and children are severed, and because the children are offered substitute care of lower quality than they would receive at home. These issues have been investigated in two partially overlapping areas of research: research on the effects of maternal employment (Chapters 2 and 3) and research on the effects of supplementary, extrafamilial care (Chapter 4).

One source of concern about maternal employment is that the roles of husband and wife will necessarily be blurred, to the detriment of harmonious interaction within the family. This concern has its origins in the notion that male and female roles complement one another and permit the couple or family to capitalize on these complementary areas of expertise. According to Parsons (Parsons & Bales, 1955), for example, women are more expressive, nurturant, and emotionally sensitive and thus should take responsibility for the management of relationships, child care, etc. By contrast, because men exhibit instrumental competence, they are suited for executive leadership of the family and for using their instrumental skills in the employment arena. However, the Parsonian assumption that heterosexual interaction is more harmonious when the parties are "appropriately" sex typed has not received empirical support. Indeed, research by Ickes and his colleagues (Ickes, in press; Ickes & Barnes, 1978) suggests that the opposite is true, and the chapters by Moen, Lamb, and Belsky, Steinberg, and Walker indicate that there is little empirical support for concerns about the harmful effects on children of maternal employment and extrafamilial care.

Studies of dual-earner families reveal that a traditional division of roles and responsibilities within the family often occurs, even when both parents are equally involved in the paid labor force (Pleck & Rustad, 1980). It could be argued, therefore, that the maintenance of traditional roles and responsibilities helps to protect children from the harmful consequences of their mothers' employment. Similar claims cannot be made about those cases in which fathers share in, or are primarily responsible for child care, while their wives share in, or are primarily responsible for the economic support of the family. The concerns expressed about role sharing and the role-reversing families are multiple, but two dominate: the belief that men are simply inferior to women in child-rearing abilities and the fear that children will be confused about gender-related social roles when they are not provided with gender-differentiated models by their parents. The first of these concerns derives from the premise that women are biologically destined to be childbearers and child rearers (Bettelheim, 1956; Brazelton, 1977; Symons, 1979). Proponents often point to the evidence that the female hormones (prolactin, progesterone, estrogen) potentiate parental behavior in nonhuman species and suggest that these hormones play a similar role in humans (Klaus & Kennell, 1976). The universality of arrangements whereby females assume primary responsibility for child care is seen as support for the claim that the arrangements are biologically ordained. Actually there is no empirical support for this claim (Lamb & Goldberg, in press), and the few relevant studies show that men and women are equivalently responsive to their own infants (Parke & Sawin, 1980), even though men tend to be less responsive to unfamiliar infants than women are (Berman, 1980; Nash & Feldman, 1981). The second concern depends on assumptions that the gender-appropriate quality of parental behavior will be lost when men become primary caretakers and women become primary breadwinners, and that the psychological adjustment of children requires the acquisition of a traditional sex role. The first of these assumptions is challenged by the evidence gathered by Lamb and his colleagues (see Chapter 5). The second assumption is faulty both because it implies a confusion between gender identity and gender role (the acquisition of a secure gender identity is developmentally important, but it need not involve conformity to a traditional gender role), and because it equates conformity to a traditional gender role with psychological adjustment. There is no justification for this assumed congruence; in fact, less traditionally sex-typed children are arguably better prepared for the egalitarian societies of the future (Hoffman, 1977).

Despite the shaky bases on which they are founded, concerns about role sharing and role reversal remain. Until recently, unfortunately, no attempts were made to study role-sharing and role-reversing families and document the effects of parental role sharing on children and parents. Several of the chapters in this volume review ongoing studies of role-sharing families: the motivations, the stresses, the effects on parental behavior, and the effects on child development.

Although concerns about maternal employment, extrafamilial child care, and role sharing/reversal are based largely on parochial prejudices and enjoy little empirical support, concerns about single parenthood are better founded. Several large-scale studies have shown that marital disharmony and hostility are more likely than any other family variable to have adverse effects, and of course such disharmony is likely to precede family dissolution (Graham & Rutter, 1973; Rutter, 1979). Furthermore, divorce is a stressful experience from which all parties (mother, father, children) take time to recover. Consequently, at the time when children are in greatest need of emotional support and reassurance, their parents are least capable of providing it. Even after the initial turmoil subsides, single-parent families are economically strained (partly because most are headed by women who still face extensive economic discrimination) and socially isolated (Hetherington, Cox, & Cox, 1978). Although such prejudices seem to be declining, divorced parents and children suffer from their own and others' perceptions that their family constellation is deviant and inferior. In addition, single parents often have difficulty obtaining temporary relief from child-care responsibilities. It is a tribute to the resilience of human personalities that the adverse long-term effects appear to be modest and the deviant outcomes quite rare.

Popular and legal prejudices also influence the composition of single-parent families. Until recently, courts upheld, in the form of "the tender years doctrine," the presumption that mothers should be awarded custody of young children following divorce because they were better suited for parenting than fathers were. Challenges by advocates of equal rights have led to removal of the legal presumption, even though this seems to have had little effect on custody decisions; as was the case a decade ago, only 10% of single-parent families today are headed by men (Glick & Norton, 1979). Perhaps this is because there remains a widespread belief that children are "better off" with their mothers. The study by Santrock and his colleagues (Chapter 10) is thus important because it represents the first attempt to determine how custodial fathers and their children fare.

OUTLINE OF THE VOLUME

Dual-Earner Families.   The following two chapters (those by Moen and Lamb) deal with the increasing participation of women—including mothers—in the paid work force. Thanks to differences in the authors' backgrounds and approaches, these two chapters complement each other very well. Moen is a sociologist by training, and her analysis reflects this discipline's concern with demographic and status variables affecting degree and type of involvement in the labor force. By contrast, Lamb's approach is more psychological—focused as it is on the personal motivations for employment and the ways in which maternal employment may affect child development.

The increased labor-force participation of women undoubtedly represents the most common deviation from the traditional pattern of family organization. Indeed, in the United States many more women are now employed than are not employed, and the rate of employment for mothers, including mothers with young children, is around 50%. Strictly speaking, therefore, maternal employment is now normative, although developmental theorists still view dual-wage-earner families as deviant, and there remain many popular misconceptions about effects on the development of young children.

By and large, the evidence suggests that maternal employment often results in an inequitable distribution of chores and responsibilities. Even when they work as many hours outside the home as their husbands do, employed mothers typically retain primary responsibility for home and child care. Fathers tend to do very little to relieve their employed wives of some traditionally "feminine" chores (Pleck & Rustad, 1980). Despite the potential dangers of role overload, however, maternal employment appears not to have adverse consequences on child development except perhaps on very young infants and elementary school-aged boys. In both cases, maternal employment per se seems less importantly involved than the values and attitudes forming the backdrop against which employment takes place. In addition, the sons and daughters of employed mothers tend to have less traditionally stereotyped attitudes about male and female roles than do children whose mothers are unemployed (see Chapter 3 for further details).

Researchers have been investigating the effects of maternal employment for decades. Even though many of the early studies were seriously flawed methodologically, and many crucial questions still have not been addressed satisfactorily, this must be deemed an established area of research. Consequently, the chapters on this topic are essentially literature reviews, rather than forums for the description of the authors' current research.

Extrafamilial Child Care. As increasing numbers of mothers with young children have entered the paid labor force, nonfamilial child care has become more important. The chapter by Belsky, Steinberg, and Walker (Chapter 4) is included in this volume for this reason. Like the two previous chapters, this chapter provides a thoughtful and integrative review rather than a description of the authors' own recent research.

Clearly, if one is to understand how changing role assignments within the family affect child development, one must also consider the impact of experiences outside the family that are correlated with the intrafamilial variables. Unfortunately, as Belsky and his coauthors point out, the published research has been concerned primarily with the effects of center-based day care, even though only 10% of the children receiving supplementary extrafamilial care are enrolled in day-care centers. The majority attend informal family day care, the effects of which have received little empirical attention. Thus even though enrollment in day care appears not to have adverse effects on socioemotional development (even in infancy), we can only conclude that nonfamilial care *need not* have adverse effects—we do not know whether developmental deviations are more likely to occur when it is employed. Among the factors affecting the influence of extrafamilial care are: the quality of care provided; consistency between the caretaking styles of parents and supplementary caretakers; the opportunity for interaction with other children; and the quality of parent–child relationships before and after enrollment in the substitute care facility. In addition, because different types of families may select different types of alternative care, there may be interactions between family and caretaker characteristics that need consideration as we strive to determine how these factors affect child development.

Increased Paternal Involvement.   Chapters 5 to 8 are concerned with a far less common characteristic of nontraditional families than maternal employment—major paternal responsibility for child care. The authors of these chapters deal with a number of issues pertaining to increased paternal involvement in child care. Among other things, they underscore the need to change male sex roles if women are to achieve equal opportunities in the educational, employment, and social spheres. Male and female sex roles are defined in relation to one another, and so neither can change greatly without complementary changes in the other. As intimated earlier, for example, increased paternal involvement is necessary if employed women are to be relieved of the role strain and overload under which many now suffer.

The four chapters concerned provide detailed discussions of ongoing studies concerned with families in which fathers are unusually involved in child rearing. For example, Lamb and his colleagues are studying more than 50 Swedish families from the third trimester of pregnancy into the second year of the infants' lives. Half of the families initially planned to divide paid parental leave in such a way that the fathers would have a prominent role in early infant care, whereas the other half planned to divide parental responsibilities in a more traditional way. Interviews of the parents during pregnancy and again 5 months after delivery allowed the researchers to enquire why the parents wished to adopt a nontraditional life-style, and to identify the correlates of various attitudes and values relating to parenthood. Observations of the parents' behavior in interactions with their infants permitted Lamb et al. to see whether fathers and mothers behaved differently depending on their degree of involvement in child care. Studies of traditional families had revealed characteristic differences between maternal and paternal behavioral styles (Lamb, 1981; Yogman, in press), but had been unable to specify whether these differences were biological or social in origin. Lamb et al. set out to address this question by comparing the behavior of mothers and fathers in traditional and nontraditional families.

In Russell's study of role-sharing Australian families (Chapter 6), all data were gathered through interviews with the parents. Consequently, although some questions concerning effects on the children were asked, Russell's primary aim was to determine why these apparently ordinary families chose to divide parental responsibilities in a nontraditional fashion, and how they evaluated this experience. Economic factors (primarily the greater employability of mothers than of fathers), mothers' and fathers' sex roles (with the fathers' scores seemingly being more influential), and political commitment seemed to be the most important determinants of role sharing. Russell reports less success in his efforts to determine why many of those who adopted a nontraditional life-style, and claimed to enjoy it, later reverted to a more traditional pattern.

Radin (Chapter 7) and Sagi (Chapter 8), meanwhile, have undertaken parallel studies of involved fathers and their preschool-aged children in Ann Arbor (Michigan) and Haifa (Israel) respectively. Deliberately using similar measures and procedures, these two investigators set out to identify the effects of paternal involvement on personality and cognitive development. Although Sagi's results appear on the whole to be somewhat clearer than Radin's, the two studies in the main yield consistent findings. Paternal involvement brings a predictable increase in the extent to which fathers influence their children and has beneficial effects on locus of control and cognitive competence. In addition, children with involved fathers seem to have less traditional attitudes about male and female roles.

Although these four studies of highly involved fathers and their families are concerned with children of varying ages and are focused on diverse issues, the researchers all report no adverse effects and, if anything, beneficial implications for child development. Indeed, the striking thing about the comparison of traditional and nontraditional parenting styles is that they appear to be remarkably similar. Of course, there remains a need for further research, particularly in the form of multimethod longitudinal studies. As a result, these pioneering studies are of heuristic as well as substantive importance.

Divorce and Its Sequelae.   From these discussions of highly involved fathers in intact families, we turn to single-parent families. Census and demographic data show that the number of single-parent families has been increasing for several decades (Glick & Norton, 1979). Although these numbers appear to be reaching a plateau, the situation is such that about 20% of today's children will spend at least part of their childhood with only a single parent. Most single-parent families are created by divorce, and 90% comprise single mothers and their children. Of all the family types discussed in this volume, single-parent families are most clearly at risk (Lamb & Bronson, 1980). Economic discrimination ensures that single mothers have great difficulty finding jobs that pay them adequately, particularly when they have been out of the work force for several years, and so do not have recent experience and skills. Further, many of the couple's friends have difficulty relating to single parents after the divorce, especially when (as is often the case) these acquaintances are work associates of the father/husband. Not surprisingly, therefore, social isolation is a frequent complaint of single parents. Further, single parents do not have partners to whom they can hand over their children when they are in need of "time out" from the incessant demands of parenting. The lack of concrete and emotional support in the face of severe socioemotional and economic stress combine to make the single parent's role an invidious one.

In the first of the two relevant chapters, Hetherington, Cox, and Cox (Chapter 9) discuss the adjustment of custodial mothers, their ex-spouses, and their children in the 2 years immediately following marital dissolution. The longitudinal study from which their data are drawn has been uniquely informative because it elucidates the processes of readjustment and allows Hetherington et al. to relate the mothers' changing emotional status to the psychological status of their children. Among many intriguing findings, the most interesting are the facts that: all parties (mothers, fathers, children) were still experiencing severe emotional stress a year after the divorce; boys were more likely to manifest continuing behavioral problems than were girls; and women who had been employed before separation coped better than those who sought employment as a result of divorce. Because Hetherington's sample is unrepresentative on both economic and geographic criteria, one can only generalize with caution from her results, but there is a clear model here for other researchers to emulate.

Generalizability may also be a problem with Santrock, Warshak, and Elliott's research on custodial divorced fathers (Chapter 10). Their data remain valuable, however, because although fathers are increasingly eligible to receive custody (full or joint) of their children, there were, until recently, no data available indicating how paternal custody affected children. The data presented by Santrock and his colleagues suggest that girls may have most difficulty adjusting when in the custody of their fathers, just as boys had the greatest problems in Hetherington's study of custodial mothers. The implication that children are better off in the care of the same-sex parent is certainly one that merits further investigation, for its ramifications are profound.

Other Alternatives.   In the volume's final chapter, Eiduson and her colleagues discuss a variety of family types that rose to prominence as part of the counterculture movement in the 1960s. These include communal living groups, single women who chose to become pregnant and remain single, and couples who preferred to avoid legal marriage. Eiduson has been studying children growing up in each of these family types for several years—her young subjects, followed since birth, have now entered public school! In their chapter, Eiduson and her colleagues discuss the child-rearing practices of parents who have adopted these alternative family styles. Perhaps because the demands of parenthood are so inflexible, one is struck by the extent to which these counterculture parents appear to be raising their children in a remarkably conventional fashion. Interestingly, their own marital relationships are becoming increasingly traditional as well.

SUMMARY

In sum, the contributors to this volume discuss a diverse array of nontraditional family types. Although the specific issues dealt with in each chapter differ, the themes outlined in the second section of this chapter predominate, and all the chapters have implications for a common question: How will this affect the children? Because nontraditional family styles are being adopted or at least considered by an increasing number of parents, the answers to this question are of manifest and growing practical importance. However, the chapters in this volume are not only of importance to social policy and applied issues. The study of nontraditional families also has significant implications for the understanding of broader developmental processes. For example, by studying sex-role development in children raised without fathers, we can appraise the "necessity" of having a male model within the family. Similarly, the relative significance of intra- and extrafamilial influences can be explored by comparing the sex roles of children whose parents' roles deviate from those adopted by the majority of men and women in the society. In addition, studies of role-reversing and role-sharing families promise to reveal whether maternal and paternal roles have a biological origin or are largely the product of gender-differentiated socialization. In general, absolutist statements equating what is normally the case with what should be the case are most readily evaluated by observing the consequences of deviations from the normative practice. The study of diverse family styles and child-rearing practices help to illustrate the complexities and potential variability of developmental processes.

REFERENCES

Aries, P. *Centuries of childhood*. New York: Vintage, 1962.

Berman, P. W. Are women more responsive than men to the young? A review of developmental and situational variables. *Psychological Bulletin,* 1980, *88,* 668–695.

Bettelheim, B. Fathers shouldn't try to be mothers. *Parents' Magazine,* 1956 (October), 124–125.

Brazelton, T. B. *Mother–father–infant interaction*. Presentation to the Conference on Family Interaction, Educational Testing Service, Princeton, N.J., December 1977.

Glick, P. C., & Norton, A. J. Marrying, divorcing and living together in the U.S. today. *Population Bulletin,* 1979, *32*(Whole number 5).

Graham, P., & Rutter, M. Psychiatric disorder in the young adolescent: A follow-up study. *Proceedings of the Royal Society of Medicine,* 1973, *66,* 1226–1229.

Hetherington, E. M., Cox, M., & Cox, R. The aftermath of divorce. In J. Stevens & M. Mathews (Eds.), *Mother/child, father-child relationships*. Washington, D.C.: National Association for the Education of Young Children, 1978.

Hoffman, L. W. Changes in family roles, socialization, and sex differences. *American Psychologist,* 1977, *32,* 644–657.

Ickes, W. Sex-role influences in dyadic interaction: A theoretical model. In C. Mayo & N. Henley (Eds.), *Gender, androgyny, and nonverbal behavior*. New York: Springer, in press.

Ickes, W., & Barnes, R. D. Boys and girls together—and alienated: on enacting sterotyped sex roles in mixed-sex dyads. *Journal of Personality and Social Psychology,* 1978, *36,* 669–683.

Klaus, M. Z., & Kennell, J. *Maternal-infant bonding*. St. Louis, Mo.: Mosby, 1976.

Lamb, M. E. The development of father–infant relationships. In M. E. Lamb (Ed.), *The role of the father in child development* (Rev. ed.). New York: Wiley, 1981.

Lamb, M. E., & Bronson, S. K. Fathers in the context of family influences: Past, present, and future. *School Psychology Review,* 1980, *9,* 336–353.

Lamb, M. E., & Goldberg, W. A. The father–child relationship: A synthesis of biological, evolu-

12   LAMB

tionary and social perspectives. In L. W. Hoffman & R. Gandelman (Eds.), *Parenting: Its causes and consequences*. Hillsdale, N.J.: Lawrence Erlbaum Associates, 1982.

Lee, R. B. *The !Kung San*. New York: Cambridge University Press, 1979.

Levine, J. A. *And who will raise the children?* Philadelphia: Lippincott, 1976.

Nash, S. C., & Feldman, S. S. Sex-role and sex-related attributions: Constancy and change across the family life cycle. In M. E. Lamb & A. L. Brown (Eds.), *Advances in developmental psychology* (Vol. 1). Hillsdale, N.J.: Lawrence Erlbaum Associates, 1981.

Parke, R. D., & Sawin, D. B. The family in early infancy: Social interactional and attitudinal analyses. In F. A. Pedersen (Eds.), *The father–infant relationship*. New York: Praeger Special Studies, 1980.

Parsons, T., & Bales, R. *Family, socialization, and interaction process*. Glencoe, Ill.: Free Press, 1955.

Pleck, J., & Rustad, M. *Husbands' and wives' time in family work and paid work in the 1975–76 study of time use*. Unpublished manuscript, Wellesley College, 1980.

Rutter, M. Maternal deprivation, 1972–1978: New findings, new concepts, new approaches. *Child Development*, 1979, *50*, 283–305.

Symons, D. *The evolution of human sexuality*. New York: Oxford University Press, 1979.

Yogman, M. W. Development of the father–infant relationship. In H. Fitzgerald, B. Lester, & M. W. Yogman (Eds.), *Theory and research in behavioral pediatrics*. New York: Plenum, in press.

2 The Two-Provider Family: Problems and Potentials

Phyllis Moen
Department of Human Development and Family Studies
Cornell University

INTRODUCTION

One of the most striking social trends of the century is the progressive influx of married women into the labor force. In 1979, half of all married women in the United States were either employed or looking for a job. This compares to only 4.5% of married women in the labor force in 1890 (Smith, 1979). Indeed, the two-provider family is rapidly becoming the norm. From 1960 to 1975 the proportion of two-earner husband/wife families grew from 23% to 30% of all households (Masnick & Bane, 1980; p. 8). The greatest change in recent years has been the increase in two-provider families with children. In 1979, over 52% of married woman with children under the age of 18 were in the labor force. Included in this group were 59% of the married mothers of school-aged children to 43% of those with children younger than 6. (US Department of Labor, 1980). Moreover, it is expected that by 1990 fully half of all mothers with preschool children will be in the labor force (Smith, 1979).

Foremost among the reasons for this remarkable growth of two-provider families are increased family financial need (especially in inflationary times), opportunities for women in service-type industries, the declining birthrate, and changes in social attitudes and prescriptions concerning the roles of women and men (Hoffman & Nye, 1974; Moore and Hofferth, 1979; Sweet, 1973). Scholars have documented the social, family, and individual factors that affect the decisions of married women to work (Moore and Hofferth, 1979; Sobol, 1974; Sweet, 1973), but there has been little systematic study of the *consequences* for families of having two earners. This chapter examines what is know as well as what is unknown about two-provider families.

Underlying Assumptions

Two assumptions guide the discussion that follows: (1) recognition of the processual aspects of the work–family connection; and (2) a picture of the active, systematic nature of families. Individuals pursue a number of "careers"; for two-provider families what is significant is the interface of the occupational and family careers. It is important to remember that the term *career* connotes change. Both work and family activities alter in intensity and significance over time; moreover, changes in one role may have inevitable consequences for the other role. For example, couples may work longer or shorter hours as a result of changes in family economic needs. Similarly, there may be changes in labor-force activity to accompany changes in a parent's time requirements—for instance, with the birth of a new baby. Investigating families with two incomes while ignoring the dynamic nature of both jobs and families would only produce a distortion of the issues.

A second assumption is a perception of the two-provider family as *active* rather than *passive*. Families can be viewed as merely responding to their existing situations or as decision-making units that make choices within the contexts of constraints, needs, and opportunities at hand. This chapter is oriented more toward the second perspective. The decision to have both husband and wife employed involves a number of considerations, including the problems and benefits that will accrue to the family as a whole.

Both opportunity factors in the labor market and family economic needs have fostered the employment of married women. But the large-scale forces producing and perpetuating the two-provider family must be considered in the light of *individual families* making *individual decisions* concerning the amount and form of each member's labor-force participation. Working couples are not merely passive victims of inflation or workplace demands. These families may resist, negotiate, or collaborate with the demands of work to varying degrees—taking another job rather than moving, for example, or refusing to work overtime. Because working husbands and wives are seen as actors rather than reactors, it is important to understand their perceptions of the problems and potentials of work, for themselves and for their families.

Major Issues

The two-provider family underscores a key issue for those concerned with families and with family well-being: *What is the nature of the relationship between families and the world of work?* When both spouses are employed, the intrusion of work into family life (and vice versa) becomes readily apparent.

A second vital concern is with *the impacts of having two earners on the family and on particular family subsystems* (such as the marital dyad or the parent–child linkage). What are the costs, in terms of family resources, of having both spouses work? Do working couples experience greater or less marital satisfaction? What are the implications of having both parents employed for the care and the socialization of their children?

Equally salient are *the impacts on society as a whole*. Individual families, across the nation, are making choices concerning who in the family will be employed outside the home. These individual decisions collectively result in widespread social change—in the make up of the labor force, in the structure of families, in the need for services, programs, and policies that take into account the phenomenon of the two-provider family.

Organization of the Chapter

The plan of the chapter is as follows: First, the more general issue of work–family linkages is discussed. Then both problems and payoffs in the form of family resources are described. Outcomes in terms of family roles and responsibilities—the division of household labor, child rearing, the marital relationship—are highlighted. The chapter concludes by placing two-provider families within the contexts of the life-course perspective as well as within a larger, societal framework.

WORK–FAMILY LINKAGES

An important outgrowth of research on two-provider families is the explication of the links between family life and the world of work. For years, scholars, employers, unions, and even workers themselves have harboured a myth of separate worlds (Kanter, 1977). Job and home life have been neatly compartmentalized; any overlap and attendant strain between them has been ignored.

But the separation of the worlds of work and family life is more illusionary than real. Notwithstanding the physical and temporal segregation of workplace and home, family and job roles clearly converge. Recent qualitative studies of individual families convincingly document the many ways in which work intrudes into the home, as well as how family life affects experiences on the job (Piotrkowski, 1979; Rapoport & Rapoport, 1976). The magnitude of this work–family conjunction is clearly suggested by findings of a recent national survey of employed workers, the 1977 Quality of Employment Survey, in which 34% of the respondents reported various forms of interference between work and family (Quinn & Staines, 1978).

In the two-provider family the links between home and work cannot be ignored, as problems from one domain are most apt to intrude upon the other. For example, couples may have difficulties in finding two jobs that mesh with their family needs. As Berger and his colleagues (1978; p.23) point out, couples seek employment opportunities: (1) in the same geographical area; (2) with hours that are compatible with household and child-care responsibilities; (3) that will allow time for them to pursue joint as well as individual interests; (4) that meet their current job expectations; and (5) that will contribute to long-term career goals. The task of locating jobs that are personally rewarding is difficult enough. Finding and maintaining two links to the labor force while at the same time meeting family obligations becomes a way of life for two-provider families that may be fraught with problems and is rarely easy.

Work–Family Strains

Strains between job and family obligations may well be inevitable in families where both spouses work. Difficulties faced by working couples have been described as *overload,* where the totality of job and family demands is simply too great, or as work–family *interference* or *conflict,* where the demands of one's job and one's family are actually contradictory (Voydanoff, 1980).

The Rapoports (1976) outline five types of dilemmas faced by working couples. The first is *overload,* which can involve social–psychological strain as well as time pressures. In the second category are *normative* dilemmas, brought about by discrepancies between one's own life-style and that valued by society. For example, a mother who is employed may feel she is not properly caring for her child according to social expectations regarding the maternal role. *Identity* dilemmas represent discontinuities between early internalized norms about the roles of men and women and the actual behavior of two-provider couples. A husband, for example, may feel that a wife's place is at home, even though his wife is employed. *Social–network* dilemmas reflect the inability of working couples to meet the expectations of and obligations to family and friends. There is little time on weekends and in the evenings for socializing when both spouses have jobs. Finally, there are *role-cycling* dilemmas, involving decisions that must be made about starting a family and the timing of major career decisions. Family and job events must be scheduled in ways that integrate childbearing and child rearing with career patterns. Moreover, couples may try to schedule job stresses so that heavy job pressures are not simultaneously experienced by both spouses.

In her study of 53 dual-career couples, Poloma (1972) found that this sample of professional women used four coping strategies in dealing with work–family overload and conflicts: (1) defining the situation of having a two-career family as positive; (2) creating a hierarchy of values (family responsibilities supersede job demands); (3) compartmentalizing home and work into separate spheres; and (4) compromising (one's career goals). A companion study of the husbands of these women (Garland, 1972) reports that the men regarded the dual-career arrangement as generally beneficial to their lives and did not feel personally threatened by their wives' careers.

The strains that Poloma and the Rapoports describe are those faced by *dual-career* families, "the type of family in which both heads of household pursue careers and at the same time maintain a family life together [Rapoport & Rapoport, 1971, p. 18].'' In comparison, working-class couples, holding down two *jobs,* not commonly regarded as careers, may well experience a different set of strains (see, for example Lein et al., 1974). In fact, a distinction is often made between dual-*worker* and dual-*career* families (Mortimer, 1978; Mortimer, Hall, and Hill, 1978). Unfortunately, most studies of two-provider families have investigated professional (career) families (Bailyn, 1970; Garland, 1972; Holmstrom, 1973; Poloma, 1972; Rapoport & Rapoport, 1971). Consequently, little is known about the experiences, orientations, and coping strategies of working-class couples (an exception: Lein et al., 1974; Working Family Project 1978), where two incomes may be defined a necessity and the requirements of jobs may be relatively inflexible and permit little freedom to deal with family concerns. For example, time off for dental appointments or for care of a sick child is much more difficult to secure in lower-level occupations (i.e., "jobs") than in professional "careers."

Differences in Work–Family Linkages

Families where both spouses are employed differ considerably, not only from single-provider families, but among themselves. For example, it is clear that dual-worker and dual-career families reflect variations in the objective requirements of the job. But working spouses may also differ in their general level of commitment to employment and the meaning they ascribe to work. Some may value work principally for the economic return it provides. Others may stress the status and social identity that are attached to particular occupations. And still others may see employment as an opportunity to socialize, to learn new skills, or to occupy otherwise unused time. These different values sought in and through employment may vary not only across working couples but within them. For example, a husband may enjoy his job principally because of its intrinsic rewards whereas his wife may be working because she appreciates the feeling of economic independence her job encourages.

Families can differ as well in terms of their ability to withstand the *costs* of the employment of both husband and wife. Dual-*career* families can usually afford to hire adequate household and child-care help to ease the domestic burden, and they may easily purchase services and laborsaving devices to reduce demands (dining out, hiring a housekeeper, household appliances, etc.) on their time and energies (Holmstrom, 1972). In working-class families, on the other hand, caring for the children and the home cannot be so easily dealt with; these couples often must juggle schedules, compromise needs, or just let things slide.

The costs of two jobs also vary by family structure and stage of the life cycle. Families with a large number of children or with preschoolers are more likely to experience difficulties meshing work and family responsibilities than are smaller families or families with school-age children. Similarly, parents who start their families relatively late in life, after job security has been achieved, are likely to experience less stress than are young parents who are simultaneously launching both their work and their family careers. To avoid or reduce the strains of coping with work and family obligations, couples may decide to delay the period of childbearing and/or choose to have smaller families (although the direction of causality is not entirely clear—see Smith-Lovin & Tickameyer, 1978; Waite & Stolzenberg, 1976). Another variation involves the patterning of labor-force patterns over the life cycle. Husbands and wives may work continuously over the life course, or one (almost always the wife) may interrupt his or her employment during the early years of childbearing and child rearing (Rapoport & Rapoport, 1976).

Finally, two-provider families can differ in terms of the employment conditions that serve to hamper or to facilite the meshing of work life with family life. Some jobs have great flexibility in terms of working hours and individual discretion, whereas others impose strict requirements concerning where and when work is accomplished. For example, college professors, among other professionals, may choose to do some of their work at home. The preponderance of jobs, however, must be performed exclusively at the workplace. Still other differential demands concern such requirements as geographical mobility, business travel, and overtime. Employers typically view their employees only as individuals and not as members of families (Renshaw, 1976), and thus are not inclined to tailor employment conditions to meet family needs. The degree to which organizations provide maternity (or parental) leaves, flexible hours, time off for the care of a sick child, and the availablity of convenient, reliable, inexpensive child-care arrangements can markedly affect the individual worker's roles both as employee and as family member.

Summary

In discussing the links between work and family life it is important to recognize the differences across two-provider families. The majority of couples do not regard their situation as voluntary; for many, two jobs are an economic necessity rather than an option. Neither do all working couples experience the same strains or the same benefits from the two-provider life-style. Some couples may take pride in meeting the challenges that jobs and family pose (Rapoport & Rapoport, 1976); others may find the same kinds of problems overwhelming. The costs and benefits of having two earners are not equally distributed among all families. It is important to remember, however, that there *are* positive as well as negative aspects of having both spouses employed. The following section discusses both the problems and potentials of this family form in terms of family resources.

FAMILY RESOURCES

Life-styles in two-provider families differ from those in traditional single-provider families, in part because of the different roles that family members play, but also because of the different resources that each family type generates. Time and money are the most obvious resources that help to determine the quality of family life. But energy and commitment are also important, as is the availability of social supports. In a somewhat different vein, personal feelings of self-worth also can be considered a "resource" that enhances the lives of working couples and can have indirect repercussions as well on the lives of their children.

The work–family connection can be conceptualized as a system of exchange (Fig. 2.1). Husbands and wives give of their skills, energies, and time in order to gain economic security, status, and a sense of purpose and identity. The nature of the exchange depends on both the structure of the family (for example, family size) and the stage of the family life cycle. For most families the benefits of having two earners far outweigh the costs. But all pay a price, particularly in respect to one scarce resource, time to get things done.

Time

The principal family resource involved in labor-force activity is time. As a fixed commodity, time allocated to employment is necessarily unavailable for other activities, including family activities. Time spent at work, therefore, offers an important and concrete measure of one dimension of employment affecting individuals and their families. The amount of time spent working, as well as which family members are employed, varies widely, both across families and within the same family over the life course.

Studies of dual-provider families too often treat employment as a simple dichotomous variable; one is either employed (or looking for employment) or out of the labor force. But treating work in this simplistic fashion may well *obscure* as much as it reveals. Employment may be full-time, part-time, or overtime, and it may involve one family member working at two jobs or two family members working at one or two jobs.

The number of work hours and their scheduling are significant because of the

FIG. 2.1.   Labor Force Participation as Exchange

strains they may induce between employment and family life (Quinn & Staines, 1978). Time constraints imposed by having two earners in the family have inevitable ramifications for the frequency and quality of family interaction and for the division of labor within the family. The employment of both parents typically creates problems of child care and conflicts between occupational and family responsibilities. Because of the cultural definitions of men's and women's roles, these burdens brought about by time constraints are apt to be disproportionately borne by the wife.

The *scheduling* of hours spent at work is no less important than their number when considering the character and quality of time available for family activities. There obviously must be a synchronization of job and family schedules (Aldous, 1969), yet such a synchronization can be problematic. Many dual-worker couples are able to use shift work as a way of reconciling the demands of two jobs with child-care responsibilities (Lein et al., 1974; Mott et al., 1965). But shift work can also impose serious strains on family life. For example, studies of fathers on afternoon shifts document the fact that these men often feel they see too little of their children because of the timing of their work (Mott et al., 1965). Mortimer's (1979) study of midwestern male college graduates revealed that 59% of those men found that the long hours and the need to work at night or on weekends was disruptive of their family life. Similarly, men and women interviewed for the Quality of Employment Survey most often mentioned time and scheduling problems as the primary form of work–family interference (Quinn & Staines, 1978).

Not enough is known about the effects of both spouses working on the amount of time for family activities. Couples may adapt to the high time demands of jobs by forgoing leisure rather than family activities. A study of couples in Seattle (Clark, Nye, & Gecas, 1979), revealed that husbands' work time was not related to marital role performance but was linked to reduced participation in recreational activity. However, for couples with preschool children a negative relationship was found between the husband's hours on the job and his participation in the child-care role (Clark & Gecas, 1977). These kinds of studies are suggestive, but far from definitive. The complex relationships among work time, family time, and leisure time are substantially underresearched. What is required are investigations that take into account the detailed work patterns of each spouse in order to trace out the specific family impacts of the time and timing of work.

Energy and Commitment

Closely related to time is another resource that is "spent" in the market place: energy. Research has convincingly documented that work can be a physical and emotional drain, and a major impediment to achieving a satisfactory and satisfying non-work life (Kornhauser, 1965; Work in America, 1973; Young & Willmott, 1973). Moreover, these are costs born not only by working parents but by their children as well. It is only reasonable to expect that parents fatigued by physically and psychologically demanding jobs will have insuffient energy to devote to family matters.

Still another resource that is related to time involves the significance of the work role, the degree of commitment to the job. Commitment is apt to be thought of as a undimensional, fixed quantity variable, with high work involvement on one end of the continuum and high family involvement at the other. Although this is a realistic portrayal of the quantity of involvement—of the relative amount of time devoted to work and family—it is not necessarily an accurate reflection of psychological investments. For example, it would be possible for parents to rate themselves as highly committed to *both* parenting and employment. It is in this instance that the strains produced by the two roles are likely to be most pronounced.

The "absorptiveness" of jobs, the degree to which one's occupation demands high emotional involvement, is a prime example of the "spillover" of work into home (Kanter, 1977). When either partner (or both) is on a career ladder, high commitment is demanded; this is often at the time of life when family responsibilities are the greatest (Mortimer, Hall, & Hill, 1978). Parents highly committed to their work have been shown to experience frequent conflict in relation to their family responsibilities (Young & Willmott, 1973). In Mortimer's study of midwestern college graduates, over half of her sample felt their families suffered strain as a result of their own fatigue or irritability due to tensions or problems at work, and 41% reported their preoccupation with work-related problems or demands was disruptive to their families.

In this area of work–family concern as in others, research to date has been provocative but incomplete. What is not known is how commitment to work and family changes over time, and research is needed to document variations in the absorptiveness of jobs over the family life cycle. Additional study of the consequences of high work commitment—for child care and family life in general—is also required.

Economic Security

The multiworker family is one remedy for the financial press of inflation, low wages, and the progressively increasing costs of raising a family. In 1978, the median family income of families in which both husband and wife were employed was $22,109 compared to $16,156 in families where the husband alone worked outside the home (US Department of Labor, 1980). This represents a significant difference in the ability of families to provide for their needs and live comfortably.

The presence of secondary earners is thus an important family resource in achieving economic security and well-being. In 1977, wives' earnings represented about one-fourth of family income. Wives working full time and year round contributed nearly 40% of their family's income (Hayghe, 1978). However, whether the earnings potential of wives can in fact be realized in order to provide for their families is determined by a host of cultural and institutional factors, including employment opportunities, prevailing wage rates, and the "costs" of employment. For women with preschool children, for example, the expenses incurred in order to work full time may be quite high (e.g., substitue child care), and they may at best be able to manage temporary or part-time employment.

Work obviously is critical to the economic well-being of families; but, by the same token, unstable or low-paying jobs can undermine that well-being. One survey reported that most American wage earners rank job security higher in importance than increased income (Yankelovich, Skelly, & White, 1975). Seventy percent of those with young children agreed with the statement that it is better to have a secure job than one that pays a lot, compared with only 44% of those families having no children.

Which two-provider families are the most economically insecure? Understandably, insecurity is most common among couples who have little education and few marketable skills. Parents in families with young children also tend to be insecure, because they more frequently lack the seniority and experience that insures stable employment and higher wage rates. A recent study found that breadwinners with children under 6 were the most likely to be unemployed, to have a longer period of unemployment in the event of job loss, and to have inadequate income in the face of unemployment (Moen, 1979, in press).

Here again, more research is needed—to clarify further the contributions to family life made by secondary wage earners, as well as the problems created in the course of making these contributions. The role of the second income in easing pressure points, especially during the early stages of child rearing, is most in need of investigation, with particular attention paid to the costs of substitute child care.

Status and Social Placement

In considering the financial benefits of having both spouses employed it is important to recognize an additional social reward in the form of *status* or, more broadly, what Scanzoni (1970) terms "integration into the opportunity structure." The location of individuals and their families within the social structure is contingent on the power, prestige, and resources that are earned through the family's linkage to the economic system. The social standing of families within the community is a critical determinant of life circumstances and experiences, the quality of the life of parents and their children. Although it is difficult, if not impossible, to separate the effects of social status from the effects of income per se, it is important to acknowledge the differential payoff that accrues to parents employed as professionals compared to that received by persons situated on the lower rungs of the occupational ladder. Success in the occupational sphere is reflected in the "respectability" of the family; moreover, parents who are ascribed low prestige may limit the occupational aspirations as well as the opportunities of their children. Status becomes a life-style contingency, opening or closing options not only to the individual worker, but to his or her family as well. (For a discussion of status mobility, see Blau & Duncan, 1967; Duncan, Featherman, & Duncan, 1968). Wives and children in an early study of blue-collar families were found to be aware of the low status of the father's occupation and expressed dissatisfaction with the low prestige of his job (Dyer, 1956). Social scientists are just beginning to examine status in two-earner families by evaluating the jobs of both spouses. Of particular interest in such research are the implications, for families, of status differentials between husbands and wives, situations where the spouses occupy widely separated positions in the occupational hierarchy.

Social Network

Another "resource" that emerges from the work–family connection is the development of a network of social contacts and relationships. In fact, one of the major complaints of mothers who are not in the labor force is their sense of social isolation (Ferree, 1976). The workplace constitutes a social setting where friendships may be fostered and information is transmitted. These, in turn, can become important family resources, social supports that are invaluable to working couples not only in times of crisis, but also in managing day-to-day problems of living. When both spouses are employed, their potential network is doubled. On the other hand, their nonworking hours are often occupied in the care and maintainance of the home and the children. This leaves little time for leisure and for social activities (Mortimer, Hall, & Hill, 1978). Even relationships with relatives may be quite circumscribed (St. Johns-Parsons, 1978). One of the limitations faced by two-earner families is the physical and social isolation of the nuclear family (Holmstrom, 1973). Working parents rarely have relatives living in the home or nearby to share the burden of child care. This isolation is compounded because of the scarcity of time for socializing with friends or those relatives who are accessible (Rapoport & Rapoport, 1976). One solution to the lack of leisure time may be socializing with others in similar circumstances and with similar time constraints. The Rapoports' study (1976) of dual-career couples reported the importance of social linkages with other dual-career families for exchanging services as well as support for their shared life-style.

Friends, neighbors, and relatives constitute an informal source of support for the two-provider family, but there are also formal ties to the community. Public and private agencies can be sources of information, child care, counseling, recreational activities, and emergency aid. Research is required to investigate the use by working couples of community services as well as informal social networks and the factors that contribute to the isolation of some families and the integration of others. The distinctions between dual-worker and dual-career families may be important in describing the utilization of social services as well as the tapping of one's personal network of kin, friends, and neighbors to ease the strains in coordinating work and family roles.

Identity and Self-Esteem

Work serves as a major basis for evaluating oneself and being evaluated by others in our society. This is especially true for men, whose identities are closely bound to their occupational positions. Although our society has long recognized the importance of work as a "validating activity" for men (Kahn, 1972; Mortimer, 1979; Rainwater, 1974a, 1974b), evidence suggests that it is now becoming increasingly salient for women as well (Hoffman, 1974; Sobol, 1974). Studies of employed mothers have shown that they express higher levels of self-esteem, competence, and general satisfaction with life than mothers not engaged in paid employment (Feld, 1963; Hacker, 1971; Hoffman, 1974). A recent study of working-class mothers of grade school children underscores the fact that women who are employed are more satisfied with themselves and their lives than are full-time homemakers (Ferree, 1976).

For women, however, the importance of work as a source of identity is less than it is for men. Historically, the wife's identity has been synonomous with the family. According to Oakley, 1976: Our language contains the phrase "a family man," but no such phrase for women—since family, for all practical purposes means women. Women's evaluation of their work experience depends heavily on their motivation and commitment (Bailyn, 1970; Dubin, 1976; Haller & Rosenmayer, 1971; Parnes, et al., 1970; Safilios-Rothschild, 1970), but it is becoming clear that the work role and its identity-bestowing qualities are significant for many wives.

What are the psychological implications of being a partner in a two-earner family? Most research has examined the consequences for employed *mothers,* rather than fathers, assuming that the strain of work–family conflicts is borne principally by the woman of the house. Some studies (Birnbaum, 1971) have found a positive link between a woman's employment and feelings of anxiety or guilt. Hoffman (1974), on the other hand, emphasizes psychic satisfactions of work and the feelings of achievement, competence, and contribution it fosters. More recent research reveals that employed women have a more positive self-image than do full-time homemakers. A study of 83 dual-career and traditional families found that the husbands and wives with dual careers were more inner-directed than traditional couples, although it fails to document differences in self-regard between working and nonworking wives (Huser & Grant, 1978). Research on married women has shown that the nature of their work experience can exert a powerful effect on their self-conceptions, social orientations, and even intellectual functioning (Kohn et al, 1979). Moreover, this research has shown that dimensions of occupation, such as time pressure, substantive complexity, and closeness of supervision have psychological consequences for both men and women. The role of the other spouse's orientations toward the two-earner family as well as attitudes concerning his or her own job may be an important factor in the mental health of the individual.

Scholars looking at two-earner families must also be sensitive to the drudgery of some jobs and to the fact that employment is not always perceived as desirable, especially for working couples with jobs, rather than careers. Although work can be a source of satisfaction and self-esteem (Form, 1973; Seeman, 1971; O'Toole, 1974), it also can foster dissatisfaction, depression, and despair (Blauner, 1964; Kornhauser, 1965; Seligman, 1965). Much of the meaning of work depends on the role orientations of the individual worker as well as the particular characteristics of the job. Whether one's job is seen as a career or an occupation—contributing both to society and to individual fulfillment—or whether it is seen as a task requiring certain skills or merely a way of earning money affects both the salience and the satisfactions of employment (Fried, 1966). For example, professionals report higher levels of job satisfaction than do workers in lower occupational categories (Kahn, 1974). Studies have found not only consistent differences in health and self-esteem by occupational level, but progressive changes in health and self-esteem as one moves up or down the occupational ladder (French, 1963; Kahn & French, 1970). A study in Baltimore and Detroit of employed, married men with small children found a positive relationship between social status (higher income and educational levels) and feelings of effectiveness and control (Gurin & Gurin, 1976). One's job status serves as an indicator of public esteem (French, 1963). Those holding low-status jobs and those whose work linkage is marginal at best are most likely to be evaluated and to evaluate themselves as inadequate and incompetent.

What is the relative importance of job and family in accounting for feelings of self-worth and general life satisfaction? Although, as suggested in the foregoing, work is a key element in individual well-being, studies of the mental health of both men and women have underscored the centrality of the family in people's lives. Douvan and colleagues (1979), for example found that the family role, pitted against work, is valued at a ratio of three to one by both men and women. And research has shown that family roles are an important source of life satisfaction. People who are happy in their marriage and family life tend to consider themselves happy in general (Gurin, Veroff, & Feld, 1957). But there is unquestionably variability in the salience of work and family across two-provider families and in the consequent effects of each on feelings of well-being.

Summary: Resource Distribution

The sharing of the breadwinning role by husbands and wives has obvious implications for the quality of family life. Financial well-being is clearly improved; the cushion of a second income also provides an added measure of economic security. But other resources—time and energy—are often constrained when both spouses are employed, curtailing opportunities for family activities and relationship among family members.

Existing knowledge and understanding about the resources of two-provider families are far from complete. Research needs to be undertaken not only on the *availability* of particular resources such as time and money but on the configuration or *distribution* of resources across families and within the same family over its life cycle. Duel-*career* couples may be able to "purchase" time, for example, by engaging domestic help or eating at restaurants. But dual-*worker* families may well have neither time nor money and may, therefore, be less equipped to manage reoccurring work–family strains. It is also likely that families with limited resources are less able to cope with unanticipated stresses, such as a sick child, than can those families with more bountiful resources. What is not clear is the relative utility or the substitutability of different types of resources. Are social supports more valuable for procuring emergency child care than is income? Similarly, how important is flexibility of working hours, relative to the income that a job generates, in dealing with points of stress in the work–family junction? Questions need to be asked, as well, about the impacts of *changes* in family resources on the relationships between husbands and wives, parents and children.

Resources constitute the materials and the tools by which families shape their day-to-day experiences, their relationships, their dreams for the future. The amount and type of resources available to two-provider families have direct repercussions for the functioning of the family. The following section examines three facets of life for two-provider families: the division of labor, the marital relationship, and parenting.

FAMILY FUNCTIONING

Household Division of Labor

In considering the division of labor within the home a distinction should be made between *participation* in domestic activities and *responsibility* for these activities. When both spouses work, husbands may share in the household tasks, but domestic roles usually remain the principal responsibility of the wife (Holter, 1970; Pleck, 1977; Slocum & Nye, 1976). Holmstrom (1973), in as study of 27 professional couples, found that most of the husbands did in fact "help out" with the domestic chores. Poloma and Garland (1971) report similar conclusions in a study of 53 employed professionals but found that only one couple shared the housework equally. Research on male managers in Britian documented that these men put in long hours on the job and did little housework (Young & Willmott, 1973). Time-budget studies in the last half of the 1960s (Robinson, 1977; Walker & Woods, 1976) reported that the amount of time wives spent working outside the home did not markedly affect the amount of time that husbands devoted to household activity, including time for child care. A more recent national time-budget study by the University of Michigan's Survey Research Center compares time use in 1975 with that in 1965 and continues to reflect the minimal involvement of husbands in domestic activities (Hill & Stafford, 1980; Stafford, 1980).However, Hoffman (1977) notes that husbands of employed wives are more likely to help with the care of children than are husbands of nonemployed wives. And in a recent national survey of employed workers (the 1977 Quality of Employment Survey), husbands in two-provider families reported spending 1.8 hours per week more in housework and 2.7 hours per week more in child care than did husbands of nonemployed wives (Pleck, 1979).

It is reasonable to expect that the division of labor between husband and wife varies according to the nature of each spouse's employment. When both spouses pursue uninterrupted careers one would anticipate that household chores are equitably divided between them. But this need not be the case, as is reported in a study (St. Johns-Parsons, 1978) of 10 dual-career families in which the wife had been continously employed. There was no sharing of household tasks, and the husband's was seen as the more important career.

The distribution of domestic chores may differ somewhat between families in which wives work full time and in those in which wives work less than full time. Weingarten (1978), in interviews with 32 Boston couples, found that professional families with wives working part time were less likely to share the household chores than were full-time employed couples. But if one considers both work on the job and domestic "work" at home, the division of labor may be more equitable in families where the wives are employed less than full time. Vickery (1979) notes that the part-time employed wife and her husband are more likely to have evenly distributed work loads than are full-time working couples, with the wife assuming major responsibility for the domestic chores, and the husband devoting most of his time to his job.

One factor that may affect the amount of time husbands devote to domestic activities is the scheduling of each spouse's job. A recent study of 750 households using time diaries found that men were more likely to do housework and care for children if their wives worked in the late afternoon or evening (Berk & Berk, 1979). This well may be the pattern of many working-class couples, who use shift work as a means of sharing the child-care role (Lein et al., 1974). However, because most research on the division of labor has focused on professional couples, little is known about the patterns of domestic activity in working-class families. In one intensive study of 14 dual-worker families, it was found that although both parents participated in child care, the responsibility for the children remained with the wife (Lein et al., 1974). And Bahr (1974) also found that even though husbands may participate more in domestic activities the *responsibilities* for home and child care remain with the wife.

The Rapoports (1976) have underscored the importance of looking at the division of responsibility as well as the actual participation of husbands and wives in domestic chores. From the literature review it would appear that what Myrdal and Klein (1956) describe as a married woman's second "primary" role, her employment, more often than not takes a back seat to her first primary role within the home. Although men may be "helping out" at home, particularly with child care, the responsibility for the household maintenance and child rearing remains with their wives. This may represent a deliberate limitation of both partners' involvement in various spheres (Bailyn, 1978); men may still be responsible for breadwinning, whereas women are accountable for the maintenance and smooth functioning of the family. But it may also reflect the difficulty of truly sharing responsibilities for work and family equally (Pleck, 1977). What Young and Willmott (1973) describe as *symmetrical* patterning, where neither spouse has a monopoly in either work or homelife, may be exceedingly difficult to achieve when both societal norms and job expectations are geared to a sexual division of labor. In traditional single-earner families the presence of two adults in the household has facilitated the occupational attachment of one by providing a "homemaker" to accomplish the nonmarket work (Hunt & Hunt, 1977). This division of labor places a serious limitation on the occupational opportunities of married women. Until normative prescriptions concerning the roles of men and women change and the structural constraints of occupations have been altered, time will be especially scarce for working wives. In addition, fathers will continue to put most of their time into providing for the family, which means a minimal involvement for them in child care and other domestic responsibilities. The full ramifications of this situation in terms of the emotional relationships between husband and wife, parent and child remain to be developed through further research. What is required is a thorough investigation of the consequences for couples and their children of various patterns of work, especially as they pertain to caring for children and maintaining a home. Potential consequences for both men and women of a decrease in the standard work week and/or greater opportunities for part-time employment are particularly deserving of attention.

The Marital Relationship

Strains resulting from simultaneously managing a job and family responsibilities may well influence the emotional relationship between husband and wife. The hidden contract in most marriages contains certain implicit expectations regarding the roles played by husbands and wives (Gowler & Legge, 1978). When working couples develop relationships that radically depart from those in conventional single-provider families, both spouses may be dissatisfied with the marriage. An extensive review of the literature on the relationship between marital problems and the wife's employment suggests that in lower-class families there is more marital satisfaction when the wife is not in the labor force (Hoffman & Nye, 1974). However, studies of middle-class families reveal no such differences; indeed, when the wife enjoys her work, working couples appear to experience greater marital satisfaction than do traditional single-earner couples (Hoffman & Nye, 1974, p. 206).

Research suggests that characteristics of the jobs as well as husbands' and wives' attitudes toward their own work and the employment of the spouse may be important conditioners of the quality of the marital relationship. For example, a study of male shift workers (Mott, et al., 1965) found that those on rotating shifts had a great deal of difficulty in coordinating family activities with their wives and reported problems in a number of areas in their roles as husbands (p. 101–130). Staines and his colleagues (1978) found that role overload of women (defined as wishing for domestic help from husbands and feeling rushed) was an important correlate of marital problems in two-earner families. Bailyn (1970) found that marital happiness in two-career families was related to the family orientations of the husbands. She suggests that: "identifying the conditions under which men find it possible to give primary emphasis to their families while at the same time functioning satisfactorily in their own careers may become more relevant to the problems of careers for married women than the continued emphasis on the difficulties women face in integrating family and work [p. 112]."

In spite of the work–family strains, couples may benefit from sharing the provider role. In a study of 54 professional couples Weingarten (1978) found that these couples were intensely involved with each other as well as with their careers using "interdependence" as a strategy for coping with the complexities of their lives. The younger couples in her sample were particularly close emotionally, sharing the setbacks as well as the successes of their respective careers. A study (Huser & Grant, 1978) of 83 university faculty couples found no difference between single breadwinner and dual-career couples in the number and types of interests shared and, in fact, found that the two-career spouses were more flexible than the more conventional couples in the sample. In considering the quality of marriage, it is important not to equate recognition of problems with marital dissatisfaction. A recent survey found, for example, an increase in awareness of difficulties concurrently with an increase in reported happiness in marriage from 1957 to 1976 (Douvan et al., 1979, p. 63).

Some writers have expressed concern that working couples might compete with one another in terms of their careers (Parsons, 1959, Parsons & Bales, 1955). The potential for marital conflict as a result of direct competition in the world of work, however, is not apt to be great because, as Oppenheimer (1977, p. 404) points out, husbands and wives rarely work in the same occupation or even in the same organization. Still while there may be no direct on-the-job conflicts, the fact that a wife earns money changes the family distribution of resources and, hence, her relative power in the marriage and in family decision making (Scanzoni, 1978).

Whether or not working couples experience marital strain or conflict it is clear that social attitudes toward the roles of husbands and wives are changing. A study by Thornton and Freedman (Institute for Social Research, 1980), using data collected from a panel of women at various intervals from 1962 through 1977, found a major shift in attitudes concerning sex roles. For example, there was an increase of 21 percentage points in the number of women who disagreed with the statement: "Some work is meant for men and other work is meant for women." Similarly, whereas two-thirds of the respondents in 1962 agreed that panel study concerning the following item: "Most of the important decisions in the life of the family should be made by the man of the house," only one-third endorsed this statement in 1972. Thornton and Freedman report that the greatest changes in sex-role attitudes has occurred among younger women, those with more education, those with better educated husbands, and those who were working in 1962.

Additional research is required to investigate the effects of such changes in sex-role attitudes. Differences in marital satisfaction between working-class couples and professional couples is another area requiring study. Much of the difference may be due to socioeconomic status and resources rather than the work roles of either spouse. Further study is also needed to examine the attitudes and behavior of spouses in "successful" two-provider families, those who appear to manage work–family overloads and conflicts with relative ease, to determine how they achieve an effective blending of roles.

Childrearing

It is commonly believed that the development of children can be enhanced by their participation in activities with valued adults (Bronfenbrenner, 1979). In our society, with the isolation of the nuclear family, the burden of the caretaking of children falls principally on the parents (Holmstrom, 1973). There are few social supports—formal or informal—to share this task. The conditions of child rearing and development are necessarily transformed when both parents work, but it is still unclear just how and to what extent parents' jobs limit their full participation in the child-care role.

One should not look at the implications for children of having both mothers and fathers employed without first placing the two-provider family in its social and historical context. In March 1977 nearly half (47.7%) of all children under 18 had mothers who were employed (Grossman, 1978). Moreover, the labor force reentry rate of employed women who bear their first child is greater than 50% (Mott & Shapiro, 1977). Thus being a child in a two-earner family is becoming the norm. Much of the literature on the effects of having both parents work is therefore dated, looking at maternal employment at a time when it was far less commonplace.

Characteristics of parent's occupations "spill over" into the lives of their children in both direct and indirect ways. For example, a parent's job responsibilities necessarily take away from the hours available to spend in family activities. In fact, it may well be that time demands are the most formidable problem of child rearing faced by two-provider families (Vickery, 1979). Because of the separation of work and home that has been a fact of life since the Industrial Revolution, hours spent on the job are almost always hours that a parent is away from the child (Oakley, 1976; Young & Willmott, 1973).

Scarcity of time is especially problematic for parents of young children who simultaneously face both high time demands for child care and high financial needs. As Rallings and Nye (1979, p. 222) point out, the years with preschool children are the most costly—both economically and psychologically—for two-provider families. The early years of child rearing are likely to be the peak years of job demands of working parents (Wilensky, 1963). They also are likely to be the period when job and financial security are the lowest (Moen, 1981).

One means of accommodating to the conflicting demands of working and parenting is to reduce working time. Women with small children who remain in the labor force are more likely to work less than are women with older children. Not quite 20 % of the employed mothers of preschoolers were working full time for 50 weeks per year in 1977, compared to over 50% of the wives without children (US Dept. of Labor, 1979). Many of those working full time would prefer to work fewer hours. A recent study (Moen & Dempster-McClain, 1981) of the working parents of preschoolers found that nearly half the mothers employed full time expressed a preference for working fewer hours in order to spend more time with their children. Noteworthy too, nearly a third of the fathers of preschoolers also would have preferred a reduced work week. A study of the work–leisure preferences of workers in California found that parents of young children were more willing to trade in income for time off than were workers at other stages of the life cycle (Best, 1978).

Time is a precious commodity for working parents of young children. One reflection of this is reduced family size. The high labor-force participation rate of married women during their childbearing years has meant a postponement in starting families as well as having fewer children (Hoffman & Nye, 1974; Waite & Stolzenberg, 1976). Another indicator of the scarcity of time is the curtailment of domestic activities. Employed mothers spend considerably less time on housekeeping chores than do mothers not working outside the home (Robinson, 1977; Walker & Woods, 1976), though differences between employed women and homemakers in time spent on housework appears to be diminishing (Pleck, 1979). Nevertheless, working mothers, in particular, are vulnerable to role overload in trying to meet the competing demands of a job and home life (Rapoport & Rapoport, 1972). This overload often results in the requirement that children assist with the housework—and in the process develop independence and resourcefulness through helping with the household task assignments—(Elder, 1974; Propper, 1972). Fathers as well as mothers are handicapped in the child-care role as a result of the hours they work. A study of 78 Seattle couples with preschoolers found that there was a negative relationship between a husband's work time and his sharing of the child-care role (Clark & Gecas, 1977).

Working parents must not only find adequate child-care arrangements, but also mesh the scheduling of these arrangements for different children of different ages with their own work schedules. When emergencies such as a child's illness or a school holiday create disruptions in the arrangements, couples must resort to their own makeshift solutions. Such problems of child care are particularly stressful for working parents of preschoolers (Bryson, Bryson, & Johnson, 1978; Rapoport & Rapoport, 1971; St. Johns-Parsons, 1978).

When the occupation of either parent requires frequent travel or relocation the whole family is affected. Jobs requiring geographical mobility mean that children must face new neighborhoods, schools, and friends. Still, geographical mobility may not be as disruptive as one might think. In one study of families who had moved, most parents said their children had little difficulty in adjusting and making new friends (Barrett & Noble, 1973).

There are also more subtle ways in which the world of work touches the lives of children. Children traditionally have seen work as something appropriate for fathers and not for mothers (Goldstein & Oldham, 1979). Changes in women's and men's roles, as well as attitudes towards them are not faithfully mirrored in the socialization process. A study of children's attitudes towards employment found that 41% of the sample of children in grades one, three, five, and seven saw women as nonworkers (Goldstein & Oldham, 1979, p. 43). The younger children were especially likely to see mothers as exempt from employment outside the home. But conventional views of the sexual division of labor are giving way to more egalitarian orientations. Children of working mothers are more likely to approve of maternal employment than are children of nonemployed mothers (Hoffman, 1977).

Working parents also serve as role models for their children. For example, daughters of all ages, from grade school through college level, are more likely to want and intend to work if their mothers worked than are daughters of nonworking mothers (Almquist & Angrist, 1971; Hartley, 1960; Smith, 1969). Several studies have shown that daughters of working mothers are also more likely to have higher career aspirations than daughters whose mothers are not employed (Almquist & Angrist, 1971; Tangri, 1972). Furthermore, the fact that fathers are taking a more active role in child rearing when the mother is employed may well lead to reduction in the sex differences between boys and girls and may facilitate the development of independence and achievement in girls. But as Hoffman (1977) notes: "the shift in women toward work is more clearly documented than is the shift in the role of men toward parenting [p. 655]."

Child rearing has traditionally been the province of the mother. Consequently, it has been logical, from a research point of view, to look at the effects of the *mother's* employment on the parenting role. But clearly the father's job also has socialization effects. Kohn (1972) has documented the effects of the father's occupational experience on parental values such as encouraging self-direction. He found that middle-class fathers (who are more likely to be rewarded on the job for self-reliance and ambition) were more likely to stress achievement values for their children, whereas blue-collar fathers underscored the importance of obedience (see review by Gecas, 1979). Although children no longer learn job skills sitting at the working parent's knee, they are taught behaviors and attitudes about work by their parents—both intentionally and unintentionally. As two-provider families become commonplace and increasingly an accepted family form, fathers may participate more fully in the care and socialization of their children. Additional research is required to examine the separate and joint effects of both parents' jobs on socialization processes and outcomes as well as the role of supplementary caregivers in the socialization process (see chapters by Belsky, Steinberg, & Walker on day care and by Lamb on maternal employment).

A LIFE-COURSE PERSPECTIVE

Families are dynamic institutions with continuously changing membership, functions, and needs over time. Work careers are similarly dynamic, changing over the years in both form and function. The two-provider family must be viewed within this context of change in order to understand fully the variations in the costs and benefits of this type of work–family linkage over the life course.

Parents with young children are the most likely to experience conflicts between work and family obligations. As children grow older, the time demands of both work and family may be considerably reduced, and the role overload of working parents should be similarly lessened. But other problems may be exacerbated at the same time. For example, the high income requirements of families with adolescents may pressure either or both parents to put in more hours on the job and, at times, take second jobs. And the degree of involvement of husbands and wives in careers over the years may make geographical mobility difficult. The Rapoports (1976) label the meshing of individual job careers with the family life cycle "role cycling." In order to understand the problems and potentials of the two-provider family the stage of the family in terms of life-cycle events needs to be considered as well as the stage of both spouses in their respective employment.

Because the existing body of knowledge is so inadequate, future research needs to explore the expanding and contracting demands of both home and work life. It has been suggested that when family and occupational responsibilities peak at the same time the husband's satisfaction with both work and family declines (Aldous, Osmond, & Hicks, 1979). But it could be that high involvement in one role encourages high involvement in another. The degree of absorption—in family and in work—over the life course is another area worthy of investigation, as are critical transition points in work and in family life.

Pleck (1980) has suggested that work–family interference may be more correctly regarded as work–*parent* interference because parents as revealed in the 1977 Quality of Employment Survey—both fathers and mothers—are more likely than nonparents to experience conflict concerning work and family roles. A far more central research question is to what extent family adjustments to having both parents employed outside the home are a function of: (1) characteristics of each spouse's job; and (2) the availability and use of community services (such as day care). In addition, the effects on families of continuities and discontinuities of each spouse's work role need to be documented, as do the impacts of transitions (as, for example from single-earner family to having both spouses work). "Career" implies an occupation with a sequential patterning that includes progressively greater responsibility, and greater rewards (Wilensky, 1961); but "career" need not necessarily imply a hierarchial sequence (as, for example, in Wilensky's discussion of "disorderly careers" 1961). Researchers need to pay greater attention to how both mothers and fathers schedule their work careers over the life cycle—in terms of moonlighting, overtime, and part-time work as well as withdrawing from the labor force—and to link this patterning with outcomes such as time spent with family, quality and quantity of parenting, and marital, parental, and work satisfactions.

Change can be viewed from the perspective of individual families as they pass through stages of the life cycle; it can also be examined from a larger historical perspective. Two-provider families are becoming the rule rather than the exception. Projections into the future indicate that there will be a substantial decrease in the number of one-provider husband/wife households, from the current 25% to about 14% of all households by 1990, whereas two-provider husband/wife households will remain at about 31% (Masnick & Bane, 1980, p. 9). (Projections also suggest an increase in both single-parent and single-*person* households.) As an increasing number of families confront the task of integrating work and family roles, new coping strategies for doing so—both formal and informal—can be expected to emerge. The sheer magnitude of this development is likely to become a potent force for change in the amount and types of support provided to working couples.

TWO-PROVIDER FAMILIES IN A SOCIETAL CONTEXT

Families do not exist in isolation; their borders are crossed, even trespassed daily. The family is vulnerable—sometimes painfully so—to the forces exerted by the structures and cultures in which it is embedded. These forces differ over time, both in strength and centrality. For example, in the Middle Ages the church was a significant shaper of European family life. In the United States, in the 1980s, there are two institutions that penetrate the lives of families in both overt and subtle ways: the economic system and the political system. This chapter concentrates on one strand of influence in which each of these institutions shares a hand: the world of work as it relates to two-provider families.

The family is an appropriate vantage point from which to examine work, because the family provides the forum through which labor-force involvement decisions are structured. It is also the filter through which labor-force activity affects dependent persons, be they children, youth, nonworking adults, or the aged. The problems of working parents are an inevitable consequence of the juxtaposition of conflicting roles. The personal crises faced by two-provider families in the management of both work and family roles are specific examples of the general, cultural ambivalence towards the responsibilities of society toward families. In the United States we view the difficulties faced by working couples (especially working parents) as essentially personal problems rather than public issues. Parents must, for the most part, manage their own problems of child care, shiftwork, geographical mobility, job security, and the rising costs of living. Working couples today deal with the strains between work and family essentially on their own. Their "coping" strategies include establishing priorities for work and family responsibilities, reducing involvement in one role (e.g., working part time, having fewer children, postponing childbearing, temporarily dropping out of the labor force) or seeking outside support (such as child-care assistance). But the real task ahead is to recast the complex social and economic environments that structure both family and work roles.

The proliferation of families in which both spouses work has implications beyond the borders of the individual family units. The economic system and society at large are shaped to a great extent by the decisions made in individual families concerning the nature and extent of their attachments to the labor force. Consequently, public policies must attend more closely and deliberately to the two-earner phenomenon or fail to respond appropriately and effectively to this emerging family form. Similarly, the private policy decisions of individual firms and labor unions must also begin to take closer account of the family contexts of worker's jobs.

Solutions to the major problems of two-provider families turn on achieving an optimal balance of work and family obligations. Provision for child care is one obvious need in families where both parents work. Equally important are options in work hours and the scheduling of work. Much of the role conflict and strain experienced by working parents emanate from the absence of such flexibility. Jobs are designed for individuals, not family members; yet, for optimal family functioning, the family roles of working parents must be coordinated with the work roles of both spouses, even as the two jobs must be coordinated one with the other.

Two possible options for two-provider families are the sharing of the same position ("job sharing") or sharing of the provider role by each working part time ("work sharing"). Job sharing has been seen by some academic couples as beneficial in reducing work–family strains (Arkin & Dobrofsky, 1978), but it may well be an opportunity limited to a few occupations. When each spouse holds a part-time job the overloads of family and work demands are considerably reduced. Gronseth (1978), in a study of 18 Norwegian couples, found that this "work-sharing" pattern was highly satisfactory to both husbands and wives. But both job sharing and part-time employment may be unrealistic for couples with high financial needs and/or low wages.

Policies concerning childbearing and infant care should be developed so as to facilitate the maintenance of stable links of both parents to the labor force where such are preferred. In addition, provision should be made to enable either fathers or mothers to interrupt their work careers in order to begin their families without sacrifice of position, benefits, or status. Temporary reductions in responsibilities and in hours on the job when children are small should be an option in all occupations, for both men and women.

A variety of points have been suggested where policy intervention might facilitate satisfactory work–family integration. Focusing on two-provider families calls attention to the constraints making labor-force attachment problematic at different stages in the life cycle, especially for women. It also underlines the strains faced by working parents. As Kanter notes, people come to work in organizations as members of families; the families are themselves affected by the policies and practices of the organization (1977, p. 3). Needs of families may well have to be taken into consideration in future organizational and public policies. Problems of part-time work, flexible hours, geographical mobility, child care, and maternal (and paternal) benefits are already intruding into the policy debate (Kreps, 1976; O'Toole, 1974; Work in America, 1974).

The larger issue of social change in the patterns of labor-force participation really turns on the changing roles of men and women—within the occupational sphere and within the family itself. Studies have documented that even when women are employed, the burden of the household and child-care tasks remain theirs. It has been suggested that this is indicative of normative constraints concerning the roles of husband and wife as well as the occupational constraints of the husband's job (Pleck, 1977). The issue of scheduling of work becomes central when facing the problems of moving from role separation to joint role performance of husband and wife in the occupational and family spheres (Bott, 1957). Changes from one earner per family to two requires corresponding changes in the workplace and in the provision of social services to meet new family "needs." Government, organizations, and families will have to re-negotiate the forms and functions of work, especially the amount and flexibility of time for work.

The connections between work and family cannot be viewed apart from their environmental context—from the structural, cultural, and occupational milieu in which families are located. An important mediator of the environment is government. The United States does not have a formal "family policy." But, if we define such a "policy" as the things government does to and for the family (Kamerman & Kahn, 1978), then government is very much involved in constraining, facilitating, and mediating the family/labor-force transaction—both deliberately and unintentionally.

CONCLUSIONS

This chapter has underscored the linkages between work and family in two-provider families as they are manifested in the form of financial security, status, conflicting obligations, and role strains. Work is essential to the economic well-being of the family; it offers parents the means to maintain or even improve the quality of their lives and the lives of their children. By the same token, the absence of a satisfactory job linkage at a living wage can be a serious impediment to husbands and wives struggling to make ends meet.

Time constraints necessarily limit the number of joint activities working couples can engage in—with their children and with each other. While this can be problematic for all families, it is especially straining in those families in which both parents work. The conflicts between work and family roles are seldom resolved, rather, they are "juggled" in a time-budgeting process that is often unsatisfactory. Because of the traditional division of labor within the family it is the woman who is seen as principally responsible for the domestic chores, including child care. The strain of role overload is most often felt, therefore, by the mother who works.

These two aspects of work—money and time—are not separate from one another; husbands and wives trade their time and skills for income, status, and security. What is particularly significant in these days of inflation is that a single income is often insufficient for a family to meet the rising costs of living. Families are being forced to give increasing amounts of time—in the form of moonlighting, overtime, as well as having two earners—in order to meet the economic squeeze. Although there are many reasons for the increase in the participation of married women in the labor force, an accurate and important point to note is that in an increasing number of cases, two earners are required to support a family.

Much of the stress of work for two-provider families is socially determined—a consequence of the structure of occupational roles and the fundamental cultural contraditions built into the economic and family systems as they exist in the United States today. Governmental as well as organizational policies have underscored these strains by viewing the worker as an individual, apart from any family context. The difficulty lies not in the family or the workplace, but in the articulation of the two.

Both public and private policies can do much to alleviate the strains faced by parents who work by altering the structure and scheduling of employment. A number of options are possible: flexible working hours, substitute child care, part-time employment (with fringe benefits and opportunities for promotion), maternal and paternal leaves of absence, a reduced work week for parents who choose to work less while their children are young, moving into regular working hours as their children grow older.

The issues raised in this chapter are important, not only from the perspective of today's two-provider families, but from the vantage point of families of the future. For a number of reasons—both ideological and economic—two-provider families are here to stay. A study of the orientations of men and women found that young women are closer to young men in the choice of work-related "self-actualization" as an important value than they are to the values of older women (Douvan et al., 1979). Moreover, evidence from the younger cohorts of men and women suggests that the attachments of mothers to the labor force are likely to become more similar to those of fathers; married women will in even greater numbers work continuously at full-time jobs (Masnick & Bane, 1980). The question remains as to whether to design of work will be transformed to enable family life to thrive within the context of two jobs.

ACKNOWLEDGMENTS

The author appreciates the comments and suggestions made by Jeylan Mortimer, Richard P. Shore, Paula Avioli, and Donna Dempster McClain on an earlier draft of this chapter.

REFERENCES

Aldous, J. Occupational characteristics and males' role performance in the family. *Journal of Marriage and the Family*, 1969, *31*, 707–712.

Aldous, J., Osmond, M., & Hicks, M. Men's work and men's families. In W. Burr, R. Hill and I. Nye (Eds.), *Contemporary theories about the family*. New York: Free Press, 1979.

Almquist, E. M. & Angrist, S. S. Role model influences on college women's career aspirations. *Merrill-Palmer Quarterly*, 1971, *17*, 265–269.

Andrisani, P. J. & Nestel, G. Internal-external control as contribution to and outcome of work experience. *Journal of Applied Psychology*, 1976, *61*, 156–165.

Arkin, W. & Dobrofsky, L. R. Job Sharing. in R. Rapoport & R. N. Rapoport (eds.), *Working couples*. New York: Harper Colophon Books, 1978.

Bahr, S. J. Effects on power & division of labor in the family. In L. W. Hoffman & F. I. Nye (Eds.), *Working mothers*. San Francisco: Jossey-Bass, 1974.

Bailyn, L. Career and family orientations of husbands and wives in relation to marital happiness. *Human Relations*, 1970, *23*, 97–113.

Bailyn, L. Accomodation of work to family. In R. Rapoport & R. N. Rapoport, eds., *Working couples*. New York: Harper Colophon, 1978.

Barrett, C. & Noble, H. Mothers' anxieties versus the effects of long distance move on children. *Journal of Marriage and the Family*, 1973, *35*, 181-188.

Bell, C. S. Should every job support a family? *Public Interest*, 1975, *40*, 109-118.

Berger, M., Foster, M. & Wallston, B. S. Finding Two Jobs. in R. Rapoport & R. N. Rapoport (eds.), *Working couples*. New York: Harper Colophon books, 1978.

Berk, R. A. & Berk, S. F. *Labor and leisure at home*. Beverly Hills, Sage, 1979.

Best, F. Preferences on worklife scheduling and work-leisure trade offs. *Monthly Labor Review*, 1978, *101*, 31-37.

Birnbaum, J. A. Life patterns and self-esteem in gifted family-oriented and career-committed women in M. M. T. Shuch (Ed.), *Women and achievement: social and motivational analyses*. New York: Wiley, 1971.

Blau, P. M. & Duncan, O. D. *The American occupational structure*. New York: Wiley, 1967.

Blauner, R. *Alienation and freedom*. Chicago: University of Chicago Press, 1964.

Bott, E. *Family and social networks*. London: Tavistock Publications, 1957.

Bronfenbrenner, U. *The ecology of human development*. Cambridge, MA: Harvard University Press, 1979.

Bryson, R., J. Bryson, & Johnson, M. Family size, satisfaction and productivity in dual-career couples. In. R. Bryson and J. Bryson (eds), *Dual career couples*. New York: Human Science, 1978.

Clark, R. A. & Gecas, V. The employed father in America: A role competition analysis. Paper presented at the annual meeting of the Pacific Sociological Association, 1977.

Clark, R. A., Nye, F. I., & Gecas, V. Husbands' work involvement and marital role performance. *Journal of Marriage and the Family*, 1978, 9-21.

Douvan, E., Veroff, J. & Kulka, R. Family roles in a twenty year perspective. *Economic Outlook USA*, 1979, *6*, 60-63.

Dubin, R. Work in Modern Society. In R. Dubin (ed.), *Handbook of Work, Organization and Society*. Chicago: Rand McNally, 1976.

Duncan, O. D., Featherman, D. L. & Duncan, B. *Socioeconomic background and occupational achievement*. U.S. Department of HEW, Office of Education, 1968.

Dyer, W. G. The interlocking of work and family social systems among lower occupational families. *Social forces*, 1956, *34*, 230-233.

Elder, G. H., Jr. *Children of the great depression*. Chicago: University of Chicago Press, 1974.

Feld, S. Feelings of Adjustment. In F. I. Nye and L. W. Hoffman (Eds.), *The employed mother in America*. Chicago: Rand McNally, 1963.

Ferree, M. M. Working-class jobs: Housework and paid work as sources of satisfaction. *Social Problems*, 1976, *23*, 431-441.

Form, W. H. Auto workers and their machines: A study of work, factory and job satisfaction in four countries. *Social Forces*, 1973, *52*, 1-15.

French, J. R. P., Jr. The social environment and mental health. *Journal of Social Issues*, 1963, *19*, 39-56.

Fried, M. A. The role of work in a mobile society. In S. B. Warner (ed.), *Planning a network of cities*. Cambridge, Mass.: MIT Press, 1966.

Garland, T. The better half? The male in the dual profession family. In C. Safilios Rothschild (Ed.), *Toward a sociology of women*. Massachusetts: Xerox Publishing, 1972.

Gecas, V. The influence of social class on socialization. in W. R. Burr, R. Hill, F. I. Nye, I. L. Reiss (eds.), *Contemporary theories about the family*, Vol. I. New York: The Free Press, 1979.

Goldstein, B. & Oldham, J. *Children and work: A study of socialization*. New Brunswick, NJ: Transaction, Inc., 1979.

Gowler, D. & Legge, K. Hidden and open contracts in marriage. in R. Rapoport & R. N. Rapoport (eds.), *Working Couples*. New York: Harper Colophon Books, 1978.

Gronseth, E. Work sharing: A Norwegian example. In R. Rapoport & R. N. Rapoport (eds.), *Working Couples*. New York: Harper Colophon Books, 1978.

Grossman, A. S. Children of working mothers. *Monthly Labor Review*, 1978, *101*, 30–33.

Gurin, G. & Gurin, P. Personal efficacy and the ideology of individual responsibility. In B. Strumpel (ed.), *Economic means for human needs*. Ann Arbor, Michigan: Institute for Social Research, 1976.

Gurin, G., Veroff, J. & Feld, S. Americans view their mental health, 1957.

Hacker, H. M. The feminine protest of the working wife. *Indian Journal of Social Work*, 1971, *31*.

Haller, M. & Rosenmayer, L. The pluridimensiondity of work commitment. *Human Relations*, 1971, *24*, 501–518.

Hartley, R. What aspects of child behavior should be studied in relation to maternal employment on children. A. Siegel (Ed.). PA: Social Science Research Center, 1960.

Hayghe, H. Marital and family characteristics of workers, March 1977. *Monthly Labor Review*, 1978, *3*, 51–54.

Hill, C. R. & Stafford, F. P. Parental care of children time diary estimates of quantity, predictability and variety. *Journal of Human Resources*, 1980, 219–39.

Hoffman, L. W. Changes in family roles, socialization, and sex differences. *American Psychologist*, 1977, *32*, 644–657.

Hoffman, L. W. Psychological factors. In L. W. Hoffman and F. I. Nye (eds.), *Working mothers*, San Francisco: Jossey-Bass, 1974.

Hoffman, L. W. & Nye, F. I. *Working mothers*. San Francisco: Jossey-Bass, 1974.

Holmstrom, L. L. *The two-career family*. Cambridge, Mass: Schenkman, 1973.

Holter, H. *Sex roles and social structure*. Oslo: Universitetsforlkaget, 1970.

Hunt, J. G. & Hunt, L. L. Dilemmas and contradictions of status: The case of the dual-career family. *Social problems*, 1977, *19*, 412–416.

Huser, W. R. & Grant, C. W. A study of husbands and wives from dual-career and traditional-career families. *Psychology of Women Quarterly*, 1978, *3*, 78–79.

Institute for Social Research Fifteen year study documents tremendous change in women's sex-role attitudes. *ISR Newsletter*, 1980, p. 3.

Kahn, R. L. The meaning of work. In *The human meaning of social change* ed. by Angus Campbell & Philip E. Converse. NY: Russell Sage, 1972.

Kahn, R. L. The work module: A proposition for the humanism of work. In J. O'Toole (Ed.), *Work and the quality of life*. Cambridge, MIT Press, 1974.

Kahn, R. L. & French, J. R. P., Jr. Status and conflict: Two themes in the study of stress. In J. E. McGarth (ed.), *Social and Psychological Factors in Stress*. New York: Holt, Reinhart and Winston, 1970.

Kamerman, S. & Kahn, A. J. (eds.) *Family Policy: Government and families in fourteen countries*. New York: Columbia University Press, 1978.

Kanter, R. *Work and family in the United States: A critical review and agenda for research and policy*. New York: Russell Sage, 1977.

Kanter, R. M. Families, family processes, and economic life: Toward systematic analysis of social historical research. *American Journal of Sociology*, 1978, *84*, supplement, 316–340.

Kohn, M. L., Miller, J, Miller, K. A. & Schooler, C. Women and work: The psychological effects of occupational conditions. *American Journal of Sociology*, 1979, *88* 66–95.

Kornhauser, A. *Mental health of the industrial worker*. New York: Wiley, 1965.

Kreps, J. (ed.) *Women and the American Economy* Englewood Cliffs, New Jersey: Prentice-Hall, 1976.

Lein, L., Durham, M., Pratt, M., Schudson, M., Thomas, R. & Weiss, H. Final report: Work and family life. National Institute of Education Project, No. 3-3094. Cambridge, MA: Center for the Study of Public Policy, 1974.

Masnick, G. & Bane, M. J. *The nation's families: 1960-1990*. Cambridge, Mass.: Joint Center for Urban Studies, 1980.

Moen, P. Family impacts of the 1975 recession: Duration of unemployment. *Journal of Marriage and the Family*, 1979, *4*, 561-572.

Moen, P. Preventing financial hardship: Coping strategies of families of the unemployed. In H. McCubbin (ed.), *Family stress, coping and social support* (in press).

Moen, P. & Dempster-McClain, D. Work time preferences of parents of preschoolers. Unpublished draft, 1981.

Moore, K. A. & Hofferth, S. L. Women and their children. In R. E. Smith (ed.), *The Subtle Revolution*. Washington, D.C.: The Urban Institute, 1979.

Molm, L. D. Sex role attitudes and the employment of married woman: The direction of causality. *The Sociological Quarterly*, 1978, *19*, 522-533.

Mortimer, J., R. Hall & Hill, R. Husbands' occupational attributes as constraints on wives' employment. *Sociology of Work and Occupations*, 1978, *5*, 285-313.

Mortimer, J. T. Dual career families: A sociological prespective. In S. S. Peterson, J. M. Richardson, G. V. Kreuter (eds.), *The two-career family—Issues and alternatives*. Washington, D.C.: University Press of America, 1978.

Mortimer, J. T. Work-family linkages as perceived by men in the early stages of professional and managerial careers. In H. Z. Lopata (ed.), *Research in the interweave of social roles: Women and men*. Greenwich: JAI Press, 1979.

Mott, F. L. & Shapiro, D. Work and motherhood: The dynamics of labor force participation surrounding the first birth. In H. S. Parnes (ed.), *Years for decision: A longitudinal study of the educational and labor market experience of young women*, Vol. 4. Columbus, Ohio: Ohio State University Center for Human Resource Research, 1977.

Mott, P. E., Mann, F. C., McLaughlin, Q., & Warwick, D. P. *Shift work: The social, psychological, and physical consequences*. Ann Arbor: University of Michigan Press, 1965.

Myrdal, A., & Klein, V. *Women's two roles: home and work*. London: Routledge & Kegan Paul, 1956.

Nye, F. I. Sociocultural context. In Lois W. Hoffman & F. I. Nye (Eds), *Working mothers*. San Francisco: Jossey-Bass, 1974.

Oakley, A. *The housewife: Past and present*. New York: Vintage Books, 1976.

Oppenheimer, V. K. The life cycle squeeze: The interaction of men's occupational and family life cycles. *Demography*, *11*, 227-246.

Oppenheimer, V. K. The sociology of women's economic role in the family. *American Sociological Review*, 1977, *42*, 387-405.

O'Toole, J. *Work and the quality of life: Resource papers for work in America*. Cambridge, Mass.: MIT Press, 1974.

Papanek, H. Men, women, and work: Reflections on the two-person career. *American Journal of Sociology*, 1973, *78*, 852-872.

Parnes, H. S., Shea, J. R., Spitz, R. S. & Zeller, F. A. *Dual careers: A longitudinal analysis of the labor market experience of women*, Vol. I. (Manpower Research Monograph). Washington, D.C. U.S. Government Printing Office, 1970.

Parsons, T. The social structure of the family. In R. Anshen (ed.), *The family: Its function and destiny*. New York: Harper, 1959.

Parsons, T. & Bales, R. F. *Family socialization and interaction process*. Glencoe, Illinois: The Free Press, 1955.

Piotrkowski, C. S. *Work and the family system: A naturalistic study of working class and lower-middle class families*. New York: The Free Press, 1979.

Pleck, J. H., Staines, G. L., & Lang, L. Conflicts between work and family life. *Monthly Labor Review*, 1980, March, 29-31.

Pleck, J. H. The work-family role system. *Social Problems,* 1977, *24*(4), 417–427.

Pleck, J. Men's family work: Three perspectives and some new data. *The Family Coordinator,* 1979, *28,* 481–487.

Poloma, M. Role conflict and the married professional women. In C. Safilios-Rothschild (ed.), *Toward a sociology of women.* Lexington, Mass.: Xerox College Publishing Co., 1972.

Poloma, M. M. & Garland, T. N. The myth of the egalitarian family: Familial roles and the professionally employed wife. In Athena Theodore (Ed.), *The Professional Woman.* Cambridge, MA: Schenknon Books, 1971.

Propper, A. The relationship of maternal employment to adolescent roles, activities, and parental relationships. *Journal of Marriage and the Family,* 1972, *34,* 417–421.

Quinn, R. P. & Staines, G. L. *The 1977 Quality of Employment Survey.* Ann Arbor, Michigan: Institute for Social Research, University of Michigan, 1978.

Rainwater, L. *What money buys: Inequality and the social meaning of income.* New York: Basic Books, 1974a.

Rainwater, L. Work, well-being and family life. In J. O'Toole (Ed.), *Work and the quality of life.* Cambridge, Mass.: MIT Press, 1974b.

Rallings, E. M. & Nye, R. I. Wife-mother employment: Family & society. In W. R. Burr, R. Hill, F. I. Nye, I. L. Reiss (Eds.), *Contemporary theories about the family,* Vol. I. New York: Free Press, 1979.

Rapoport, R., & Rapoport, R. *Dual-career families.* Baltimore, MD: Penguin, 1971.

Rapoport, R., & Rapoport, R. The Dual-career family: A variant pattern and social change. In Safilios-Rothschild, C. (Ed.), *Toward a sociology of women.* Lexington, MA: Xerox, 1972.

Rapoport, R., & Rapoport, R. *Dual-career families re-examined: new integrations of work and family.* New York: Hoper Colophon, 1976.

Renshaw, J. An exploration of the dynamics of the overlapping worlds of work and family. *Family Process,* 1976, *15,* 143–65.

Robinson, J. *How Americans use time: A social-psychological analysis.* New York: Praeger, 1977.

Safilios-Rothschild, C. The influence of wives' degree of work commitment upon some aspects of family organization and dynamics. *Journal of Marriage and the Family,* 1970, *24,* 681–691.

Scanzoni, J. *Opportunity and the family: A study of the conjugal family in relation to the economic opportunity structure.* New York: Free Press, 1970.

Scanzoni, J. *Sex roles, women's work and marital conflict.* Lexington, Mass.: Lexington Books, 1978.

Seeman, M. The urban alienations: Some dubious theses from Marx to Marcuse. *Journal of personality and social psychology,* 1971, *19,* 135–143.

Seligman, B. B. On work, alienation and leisure. *American Journal of Economics and Sociology,* 1965, *24,* 337–339.

Slocum, W. L. & Nye, F. I. Provider and housekeeper roles. In F. Ivan Nye et al. (Eds.), *Role structure and analysis of the family.* Beverly Hills: Sage Foundation, 1976.

Smith, H. C. *An investigation of the attitudes of adolescent girls toward combining marriage, motherhood, and a career.* Unpublished doctoral dissertation, University microfilms 69–8089, Columbia University, 1969.

Smith, R. E. *The subtle revolution.* Washington, D.C.: The Urban Institute, 1979.

Smith-Lovin, S. & Tickameyer, A. S. Non-recursive models of labor force participation, fertility behavior and sex role attitudes. *American Sociological Review,* 1978, *43,* 541–547.

Sobol, M. G. Commitment to work. In L. W. Hoffman and F. I. Nye (Eds.), *Working mothers.* San Francisco: Jossey-Bass, 1974.

St. Johns-Parsons, D. Continuious dual-career families: A case study. *Psychology of Women Quarterly,* 1978, *3,* 30–42.

Stafford, F. P. Women's use of time converging with men's. *Monthly Labor Review,* 1980, 57–59.

Staines, G. L., Pleck, J. H., Shepard, L. J., & O'Connor, P. Wives' employment status and marital adjustment: Yet another look. In Bryson & Bryson (eds.), *Dual-career couples*. New York: Human Services Press.

Sweet, J. A. *Women in the labor force*. New York: Seminar, 1973.

Tangri, S. S. Determinants of occupational role innovation among college women. *Journal of Social Issues*, 1972, *28*, 177-199.

U.S. Department of Labor *Marital and family characteristics of workers, 1970 to 1978*. Special Labor Force Report 219. Washington: Bureau of Labor Statistics, 1979.

U.S. Department of Labor *Perspectives on working women: A databook*. Bulletin 2080. Washington, D.C.: U.S. Bureau of Labor Statistics, 1980.

Vickery, C. Women's economic contribution to the family. In R. E. Smith (Ed.), *The subtle revolution*. Washington, D.C.: Urban Institute, 1979.

Voydanoff, P. Work-family life cycles. Paper presented at Workship on Theory Construction, National Council on Family Relations, October, 1980.

Waite, L. J. & Stolzenberg, R. M. Intended childbearing and labor force participation of young women: Insights from nonrecursive models. *American Sociological Review*, 1976,*41*, 235-51.

Waldman, E. et al. Working mothers in the 1970's a look at the statistics. *Monthly Labor Review*, 1979, 39-48.

Walker, K. E. & Woods, M. E. *Time use: A measure of household production of family goods and services*. Washington, D.C.: American Home Economics Association, 1976.

Weingarten, K. The employment pattern of professional couples and their distribution of involvement in the family. *Psychology of Women Quarterly*, 1978, *3*, 43-52.

Wilensky, H. L. The moonlighter: A product of relative deprivation. *Industrial Relations*, 1963, *3*, 105-124.

Wilensky, H. L. The uneven distribution of leisure. *Social Problems*, 1961, *9*, 32-56.

Work in America. Report of a Special Task Force to the Secretary of Health, Education and Welfare. Cambridge, Mass.: MIT Press, 1973.

Working Family Project. Parenting. In R. Rapoport and R. Rapoport (eds.), *Working couples*. New York: Harper Colophon Books, 1978.

World of Work Report. *Part-time workers constitute fast-growing work force segment*, 1977.

Young, M. & Willmott, P. *The symmetrical family*. New York: Pantheon Books, 1973.

Yankelovich, Skelly, & White. *The general mills American family report 1974-75*. Minneapolis, Minn., 1975.

3 Maternal Employment and Child Development: A Review

Michael E. Lamb
University of Utah

Most of the family styles discussed in this volume involve relatively uncommon deviations from the traditional pattern, comprising a male breadwinner with a wife responsible for child rearing and homemaking. However, several of the chapters, including this one, deal with family characteristics that, though nontraditional, are at least as common today as—if not more common than—traditional family styles. As the authors note, dual-provider families, maternal employment, and the use of nonfamilial supplementary child care have become normative practices in contemporary Western nations.

According to tradition, adult women should withdraw from the paid work force when they are married, becoming full-time homemakers and (shortly thereafter) mothers from that point on. Historically, the first notable deviation from this pattern occurred when the widespread availability of contraceptives made it possible for couples to postpone childbearing for several years; in many cases, women could and did continue to work outside the home until the birth of their first child. More recently, however, an increasing number of women have chosen to remain in paid employment not only before but also after their children are born. By 1978, 50% of the women in the United States and 44% of the married women with husbands present were in the paid labor force; the number of employed women is expected to rise to 57% by 1995 (Glick, 1979). Employment rates are not that much lower today for married mothers in intact families than for women in general: In 1975, 52% of the mothers of school-aged children (6- to 17-year-olds) and 36% of the mothers of infants and preschool-aged children were employed, although some of these women were employed part time (Glick & Norton, 1979). Employment rates are even higher for single mothers and for married black women in intact families (Glick & Norton, 1979). Most single mothers are employed, and 16% of the children under 18 live with single mothers. The employment rate among married black mothers exceeds 60%. In all, therefore, a substantial minority of the children in the United States have both parents employed outside the home, or else have only one parent who is almost certain to be in paid employment. Another way of viewing these statistics is to observe that only 23% of the households in the United States now fit the traditional pattern, with father as sole breadwinner and mother at home caring for one or more children (Pleck & Rustad, 1980).

Maternal employment has not always been so common, of course. The proportion of employed married women increased 28% between 1960 and 1975, while the proportion of mothers of preschoolers who were in paid employment increased 57% during the same period (Glick & Norton, 1979). Increases are even more dramatic if we compare current rates of maternal employment with those of the 1940s and 1950s. These historical trends are extremely important when evaluating research on maternal employment; because today's normative practices were deviant a few decades ago, it is likely that maternal employment was regarded and evaluated very differently (by working women themselves, their spouses and peers, those who helped care for their children, and researchers) in 1940 than it is viewed today. Just a generation ago, for example, the working mother (especially one with young children) was considered selfishly derelict in her maternal responsibilities, and her husband (if there was one) was considered a shamefully inadequate provider and/or a weak husband because he "permitted" his wife to work. Such hostile attitudes toward maternal employment may have increased the likelihood that maternal employment would adversely affect children's development, either directly or indirectly. By contrast, popular attitudes toward maternal employment are much more accepting today. As a result, it is doubtful how much the findings of early studies tell us about the effects of maternal employment on children growing up in the 1980s.

In this chapter, I first review evidence and speculations about the various reasons why so many mothers are employed today before discussing in the second section the effects of maternal employment on family dynamics. In both sections, I stress that working mothers do not constitute a single homogeneous group—far from it. The evident heterogeneity among them is important, for maternal employment is likely to have different effects on family functioning and parenting depending on the individual's circumstances and motivations. Thereafter, I review evidence concerning the effects of maternal employment on infants, young children, and adolescents in three separate sections. Research concerning the different age groups differs in thoroughness, consistency, and degree of attention to mediating variables; consequently, these sections are not equally long or equivalently conclusive. In the final section, I attempt to clarify the demonstrated effects by discussing them in social context.

WHY MOTHERS SEEK EMPLOYMENT

One can divide the reasons why mothers seek paid employment into two broad classes: economic and personal. These distinctions are useful for analytic purposes, but they are not rigid. Furthermore, the various reasons mentioned here are not mutually exclusive and my discussion is by no means exhaustive.

Economic Reasons

A large number of mothers are employed by virtue of economic necessity; maternal employment is the only way that many families can afford their chosen standard of living. Economic necessity is hard to define absolutely in an affluent, consumer-oriented society; certainly, most two-parent families do not *need* two incomes to bring themselves above the official poverty level although many of them do "need" two incomes in order to achieve or even approach the life-style to which they aspire. The statistics and tables presented by the United States Census Bureau quantify and illustrate the obvious: The total income of families with two wage earners is substantially and significantly higher than that of families with only one wage earner. Even when one takes into account the increased costs of supplementary child care in dual-provider families, it is clear that families that can count on two incomes are economically better off than those that must rely on only one.

For married women with children, therefore, the choice is between paid employment and acceptance of a lower standard of living. Two incomes have always been larger than one, but recent socioeconomic changes have changed the relative costs and benefits of employment and homemaking. First, consumer aspirations, in the context of accelerating and apparently uncontrollable inflation, have risen more rapidly than have average incomes. This has accentuated the perceived need for a second income. Second, the slowdown of the United States economy in the decade since the Vietnam War has made the prospect of temporary or permanent unemployment a fact of life for many adults, and this has made a second wage earner seem like a sensible insurance against economic uncertainty. Third, there is much less prejudice against maternal employment today then there was decades ago and there are many more options for alternative child care.

Many employed mothers, however, do not have the luxury of choice; single mothers generally have to work in order to support themselves and their families even at an impoverished level. Single mothers no longer constitute a small group; the number of single-parent families has grown dramatically in the last few decades. Current statistics indicate that one in five children in the United States spends at least a portion of his or her childhood in a single-parent family (Glick,

1979; Glick & Norton, 1979). Thus rising divorce rates have contributed substantially to increases in the rates of maternal employment.

Personal Reasons

A number of secular attitudinal trends seem related to the steady increases in the rate of maternal employment, although the correlational nature of the evidence makes it difficult to distinguish clearly between causes and effects.

The most important of these attitudinal changes can be attributed to the women's liberation movement. The women's movement has successfully promoted the beliefs that women deserve educational opportunities equivalent to those of men and that they should have equal opportunities of employment in positions for which they are qualified. The rhetoric of feminist leaders has legitimized, if not accentuated, the ambitions of work- and career-oriented women by repeatedly emphasizing that women need not feel limited to careers as homemakers and mothers. Whether or not the feminist movement caused, catalyzed, or simply articulated previously unspoken desires, the reality is that many women today want to be employed. For many of these women, especially those who are well educated, maintenance of a sense of self-worth depends on the rewards of employment—either because employment per se or the satisfaction of the particular job are intrinsically rewarding, or because esteem derives from contributing to the economic support of the family. The perceived psychological value of employment relative to homemaking and motherhood has also been enhanced by the pervasive devaluation of child care and housework; especially in professional and middle-class circles it is often rather shameful to admit being "only a housewife and mother."

These social and psychological pressures make employment desirable regardless of the family's economic circumstances. Thus, a national survey conducted in 1976 found that 75% of the women who were employed said they would remain employed even if it were not economically necessary (Dubnoff, Veroff, & Kulka, 1978). The most common reason given for this desire to remain employed was "to fill the time"; only 10% of the women interviewed said that they worked to fulfill achievement aspirations (Dubnoff et al., 1978). Meanwhile, educated women who are unemployed may become overprotective mothers who suffer a decline in self-esteem as their full-time availability comes to exceed the decreasing needs of growing children (Birnbaum, 1975).

Attitudinal changes supportive of maternal employment have been paralleled by declines in average fertility rates. As a result, average family size has fallen dramatically throughout the industrialized world in the last few decades. In many western European and communist countries, the average family now has fewer than two children and, in the United States, the average is just over two (Glick & Norton, 1979). Viewed in the context of scientific and medical advances that have increased average life expectancy to 73 years (Richmond, 1980), reduced family size means that childbearing and child rearing make demands on a relatively small (and declining) portion of the average person's life-span. Furthermore, because it is less taxing to care for two children than for six, the child-rearing years themselves are less demanding today than they were in the past.

Finally, today's families are not only smaller but are being formed later; many more married and cohabitating couples defer childbearing now than did so in preceding decades (Glick & Norton, 1979). Before deciding to have children, many women obtain educational qualifications, work experience, and seniority. They also get accustomed to being employed, and their families come to rely on the income they provide. Consequently, many of these women are unwilling to withdraw from the work force when they become mothers, other than for the parental leave that they are permitted to take without losing their jobs.

Summary

Singly or in diverse combinations, the foregoing factors explain why so many women now seek to combine motherhood and employment. The relative importance of these rationales or motivations varies substantially from one mother to the next, and this has significant implications for attempts to explore the effects of maternal employment. If we are to understand whether and how maternal employment affects child development, it is necessary to determine first why the mother is employed and how she feels about it, because this helps determine how maternal employment is viewed by the woman and her peers. This in turn permits us to define the psychological and social context of her employment and thus makes it easier to specify its probable effects. Although researchers seldom acknowledge it, there is a world of difference between the woman who has to work although she does not want to do so and the mother who has carefully prepared herself for the combination of parenthood and career because both are intrinsically important to her. Both are employed, but they are likely to behave differently toward their children and so affect their development in distinctly different ways. Unfortunately, it is difficult to substantiate such speculations empirically. Most studies have simply compared employed mothers and/or their children with unemployed mothers and/or their children without regard for the vast diversity within these two heterogeneous groups. Employed mothers differ among themselves with respect to: when in their children's lives they resumed work; why they did so; how they feel about combining motherhood and employment; how their spouses, families, and peers feel about maternal employment; how much they work (e.g., part or full time); and how flexible their working hours are. All these differences surely affect the impact of maternal employment on the family and on the children's development, although in the absence of the necessary research we can only speculate about the importance of these factors.

EFFECTS OF MATERNAL EMPLOYMENT ON FAMILY
DYNAMICS

In this section, I turn attention to the attitudes and values of the employed mother, her spouse (if she has one), and her reference group of family and friends. Of the issues discussed here, the most important concern: whether the woman is employed because she wants to work or because she has to; whether her spouse approves of or feels threatened by her employment; the relative importance of motherhood and work to the mother; and the amount of practical and emotional support she receives from her husband and reference group. Together, these factors seem likely to affect both the emotional status of the employed mother and the extent to which her household and child-care responsibilities are reduced by the increased involvement of others.

The research on the relationship between maternal employment and marital satisfaction is of varying quality and the findings are somewhat inconsistent. On the whole, however, it seems that working women tend to be as satisfied as, or more satisfied than, homemakers, whereas the husbands of employed women tend to be less satisfied than the husbands of unemployed women (Glenn, 1975; Moore & Hofferth, 1979). It seems likely that there would be a social class difference in this regard. Although the correlation between social class and attitudes regarding sex-role stereotypes is highly imperfect, it is still the case that the attitudes of lower- and working-class individuals are more conservative and traditional than those of middle-class men and women. As Komarovsky (1962) graphically reported many years ago, working-class men feel that they are responsible for supporting their wives and families, and thus that they may be viewed as failures if their wives "have to" work, too. Their wives tend to share these conservative attitudes, and thus when lower-class women are employed, it is often by necessity rather than by choice. Their conservative husbands are least likely to assist with home and child-care chores, regardless of their wives' employment status. In such circumstances, therefore, maternal employment undermines the husband's status and increases the likelihood of role strain in the employee/wife/mother, without bringing compensating benefits such as enhanced self-esteem for the woman.

It is among the well-educated middle class that the most dramatic attitudinal changes have taken place in recent years. Men and women from such backgrounds at least claim to support the right of women to seek personal fulfillment and economic rewards through paid employment. Many middle-class women want to be employed whether or not it is financially necessary because employment constitutes a significant aspect of their self-definition and is thus a significant source of self-esteem. Although these women retain primary responsibility for most household and child-care chores regardless of their employment status, their husbands do spend slightly more time in household and child-care tasks (Pleck & Rustad, 1980). This increase in men's family work, coupled with a major decline in the amount of time employed women devote to such activities, means that in relative terms, employed women perform a substantially smaller proportion of the necessary work around the home than do unemployed women (Blood & Hamblin, 1958; Hall & Schroeder, 1970; Hoffman, 1977; Holmstrom, 1972; Kliger, 1954; Pleck, 1979; Pleck & Rustad, 1980; Szolai, 1966; Walker, 1970; Weil, 1961). Consequently, adverse effects of role overload due to these mothers' efforts to be primary parents and primary housekeepers, as well as economic providers, are likely to be offset, as least in part, by the enhancement in self-esteem derived from employment and by their husbands' assistance and support. Stated differently, if such women were forced to withdraw from employment against their will, they might benefit from having more time to devote to their children, but the quality of their parenting might suffer due to dissatisfaction and declining self-esteem. Although their husbands do not come close to sharing household and child-care responsibilities, they are at least emotionally and attitudinally supportive, as are most friends. This fact should moderate any adverse effects of maternal employment (and consequent inaccessibility) in the children.

Attitudes and values are also important in determining the amount of guilt experienced over the dereliction of maternal responsibilities. As values change and maternal employment becomes more common, guilt is less likely to occur, except perhaps among employed mothers of young infants. Nevertheless, when women fear, and others gloomily confirm, that maternal employment will adversely affect their children's development, employed mothers may feel guilty about their decision to work, especially when that decision appears to have been selfishly motivated rather than economically necessary.

Furthermore, it is important to recognize that, quite apart from its economic costs, the decision *not* to work may have adverse implications for the child's care and development. It seems unlikely that a child is materially better off with a dissatisfied full-time mother who would prefer to be working than with a part-time mother who is contented and fulfilled, assisted by a consistent extrafamilial caretaker during working hours (Yarrow, Scott, DeLeeuw, & Heinig, 1962). Thus Farel (1980) reported that the most poorly adjusted children were those who had mothers who wanted to be, but were not, employed. When a mother is employed, the development of her child is affected not simply by the mother's regular absences, but also by the quality of interaction when she is present, the stability and quality of the supplementary care arrangement, the similarity between the parenting styles experienced at home and in supplementary care settings, and the additional interaction with peers that most extrafamilial settings assure (see also Belsky, Steinberg, & Walker, chapter 4). In addition, to the extent that the father's involvement in child care increases when his wife is employed, the relative formative importance of the father–child relationship is likely to increase (Lamb, 1981). This too must be taken into account when appraising the effects of maternal employment on child development.

In several recent publications (Lamb, Chase-Lansdale, & Owen, 1979; Lamb & Easterbrooks, 1981; Lamb, Owen, & Chase-Lansdale, 1980), I have speculated about the processes whereby variations in parental attitudes about work and child rearing may affect the socioemotional development of infants and young children. I have argued that parental sensitivity or responsiveness is most likely to be affected by the mother's satisfaction or dissatisfaction, the relative subjective evaluation of parenthood and work, the mother's guilt, the supportiveness of her spouse and friends, and the perceived oppressiveness of her combined role demands. Thus women who feel unfulfilled or dissatisfied, to whom parenthood is not intrinsically important, who feel guilty because they are employed, and who receive little or no support from family and friends, are likely to be less sensitive parents who establish relationships of poorer quality with their children. Analogously, maternal employment may not affect or may even enhance the quality of parent–child relationships when it brings enhanced self-esteem, satisfaction, and the support of husbands and friends.

Summary

Just as the motivations for maternal employment vary, so also is there diversity in the ways in which maternal employment is appraised. The attitudes of the employed mother and her husband are especially important in determining whether she feels badly about being employed, how greatly she is overburdened by her combined roles, and how much psychological gratification she obtains from employment. All these factors are likely to affect the quality of the child's experiences within the family. These factors, along with differences among substitute care settings, together determine how maternal employment affects child development. Maternal employment is likely to have very different effects on children's development, depending on the characteristics of individual families, but few studies have taken this heterogeneity into account.

EFFECTS OF MATERNAL EMPLOYMENT ON CHILDREN

Infants, Toddlers, and Preschoolers

There have been many published reviews on the effects of maternal employment on child development—a fact testifying to the longstanding concern that maternal employment might have adverse effects on children (Etaugh, 1974; Hoffman, 1974a, 1979; Nye & Hoffman, 1963; Siegel & Haas, 1963; Stolz, 1960; Yudkin & Holme, 1963). Each of these reviews—even those published most recently—has observed that least is known about the effects of maternal employment on the socioemotional development of infants and toddlers, because this age group has been least extensively studied. In part, this is because maternal employment has traditionally been least common among mothers with small children, and in part it is because developmental theorists have long had fewer doubts about the effects of maternal employment on young children than about its effects on school-aged children. Most developmentalists agreed that maternal employment during these years was more likely to affect development adversely (Bowlby, 1973). Researchers such as Blehar (1975) have explicitly suggested that: "many repetitions of minor [i.e., daily] separations may have effects similar in form to major separation [p. 294]." Unfortunately, many of the studies that ostensibly might allow us to investigate these dire predictions were designed as studies on the effects of day care rather than studies on the effects of maternal employment. This may be an important point, because although both maternal employment and day care involve repeated daily separations from mothers and although most employed mothers do seek supplementary extrafamilial care for their children, most children are not enrolled in day-care programs ("family day care" is much more common). Further, the attitudinal and motivational variables discussed in the previous sections are not relevant to the effects of day care and have not been considered. For these reasons, and also because the data are reviewed more thoroughly by Belsky and his colleagues in Chapter 4, this volume, I review these data briefly, focusing primarily on those studies in which maternal employment was explicitly considered.

Most researchers have simply compared children enrolled in day-care centers with those who are cared for by their mothers. The findings of such studies indicate that children establish preferential attachments to their mothers even when they are in supplementary day care (Farran & Ramey, 1977; Fox, 1977; Kagan, Kearsley, & Zelazo, 1978; Maccoby & Feldman, 1972), although they also form attachments to consistent supplementary caretakers (Willis & Ricciuti, 1974). Contrary to theoretically derived predictions, day care appears to have no adverse effects on the child–mother attachment (Brookhart & Hock, 1976; Cochran, 1977; Doyle, 1975; Doyle & Somers, 1975; Feldman, 1974; Lieberman, 1976; Moskowitz, Schwarz, & Corsini, 1978; Ragozin, 1980; Roopnarine & Lamb, 1978). Blehar (1974) reported divergent findings, suggesting that children who entered day care around 2 years of age were likely to avoid their mothers after a brief separation, whereas those who entered day care at 3 behaved angrily toward their mothers. However, others have not been able to replicate these findings (Blanchard & Main, 1979, Moskowitz et al., 1978; Ragozin, 1979; Roopnarine & Lamb, 1978), leading Blanchard and Main (1979) to suggest that Blehar had observed temporary adjustment difficulties right after enrollment, rather than enduring effects. Further, few studies involve preenrollment assessments to determine whether the day-care and home-care groups are initially comparable (Frye, 1979); those that have done so (Roopnarine & Lamb, 1978, 1980) suggest that preenrollment differences may by greater than the later differences! In one of the only longitudinal studies yet conducted, Moore (1975) followed a group of English children for many years and reported that unstable supplementary care in the preschool years predicted maladjustment in adolescence. However, this finding is hard to evaluate because the stability of the caretaking arrangements was confounded with familial stability. In all, therefore, the evidence suggests that day care generally does not have adverse effects on the development of young children, but these studies tell us little about the effects of maternal employment.

Perhaps because so many reviewers have urged researchers to investigate the effects of maternal employment on infants and young children, there have recently been several intensive studies of employed mothers with very young children. Their findings are not entirely consistent, however, and so there remains a need for further research on this topic. Nevertheless, the studies are impressive because here at least researchers have clearly tried to view both employed and unemployed mothers as representatives of heterogeneous rather than homogenous groups and thus have sought to determine, by way of within-group analyses, what factors other than maternal employment per se affect the psychosocial development of young children. I have argued elsewhere (Lamb et al., 1979, 1980; Lamb & Easterbrooks, 1981) that such studies promise to tell us most about social development and about the processes whereby maternal employment or unemployment affects child development.

Comparing the mother–infant interactions involving employed and unemployed mothers of preterm infants, Cohen (1978) reported no group differences during the first year of life. In the second year, however, she found that the nonworking mothers had more positive interactions with their infants, who vocalized more and had higher developmental quotients. Unfortunately, the groups differed initially, in that the women who later sought employment had smaller and lighter infants and were more likely to be single parents. Consequently, it is not clear that the group differences can be attributed to maternal employment status.

Ellen Hock (1978, 1980; Hock, Christman, & Hock, 1980) has recently completed a prospective study of employed and unemployed mothers recruited around the time of delivery. Analyzing data gathered around delivery and when the infants were 3 months old, she found that those who resumed paid work within the infants' first trimester reported less infant distress at separation, were themselves less anxious about separation, and trusted supplementary caretakers more than did uemployed mothers (Hock, 1978). Predictably, the employed mothers were more career oriented than the unemployed mothers. Interestingly, career orientation was differently correlated with other attitudes among working and nonworking mothers. Among employed mothers, the correlations were all negative; the higher the career orientation, the less the reported distress at separation, the less the mothers' anxiety about separation, and the less the mothers' apprehension about other caretakers. These three variables were positively correlated with career orientation among the unemployed mothers.

In a later report, Hock (1980) factor-analyzed interview and observational data gathered during the first year of the infants' lives. She reported that compared with unemployed mothers, working mothers were less likely to believe that they alone could meet their infants' needs adequately (which is not surprising) and that unemployed mothers seemed to have a greater need for reassurance and guidance from others. This last finding was consistent with a comparable report by Burke and Weir (1976) concerning employed and unemployed mothers with older children. The only behavioral difference related to maternal employment status was that the infants of unemployed mothers displayed more resistant (i.e., angry) behavior toward the stranger (*not* their mothers) in Ainsworth's Strange Situation procedure (Ainsworth, Blehar, Waters, & Wall, 1978). There were no group differences in maternal behavior. However, the generalizability of these findings may be limited by characteristics that make the group of employed mothers rather unusual. All their infants were cared for by a consistent caretaker, in a home setting, with no more than one other child present; these unusually good caretaking arrangements may help account for the absence of adverse effects attributable to maternal employment.

Hock et al. (1980) subsequently compared the unemployed mothers with mothers who originally planned not to work but later changed their minds and decided to seek paid employment. Those who changed plans regarding employment were much less likely to have planned the pregnancy and were much more career oriented than were those who followed through on their decisions not to seek employment. Those who changed plans perceived infant distress as a personal affront and reported being more upset by their infants' fussiness than the unemployed mothers were. According to Hock et al., 1980: "From the baby's birth to 3 months of age, [those who changed plans] grew less positive in attitude toward the maternal role whereas [the nonworkers] tended to grow more positive. [Those who changed plans] perceived their babies as less dependent on their own unique caregiving characteristics [p. 536]." Unfortunately Hock et al. did not report how the infants fared, but it seems reasonable to predict that these attitudinal differences are significant, especially when mothers are forced into an undesirable (un)employment status.

In another prospective longitudinal study, my colleagues and I (Owen, Chase-Lansdale, & Lamb, in preparation) found that employed mothers with infants valued work more and parenthood less than did nonemployed mothers. Working mothers also reported less support from family and friends for their child-care plans. They reported marginally more help in child care from their husbands, whereas the fathers themselves reported that they provided substantially more help than did the husbands of the unemployed mothers. Satisfaction with parenthood was positively correlated with the value of parenthood and was negatively correlated with both the perceived value of work and resentment of the infant's intrusion. Infants who were securely attached at 1 year tended to have mothers who valued parenthood highly whereas those who were insecurely attached tended to value work highly and parenthood less. Mothers who were employed—especially those who were employed full time—were more likely to have infants who were insecurely attached to them than were unemployed mothers. However, when employed mothers valued both parenthood and work, their infants tended to develop secure attachments, indicating that maternal employment per se did not necessarily result in insecure mother–infant attachments. Rather, it was the perceived importance of parenthood that was critical.

Two other recent studies confirm the relationship between maternal employment and insecure infant–mother attachment. Both Thompson, Lamb, and Estes (in press) and Vaughn, Gove, and Egeland (in press) reported that insecure infant–mother attachments were more likely to develop when the mothers were employed outside the home and their infants thus experienced regular nonmaternal care. The infants of employed mothers notably seemed to avoid rather than seek interaction with their mothers (Vaughn et al., in press). In addition, Thompson et al. reported that the security or insecurity of the attachment relationships were more likely to change between 12 and 19 months of age when mothers worked outside the home than when they did not.

The recent spate of investigations concerning maternal employment and infant development has not been matched by a comparable flurry of activity regarding slightly older children. However, Gold and Andres (1978c; Gold, Andres, & Glorieux, 1979) have recently conducted two careful studies involving middle-class English- and French-speaking Canadian 4-year-olds and their mothers, many of whom had been employed since the children's births. Gold and her colleagues reported better adjustment among the children of employed mothers than among the children of unemployed mothers, although in the English sample the sons of employed mothers had lower IQs. The suggestion that maternal employment adversely affects achievements by sons is interesting because it is consistent with findings obtained in several studies involving adolescents and preadolescents (see below). Most of the earlier studies that focused on the effects of maternal employment on young children reported no differences in psychological adjustment between preschool-aged children whose mothers were and were not employed (Chu, 1970; Nye, Perry, & Ogles, 1963; Siegel, Stolz, Hitchcock, & Adamson, 1963).

Effects on child development were not assessed in two other recent studies comparing employed and unemployed mothers with preschool-aged children, but the studies are interesting nevertheless. Goldberg (1977) reported that employed and unemployed middle-class mothers spent equivalent amounts of time in one-to-one interaction with their children. This finding suggests that maternal employment does not necessarily reduce the amount of parent–child interaction and makes it even more important to explore further the qualitative factors mediating parental influences on their children's development. Goldberg's finding also implies that employed mothers need not fear that their jobs deprive them of the interaction that unemployed mothers and their children enjoy (Birnbaum, 1971; Hoffman, 1963b; Kliger, 1954). In a larger time-use survey, Hill and Stafford

(1978) confirmed Goldberg's finding where highly educated mothers were concerned. However, they found that less educated mothers reduced their involvement with their children as their involvement in the labor force increased.

Early and Middle Childhood

Many of the studies of elementary school-aged children were designed to appraise the widespread assumption that maternal employment had predictably
adverse effects on children's development. Consequently, most researchers have
examined the effects on psychological adjustment and sex-role stereotyping.
(Sex-role stereotyping was once viewed as an index of psychological adjustment.) I discuss research on these two topics separately here.

Psychological Adjustment.   The results of studies focused on psychological
adjustment are somewhat inconsistent. One investigation of Belgian children
(Dits & Cambier, 1966) reported that the sons of employed mothers were more
poorly adjusted than the sons of unemployed mothers, another study reported that
maternal employment was associated with better adjustment among Israeli children (Rabin, 1965), whereas several reported no group differences (Hand, 1957;
Hoffman, 1963b; Rouman, 1956; Schreiner, 1963; Yarrow, 1961; Yarrow,
Scott, deLeeuw, & Heinig, 1962). Each study has identified some poorly adjusted children, of course, and two researchers have tried to determine what
factors are associated with maladjustment in the children of both employed and
unemployed mothers. Hoffman (1963b) reported that the children of dissatisfied
working mothers were most poorly adjusted, and Woods (1972) reported that
employed mothers who had the most positive attitudes about work had the best
adjusted children. These findings led Etaugh (1974) to conclude that mothers
who are satisfied with their lives have the best adjusted children, regardless of
their employment status. Perhaps this is because life satisfaction increases the
effectiveness of parents (Gold & Andres, 1978b; Hoffman 1974a).

Other studies have reported that maternal employment affects boys from
lower- and middle-class families rather differently. In lower-class families, maternal employment is associated with strains in father–son relationships and resulting reductions in the extent to which the boys respect and admire their fathers
(Douvan, 1963; Gold & Andres, 1978b; Hoffman, 1974a; Kappel & Lambert,
1972; McCord, McCord, & Thurber, 1963; Propper, 1972; Romer & Cherry,
1978). These strains may account for the finding that the sons of lower-class
employed mothers are more poorly adjusted than any other group (Douvan,
1963; McCord et al., 1963). In middle-class families no comparable strains in
parent–child relationships are reported, and although the sons of employed
mothers may do more poorly at school than the sons of unemployed mothers
(Brown, 1971; Burchinal, 1963; Dits & Cambier, 1966; Frankel, 1964; Gold &
Andres, 1978a; Rees & Palmer, 1970), the effects on psychological adjustment

remain unclear. Three studies have reported that maternal employment has no effect (Burchinal, 1963; Roy, 1963; Schooler, 1972), two found positive effects (Farley, 1968; Nelson, 1971), and one reported adverse effects (Brown, 1970) on the adjustment of middle-class boys. Presumably, maternal employment has worse effects on boys from lower-class families because members of this subculture tend to have more traditionally sex-stereotyped expectations and are thus likely to regard maternal employment as evidence of the fathers' failure to provide for their families. This would make the fathers seem poor models with whom to identify. It is not at all clear, however, why employed mothers in middle-class families should have sons who perform more poorly at school than do unemployed mothers.

Sex Roles.   There is much less inconsistency in the results of studies focused on gender-related attitudes and values than in the research concerned with psychological adjustment. Both girls (Baruch, 1972; Duvall, 1955; Finkelman, 1966; Gold & Andres, 1978c; Hartley, 1960; Hoffman, 1963b; Hoffman & Nye, 1974; King, McIntyre, & Axelson 1968; Meier, 1972; Miller, 1975; Romer & Cherry, 1978) and boys (Gold & Andres, 1978c; Hoffman, 1963b, 1974a; Romer & Cherry, 1978) have less sex-stereotyped expectations and attitudes when their mothers are employed than when their mothers are unemployed. These studies, and those concerning adolescents, which are reviewed later, also indicate that the daughters of employed mothers are more career oriented and aspire to more nontraditional roles than do the daughters of unemployed mothers.

Other Findings.   Finally, studies of school-aged children and adolescents reveal that compared with those whose mothers are unemployed, children are more likely to have responsibility for household chores when their mothers are employed (Douvan, 1963; Hoffman, 1963b; Johnson, 1969; Propper, 1972; Roy, 1963; Walker, 1970a; Yarrow et al., 1962). This may be important, as the assignment of responsibility for household chores appears to enhance self-esteem (Smokler, 1975). Employed mothers are also more likely than unemployed mothers to train their children to be independent (Birnbaum, 1971; Burchinal & Lovell, 1959; Hoffman, 1963b; McCord et al., 1963; Yarrow et al., 1962).

Adolescence and College Age

Psychological Adjustment.   Because paper-and-pencil measures can easily be used to obtain self-report information from adolescents and college students, many researchers have compared groups of adolescents (especially female students) having employed and unemployed mothers. The reported behavior of employed and unemployed mothers does not differ systematically (Finkelman, 1966; Franke, 1972; Propper, 1972; Woods, 1972). There are also no consistent differences in psychological adjustment related to maternal employment status (Armstrong, 1967; Baruch, 1972b; Burchinal, 1963; Dawson, 1970; Fish, 1970; George & Thomas, 1967; Nelson, 1971; Nye, 1963; Rabin, 1965; Roy, 1963), although one study reported that maternal employment adversely affected sons (Brown, 1970), and several reported that it had favorable consequences for both sons and daughters (Farley, 1968; Gold & Andres, 1978a; Stott, 1965; Whitmarsh, 1965). In one large-scale study, Kappel and Lambert (1972) reported increased self-esteem and respect for parents among adolescent girls whose mothers worked for self-oriented reasons (e.g., achievement), but not among those whose mothers worked for family-oriented reasons (e.g., to support the family). Unfortunately, such distinctions are seldom made by researchers, for the methodological quality of the work tends to be extremely poor. Many researchers have failed to specify factors such as when the mothers began employment, what sorts of jobs they had, whether they worked part time or full time, and even— incredible as it may seem—the sex or socioeconomic background of the subjects! This may account for some of the inconsistency among studies. The most parsimonious conclusion seems to be that maternal employment usually does not affect the adjustment of adolescents adversely. In fact, recent studies like those of Gold and Andres (1978a, 1978b) report better adjustment among adolescents (especially those from middle-class families) whose mothers are employed— perhaps because unemployed mothers suffer loneliness and a decline in self-esteem as their adolescent children grow older and their maternal responsibilities diminish (Birnbaum, 1975).

Achievement.   The adolescent daughters of employed mothers today appear more outgoing, independent, active and motivated to achieve than the daughters of unemployed mothers (Almquist & Angrist, 1970; Tangri, 1969). By contrast, maternal employment sometimes appears to have adverse consequences on the achievement motivation of sons (Banducci, 1967; Brown, 1970; Burchinal, 1963; Dits & Cambier, 1966; Frankel 1964; Gold & Andres, 1978a), although some studies have failed to replicate such effects (Keidel, 1970; Nelson, 1969; Roy, 1963; Schreiner, 1963), and Banducci (1967) reported adverse effects only among upper-class boys. The effects on achievement motivation are not readily explained, and in at least two cases (Frankel, 1964; Jones, Lundsteen, & Michael, 1967) the effects have been traced, not to maternal employment, but to the prestige of the mothers' jobs and their level of education. Consequently, considerably more research is needed before we will understand whether and how maternal employment affects achievement motivation in sons.

Sex Roles.   As in the case of younger children, studies of sex-role conceptions among high school pupils, college students, and young adults repeatedly find that the sons and daughters of employed mothers have more egalitarian and less sex-stereotyped attitudes than do the children of unemployed mothers

(Almquist & Angrist, 1970; Astin, 1969; Banducci, 1967; Baruch, 1972a; Below, 1969; Birnbaum, 1971; Douvan, 1963; Frieze, Parsons, & Ruble 1972; Hoffman, 1963c; King et al., 1968; Meier, 1972; Peterson, 1958; Roy, 1963; Siegel & Curtis, 1963; Smith, 1969; Tangri, 1972; Vogel, Broverman, Broverman, Clarkson, & Rosenkrantz, 1970; White, 1967; Zissis, 1964). Presumably, this is because employed mothers provide less traditional role models than do unemployed mothers. In addition, because the husbands of employed women perform a greater proportion of household tasks than do the husbands of full-time homemakers, they too provide less traditional role models (Hoffman, 1977).

Summary

Evidently, researchers are now responding to the repeated assertions by reviewers that the effects of maternal employment of infants have been studied insufficiently. Several studies involving young children have recently been undertaken; their results suggest that insecure infant–mother relationships are more likely to develop when mothers of young infants are employed than when they are not. Insecure infant–mother attachments are not inevitable in such circumstances, however. Effects on the security of infant–mother attachment appear to vary depending on the perceived value of employment and parenthood to the mother and the nature of the supplementary care arrangement. The age of children when their mothers return to work may also be important: Multiple caretaking may have fewer adverse effects when infants are exposed to two or more consistent caretakers earlier rather than later in their lives (Hock, 1978).

From the multitude of studies conducted, the firmest conclusion is that the sons and daughters of employed mothers have less sex-stereotyped expectations and values than do the children of unemployed mothers. Studies focused on other outcome measures reveal less clear-cut group differences. In general, there is substantial evidence that mothers who are satisfied with their lives—whether or not they are employed—have well-adjusted children. On the other hand, boys from lower-class families appear in some studies to be poorly adjusted, whereas boys from middle- to upper-class families appear to suffer declines in achievement motivation. Both findings are not consistently reported, however, and the reasons for any such effects have not been explored. There remains a substantial need for research designed to determine *how* maternal employment affects child development—positively or negatively.

EFFECTS IN CULTURAL CONTEXT

Perhaps the most consistent effect emerging from a review of the literature on the effects of maternal employment (see the foregoing) is that children with employed mothers have less stereotyped or more egalitarian sex-role concepts than do children with unemployed mothers. Researchers interpreting these results a few years ago would have described the daughters of employed mothers as less feminine or more masculine (and sons as more feminine/less masculine) than the children of unemployed mothers. Implicitly or explicity, this would have been portrayed as an adverse effect of maternal employment, because psychological adjustment was believed to demand appropriate (sic) sex typing. By contrast, conformity to traditional sex-stereotyped roles is no longer viewed as a desired ideal; rather, those who combine high masculinity and high femininity are believed to be well adjusted (Bem, 1975; Bem & Lenney, 1976; Bem, Martyna, & Watson, 1976), and conformity to sex roles is considered less important to adjustment than the security of gender identity (Lamb & Urberg, 1978). In addition, previous reviews of the maternal employment literature (Hoffman, 1974a, 1979) have argued that we must view the effects of maternal employment in light of the sort of society that is likely to exist when today's children become adults. Although sex discrimination continues and sex-role stereotypes remain, the trends are for fewer and fewer women to become full-time homemakers and mothers and, to a lesser extent, for men to assume increasing responsibility for home and child care. Consequently, because of the more egalitarian attitudes they develop, children whose mothers were employed are better prepared for their future adult roles than are the children whose mothers were unemployed. Employed mothers also encourage independence in their children—again, an advantage rather than a disadvantage, especially for young women (Hoffman, 1977). In all, therefore, many of the more reliably reported effects of maternal employment must be viewed as beneficial rather than harmful consequences.

The same secular changes in societal values also alter the subjective status of employed women and mothers. Where they once occupied atypical and somewhat disapproved roles, employed mothers are now in the majority. Unemployed mothers, because they are "only" housewives and mothers, are now the brunt of implicit disapproval. Unfortunately, no one has traced changes in the self-concepts of young employed mothers over the last four decades, but one would expect to find significant trends. Further, dramatic increases in women's educational attainments have enabled them to obtain more satisfying employment and have also increased their motivation to do so (Hoffman, 1974b, 1979). A national survey conducted in 1976 indicated that 76% of the employed women in the United States would continue to work even if this were not economically necessary (Dubnoff et al., 1978), suggesting that many women would be bored (Dubnoff et al., 1978) or unfulfilled (Lamb et al., 1980) if they were not employed outside the home. Presumably, this would leave them dissatisfied—an important point in light of the evidence that the best adjusted children are those whose mothers are satisfied with their lives, whether or not they are employed (Etaugh, 1974; Hoffman, 1974a).

On the other hand, employed mothers continue to face one major, potentially pathogenic problem—role overload or personal overextension. Labor-saving appliances have reduced the amount of time involved in household maintenance, but the total amount of time that employed women must invest in housework, child care, and their jobs remains substantially higher than the amount of time unemployed mothers devote to child care and housework (Pleck, 1980). The long-term effects of this overextension are unknown. There may be some compensating benefits as far as the children are concerned, however. To alleviate the pressures somewhat, many employed women substantially reduce the amount of time they invest in housework and child care (Pleck & Rustad, 1980), and their husbands marginally but significantly increase the amount of time they devote to housework and child care. The decrease in women's involvement and the modest increase in men's involvement produce an impressive shift in the *relative* involvement of men and women in home and child care (Hoffman, 1977). Consequently, the children of employed mothers are provided with more egalitarian male and female roles within the home. Further, the increased involvement of fathers promises to be beneficial to sons and daughters alike (Lamb, 1979, 1981).

The benefits mentioned in the last paragraph do not, of course, accrue to the children of single employed mothers. Although these mothers provide nontraditional models for their children, it is naive to be sanguine about their situation. Women are generally paid more poorly than men, and so single mothers— especially single black mothers—often suffer under severe economic stress (Glick & Norton, 1979). Furthermore, single parents lack a partner to reinforce their efforts at socialization, and to take over temporarily when the stresses increase (Maccoby, 1977). Parenting failures—including child abuse and neglect—are more likely to occur in such circumstances (Belsky, 1980; Garbarino, 1976; Garbarino & Sherman, 1980). An increasing number of children spend at least part of their childhood with single parents, and so we cannot ignore the fact that these children must be deemed "at risk." On the other hand, maternal employment per se is not the cause of these families' problems. In fact, when mothers are employed before their marriage breaks up, they are better able to cope (emotionally and economically) with the divorce (Hetherington, 1979). As a result, the adverse effects on their children are that much less. It is especially hard on children when the family dissolution brings about the need to adjust simultaneously to the new demand of single parenthood and employment. In addition, women who have not been employed are unlikely to have the experience, skills, and seniority that assure a satisfactory income.

CONCLUSION

Two to three decades ago, it was widely believed that maternal employment had adverse effects on child development, with the seriousness of these effects increasing in proportion to the youthfulness of the children when their mothers began to work. As the foregoing review indicates, empirical studies have failed to substantiate these pessimistic conclusions. It is not the case, however, that maternal employment has no effects on child development. Infants and young children may be especially vulnerable, and although insecure mother–infant relationships are not inevitable when mothers of very young children are employed, they do seem more likely to occur. As with older children, however, it is not maternal employment per se, but rather the attitudes, values, and circumstances of the employed women that are pathogenic. Considerably more research is needed to define how these factors affect child development and thus how these adverse effects might be alleviated or eliminated. Some speculations are presented in the first half of this chapter.

As far as school-age children and adolescents are concerned, there is substantial evidence that children have less stereotyped conceptions of male and female roles, and daughters are more achievement oriented when their mothers are employed than when they are not. Maternal employment is sometimes associated with reduced psychological adjustment among school-aged children, but these effects are reported so rarely that we cannot consider maternal employment per se to be the necessary and sufficient causal factor. Rather, the mothers' life satisfaction, regardless of employment status, appears to be the crucial intervening variable. Satisfaction is likely to vary depending on whether a mother wants to work and why, whether she does work, whether she enjoys her job, whether her husband approves of her employment, whether he assists with housework and child care, and so forth. Unfortunately, very few studies have considered variables such as maternal satisfaction—let alone the origins of satisfaction and dissatisfaction.

The fact is, however, that maternal employment is simply a status variable; it has little explanatory value unless attempts are made to view a woman's employment status in the context of her social and family circumstances as well as her values and goals. Only in this way can psychologically important causal networks be elucidated. The first, second, and final sections of this chapter illustrate the factors affecting the diverse meanings of and motivations for, employment, as well as the secular changes that have altered popular attitudes concerning maternal employment as well as the desired outcomes of socialization. By discussing these factors, I hope to have identified clearly the factors demanding consideration in future attempts to explore the relationship between maternal employment and child development.

REFERENCES

Ainsworth, M. D. S., Blehar, M., Waters, E., & Wall, S. *Patterns of attachment.* Hillsdale, N.J.: Lawrence Erlbaum Associates, 1978.

Almquist, E. M., & Angrist, S. S. Career salience and atypicality of occupational choice among college women. *Journal of Marriage and the Family,* 1970, *32,* 242-249.

Armstrong, R. F. *Working mothers and teenage children in an Iowa community.* Unpublished doctoral dissertation, University of Iowa, 1967.

Astin, H. S. *The woman doctorate in America.* Hartford, Conn.: Russell Sage Foundation, 1969.

Banducci, R. The effect of mother's employment on the achievement, aspirations, and expectations of the child. *Personnel and Guidance Journal,* 1967, *46,* 263-267.

Baruch, G. K. Maternal influences upon college women's attitudes toward women and work. *Developmental Psychology,* 1972, *6,* 32-37. (a)

Baruch, G. K. *Maternal role pattern as related to self-esteem and parental identification in college women.* Paper presented to the Eastern Psychological Association, Boston, April 1972. (b)

Below, H. I. *Life styles and roles of women as perceived by high school girls.* Unpublished doctoral dissertation, Indiana University, 1969.

Belsky, J. Child maltreatment: An ecological integration. *American Psychologist,* 1980, *35,* 320-325.

Bem, S. Sex role adaptibility: One consequence of psychological androgyny. *Journal of Personality and Social Psychology,* 1975, *31,* 634-643.

Bem, S., & Lenney, E. Sex-typing and the avoidance of cross-sex behavior. *Journal of Personality and Social Psychology,* 1976, *33,* 48-54.

Bem, S., Martyna, W., & Watson, C. Sex-typing and androgyny: Further explorations of the expressive domain. *Journal of Personality and Social Psychology,* 1976, *34,* 1016-1023.

Birnbaum, J. A. *Life patterns, personality style, and self-esteem in gifted family-oriented and career-oriented women.* Unpublished doctoral dissertation, University of Michigan, 1971.

Birnbaum, J. A. Life patterns and self-esteem in gifted family-oriented and career-oriented women. In M. S. Mednick., S. S. Tangri, & L. W. Hoffman (Eds.), *Women and achievement.* Washington, D.C.: Hemisphere, 1975.

Blanchard, M., & Main, M. Avoidance of the attachment figure and social–emotional adjustment in day-care infants. *Developmental Psychology,* 1979, *15,* 445-446.

Blehar, M. C. Anxious attachment and defensive reactions associated with day care. *Child Development,* 1974, *45,* 683-693.

Blehar, M. C. Anxious attachment and defensive reactions associated with day care. In U. Bronfenbrenner & M. A. Mahoney (Eds.), *Influences on human development.* New York: Holt, Rinehart, & Winston, 1975.

Blood, R. O., & Hamblin, R. L. The effect of the wife's employment on the family power structure. *Social Forces,* 1958, *36,* 347-352.

Bowlby, J. *Separation: Anxiety and anger.* New York: Basic Books, 1973.

Brookhart, J., & Hock, E. The effects of experimental context and experiential background on infants' behavior toward their mothers and a stranger. *Child Development,* 1976, *47,* 333-340.

Brown, S. E. *Husband's attitude toward and consequences of wife–mother employment.* Unpublished doctoral dissertation, Florida State University, 1971.

Brown, S. W. *A comparative study of maternal employment and nonemployment.* Unpublished doctoral dissertation, Mississippi State University, 1970.

Burchinal, L. B. Personality characteristics of children. In F. I. Nye & L. W. Hoffman (Eds.), *The employed mother in America.* Chicago: Rand McNally, 1963.

Burchinal, L. B., & Lovell, L. *Relation of employment status of mothers to children's anxiety, parental personality, and PARI score.* Unpublished manuscript, Iowa State University, 1959.

Burke, R., & Weir, T. Some personality differences between members of one-career and two-career families. *Journal of Marriage and the Family,* 1976, *38,* 453-458.

Chu, C. A study of the effects of maternal employment for the preschool children in Taiwan. *Acta Psychologica Taiwania,* 1970, *12,* 80-100.

Cochran, M. M. A comparison of group care and family child-rearing patterns in Sweden. *Child Development,* 1977, *48,* 702-707.

Cohen, S. E. Maternal employment and mother–child interaction. *Merrill–Palmer Quarterly,* 1978, *24,* 189–197.

Dawson, F. *An analytical study of the effects of maternal employment, of same-sex chum denial in preadolescence, and of residential mobility on self-actualization achievement in a sample of adolescents.* Unpublished doctoral dissertation, American University, 1970.

Dits, A., & Cambier, A. L'absence de la mere tors de retour de l'enfant de l'ecole. *Enfance,* 1966, *1,* 99–111.

Douvan, E. Employment and the adolescent. In F. I. Nye & L. W. Hoffman (Eds.), *The employed mother in America.* Chicago: Rand McNally, 1963

Doyle, A-B. Infant development in day care. *Developmental Psychology,* 1975, *11,* 655–656.

Doyle, A-B., & Somers, K. *The effect of group and individual day care on infant development.* Paper presented to the Candian Psychological Association, Quebec, June 1975.

Dubnoff, S. J., Veroff, J., & Kulka, R. A. *Adjustment to work: 1957–1976.* Paper presented to the American Psychological Association, Toronto, August 1978.

Duvall, E.B. *Conceptions of mother roles by five- and six-year-old children of working and non-working mothers.* Unpublished doctoral dissertation, Florida State University, 1955.

Etaugh, C. Effects of maternal employment on children: A review of recent research. *Merrill–Palmer Quarterly,* 1974 *20,* 71–98.

Farley, J. Maternal employment and child behavior. *Cornell Journal of Social Relations,* 1968, *3,* 58–71.

Farel, A. M. Effects of preferred maternal roles, maternal employment, and sociodemographic status on school adjustment and competence. *Child Development,* 1980, *51,* 1179–1186.

Farran, D. C., & Ramey, C. T. Infant day care and attachment behavior toward mothers and teachers. *Child Development,* 1977, *48,* 1112–1116.

Finkelman, J. J. *Maternal employment, family relationships, and parental role perception.* Unpublished doctoral dissertation, Yeshiva University, 1966.

Fish, K. D. *Paternal availability, family role structure, maternal employment, and personality development in late adolescent females.* Unpublished doctoral dissertation, University of Massachusetts, 1970.

Feldman, S. S. *The impact of day care on one aspect of children's social-emotional behavior.* Paper presented to the American Association for the Advancement of Science, San Francisco, February 1974.

Fox, N. Attachment of kibbutz infants to mother and metapelet. *Child Development,* 1977, *48,* 1228–1239.

Franke, H. B. *A comparison of perceived parental behavior characteristics of eighth-grade children of working and nonworking mothers.* Unpublished doctoral dissertation, University of Florida, 1972.

Frankel, E. Characteristics of working and nonworking mothers among intellectually gifted high and low achievers. *Personnel and Guidance Journal,* 1964, *42,* 776–780.

Frieze, I., Parsons, J., & Ruble, D. *Some determinants of career aspirations in college women.* Unpublished manuscript, University of California at Los Angeles, May 1972.

Frye, D. *The problem of infant day care.* Unpublished manuscript, Yale University, 1979.

Garbarino, J. A preliminary study of some ecological correlates of child abuse: The impact of socioeconomic stress on mothers. *Child Development,* 1976, *47,* 178–185.

Garbarino, J., & Sherman, D. High-risk neighborhoods and high-risk families: The human ecology of child maltreatment. *Child Development,* 1980, *51,* 188–198.

George, E. I., & Thomas, M. A comparative study of children of employed mothers and unemployed mothers. *Psychological Studies,* 1967, *12,* 32–38.

Glenn, N. D. The contribution of marriage to the psychological well-being of males and females. *Journal of Marriage and the Family,* 1975, *37,* 594–601.

Glick, P. C. Future American families. *COFU Memo,* 1979, *2*(3), 2-5.

Glick, P. C., & Norton, A. J. Marrying, divorcing, and living together in the U.S. today. *Population Bulletin,* 1979, *32,* whole number 5.

Gold, D., & Andres, D. Comparisons of adolescent children with employed and unemployed mothers. *Merrill-Palmer Quarterly,* 1978, *24,* 243-254. (a)

Gold, D., & Andres D. Developmental comparisons between ten-year-old children with employed and unemployed mothers. *Child Development,* 1978, *49,* 75-84. (b)

Gold, D., & Andres, D. Relations between maternal employment and development of nursery-school children. *Canadian Journal of Behavioural Science,* 1978, *10,* 116-129. (c)

Gold, D., Andres, D., & Glorieux, J. The development of Francophone nursery-school children with employed and nonemployed mothers. *Canadian Journal of Behavioural Science,* 1979, *11,* 169-173.

Goldberg, R. J. *Maternal time use and preschool performance.* Paper presented to the Society for Research in Child Development, New Orleans, March 1977.

Hall, F. T., & Schroeder, M. P. Time spent on household tasks. *Journal of Home Economics,* 1970, *62,* 23-29.

Hand, H. B. Working mothers and maladjusted children. *Journal of Educational Sociology,* 1957, *30,* 245-246.

Hartley, R. E. Children's concepts of male and female roles. *Merrill-Palmer Quarterly,* 1960, *6,* 83-91.

Hetherington, E. M. Divorce: A child's perspective. *American Psychologist,* 1979, *34,* 851-858.

Hill, C. R., & Stafford, F. P. *Parental care of children: Time diary estimates of quantity, predictability, and variety.* Unpublished manuscript, Institute of Social Research, University of Michigan, 1978.

Hock, E. Working and nonworking mothers with infants: Perceptions of their careers, their infant's needs, and satisfaction with mothering. *Developmental Psychology,* 1978, *14,* 37-43.

Hock, E. Working and nonworking mothers and their infants: A comparative study of maternal caregiving characteristics and infant social behavior. *Merrill-Palmer Quarterly,* 1980, *26,* 79-101.

Hock, E., Christman, K., & Hock, M. Factors associated with decisions about return to work in mothers of infants. *Developmental Psychology,* 1980, *16,* 535-536.

Hoffman, L. W. Effects on children: Summary and discussion. In F. I. Nye & L. W. Hoffman (Eds.), *The employed mother in America.* Chicago: Rand McNally, 1963. (a)

Hoffman, L. W. Mother's enjoyment of work and effects on the child. In F. I. Nye & L. W. Hoffman, (Eds.), *The employed mother in America.* Chicago: Rand McNally, 1963. (b)

Hoffman, L. W. Parental power relations and the division of household tasks. In F. I. Nye & L. W. Hoffman (Eds.), *The employed mother in America.* Chicago: Rand McNally, 1963. (c)

Hoffman, L. W. Effects of maternal employment on the child: A review of the research. *Developmental Psychology,* 1974, *10,* 204-228. (a)

Hoffman, L. W. The employment of women, education, and fertility. *Merrill-Palmer Quarterly,* 1974, *20,* 99-119. (b)

Hoffman, L. W. Changes in family roles, socialization, and sex differences. *American Psychologist,* 1977, *32,* 644-657.

Hoffman, L. W. Maternal employment: 1979. *American Psychologist,* 1979, *34,* 859-865.

Hoffman, L. W., & Nye, F. I. *Working mothers.* San Francisco: Jossey-Bass, 1974.

Holmstrom, L. L. *The two-career family.* Unpublished manuscript, Radcliffe College, 1972.

Johnson, C. L. *Leadership patterns in working and nonworking mother middle-class families.* Unpublished doctoral dissertation, University of Kansas, 1969.

Jones, J. B., Lundsteen, S. W., & Michael, W. B. The relationship of the professional employment status of mothers to reading achievement of sixth grade children. *California Journal of Educational Research,* 1967, *18,* 102-108.

Kagan, J., Kearsley, R., & Zelazo, P. *Infancy: Its place in human development*. Cambridge, Mass.: Harvard University Press, 1978.

Kappel, B. E., & Lambert, R. D. *Self-worth among children of working mothers*. Unpublished manuscript, University of Waterloo, 1972.

Keidel, K. C. Maternal employment and ninth grade achievement in Bismarck, North Dakota. *Family Coordinator*, 1970, *19*, 95–97.

King, K., McIntyre, J., & Axelson, L. J. Adolescents' views of maternal employment as a threat to the marital relationship. *Journal of Marriage and the Family*, 1968, *30*, 633–637.

Kliger, D. *The effects of employment of married women on husband and wife roles: A study in culture change*. Unpublished doctoral dissertation, Yale University, 1954.

Komarovsky, M. *Blue-collar marriage*. New York: Random House, 1962.

Lamb, M. E. Paternal influences and the father's role: A personal perspective. *American Psychologist*, 1979, *34*, 938–943.

Lamb, M. E. The development of father–infant relationships. In M. E. Lamb (Ed.), *The role of the father in child development* (Rev. ed.). New York: Wiley, 1981.

Lamb, M. E., Chase-Lansdale, P. L., & Owen, M. T. The changing American family and its implications for infant social development: The sample case of maternal employment. In M. Lewis & L. A. Rosenblum (Eds.), *The child and its family*. New York: Plenum, 1979.

Lamb, M. E., & Easterbrooks, M. A. Individual differences in parental sensitivity: Origins, components, and consequences. In M. E. Lamb & L. R. Sherrod (Eds.), *Infant social cognition: Empirical and theoretical considerations*. Hillsdale, N. J.: Lawrence Erlbaum Associates, 1981.

Lamb, M. E., Owen, M. T., & Chase-Lansdale, P. L. The working mother in the intact family: A process model. In R. R. Abidin (Ed.), *Parent education and intervention handbook*. Springfield, Ill.: C. C. Thomas, 1980.

Lamb, M. E., & Urberg, K. The development of gender role and gender identity. In M. E. Lamb (Ed.), *Social and personality development*. New York: Holt, Rinehart, & Winston, 1978.

Lieberman, A. *Preschoolers' competence with a peer: Relations with attachment and peer experience*. Unpublished doctoral dissertation, Johns Hopkins University, 1976.

Maccoby, E.E. *Current changes in the family and their impact upon the socialization of children*. Paper presented to the American Sociological Association, Chicago, September 1977.

Maccoby, E. E., & Feldman, S. S. Mother attachment and stranger reactions in the third year of life. *Monographs of the Society for Research in Child Development*, 1972, *37*, whole number 146.

McCord, J., McCord, W., & Thurber, E. Effects of maternal employment on lower-class boys. *Journal of Abnormal and Social Psychology*, 1963, *67*, 177–182.

Meier, H. C. Mother-centeredness and college youth's attitudes toward social equality for women: Some empirical findings. *Journal of Marriage and the Family*, 1972, *34*, 115–121.

Miller, S. M. Effects of maternal employment on sex-role perception, interests and self-esteem in kindergarten girls. *Developmental Psychology*, 1975, *11*, 405–406.

Moore, K. A., & Hofferth, S. L. Effects of women's employment on marriage: Formation, stability, and roles. *Marriage and Family Review*, 1979, *2*, 27–36.

Moore, T. W. Exclusive early mothering and it alternatives. *Scandinavian Journal of Psychology*, 1975, *16*, 256–272.

Moskowitz, D., Schwarz, J. C., & Corsini, D. Initiating day care at three years of age: Effects on attachment. *Child Development*, 1978, *49*, 239–242.

Nelson, D. D. A study of school achievement among adolescent children with working and nonworking mothers. *Journal of Education Research*, 1969, *62*, 456–457.

Nelson, D.D. A study of personality adjustment among adolescent children with working and nonworking mothers. *Journal of Educational Research*, 1971, *64*, 1328–1330.

Nye, F. I. The adjustment of adolescent children. In F. I. Nye & L. W. Hoffman (Eds.), *The employed mother in America*. Chicago: Rand McNally, 1963.

Nye, F. I., & Hoffman, L. W. (Eds.), *The employed mother in America,* Chicago: Rand McNally, 1963.

Nye, F. I., Perry, J. B., & Ogles, R. H. Anxiety and anti-social behavior in preschool children. In F. I. Nye & L. W. Hoffman (Eds.), *The employed mother in America.* Chicago: Rand McNally, 1963.

Owen, M. T., Chase-Lansdale, P. L., & Lamb, M. E. *Mothers' and fathers' attitudes, maternal employment, and the security of infant-parent attachment.* Unpublished manuscript, 1981.

Peterson, E. T. *The impact of maternal employment on the mother–daughter relationship and on the daughter's role orientation.* Unpublished doctoral dissertation, University of Michigan, 1958.

Pleck, J. H. Men's family work: Three perspectives and some new data. *Family Coordinator,* 1979, *28,* 481–488.

Pleck, J. H., & Rustad, M. *Husbands' and wives' time in family work and paid work in the 1975-76 study of time use.* Unpublished manuscript, Wellesley College, 1980.

Propper, A. M. The relationship of maternal employment to adolescent roles activities, and parental relationships. *Journal of Marriage and the Family,* 1972, *34,* 417–421.

Rabin, A. I. *Growing up in the kibbutz.* New York: Springer, 1965.

Ragozin, A. Attachment behavior of day-care children: Naturalistic and laboratory observations. *Child Development,* 1980, *61,* 409–415.

Rees, A. N., & Palmer, F. H. Factors related to change in mental performance. *Developmental Psychology Monographs,* 1970, *3*(2, part 2).

Richmond, J. *The Surgeon General's Report on the Health of Americans: 1980.* Washington, D.C.: Department of Health and Human Services, 1980.

Romer, N., & Cherry, D. *Developmental effects of preschool and school age maternal employment on children's sex-role concepts.* Unpublished manuscript, Brooklyn College, 1978.

Roopnarine, J. L., & Lamb, M. E. The effects of day care on attachment and exploratory behaviors. *Merrill-Palmer Quarterly,* 1978, *24,* 85–95.

Roopnarine, J. L., & Lamb, M. E. Peer and parent–child interaction before and after enrollment in nursery school. *Journal of Applied Developmental Psychology,* 1980, *1,* 77–81.

Rouman, J. Schoolchildren's problems as related to parental factors. *Journal of Educational Research,* 1956, *50,* 105–112.

Roy, P. Adolescent roles: Rural–urban differentials. In F. I. Nye & L. W. Hoffman (Eds.), *The employed mother in America.* Chicago: Rand McNally, 1963.

Schooler, C. Childhood family structure and adult characteristics. *Sociometry,* 1972, *35,* 255–269.

Schreiner, M. Auswirkungen mutterlicher Erwebstatigkeit auf die Entwicklung von Grundschulkindern. *Archiven fur die Gesamte Pschologie,* 1963, *115,* 334–382.

Siegel, A. E., & Curtis, E. A. Familial correlates of orientation toward future employment among college women. *Jouranl of Educational Psychology,* 1963, *54,* 33–37.

Siegel, A. E., & Haas, M. B. The working mother: A review of research. *Child Development,* 1963, *34,* 573–542.

Siegel, A. E., Stolz, L. M., Hitchcock, E. A., & Adamson, J. Dependence and independence in children. In F. I. Nye & L. W. Hoffman (Eds.), *The employed mother in America.* Chicago: Rand McNally, 1963.

Smith, H. C. *An investigation of the attitudes of adolescent girls toward combining marriage, motherhood, and a career.* Unpublished doctoral dissertation, Columbia University, 1969.

Smokler, C. S. *Self-esteem in preadolescent and adolescent females.* Unpublished doctoral dissertation, University of Michigan, 1975.

Stolz, L. M. Effects of maternal employment on children: Evidence from research. *Child Development,* 1960, *31,* 749–782.

Stott, D. H. Do working mothers' children suffer? *New Society,* 1965, August 19, 8–9.

Szolai, A. The multinational comparative time budget: A venture in international research cooperation. *American Behavioral Scientist,* 1966, *10,* 1–31.

Tangri, S. S. *Role innovation in occupational choice.* Unpublished doctoral dissertation, University of Michigan, 1969.

Tangri, S. S. Determinants of occupational role innovation among college women. *Journal of Social Issues,* 1972, *28,* 177-200.

Thompson, R. A., Lamb, M. E., & Estes, D. Stability of infant–mother attachment and its relationship to changing life circumstances in a representative middle-class sample. *Child Development,* In press.

Vaughn, B., Gove, F., & Egeland, B. The relationship between out-of-home care and the quality of infant-mother attachment in an economically disadvantaged population. *Child Development,* 1981, in press.

Vogel, S. R., Broverman, I. K., Broverman, D. M., Clarkson, F. E., & Rosenkrantz, P. S. Maternal employment and perception of sex roles among college students. *Developmental Psychology,* 1970, *3,* 384-391.

Walker, K. E. How much help for working mothers? The children's role. *Home Ecology Forum,* 1970, *1,* 13-15. (a)

Walker, K. E. *Time-use patterns for household work related to homemakers' employment.* Unpublished manuscript, Cornell University, 1970. (b)

Weil, M. W. An analysis of the factors influencing married women's actual or planned work participation. *American Sociological Review,* 1961, *26,* 91-96.

White, K. Social background variables related to career commitment of women teachers. *Personnel and Guidance Jurnal,* 1967, *45,* 648-652.

Whitmarsh, R. E. Adjustment problems of adolescent daughters of employed mothers. *Journal of Home Economics,* 1965, *57,* 201-204.

Willis, A., & Ricciuti, H. N. *A good beginning for babies.* Ithaca, N.Y.: College of Human Ecology, Cornell University, 1974.

Woods, M. B. The unsupervised child of the working mother. *Developmental Psychology,* 1972, *6,* 14-25.

Yarrow, M. R. Maternal employment and child rearing. *Children,* 1961, *8,* 223-228.

Yarrow, M. R., Scott, P., deLeeuw, L., & Heinig, C. Child rearing in families of working and nonworking mothers. *Sociemetry,* 1962, *25,* 122-140.

Yudkin, S., & Holme, A. *Working mothers and their children.* London: Michael Joseph, 1963.

Zissis, C. A study of the life planning of 550 freshman women at Purdue University. *Journal of the National Association of Women Deans and Counselors,* 1964, *28,* 153-159.

4 The Ecology of Day Care

Jay Belsky
The Pennsylvania State University

Laurence D. Steinberg
University of California, Irvine

Ann Walker
Child Development Council of Centre County
Bellefonte, Pennsylvania

There is a difference between what is traditional and what is typical, and, by the same token, there is a difference between what is nontraditional and what is atypical. Anyone familiar with the changing demographic profile of the American family is well aware that the *traditional* American family—two-parent, nuclear, nonworking mother—is no longer the *typical* American family. Indeed, if we hold to this definition of the traditional family, we find that the vast majority of families in America have broken with tradition.

Despite the fact that the typical American family has changed substantially over the past quarter-century, the image of this traditional family remains. It is for this reason that a chapter on day care earns its place in a volume on child rearing in nontraditional families: Although supplementary child care[1] has an important place in the daily life of millions of American families, it is still viewed as nontraditional. This image has two bases: First, when viewed within a historical context, any form of nonparental child care appears to depart from what has typically been viewed as the "traditional" means of child rearing in this country. And second, it is precisely those families whose structure is

---

[1] We deliberately eschew the term "substitute" care because we believe that quality day care supplements, but does not take the place of child care in the family.

71

nontraditional—single-parent families and families with working mothers—who have been, and who continue to be most likely to use some form of day care. Day care then, is doubly nontraditional: It is an unconventional approach to child rearing relied upon primarily by nontraditional families.

Our contention that a discussion of day care belongs in a volume on child rearing in nontraditional families is supported by two sources of information. The first is historical in nature and illustrates both the ambivalence of American society toward day care as a social institution—an ambivalence that derives, we believe, from the view that nonparental child rearing is too unorthodox—as well as a general tendency for day care to be used either by those families seen as out of society's mainstream (and for whom, ostensibly, breaking with tradition is more acceptable) or by traditional families during unusual times (again when breaking with tradition is not necessarily taboo). The second body of data is demographic in nature and provides support for the notion that day care is more popular today among families with nontraditional forms.[2] As the number and proportion of single-parent families and families with working mothers have grown, so have the utilization of and demand for day care. In this regard, child rearing in nontraditional families cannot be fully understood or thoroughly discussed without consideration of child rearing through day care.

Historical Analysis: Day Care as an Emergency or Problem Service

America's ambivalence toward day care and, in particular, toward government-sponsored day care, stems, in part, from traditions that stress individualism and the sanctity of the family. Children are considered to "belong to" their parents, rather than to the larger society, which "grants" custody to parents during the formative years, as tends to be the prevailing view in many European nations (Peters, 1979). Hence, responsibility for child care in America has historically been viewed as primarily that of the family.

Consideration of the history of day care in America, which dates back to the mid-1800s, indicates that when out-of-home child care has been sponsored by the government, it has rarely reflected a direct concern for the welfare of children. Indeed, supplementary child care traditionally has emerged in response to adult

---

[2]We are aware, of course, that many families traditional in structure and composition themselves break with tradition by using some form of supplementary child care. Although it would be interesting to know whether and how the utilization of day care differentially affects members of traditional and nontraditional families, we can find no research that examines interactions between family type and child-rearing mode. Thus, we have no idea, for example, of whether children from divorced families are affected differently by experience in day care than are children from intact homes; indeed, few day care researchers provide any information at all on the family structures from which their study samples are drawn.

concerns (Lieberman, 1978)—initially, and most recently, to the needs of working parents and, from time to time, in response to national crises.

The first day care center in this country was established in 1854 in New York City for children of nontraditional families—those with working mothers. This and other 19th-century day nurseries emerged in response to the labor demand of industrialization and to the influx of over 5 million immigrant families between 1815 and 1860. Because immigrant women recruited into industry had few available relatives with whom to leave their children, privately sponsored childcare facilities developed. In meeting the needs of working women, the primary purpose of these institutions was to provide custodial services, although some settlement houses did construe the socialization of young immigrant children into the American way of life to be one of their missions (Kamerman & Kahn, 1978; Lieberman, 1978; Ruderman, 1968).

Ruderman (1968) argues that because social workers were the first professionals to involve themselves in day care, supplementary child care came to be seen as a response to family inadequacy, that is, as a problem service for problem families. Vestiges of this perspective are still evident today; most contemporary federal day care legislation is directed at the poor, often with the expressed purpose of reducing the welfare roles by providing child care so that impoverished parents can work. The initial conceptualization of day care as a service for problem families has undoubtedly impeded widespread public acceptance of federal sponsorship of day care.

Although the federal government established a limited number of centers following the Civil War, it was not until the Great Depression that Washington made its first major commitment to child care, indicating at least tacit acceptance of the idea that even traditional families might need to turn to supplementary child care—but only during times of crisis. In fact, this involvement marked the beginning of what would become a crisis-determined cycle of federal support (Fein & Clarke-Stewart, 1973). As Steiner (1976) notes in his insightful volume on the politics of child care in America: "Before Head Start, federal support for child care was accomplished only when explicitly tied to a national emergency—to winning a war or overcoming economic depression [p. 15]."

That supplementary child care for traditional families has been essentially an unacceptable idea in this country is most clearly reflected in the fact that day care has never been justified on the basis of its potential contribution to the welfare of children. Rather, it has typically been adult concerns, often exacerbated by national emergencies, that have been used to rationalize the use of day care by mainstream families. To do otherwise would have meant to approve day care as a child rearing mode with value in its own right.

As a case in point, the establishment of day care centers during the depression (beginning in 1932) provided a means of employing out-of-work school personnel; consequently, it was administered by the Works Project Administration

(WPA). And by 1937, 1900 nurseries were established to serve over 40,000 children. However, because these centers were not established out of concern for the welfare of children, federal involvement in day care was terminated with the start of World War II, when mobilization for war made the WPA unnecessary (Kamerman & Kahn, 1978).

After a brief period, national-defense womanpower needs resulted in increased federal support for child care. In 1942, with the passage of the Community Facilities Act (also called the Lanham Act), the federal government made available 50% matching funds to private industries to establish and operate child care centers in war-impacted areas. Once again the intent behind this act was clear, and the legislation never extended to government sponsorship of child care outside the defense-emergency framework (Emlen & Perry, 1974). Thus this program, which served 105,000 children and cost 51 million dollars, was, in Steiner's (1976) words: "a win-the-war program, not a save-the-child program [p. 16]." Consequently, by 1946 and the war's end, funds were withdrawn and programs dismantled—despite the fact that many mothers continued to work. Public sentiment not only supported the idea that mothers belonged at home, but governmental involvement in family life came to be viewed with suspicion (Kamerman & Kahn, 1978).

The federal government's involvement in day care did not surface again until the 1960s, with the passage of ammendments to the Social Security Act authorizing grants-in-aid to states for day care services (Emlen & Perry, 1974; Peters, 1979; Steiner, 1976). Unlike the depression and World War II experience, however, during the War-on-Poverty years day care was conceptualized and implemented as a means of taking women off the welfare rolls. Day care had thus come full circle, returing to its 19th-century conception as a service for inadequate families with problems.

The Social Security Act of 1935 authorized grants-in-aid for child welfare services, some of which included day care—usually on a project or demonstration basis. The 1962 ammendment to this act raised service reimbursements to 75% and authorized limited matching funds to states for the development of licensed day-care facilities for children of welfare recipients. Additional ammendments in 1967 significantly altered and enlarged federal authorization to pay for child welfare services. For example, under Title IV-A, intended to encourage state departments of public welfare to develop day care facilities, federal reimbursement to states was substantially increased to a 75:25 matching-funds formula. In 1974, under this law, which targeted programs for the economically impoverished, child care was provided to over one-half million children at a cost of 464 million dollars (Kamerman & Kahn, 1978).

In 1975, states were given more freedom to spend monies earmarked for social services, as the Title XX ammendment to the Social Security Act made available block grants to states (i.e., revenue sharing). And although social services (including day care) were still primarily targeted for the poor, eligibility became more universal—at least in theory. For families with incomes below 65% of the state median income, day care services were to be available for free; graduated fees were mandated for those with income ranging from 65% to 115% of the median. But because total expenditures under Title XX were and still are limited by a ceiling level, and because half of all services must be reserved for welfare recipients, Title XX services are not always available to those who are eligible for them (Kamerman & Kahn, 1978).

In addition to these revisions of the Social Security Act, other federal programs have been developed to provide day care services for poverty families. In 1962, for example, Title II of the Manpower Training Act mandated the provision of child care for children of the hard-core unemployed who were provided jobs or vocational training. Similarly, a 1972 amendment (Title IV-C) of the 1967 Work Incentive Program (WIP) required states to provide child care for children whose welfare-recipient parents were required to obtain work or undergo job training. Although WIP specifically excluded parents with children under 6 from this work requirement, in 1975 78,000 such children were receiving child care under WIP's auspices (Kamerman & Kahn, 1978).

As a final piece of evidence supporting our view that day care has never been viewed in this country as an acceptable alternative or even adjunct to full-time child rearing in a traditional home environment, we remind the reader of President Nixon's 1971 veto of the Comprehensive Child Development Act, which was attached to the Economic Opportunity Amendments. This act would have provided child care services to all families (although it gave priority to low-income children). Nixon claimed, consistent with what had always been America's attitude toward day care, that government sponsorship of supplementary child care would "commit the vast moral authority of the national government to the side of communal approaches to child rearing over and against the family centered approach." The fact, however, that Nixon considered day care to be beneficial to children from impoverished families underscores the interpretation that supplementary child care has been, and continues to be viewed as acceptable for certain (i.e., nontraditional) families, as many of the families categorized as impoverished under this definition would also be nontraditional in structure.

This brief history of day care in America, supporting our thesis that supplementary child care typically has been viewed as an acceptable mode of child rearing only for nontraditional families, suggests that as the number of such families increases so should the demand for and utliziation of day care services. An examination of the changing demographics of the American family alongside figures of day care use and demand bears out this contention.

Demographic Analysis: The Changing American Family

Between 1940 and 1975, the number of women participating in the American labor force doubled, and the number of working mothers increased eightfold

(Hill, 1977,1978). Whereas only 18% of mothers with children under 6 years of age were employed outside the home in 1955 (Office of the Assistant for Planning and Evaluation, DHEW, 1978), 10 years later the figure was 20%, and in 1977, 41% (Hofferth, 1979). Thus, in 1976, 516 million women with young children were working—a tripling of the 1970 figure. Projections reveal that this rate of growth will continue to escalate to an *expected 6 million working mothers with children under 6 by 1985*—a 32% increase over a brief 10-year period (Hill, 1978). Indeed, it is estimated that by 1990, three of every four mothers will work, and that there will be 10.5 million very young children in need of day care (Urban Institute, 1980).

Further evidence of the changing nature of the American family can be found in census bureau data on single-parent families compiled by Bronfenbrenner (1975). From 1948 to 1975, the proportion of households with only one parent increased dramatically, with the largest increase taking place during the period from 1964 to 1974. In fact, as of 1974, one of every six American children under the age of 11 lived in a single-parent family—almost double the 1948 rate. Most importantly in the context of this chaper, this rise was most rapid among families with children under 6. By 1974, one of every eight children under 3 was living in a single-parent household. And, across all ages, 80% of these single parents who were household heads were employed full time.

According to the most recent data gathered by the United States Department of Health, Education and Welfare, as of June 1978, 11 million children under 14 years of age spend a substantial part of their week in supplementary child care arrangements. When broken down by age, these data indicate that 2.5 million infants and toddlers, 3.7 million preschoolers, and 4.9 million school-age children spend a sizable amount of their waking day being cared for by someone other than their parents (Office of the Assistant for Planning and Evaluation, 1978).

Recent census bureau projections, which estimate an average 2.1 children per family, suggest that the demographic pressures that affect demand for supplementary child care will increase still further over the next decade (Hofferth, 1979). This is because the children of the ''baby-boom'' era (1946–1964) will, as parents, produce a sizable increase in the number of preschoolers in the American population over the next decade. Specifically, the population of 0–5-year-olds is expected to rise from a low of 17.1 million in 1977 to a high of 23.3 million in 1990; about one-half of the mothers of these preschoolers, projections indicate, will return to work before their offspring reach their sixth birthday.

How will America respond to the coming demands for supplementary child care? The answer is not clear. We can be relatively certain, however, that as nontraditional family forms become more prevalent among the middle class, families in need of day care will come to form an increasingly sizable, politically powerful group that will, in all likelihood, not stand for the lukewarm, vascillating commitment to supplementary shild care that has characterized American society over the past century.

Overview

The projected increase in supplementary child care demand over the next deacde provides all the more impetus for research on the impact of day care on children, families, and society. As we have written clscwhcrc (Belsky & Steinberg, 1978), a comprehensive understanding of the effects of day care must be grounded in an ecological framework, a framework that extends beyond typical questions concerning the direct effects of day care on the individual child. We shall see that, when considered from this ecological perspective, we know alarmingly little about the place and impact of day care within contemporary American society.

In this chapter we discuss what is known and, more importantly, if we are to better prepare ourselves for the coming decade, what *needs* to be known about day care. The discussion is organized into three subsections: (1) an examination of the variety of day carc services presently offered, with special attention paid to their unique characteristics; (2) an update of a recent view of existing research on the effects of day care on child development (Belsky & Steinberg, 1978); and (3) a speculative analysis of the relatively unstudied affects of, and influences on day care. In sum, it is our purpose to examine the ecology of day care.

DAY CARE TODAY

In this part of the chapter we briefly describe three generic types of supplementary child care, examine their present rates of usage, and consider in detail their unique characteristics. The three types of care we are concerned with are center day care (CDC), family day care (FDC), and home care (HC). As its label implies, CDC is provided in a center, such as a church basement or community recreation facility, and usually serves 12 or more children. FDC is provided in a private family home and, by federal regulation, cannot serve more than six children. Finally, HC defines what is often referred to as baby-sitting—a person coming into the child's home to provide care.

Rates of Use

According to the most recent data gathered by the United States Department of Health, Education, and Welfare, as of June 1978, 11 million children under 14 years of age spend a substantial part of their week in supplementary child care arrangements. When broken down by age, these data indicate that 2.5 million infants and toddlers, 3.7 million preschoolers, and 4.9 million school-age children spend a sizable amount of their waking day being cared for by someone other than their parents (Office of the Assistant for Planning and Evaluation, 1978). When these data are considered in terms of the type of supplementary care used, we find that about 2.6 million families use in-home care for more than 10 hours per week, 3.4 million rely on family day care, and 1.3 million rely on center care. What we see here, then, is that the type of care that is most publicly visible (CDC) is the least used. And, as we shall see when we review the effects of day care, we know most about this kind of care, which we have least of, and far less about the kinds of care that are most widely employed.

According to Hill (1977, 1978), in-home care is the most widely preferred mode of care, and the most critical determinants of type of care utilized are the size and age composition of the family. The absence of teenage girls or other adults in the family, or a one-parent family, sharply increase the likelihood that extrafamilial care will be employed. Once the decision is made to go outside the home, cost is the most critical factor; FDC tends to be less expensive than CDC. In general, though, social class does not appear to be a major determinant of type of care selected by a family (Hill, 1978).

As part of an in-depth study of a group of middle-class day care users, Steinberg and Green (1979) have identified additional reasons for the selection of particular types of care. In general: "center day care is chosen for its school-like atmosphere, family day care for its similarity to the home environment, and in-home care for its convenience and reliability [p. 11]."

Variation in Day Care

Like social class, day care is often considered in class-theoretic terms (Bronfen-brenner, 1979) when comparisons are made between the development of home- and day-care-reared children. Yet anyone who has had any contact with "day care" is aware that child care programs vary immensely. In this section, then, it is our purpose to examine the particular attributes of the three kinds of supplementary care we have described. Consideration of such variability, both between and within various generic types of supplementary child care, is essential if we hope to understand the effects of day care.

Center Day Care.   Center day care has received the most systematic attention of investigators concerned with the microsystem of day care. In this section, we first consider research comparing center and other types of day care, and then investigations examining variation within center programs and its effect on children's experiences. Before reviewing these studies, several general comments are offered regarding the general advantages and disadvantages of CDC.

The greatest strength of center programs is their stability and predictable hours of operation. Such strengths, we should point out, can also be weaknesses, as centers tend to have fixed hours of operation that often limit their ability to respond to the individual and special needs of working parents. As additional advantages, CDC programs tend to offer a wider variety of formal learning experiences; are always licensed (as they are publicly visible); and are most likely to employ at least some trained professionals and staff. On the negative side, centers rarely provide care for children under 2 years of age and, because of the professionalism of the staff, can create an undesirable distance between parents and caregivers, as these persons may not always share child-rearing or other values. Centers also lack a home atmosphere, which, as we have already noted, Steinberg and Green (1979) found to be one reason why many parents in their middle-class, southern California sample chose to make arrangements with family day care providers. Having made these general comments, we now consider empirical work comparing CDC with other child-rearing arrangements.

Rubenstein and Howes (1979) compared the daily experience of 17–20-month-olds in five community-based, nonprofit, day care centers with those of matched children cared for at home by their mothers. Naturalistic observations revealed that infants cried more, smiled less, wandered more, and showed less competent play at home than in CDC. This pattern of infant differences was associated with less adult smiling and holding and more adult restrictive/controlling behavior in the home. No setting differences were evident, however, in verbal and cognitive stimulation offered the children by their caregiver. Peers, it appeared, were primarily responsible for the enhanced play competence of the day care children, because when home-reared toddlers who had regular playmates were observed interacting with them, CDC–HC differences in cognitive sophistication of infant play disappeared. These data clearly suggest that, at least in some regards, center day care may be more supportive of early development than many homes. In fact, Howes and Rubenstein (1980c) suggest, on the basis of their data, that child care may be less difficult and more pleasurable when adults and children are not isolated from peer contact, as is the case in group-rearing situations. Not only do children have options for choosing between caregivers to interact with, but for the adults, child care is a shared activity in which there exist opportunities to verbalize frustration to another adult and seek immediate support and assistance when relationships become particularly disharmonious.

Instead of examining HC and CDC simultaneously, other investigators have shed light on the nature of center care by comparing children's experiences in FDC and CDC. In the New York City Infant Day Care study, for example, CDC programs were found to be superior to FDC programs in the play materials, equipment, and space made available to children. The importance of such advantages is suggested by Prescott and David's (1976) analysis of research on the physical characteristics of the day care environment. As the number of children per square feet increases, these critics noted, so do aggressiveness, destructiveness, and unoccupied behavior (Rohe & Patterson, 1974). Because availability of resources is also important, Prescott and David concluded that an environment low in density and high in resources is optimal for the preschool child.

In our minds, the most important, and potentially influential difference that distinguishes the microsystems of CDC and FDC concerns the general types of experiences available to children in each context. As Papousek (1970) observed quite some time ago, day care centers provide children with playful and other useful experiences, but tend to detach the child from everyday contacts with the broader environment. In commenting on the same point, Prescott and Jones (1971) noted that day care centers tend to be modeled after nursery school programs that present children: "a *protected* environment scaled to their developmental level and designed to promote experiences of mastery within a child-sized manageable world [p. 54, emphasis added]."

Because nursery school is intended to balance "the child's home and community life which takes place in an adult-sized, complex environment, full of problems, emotions and demands [Prescott & Jones, 1971, p. 54]," such a design and programming philosophy is appropriate. We suspect that this nursery school model may not be best, though, for children cared for outside of the home in a group setting on a full-time, rather than a part-time basis. Day care designed on a nursery school model may inadvertently isolate the child from the world of adults engaged in noncaregiving roles (Belsky, 1980b). Work by Rubenstein and Howes (1979) and by Cochran (1977) clearly suggests that in this regard FDC may be less isolating; in FDC homes (as in the child's own home) the caregiver must perform multiple tasks and the environment is not totally designed to meet the child's needs, as tends to be the case in CDC programs. Unfortunately, there is, as yet, no work that has examined the consequences of such differences for children's development.

Simply because a day care program exists in a church basement, school classroom, or community center, and thus qualifies as a center-based program, does not mean that it is like all other CDC programs. In fact, variation within CDC programs can be as great as that that we have just noted exists between CDC and other caregiving contexts (i.e., HC, FDC). It is just such variation that we now consider, before turning attention to an analysis of the particular strengths and limitations of FDC. Consideration of such variation, we believe, is essential to understanding the effects of day care, be it center, family, or home based, because it is likely to be the experiences the child has, not the type of program she or he is in, that will exert an influence on development. Type of program simply represents a statement of probability regarding the kinds of experiences that are more or less likely.

Center/group size and child–caregiver ratio are the characteristics of centers that have received the most empirical attention in efforts to understand how variation in programs affect children's experience. In an early observational study of 69 California preschool day care programs, Prescott, Jones, and Kritchevsky (1967) found that when center population exceeded 60, more emphasis was placed on rules and routine guidance than when size ranged from 30–60 children. Teachers, in fact, placed twice as much emphasis on control in the large groups, possibly accounting for the observation that in small centers children displayed more pleasure, wonder, and delight. Additional evidence from this study revealed that large centers were less flexible in their scheduling, offered children fewer opportunities to initiate and control activities, and had teachers who displayed less sensitivity to the individual needs of the children (Heinicke, Friedman, Prescott, Puncel, & Sale, 1973).

Recently, most of these results have been replicated in a large-scale national study of 57 day care centers in Atlanta, Detroit, and Seattle (hereafter referred to as The National Day Care Study or NDC Study). Travers and Ruopp (1978) reported that for children 3 to 5 years of age, group size was the single most important determinant of the quality of children's experience. In groups of less than 15–18 children, caregivers were involved in more embellished caregiving (e.g., questioning, responding, praising, comforting), less straight monitoring of children, and less interaction with other adults. And in these smaller groups, children were more actively involved in classroom activities (i.e., considering and contemplating, contributing ideas, cooperating, persisting at tasks). As we shall see when we consider processes of influence that may determine the effects of day care, such caregiving styles and childhood experiences are predictive of social and intellectual functioning.

Interestingly, the NDC study found that child-to-caregiver ratio had little effect on the quality of *preschoolers'* experience in day care, though it was an important determinant of *infants'* experiences. More overt distress was observed among children under 3 as the number of children per caregiver increased. Additionally, in such high-ratio infant and toddler programs, staff spent more time in management and control interactions, and engaged in less informal teaching (Connell, Layzer, & Goodson, 1979; Travers & Ruopp, 1978). Biemiller, Avis and Lindsay (1976) reported similar findings in a small study comparing two infant day care programs.

Day care centers also vary in their "curricula," and such variation appears to be of particular concern to parents when selecting a child-care program. In fact, Joffee (1977) discerned racial preferences in her sociological study of the relationship between parents and school-administered programs in Berkeley, California. Blacks preferred a formal school atmosphere with special attention paid to discipline, the structuring of activities, and an academic curriculum, whereas whites desired less structured programs emphasizing socioemotional concerns. In an independent study, Prescott (1973) compared the experiences of 112 children in just such "closed"- and "open-structured" day care programs. Observations revealed that, consonant with their philosophy, closed programs, such as the ones black parents preferred, set clear limits, lacked opportunity for the exercise of autonomy and initiative, and afforded little positively affective, adult–child interaction. Open structure, on the other hand, encouraged autonomy and warm relations with caregivers, but offered less frequent intellectually stimulating activities. On the basis of these comparisons it should be evident that all CDC is not alike (see also Sheehan & Abbott, 1979).

Another characteristic in which programs differ is the opportunity for contact with mixed age peers. In most centers children are grouped in narrow age bands. Beller, Litwok, and Sullivan (no date) found, however, in their observational study of 22 classrooms providing care for 80 lower-income 2–3 year-olds, that age integration can have positive effects. Specifically, children in mixed aged groups spent more time engaged in complex social interaction such as that demanded by imaginative play, and teachers were more nurturant and complied more often to the demands of the children in such classrooms. The fact that Fein and Clarke-Stewart (1973) concluded, upon reviewing the literature on age integration in nursery school populations, that conflicts are more common and long lasting in age-segregated groups, and that there is less affection, teaching, and more competition displayed in such groupings, suggests to us one possible strength of family day care programs, as age integration is the norm rather than the exception in this type of care (Howes & Rubenstein, 1980a). This advantage may not become operational, however, until children reach 3–4 years of age, as a study by Howes and Rubenstein (1980a) comparing the experiences of FDC- and CDC-reared toddlers found few setting differences in peer interaction (on only two of 19 behaviors). In fact, even though the FDC programs studied had a greater mix of children of various ages, the ages of the study children's primary playmates were not different across day care contexts and tended to be similar to the target child's.

Family Day Care. As noted already, FDC constitutes the single largest system of out-of-home care in this country, both in terms of the number of families using care and the number of children served. An estimated 1.3 million FDC homes serve an estimated 2.4 million full-time children (over 30 hours per week), 2.8 million part-time children (10–29 hours per week), and 16.7 million children in occasional care (less than 10 hours per week). Over 50% of the full-time children in FDC are less than 6 years of age, with the greatest proportion of these children under 3. FDC also represents the most prevalent mode of care for the 5 million school children between 6 and 13 whose parents work (Fosburg, 1980).

It is important to note that three different types of FDC homes can be identified. *Unregulated homes* are those that are not licensed or registered by a public agency. Unregulated care, although illegal in many cases, is the most prevalent form of FDC. Indeed, a 1971 survey estimated that unlicensed care constituted 90% of all day-care arrangements (Westinghouse/Westat, 1971). In *regulated or licensed care,* the provider has been licensed by a state, county, or local government agency (e.g., department of human resources, county board of health). Across the nation there is considerable variation in licensing standards, but most deal with group composition (i.e., staff–child ratio) and basic health and safety measures. Licensed homes are visited (often irregularly) by local officials who review the health and safety of the environment. Finally, *sponsored or supervised homes* are part of networks or organizations of child care providers. These are groups of licensed caregivers whose organization provides them with referrals and training or other child support services (e.g., play material). Such networks frequently work on the assumption that provision of training and assistance to caregivers improves the quality of care provided.

In the course of the preceding discussion of the microsystem of CDC, we touched upon two possible strengths of family day care: (1) the daily and close contact it affords children with mixed-age peers; and (2) its limited isolation from the noncaregiving world. Other advantages we see are its more flexible hours, convenient location, and the freedom FDC affords parents in selecting caregivers with values similar to their own. For children without fathers another strength is suggested, as it has been our experience that the man of a family day care home frequently has contact with the children enrolled in a program. Of course, family day care has its own unique disadvantages. As Steinbeerg and Green(1979) and Saunders and Keister (1972) discovered, FDC programs tend to be unstable, making this kind of service unreliable across the long term. Additionally, there is often little assurance that the provider has any formal training in child care, though most are experienced parents. More often than not, however, these caregivers lack the licensing *and* supervision that can help to assure quality care. It is not surprising, then, that Steinberg and Green (1979) found that many parents deliberately chose not to employ FDC providers because they view this type of care arrangement as lacking a formal education program (i.e., a curriculum).

Our own experience demonstrates that when FDC homes are both licensed and supervised—by a child development council, for example—quality of care can be maintained. A recent study of 41 sponsored (i.e., supervised), 35 licensed, and 23 unlicensed FDC homes corroborates this points. On the basis of lengthy, naturalistic observations, Hawkins and her colleagues (Carew, 1979; Hawkins, Wilcox, Gillis, Porter, & Carew, 1979) found that sponsored caregivers were most involved with their children (e.g., teaching, helping, offering direction) whereas providers in unlicensed homes were least involved. Moreover, these sponsored homes were found to offer safer physical environments (Stallings & Porter, 1980). Probably as a consequence of such differences between types of FDC homes, toddlers in the unlicensed homes were more likely to spend time on their own, not interacting with anyone; were most frequently unhappy; and were most inclined to engage in antisocial behavior (Carew, 1979). Such differences in caregiving environments and children's experiences in FDC are probably a function, at least in part, of the fact that unlicensed homes tend to have less favorable adult–child ratios than do licensed and supervised homes (Emlen, 1977; Hall & Weiner, 1977). On the basis of these data it should be clear that, under certain circumstances, variation with a single type of care (in this case FDC) can be as great as that between types (Prescott, 1973).

This comment notwithstanding, the most significant difference that has been observed between FDC and CDC involves social contact with adults. In Prescott's (1973) comparative study of 28 day care programs, FDC children received assistance from adults more often than did CDC children. The FDC children were also more frequently involved in an activity and spent less time involved in transitions between activities (e.g., lining up to go outside, waiting for lunch). The results of the New York City Infant Day Care Study corroborate these results almost exactly. These findings highlight a potential strength of FDC, which we believe stems from the individualized attention the FDC provider can administer: the personalized relationship that the child can establish with the FDC caregiver. We describe this strength as potential because it is unfortunately the case that such close individual child/individual caregiver relationships are short lived, as FDC programs frequently prove unstable (Steinberg & Green, 1979).

In addition to differences in quantity of attention provided children, FDC differs from CDC and HC in the quality of attention children receive. Both Cochran (1977) and Howes and Rubenstein (1980c) have reported, for example, that caregivers are more controlling in homes than in centers (see also Stallings & Porter, 1980). The fact that children reared in home environments experience more restrictions and directives should not be surprising, given the different demand characteristics of physical environments that are employed only for child care (i.e., centers) and those that serve both residential living and care functions (i.e., homes).

A recent comparative study of FDC and HC indicates that the individual doing the caregiving may be as important as the physical environment in determining the different experiences that children have in various child care arrangements. Data gathered during naturalistic observations of 76 infants and toddlers revealed that mother–child interactions were affectively charged (positively and negatively) three and one half times as often as caregiver–child interaction in FDC homes. Possibly as a consequence, the children reared by their mothers made two and one half times more bids for attention than did their FDC-reared counterparts (Rubenstein & Howes, 1979).

In-Home Care.   In-home care is the least studied of the three types of care we consider. Its advantages include flexible scheduling, a single caregiver who is well known to the child (like FDC) and can perform functions other than child care (e.g., housework), and a setting that is very familiar to the child. Its most obvious disadvantages are expense, absence of peer experience, and the great variability in caregiver competence.

To our knowledge, only two comparative studies have been carried out with children reared at home by non-family members. Rubenstein, Pedersen, and

Yarrow (1977) compared two groups of 5–6-month-olds reared at home by their mothers ($N = 38$) or by substitute caregivers (15 by relatives, 12 by nonrelated baby-sitters) in their own or in the caregiver's home. The two groups of children, all from a low-income urban area, were comparable on a host of child and family characteristics (e.g., sex, birth order, parental education, father absence). Six hours of observation of caregiver/mother–infant interaction revealed according to Rubenstein et. al. (1977): "that mothers provided a more stimulating and responsive environment than did substitute caregivers [p. 530]." However, these differences became less noticeable the longer the caregiver cared for the child, suggesting that, over time, baby-sitter care approximates mother care.

The most comprehensive investigation of variation across types of care is a recently completed study by Clarke-Stewart (1979), which included mother-reared, in-home-babysitter-reared, FDC-reared, and CDC-reared preschoolers. As was expected, the home-reared children (cared for by babysitters or mothers) had more contact with adults but were exposed to fewer peers and adults other than their own parents than were the children reared outside their own homes. Findings regarding the differential effects of these modes of care will be considered when we discuss the effects of day care in the following section of this chapter.

Summary

In this section we have considered utilization of and variation in day care. Usage data reveals that in-home care is the preferred type, but the most expensive; that family day care is the most widely employed; and that center day care the least widely used. We should note that the growth rate of FDC exceeds that of CDC (Emlen & Perry, 1974). Ironically, CDC is the most studied (Belsky & Steinberg, 1978).

Consideration of variation in day care underscored the fact that day care experiences vary immensely, both within and among the three types identified; so much so, in fact, that the variability within types often exceeds that among types. The fact that this variation has rarely been considered in efforts to determine the effects of day care represents one of the major weaknesses of the day care literature. As Ricciuti (1976) has noted, only by paying careful attention to such variability across programs will it be possible to determine the processes by which day care exerts its influence.

THE EFFECTS OF DAY CARE

In an earlier report (Belsky & Steinberg, 1978), we provided a comprehensive and critical review of the research literature on the effects of day care. For purposes of this chapter we have chosen to summarize our initial conclusions and, where appropriate, update them on the basis of data that have become available since the publication of our earlier report. For the details that led to our original conclusions, the interested reader is encouraged to examine the Belsky and Steinberg (1978) review.

Before reporting the conclusions that emerged from our review, we shall reiterate the limitations that characterize the literature we examined. To an overwhelming degree, research on day care has focused on university-connected centers with high staff–child ratios and well-designed programs directed at fostering cognitive, emotional, and social development. Obviously, such care is not representative of that experienced by most children in this country. Although this may limit the degree to which this data base can be generalized, this does not necessarily mean that these studies are without significance. Where the evidence indicates that high quality day care is not detrimental to development, there is good scientific reason to refute the claim that daily separation of the young child from mother *necessarily* impairs the child's psychological functioning (Fraiberg, 1977).

The second limitation of much day care research is its restriction to immediate effects. As we shall see, we know little about the long-range consequences of day care. To the extent that "sleeper effects" of the kind discerned by Moore (1975) in the only long-term follow-up of day care children are representative of the day care experience more generally, there is reason to be hesitant about concluding too quickly that day care has no negative (or positive) effects.

The third major limitation of day care research concerns the comparability of samples. The assumption that day care and home-reared children are comparable is, in all likelihood, invalid. As Hock (1976, 1979) and Sibbison (1973) have documented, families that place their children in day care differ in important respects from those that do not (e.g., attitudes toward maternal role). And as Roopnarine and Lamb (1980) have recently discovered, home-care/group-care differences between children may antedate enrollment in child care programs. Consequently, except under unusual circumstances (e.g., random assignment of day care and home-care groups), it can not be presumed that observed home-care/day care differences are the result of rearing environment per se.

In what follows, we consider the effects of day care upon intellectual, emotional, and social development. In each subsection we consider, data permitting, how type of day care affects child functioning. Finally, before summarizing the results of our analysis, we pay special attention to evidence bearing on processes of influence; that is, to studies that go beyond home-care/day care comparisons in an effort to link characteristics of the day care experience with developmental outcomes.

Intellectual Development.   We noted in our initial review that the effects of day care on cognitive functioning have been extensively researched, but almost entirely with standardized assessments. Thus, very little is known about how day care affects the application of cognitive skills to real-world tasks and problem-solving situations. Rubenstein and Howes' (1979) previously cited study does indicate, though, that at least during children's time in care, center rearing encourages more cognitively sophisticated play activity than does home rearing. Nevertheless, according to Belsky and Steinberg (1978): "the overall picture of evidence, duly qualified, suggests that the day care experience has neither salutary nor adverse effects on the intellectual development . . . of most children. For economically disadvantaged children, however, day care may attenuate declines in test scores typically associated with high-risk populations after 18 months of age [p. 931]."

No evidence has become available since we made this statement to alter our conclusions. In fact, Craig Ramey has reported follow-up data on the infants enrolled in his day care/intervention program that serve to strengthen our original statements. Such data are considered especially important because it was data from Ramey's study and from the New York City Infant Day Care Study (Golden, Rosenbluth, Grossi, Policave, Freenan, & Brownlee, 1978) that figured most importantly in the conclusions we reached regarding day care, intellectual development, and high-risk populations.

At the time of our initial report, Ramey had followed his infants, who began full-time day care in the first half of the first year of life, through their third birthday. At that time, the day care group's mean level of functioning on the Stanford–Binet was 96, whereas, the randomly assigned, home-reared control group's mean was 81. Twenty-eight of the 53 children tested at 3 years have now been tested at 4 years and the earlier differences remain (day care $\bar{X} = 93$; home care $\bar{X} = 81$; $p < .01$; Ramey & Campbell, 1979a). Additional follow-up data indicate, possibly more importantly, that whereas only 11% of the day care-reared children are scoring in the range of cognitive–educational handicap (i.e., IQ ≤ 85) at age 5, a full 35% of the home-reared controls are scoring below this level of functioning (Ramey & Haskins, 1981). Lest the significance of this investigation be misunderstood, we must once again emphasize that this research does *not* indicate that day care enhances cognitive functioning. Rather, it demonstrates that in the case of high-risk infants, center day care prevents the decline in intellectual performance so frequently observed in home-reared children after the age of 2.

Three recent reports provide additional evidence that it is only under such conditions that an effect of day care on intellectual development can be discerned. In a long-term follow-up of 102 of 120 children initially studied by Cochran (1977) during infancy, Gunnarson (1978) found no IQ differences among three groups of children varying in rearing experience when the children were 5½ years old. In this longitudinal Swedish study, some of the children had been continuously reared in centers since infancy, some continuously at home (either by their own mother or a FDC provider), and some had experienced both home and center rearing. Hock (1979) also discerned no differences in intellectual functioning between baby-sitter- and mother-reared infants, as did Doyle and Somers (1978) in comparing FDC- and CDC-reared preschoolers. These investigations lead us again to conclude that, with the exception of center-reared children from impoverished homes, day care has neither salutary nor adverse effects on cognitive development (as measured by standardized developmental assessments and IQ tests).

Emotional Development.   Historically, the mother–child bond has been of prime concern to those interested in the influence of early experience on emotional development. Psychoanalytic theory and early research on institutionalized children (Bowlby, 1951; Goldfarb, 1943; Spitz, 1945) suggested that any arrangement that deprived the child of continuous access to the mother would impair the development of a strong maternal attachment and thereby adversely affect the child's emotional security. Because day care, by its very nature, entails the daily separation of mother from child, a good deal of attention has been devoted to discovering whether child care outside the home does indeed disrupt the child's emotional tie to his mother. The major strategy for making such an appraisal has been to observe young children's response to separation from and reunion with their mothers (usually in an unfamiliar laboratory playroom) and to see whether children prefer to interact with their mothers, their caregivers, or a stranger in free-play situations.

We concluded in our earlier report (Belsky & Steinberg, 1978), that: "the total body of evidence reviewed regarding the effect of day care on the children's attachments to their mothers offers little support for the claim that day care disrupts the child's tie to his mother [p. 939]." Across the entire set of studies reviewed, the day care experience did not appear to foster anxious as opposed to secure attachments, or to encourage in children a preference for their caregivers over their mothers. Data that have become available since our earlier review provides additional support for these conclusions, with the exception of one investigation (Vaughn, Gove, & Egeland, 1980). Because this study is unique in a variety of ways, we shall consider it only after reviewing the evidence that supports our earlier conclusion.

Before proceeding to examine these recent researches, we feel it necessary to express a change of opinion. In our earlier report we were critical of the methodology employed by most investigators to study emotional development. Specifically, we questioned the validity of Ainsworth and Wittig's (1969) much used and (abused) Strange Situation paradigm as a means of evaluating the effect of day care and, more generally, emotional development. For readers not familiar with this laboratory procedure, it involves subjecting the young child to increasing levels of stress by repeatedly separating him or her from his or her mother and introducing him or her to a strange adult. The assumption underlying this experimental situation is that the child's approach–avoidance reponses to mother and stranger, and willingness to explore the unfamiliar environment, index the quality of the infant–mother attachment bond. Since 1978 several research reports have appeared that definitively validate this assumption (see Sroufe, 1979, for a review). Specifically, infants characterized as being securely attached to their mothers, as evidenced by their strong and unambiguous proximity seeking of her during the reunion episodes of the experiment, display greater problem-solving ability and cooperative help seeking when they are 2 years of age (Matas, Arend, & Sroufe, 1978), and more skill in interacting with peers and adapting to novel situations when they are 5 (Arend, Gove, & Sroufe, 1979; Waters, Wippman, & Sroufe, 1979). In light of these convincing data, we rescind our earlier criticisms of the Strange Situation that derived from our concern for its undemonstrated predictive utility. It is not our contention that strategies of assessment that focus on the child's performance in more naturalistic situations should not be developed and deployed in day care research, but, rather, that the Strange Situation now appears to be one efficient and effective method for meaningfully diagnosing the quality of early emotional development.

We must point out though that rarely has the Strange Situation methodology been employed appropriately by day care researchers. To date, the validity of the assessment procedure has been demonstrated only when global classifications of attachments are made (secure, anxious–avoidant, anxious–resistant) during the period of 12–18 months. Many day care studies, however, rely on frequency scores of discrete behaviors (e.g., separation distress, proximity seeking) shown in the Strange Situation by children 2 and even 3 years of age. Thus, interpretations of such investigations must be made with great caution because the meaning of the behaviors studied, and thus the study findings, are not totally clear.

We noted in our initial review that only Blehar (1974) had documented "the existence of substantial, systematic differences between day care-reared and home-reared children [Belsky & Steinberg, 1978, p. 939]," and that other, more carefully controlled studies repeatedly failed to replicate her results. We cautioned, moreover, against overinterpreting group differences on single variables in the face of more pervasive similarities between home- and day care-reared children and concurred with Portnoy and Simmon's (1978) suggestion that Blehar's findings may have been an artifact of "a transient distress reaction" associated with new day care arrangements. These investigators had accurately observed that whereas the children in the Blehar study had been in supplementary care for less than 5 months, those in replication studies had been cared for outside the home for longer periods of time.

Recent reports provide evidence that substantially enhances the credibility of the hypothesis advanced by Portnoy and Simmon. In Hock's (1979) investigation, baby-sitter-reared infants who had been in supplementary care for 9 months did not differ from mother-reared infants in proximity seeking and reunion behavior directed toward mother when observed at 1 year of age in Ainsworth and Wittig's (1969) Strange Situation paradigm. Similarly, 18–24-month-olds who had been in day care for an average of 10 months made visual contact with, sought proximity to, and searched for and avoided their mothers as frequently as did a group of home-reared infants in Wynn's (1979) study, which employed a slight modification of the Ainsworth and Wittig separation–reunion procedure.

In each of these investigations, minor differences were observed between the two rearing groups. In the Wynn study, day care children were more inclined to engage in exploratory behavior (as indexed by time and distance away from mother), whereas, in the Hock investigation, children cared for by their non-working mothers more frequently resisted contact with the strange adult when she attempted to comfort the child. Minor group differences were also reported by Rubenstein, Howes, and Boyle (1979), in their comparative investigation of a small group ($n = 10$) of $3\frac{1}{2}$-year-old children reared in day care since 12 months of age and a matched group of home-reared preschoolers. But, in light of the vast similarities between the two groups of children, we find their claim that day care children have difficulty resolving the developmental task of individuation–autonomy unconvincing. Although the day care children were less cooperative with mother during a boring task, they did not differ from their home-reared counterparts in their responses to separation from and reunion with mother, on scores on a behavior-problem checklist, and in anxiety displayed while being tested. In sum, then, we view these three studies as providing additional evidence that the emotional development of young children is little influenced by their day care experience.

Perhaps the most convincing evidence of the importance of the duration of the child's day care experience in determining the effect of supplementary child care on emotional development comes from Blanchard and Main's (1979) recent study of 1- and 2-year-olds. They found avoidance of mother, both during daily pickup from day care and in a structured laboratory situation, to be negatively related to months in alternate child care. This discovery led these investigators to conclude that: "the stronger avoidance shown by Blehar's (1974) subjects . . . was due in part to their much briefer day care experience [Blanchard & Main, 1979, p. 446]." These data suggest to us that young children may go through a period of stressful adaptation to supplementary child care. But once they come to understand that regular separation from parent need not imply loss of the attachment figure, adaptation is achieved and problematic behavior is reduced.

Serious consideration of this explanation and Portnoy and Simmons' (1978) notion of a "transient distress syndrome" associated with initial day care experience may help to account for one set of discrepent findings that emerge from another day care study. Clarke-Stewart (1980) found that 2- and 3-year-olds cared for on a full-time basis in CDC were, in comparison to parent-reared, baby-sitter-reared, FDC-reared, and part-time-CDC-reared children, disproportionately likely to display low interaction and physical contact with mother upon reunion in a structured separation situation, and disproportionately unlikely to display interested interaction and positive affect. Like Blehar's subjects, however, Clark-Stewart's children had been in day care for a relatively short time (i.e., less than 6 months) when child–mother attachment was evaluated. Given the results of other studies in which children were evaluated after more day care experience, there is reason to believe that Clarke-Stewart's data might have been different had she assessed her children after another 4 to 6 months of day care. Inasmuch as baby-sitter- and FDC-reared children were not as disinterested in mother nor as nonreactive to a brief separation as were their full-time CDC counterparts, yet had been in day care just as long, a "transient distress" explanation cannot completely account for Clarke-Stewart's data. As we shall see when we consider the process through which day care exerts its influence on child development, this investigator identifies experience at home as the primary variable that accounts for her attachment findings.

The importance of home experience is also implicated in the one investigation cited earlier as forcefully contradicting our conclusion that day care does not disrupt children's emotional relationships with their mothers. Vaughn, Gove, and Egeland (1980) have recently reported that the absence of a man in the home increases the likelihood that a mother will seek employment before her infant reaches 18 months of age, which, when initiated prior to the child's first birthday, undermines the quality of infant–mother attachment. This does not seem to be the case if out-of-home care is initiated after the attachment relationship has been formed (i.e., after 12 months of age).

Several factors are important to note in considering the Vaughn et al. data. First, the subjects of this study experienced generally unstable, as well as varied, out-of-home care arrangements. Eighty percent of the infants whose attachment relations were studied at 12 and 18 months and who were in day care during this period experienced a change in supplementary caregiver. Moreover, few of the infants studied received their care in licensed day care centers; most often care was provided by an adult female, often a relative or friend of the infant's mother, in the alternate caretaker's home. Thus, what Vaugh et al. are most likely documenting are the effects of unstable and, quite possibly, low quality supplementary child care. As they note, though, this is exactly the quality of care most usually available to families from high-risk environments.

A second important point to consider is that Vaughn et al. did not find that day care enrollment prior to the first year increased the probability of an anxious versus secure infant–mother attachment relationship. Rather, it increased the probability of a particular kind of anxious attachment—and one that was predicted to occur with greater frequency on the basis of the Ainsworth/Bowlby attachment theory. Because out-of-home care was expected to make the mothers of these children more psychologically unavailable to their infants at the time when the attachment relationship was still "in the making," it was predicted—and found—that early out-of-home care would increase the probability of anxious–avoidant attachments (i.e., attachments that manifest themselves through avoidance of contact with mother following separation and/or ignorance of mother's initiations of interaction during periods of reunion). Such attachment relations, it is important to note, have been found to predict problems in adjusting to peers during the preschool years (Arend, Gove, & Sroufe, 1979).

It seems, then, that our conclusions regarding the effect of day care on emotional development need to be qualified. Supplementary child care seems to exert little influence on the child's emotional ties to his or her mother except when children are from high-risk environments and are enrolled in unstable day care arrangements prior to their first birthday. Under such conditions, infants will be more likely to develop a particular kind of disturbance in their relations with their primary attachment figure: They will be likely to avoid her. Because this avoidance is presumed to result from mother's psychological unavailability, it is reasonable to speculate that even under the conditions described previously, avoidant attachment relations with mother are not inevitable if the quality of maternal care is not compromised during those periods of the day when she is with the infant. Indirect support for this hypothesis comes from the Vaughn et al. (1980) study, as a full 50% of the infants whose mothers went to work prior to their first birthday had established secure attachments to their mothers by the time they were 18 months of age.

Social Development.   In our earlier review, we defined social development in terms of relations with peers and nonparental adults and concluded on the basis of the available evidence at that time that day care children, when compared to age-mates reared at home, interact more with peers—in both positive and negative ways. Some evidence suggested, moreover, that children enrolled in day care for extended periods displayed increased aggression toward peers and adults, and decreased cooperation with adults and involvement in educational activities once they entered school.

Lest these findings be taken as a sweeping indictment of day care rearing, we qualified our conclusions in the following manner:

> like all social and educational efforts, day care programs are likely to reflect, and in some measure achieve, the values held explicitly or implicitly by their sponsors and, through them, by the community at large.
>
> From this perspective, the tendency we have observed for all-day group care to predispose children toward greater aggressiveness, impulsivity and egocentricism may represent a phenomenon specific to American society, for these outcomes have been identified as characteristic of socialization in age-segregated peer groups in America generally. . . . That the phenomena may indeed by culturebound is indicated by . . . comparative studies of peer group socialization in the United States, the USSR, Israel, and other contemporary societies, which show that, depending on the goals and methods involved, group upbringing can lead to a variety of consequences, ranging from delinquency and violence at one extreme to unquestioning conformity at the other [Belsky & Steinberg, 1978, p. 942].

Ambron's (1980) recent suggestion that day care staff are more permissive, more tolerant of disobedience and aggression, and less inclined to set behavior standards than parents lends credence to these conclusions. So too does Macrae and Herbert-Jackson's (1975) claim that the effects of day care may be program specific. Thus, if caregivers were to adopt more authoritative child-rearing styles (Baumrind, 1967), we suspect that many day care children would evidence less problem behavior in their social relationships with both peers and adults.

Since the publication of our initial review, three studies dealing with the social development of day care children have been reported. Interestingly, these investigations provide additional support for our original conclusions that day care can have both positive and negative effects on relations with peers and nonparental adults. With respect to peer relations, interviews with the teachers of children initially enrolled in the Ramey day care/early-intervention program revealed that these children were more hostile during the fall of their kindegarten years than were control children who had not been in the program during their infancy and preschool years (as determined by teacher ratings on the Schaeffer Classroom Behavior Inventory) (Ramey, Dorval, & Baker-Ward, 1981). When these experimental and control children were compared at 6, 12, and 18 months on their reactions to examiners conducting developmental assessments (via the Bayley Infant Behavior Record), however, the day care children were found to be more socially confident at each age and less fearful of the unfamiliar adult conducting the assessments (Ramey & Campbell, 1979b; Ramey, MacPhee, & Yeats, 1981).

A study by Gunnarson (1978), also involving a follow-up of children first studied in infancy (Cochran, 1977), contradicts several earlier studies that suggested that day care may reduce children's prosocial orientation toward adults and increase their negative interaction with peers (Schwarz, Strickland, & Krolick, 1974). Naturalistic observations revealed no rearing-group differences in children's compliance and cooperation with, and positive affect expressed towards adults in the Gunnarson (1978) research. Moreover, structured doll play assessments of these 5-year-olds revealed that day care children were no more likely than home-reared children to transgress against adult wishes in the face of peer pressures to do so. The fact that such findings were not qualified by family structure (single-parent versus two-parent homes) suggests that, at least in Sweden, the effects of day care on orientation toward adults is similar regardless of the kind of home the child comes from. Whether or not the same is true of American society is unknown, as American day care studies have evidenced little concern for the interaction of home-care and day care experience.

Because the children reared in Swedish day care centers, in comparison to those reared in homes (by FDC providers or mothers), engaged more frequently in information sharing, compliance, and cooperation with peers, Gunnarson's (1978) study provides additional evidence that day care promotes positive peer skills. But the fact that negative peer interactions were no more frequent in any rearing environment leads us to reaffirm the conclusion quoted earlier from our initial review: The effect of day care on social development will likely depend on the community and cultural context in which day care is employed as well as the particular practices of the day care program.

The third investigation concerned with the effects of day care on social development that has appeared since out initial report indicates that much more can be learned about the effects of day care when variation in supplementary care is examined (Clarke-Stewart, 1979, 1980). Initial analyses of data gathered during structured experimental probes revealed only modest differences between home-reared and day care-reared 2- and 3-year-olds. Although children cared for by their parents or by a baby-sitter in their own home displayed *less* cooperation with a strange peer while playing and were less able to appraise accurately the perspective of another (social cognition) and to provide assistance to a strange adult (social competence) than were agemates cared for outside of their own home, Clarke-Stewart (1979) found no home-care/day care differences on six other measures of social development.

Analyses that went beyond a simple day care/home-care dichotomy qualified these results in several important respects. On the measures of social competence and cooperation with a strange peer, full-time, center-reared children, who had the most exposure to different people, scored higher than their peers cared for on a part-time basis in nursery school. These part-time preschoolers scored higher than FDC-reared children, who themselves exceeded baby-sitter- and mother-reared 2- and 3-year-olds. Although these data may be explained by the differential exposure that children had to different people, the same explanation fails to account for data gathered on social cognition, as FDC children scored below home-reared children on the perspective-taking measure, whereas, part-time nursery-school children scored above full-time CDC children. Thus the group with the most exposure to different people (CDC) did not score highest as they had on the measures of social competence and cooperation with a strange peer, and the group with the least such exposure (HC) did not score lowest.

The fact the FDC children performed most poorly on the assessments of compliance with adults (i.e., willingness to pickup play materials at clean-up) and prosocial behavior (i.e., showing sympathy for and offering help to an injured adult) raises serious concerns about the influence of FDC on social development, especially because children experiencing such rearing also scored lowest on the perspective-taking measure. Given our earlier defense of this family-centered approach to supplementary child care, we were surprised by these findings.

However, few of the FDC homes Clarke-Stewart studied were licensed, much less supervised (personal communication), and the importance of such supervision for child development is suggested by jointly considering Clarke-Stewart's internal analysis of her data and the earlier reviewed Carew (1979) investigation of FDC homes. Clarke-Stewart (1980) found that prosocial behavior was positively related to the amount of verbal interaction children experienced during the day with adults and that social cognition was similarly related to the frequency with which adults engaged in teaching behavior. Not only do we know from our own experience that supervised FDC programs (at least in central Pennsylvania) often provide special training to caregivers to encourage just such types of interaction, but, on a more empirical level, Carew's (1979) data demonstrate that caregivers from supervised FDC homes exceed their counterparts from unlicensed and unsupervised homes in just such growth-promoting caregiving styles. This suggests, of course, that we need to consider variation within types of day care programs if we hope to understand the effects of supplementary child care.

Processes of Influence.   The simple documentation of group differences in day care and home-reared children permits us only to speculate on the causes of such differences. As such, group comparison studies offer limited guidance for designing (or redesigning) programs to enhance positive developmental outcomes and minimize the negative consequences of group rearing. Only in the last several years have investigators moved beyond the group-comparison stage of day care evaluation research in an effort to understand the mechanisms that influence differences discerned between day care- and family-reared children.

In the National Day Care Study, Travers and Ruopp (1978) found that group size and training of caregivers were the most important determinants of variation in children's development across 57 day care centers in three cities. Specifically, children cared for in small groups (which we have already noted are characterized by more active teacher involvement and less aimless wandering by children) showed greater improvement across testing periods on examinations designed to measure kindergarten and first-grade reading readiness. Specialized training in subject areas pertinent to child care were related not only to positive classroom caregiver behavior (e.g., social interaction with children, less adult-adult interaction, less management-oriented activities), but also to child achievement. It appears, then, that small group size and caregiver training enhance children's daily experiences in day care, which in turn facilitates cognitive/motivational development.

This interpretation receives support from select findings from two large-scale investigations of infant day care and a small study of early out-of-home rearing. In the New York City infant day care project- Golden et al. (1978) found that 2-year-olds who experienced high levels of cognitive stimulation and social interaction with their caregivers in FDC homes and in centers scored high on measures of social competence and language comprehension when they were 3. Researchers from Stanford University following over 225 infants in various child-care arrangements found that children reared in low-quality environments (indexed by infrequent play and instructional interactions with caregivers, and frequent negative interactions) were less sensitive to experimental mother–infant separations than were those reared in high-quality centers (Kermoian, 1980). The infants' failure to get distressed during separation or to reduce their exploratory activity suggested to these investigators that low-quality care may increase the development of avoidant attachment relations. Because reunion data are not yet available on these infants from programs of varying quality, this interpretation awaits more rigorous documentation.

Rubenstein et al.'s (1979) small-scale study of infant day care also highlights the importance of quality of care, specifically, caregiver involvement. In their follow-up study of 10 $3\frac{1}{2}$-year-olds cared for in centers since 12 months of age, they reported that frequency of social play with caregiver predicted subsequent greeting behavior upon reunion with mother ($r = .70$), whereas caregiver directiveness (i.e., intrusiveness) predicted future temper tantrums ($r = .67$). The possibility is raised in this study that these day care experiences that appeared to influence later development may have been instigated by the children themselves; for example, infants who were more socially oriented tended to elicit more playful interaction from their caregivers. Another study by these same investigators (Howes & Rubenstein, 1980b) revealed that quality of mother–infant interaction and infants' competent play with toys at home prior to enrollment in day care strongly predicted infants' capacities to explore the day care milieu and to establish new relationships with peers, toys, and adults in day care (multiple Rs range from .63 to .97). When considered jointly, the data from these two studies suggest that skills, expectations, and emotional security developed at home facilitate positive adaptation in the new day care environment, which itself predicts future development.

Stability of care is another dimension of quality that needs to be considered in examining process of influence. Unfortunately, and surprisingly, very little work exists on this important topic. Rubenstein and Howes' (1979) recent study of experiences at home and in day care suggests that in addition to the frequent claim that a low turnover rate among staff is in the child's best interest, so too is a stable peer group. Stability has also been implicated as an important dimension of quality care in Cummings' (1980) recent investigation of behavior during separation from mother during daily morning drop-offs at day care. Children averaging 22 months of age were more likely to be distressed when left with a caregiver identified as unstable than when left with one with whom the child was very familiar. Finally, the earlier reviewed Vaughn et al. (1980) findings regarding the effect of day care on attachment when supplementary care is unstable also underscore the importance of this dimension of the day care experience.

The significance of stable rearing is likely to be most pronounced when home environment is relatively unstable; for example, when parents are either inconsistent in their own caregiving demands or when there is frequent change in persons moving in or out of the home. In her review of the effects of divorce, Hetherington (1980) makes a similar argument: Constructive relationships with teachers and peers in school, and a relatively structured and predictable environment can attenuate the negative effects of a stressful home experience. Because many day care centers and family day care homes create just such an atmosphere via regularly scheduled routines and activities, it is likely that a quality day care experience may be especially important in offsetting the negative effects of divorce. In fact, this possibility, and the fact that so many day care-reared children are from single-parent homes, led us to advise that requirements of scheduling and routine be included in the revised Federal Interagency Day Care Requirements (Belsky, Walker, & Anderson, 1979). This would insure children of at least one structured and predictable rearing environment.

Clarke-Stewart's (1979) aforementioned comparative study of home care, baby-sitting, FDC, and CDC also provides support for the contention that consideration of the child's home environment will enhance our understanding of the effects of day care. She found, for example, that preschoolers who showed ambivalent attachments in a structured separation–reunion situation (i.e., more interaction with *and* anger displayed toward mother) had nearly four times as much interaction with their peers in the evening as did the other study children—as revealed by detailed, dinnertime observations in the home. This finding suggested to Clarke-Stewart that such children did not receive sufficient parental attention and that quality of attachment is determined more by what transpires in the home than at day care.

The same appeared true of friendliness toward strange adults. In fact, on the basis of a positive correlation between the number of people the child interacted with during dinner at home and positive response to a strange adult, and a negative association between the number of people the child contacted during the day and the same dependent measure, Clarke-Stewart concluded that sociability is fostered in the family, and not by daily exposure to strange adults.

Hock's (1979) recent study also underscores the importance of home experience for understanding the effect of supplementary child care. She observed that mothers whose infants were cared for by a baby-sitter while they worked, but who expressed attitudes that stressed the importance of exclusive maternal care, had 1-year-olds who were likely to display negative reunion behavior following separation from mother. This suggests to us that when mothers are in conflict over what they have to do (i.e., work) and what they want to do (i.e., provide exclusive care for their children), they provide less sensitive care for their children, which we know can impair the development of a secure infant–mother attachment (Ainsworth, 1979). This, of course, is unlikely to be the situation of dual-career families where both parents are working for reasons of choice rather than necessity. It is quite possible, then, that the effects of day care will be mediated by family type. In families where both parents work but at least one would rather be home with the child, the conflict between desires and activity may undermine the child's development. When such conflict does not exist, however, supplementary rearing may truly function as a family support system that enhances the child's development. Clearly, work is needed that begins to consider family and day care characteristics simultaneously.

Summary

This update of our earlier review of research on the effects of day care provides additional support for, and some qualifications of the conclusions we reached in 1978. With respect to cognitive development, there is still no evidence that day care influences the intellectual functioning of children other than those from impoverished homes who are reared in centers during infancy. Exactly how long such supplementary child care experience buffers these children from the intellectual declines so frequently observed among their home-reared counterparts remains to be seen. Although the most recent data from Craig Ramey's project are encouraging, it must be noted that at the time of the 4-year-old assessment, Ramey's children were still being cared for in a very high quality, university-sponsored day care program. As Ramey himself is aware, conclusive evidence of the long-term influence of this early experience will not be available until these children leave day care and enter public school. Although initial evaluations of other early intervention projects documented "wash-out effects" of early IQ gains once programs terminated (Bronfenbrenner, 1974) and thus leave little room for optimism, more recent and long-term follow-up studies of these same children suggest that academic achievements may be positively influenced throughout the school career (Lazar, Hubbell, Murray, Rosche, & Royce, 1977). In the long term, Ramey's carefully controlled study should provide important evidence for selecting between these two alternative conclusions.

With respect to emotional development, available evidence generally fails to support the notion that supplementary child care negatively affects the child. Indeed, new evidence suggests that many of the negative effects that have been found for day care vis-à-vis infant–mother attachment may be more a function of the timing of assessment than supplementary care per se. After 6 months of day care experience, young children seem to adapt successfully to their supplementary care arrangements so that they are virtually indistinguishable from their home-reared counterparts. Where group differences are evident, little consistency across studies can be found, suggesting that the discerned effects of day care rearing are program specific or unreliable.

These conclusions seem to hold true except under circumstances in which children from impoverished homes are enrolled in unstable care prior to their first birthday (Vaughn et al., 1980). As noted earlier, such arrangements increase the likelihood that an anxious–avoidant attachment relationship will develop.

Finally, with respect to social relations with peers and nonparental adults, the data still indicate that day care can have both positive and negative effects. But Clarke-Stewart's (1979, 1980) recent study teaches us that a day care/home-care dichotomy may not be useful in teasing apart the effects of supplementary child care. And Hocks' (1979) investigation suggests that characteristics of the home environment may be important to consider in teasing apart processes of influence. More than ever, then, there is a need to examine the specific experiences of children in multiple settings in order to achieve an understanding of the effects of any type of child care.

THE WIDER ECOLOGY OF DAY CARE

Our analysis of supplementary child care through this point reveals the disciplinary narrowness that characterizes day care research to date. For example, although developmentalists have examined the psychological effects of supplementary care on children, they have failed to consider in these researches the changing nature of the American family. Similarly, sociologists and demographers who have charted recent increases in the utilization of out-of-home care, and the reasons for its adoption, have evidenced little concern for its developmental consequences. One result of this state of affairs is that we know virtually nothing about how parents' reasons for using day care mediate its effect on child development—this despite an abundance of information on day care effects and on the rise in single parenthood, maternal employment, and disenchantment with traditional female roles. Thus, for example, we know virtually nothing about how day care affects children from single-parent homes, dual-career families, or families in which traditional parental sex roles may be reversed (i.e., nontraditional families).

This absence of information represents only one limitation of our present understanding of the phenomenon of supplementary child care. Also lacking is systematic research on day care's influence on the family, the community, and American society, as well as on the reciprocal influence of these social units on day care itself. What we have yet to develop as social scientists, then, is an understanding of the linkages interconnecting the individual child in day care with the family, community, and cultural/historical contexts in which the child is embedded—that is, an ecology of day care. Coordinated inquiry at several levels of analysis is required if progress is to be made in developing an ecology of day care.

To achieve such a goal, conceptual tools are needed that are capable of bridging disciplines and overcoming handicaps of professional specialization. In our mind, Bronfenbrenner's (1977, 1979) concentric-circle model of the ecology of human development represents just such a conceptual device, as it conceives the individual to be embedded within several nested levels of context. Progressing outward from the center are the layers of the micro-, meso-, exo-, and macrosystems. According to Bronfenbrenner, the microsystem represents any immediate setting containing the developing individual; the mesosystem the interrelation of these major settings; the exosystem the formal and informal social structures that do not themselves contain the developing person but impinge upon or encompass the immediate settings, thereby influencing what goes on there; and the macrosystem the overarching patterns of ideology and organization that characterize a particular culture or subculture.

Having found this conceptual framework to be especially useful in analyzing other social-policy-related concerns of social science (child abuse: Belsky, 1980a; adolescent labor: Steinberg & Greenberger, 1979), we employ it in this final section of this chapter to guide our inquiry into: (1) *influences on;* and (2) *the broader effects of* supplementary child care. (We do not consider the microsystem of day care in our analyses, however, as we have done so already in our earlier comparative examination of CDC, FDC, and HC.) Although the discussion to follow is organized into separate subsections corresponding to the meso-, exo-, and macrosystems, respectively, it is not our intent to suggest that the multiple levels of this ecological framework can be viewed independently. Quite the contrary, we argue for an awareness of how factors at one level of analysis can influence the shape of events at others. In other words, in the ecology of day care, as in the ecology of human development more generally, levels of analysis are necessarily interconnected.

Before proceeding to consider the mesosystem of day care, one further comment is in order. To a great extent, much of what is to follow remains speculative, as relatively little data has been gathered on this wider ecology of day care. Where appropriate, then, we rely on the actual experiences of one of us (AW) in the day-to-day provision of day care services in one community to suggest avenues for future empirical inquiry.

The Mesosystem.   In this subsection concerned with the interrelation of child-rearing environments, we focus on the interface of day care and the family. Available research indicates that this interface has been examined in two general ways—by studying parent–caregiver communication and the effects of day care on the family. In neither case do we believe that available work goes far enough in exploring the mesosystem of day care.

Douglas Powell of the Merrill–Palmer Institute has conducted the most extensive examination of parent–caregiver communication (Powell, 1977, 1978a, 1978b, 1979, 1980). And his in-depth interviews of 212 parents and 89 caregivers in 12 metropolitan day care centers in Detroit reveals that few efforts are made to coordinate children's socialization across contexts. In fact, Powell concludes on the basis of his work that "fragmentation and discontinuity" characterize the social world of day care children.

Powell's detailed typology of parent–caregiver communication patterns indicates, however, that experiences across day care and home are not the same for all children. A small group of "interdependent" parents, Powell discovered, believe strongly that family information (on a wide variety of topics) should be shared with day care workers. And such parents practice what they preach, engaging in frequent communication with caregivers. "Independent" parents, in contrast, maintain a significant social distance between themselves and their children's caregivers, most probably because they conceive of family and day care as two separate rearing environments. Finally, a third group of "dependent" parents were identified who view the family/day care relationship as a one-way street in which information flows only from day care to the home.

It is unfortunate that although Powell's work was based on the assumption that the nature of cross-context communication has consequences for the child's development, no efforts were made to determine whether the children of these various types of parents had different experiences at home or in day care as a result of the information exchanged between the two sets of child rearers. We suspect that they did, because it has been our experience that when parents and caregivers inform each other of their children's experiences at home and in day care, children are more sensitively reared in each locale. The case of a $2\frac{1}{2}$-year-old receiving care in a supervised FDC home illustrates this point. This child, who had frequent toileting accidents in day care that generated many caregiving problems, was struggling to come to terms with inconsistent toilet-training demands. The problem, it seemed, stemmed from the child's inability to understand the caregiver's queries regarding the child's need to go to the bathroom. As soon as home and day care language systems were coordinated, toileting proceeded smoothly and caregiver frustration all but disappeared.

Inconsistent language is not the only cause of discontinuous care between home and day care. General child-rearing practices (e.g., regulatory strategies for dealing with curiosity, hostility, anxiety), physical environments (e.g., freedom of movement, opportunity for privacy), and value codes (e.g., delayed versus immediate gratification, justifiable aggression versus intolerance of aggression) represent other areas of potential home-care–day care discrepancies (Powell, 1980). Oviously, it is not entirely possible to maintain continuity across all these domains, nor is it necessarily advantageous to do so. In the case of young children, however, we do believe that such continuity, which is enhanced by frequent parent–caregiver communication, serves to support optimal development by providing the child with a consistent and, thus, predictable social world (Lippitt, 1968). In the case of older children, it is possible that continuity is less important. Indeed, as Lightfoot (1975) suggests, dissonance between family and other rearing environments may make children more malleable and responsive to a changing world, whereas homegeneity across rearing contexts could discourage the development of adaptive functioning. Unfortunately, we are aware of no research, basic or applied, that addresses this important issue.

We noted earlier in introducing this section of the chapter that levels of analysis in Bronfenbrenner's ecological scheme are necessarily intertwined. Several conclusions Powell draws from the results of his study illustrate this point by highlighting the potential influence of the mesosystem (parent–caregiver communication) on the microsystem (the design of day care environments). Because the bulk of information exchange occurred at transition points in the child's day (drop-off and pickup times), Powell recommended that centers be physically designed to encourage parent–caregiver interaction (e.g., coffee tables) and that personnel be available for just this purpose early in the morning and late in the afternoon. Recognition of the importance of such communication also suggests that caregiver training programs emphasize the importance of transition points for parents, not just children, and that listening skills be developed to assist caregivers in working with parents.

As we noted in our 1978 review of day care research, several studies have looked at the effect of day care on the family, and thus qualify as mesosystem researches. Ramey and Mills (1975) and Falender and Heber (1976), for example, found that mothers whose infants were randomly assigned to a day care program engaged in more frequent and positive interactions with their children than did mothers denied access to the program who reared their children at home. Both sets of investigators offered the provocative hypothesis that parents of day care children were influenced by the social skills their infants developed in day care. Subsequent analyses of a larger sample of Ramey and Mills' subjects cast doubt on this possibility (Farran & Ramey, 1980; Ramey, Farran, & Campbell, 1979), though, as do the recent results of Clarke-Stewart's (1979, 1980) day care study, because in each investigation reliable rearing-group differences in parent–child interaction could not be found. More recent and in-depth analyses of mother–infant interaction in the laboratory, however, suggest that these day care-to-child-to-parent effects may simply take time to emerge. Refined analyses of videotapes of the 20-month sessions of the Ramey, Farran, and Campbell (1979) subjects revealed that day care infants communicated to their mothers at significantly higher levels than controls, especially in terms of requesting behaviors (O'Connell & Farran, 1980). And when infants were 36 months of age, observations revealed that not only were the day care children four times as likely to attempt to modify their mothers' behavior—by asking mothers to watch their activity, read them a story, or join their play—but also that mother–child exchanges in the course of mutual play lasted twice as long in their experimental-group dyads (Farran & Haskins, 1980). Thus it appears that day care, at least under some conditions, may indirectly affect parents, by directly influencing child behavior. Indeed, it seems reasonable to speculate that the effects of day care on parental behavior will be especially pronounced with certain types of families. For example, teenage mothers may prove especially susceptible to day care influences given their lack of experience in parenting and great need for support.

Our experience in one community also convinces us that day care can have a powerful and positive influence on families by informally providing parent education. The case of one little girl from a single-parent family should illustrate this point. The mother of this girl was quite young, completely inexperienced in child care, and lacking the kind of supportive assistance that is often provided by a spouse or by relatives living nearby. Consequently, she literally let her child run her own life, eating and sleeping when she wanted to and, more generally, doing as she pleased. The discontinuity in socialization demands between home and day care were so great that the child was a virtual terror in the family day care program in which she was enrolled. Working with the support and encouragement of her supervisor, the day care provider succeeded in making this parent understand the importance of consistency and control. Moreover, she was able to develop in the mother more reliable parenting practices that, when implemented, not only made the caregiver's and the child's lives easier, but the mother's as well. Exactly how much such parent education goes on in day care remains an unstudied empirical question. Steinberg and Green (1979) do report, though, that parents with children in centers claim to learn more about parenting than do those with children in FDC homes. This may be a function, at least in part, of the expectancies that parents bring to the child care facilities they employ, as they often view CDC workers as persons specially trained in child care.

Some evidence that day care can effect parental attitudes comes from the Ramey day care project. Although mothers whose children were enrolled in the program since infancy did not differ from mothers whose children were not enrolled in the program in terms of locus of control when their infants were 3 months of age or in terms of authoritarian, hostile, rejecting, or democratic attitudes toward parenting when their offsrping were 6 and 18 months old, significant attitudinal differences did emerge by the time children had graduated from the day care program and were in kindergarten. Specifically, mothers of day care-reared children were less likely to say they were powerless to influence the school, that teaching is not the parent's job, and that the future is more important then the present. Moreover, these same mothers were more likely to profess attitudes supporting children's rights to have their own opinions and to be free to express them (Ramey, Dorval, & Baker-Ward, 1981).

In addition to influencing the parent–child relationship, we suspect that day care can affect the family in other ways—and there is some recent evidence to support this claim: Interviews with mothers of children in the Ramey day care program and with control-group mothers revealed that whereas these two groups of parents were equivalent in years of schooling in the year of their child's birth, by the time their children were 54 months old, the day care mothers had significantly more education than their control counterparts ($\bar{X}$s: 11.9 yrs. versus 10.3 yrs.) (Ramey, Dorval, & Baker Ward, 1981). Lally (1973) reports data indicating similar effects of day care on the family. Ramey, Dorval, and Baker-Ward (1981) also find that having their children enrolled in day care positively influenced mothers' work-related skills, as day care mothers were significantly more likely to be employed in skilled or semiskilled occupations by the time their children were 54 months of age, whereas control-group mothers were more likely to be unemployed or in unskilled jobs. The effect of such employment-related influences of family income should be obvious, and indeed has been documented as part of the Pennsylvania day care study, which surveyed and compared families using various types of day care and those on waiting lists hoping to enroll their children in these same day care programs (Peters, 1973).

In terms of its further effect on the family, we suspect that under two conditions day care may positively influence a marriage: when it frees a parent from the unsatisfying responsibilities of providing full-time child care and when it enables a second parent in an economically stressed family to seek gainful employment. Because a harmonious marital relationship provides support for parents in their caregiving roles (Belsky, 1981), such an unstudied effect of day care not only has the potential for positively influencing the husband–wife relationship, but the child as well. We suspect that this possible influence of day care has been ignored largely because it has been developmental psychologists who have investigated day care effects, yet it is family sociologists who study the marital relationship (Aldous, 1977).

What transpires in day care is most certainly affected by forces and contexts with which the child is not directly involved. Moreover, the effects of day care most assuredly extend beyond the child and what transpires in his or her family. Consideration of such influences on and effects of supplementary child care demands an examination of the exosystem of day care.

The Exosystem.   Recall that Bronfenbrenner (1977) defines the exosystem as those formal and informal social structures that do not themselves contain the developing child but nevertheless impinge upon and encompass the immediate settings in which the child is contained. In this exosystem analysis of day care, then, we consider how the workplace, government, and supervisory child development councils affect and/or are affected by day care.

Day care's influence on the world of work is most evident when parents' reasons for utlizing supplementary child care are considered. For most families, day care makes the employment of at least one parent (often the second parent) possible. But we suspect that day care may influence the working world in ways other than through this general effect. Specifically, the establishment of a *stable* caregiving arrangement is likely to reduce, if not eliminate entirely, the time and effort that goes into making child care plans on a week-by-week or month-by-month basis. To the extent that this is so, we hypothesize that day care effectively reduces absenteeism from the work place and, thereby, enhances employee productivity. If a day care program has the resources to care for a sick child, such effects are likely to be especially pronounced. In this regard, Steers and Rhodes (1978) note, in their recent review of the causes of employee absenteeism, that caring for a child who is ill is the major determinant of missed workdays by female employees. Stable child care is thus likely to be a vehicle for advancing the career development of women in this society.

In addition to being influenced by day care, the world of work exerts an influence on it. The general absence of flexible work hours, for example, makes supplementary child care a necessity in many families. Indeed, when parents are able to structure their working hours to accommodate the demands of child care, the very need for day care is reduced (Hofferth, 1979). Lein (1979) reports, for example, that in some families parents are able to work alternate shifts and avoid supplementary care entirely. Note that this effect of the workplace on day care has implications for child development. If parents are able to arrange their schedules so that supplementary care is not necessary or only minimally necessary, then the child will spend substantial time in the primary care of father as well as mother. By altering traditional sex roles, this indirect influence of the workplace should influence the child's sex-role development.

Spatial and temporal factors clearly influence transitions between the workplace, home, and the day care environment (see Martensson, 1977; Michelson, 1980), although little systematic research on the spatial/temporal context of child rearing exists. We know, however, that work schedules often do not coincide with the schedules of child care providers. Because parents may have little say over either, many families are caught between the time demands of different institutions and, for them, time-allocation and scheduling conflicts are commonplace. These problems are likely to be most severe among families with two parents in the full-time labor force or single-parent families in which the parent is employed full time (Michelson, 1980).

Whereas certain temporal variables operate independent of the spatial relation between the various settings in which families must function (e.g., the schedules of various institutions), others are clearly linked to the physical ecology of the community. The location of available child care arrangements in relation to the family's home and parents' workplace obviously affects the selection of a day-care provider and determines subsequent patterns of what Martensson (1977) refers to as "activity-participation." Unfortunately, little is known about the effects of variations in family activity-participation patterns on family functioning or child development. We suggest, however, that an inconvenient spatial or temporal relation among home, the child care setting, and the workplace may necessitate increased commuting time, impinge upon other important activities (e.g., family meals, recreation, household errands, sleeping), and tax the adaptational resources of the family and child alike.

The sheer time and energy demands of working, regardless of the location of the workplace, also place strains on day care programs and the families using them. All too often, employers are insensitive to family dependency on day care services. We have found in our small community in Pennsylvania, for example, that required overtime, sometimes on short notice, generates conflict between day care provider and parent, as parents are late to pick up their children or want (and frequently expect) their caregivers to put in greater hours than are contracted. Consideration of our earlier discussion of the mesosystem of day care suggests that such conflict between parent and caregiver could negatively influence the child. Even more distressing, though, is the possibility that such overtime demands on the caregiver could lead to the breakup of a stable caregiving arrangement. Although we are aware of no studies that explicitly examine the effects of multiple changes in caregiving arrangements, we strongly suspect that frequent placement change accounts for a large proportion of variance in any negative consequences associated with supplementary child care.

When industries make day care facilities available to employees, as some have already done (Kleinman, 1973), a giant step is made in overcoming conflicts that may develop between the world of work, child care, and the family. It is for this reason, and the fact that businesses reap large rewards from day care, that we believe industry ought to be encouraged, via tax incentives, for example, to develop programs for meeting the child care needs of their employees. In so doing, there can be little doubt that they will make life less stressful for dual-worker families.

Community organizations that supervise day care networks play an instrumental role in assuring that quality child care is provided and that families have access to it. They can also serve as a vehicle for linking families with the larger community. In our small Pennsylvania community, for example, a child development council is responsible not only for supplying materials to family day care homes, but also for providing in-service training to and supervising caregivers. The significance of this agency is demonstrated whenever a caregiver–parent conflict needs mediation, a child or family requires special services, or an emergency arises. In our community, for example, a day care center was recently closed down on short notice when its lease was not renewed. In many unsupervised communities such an event would surely have wreaked havoc on a large number of families. This was not the case, however, because the local child development council was responsible for overseeing center as well as family day care programs. Thus, a large number of children were smoothly transferred from the to-be-closed center program to FDC home programs that were either already in operation or quickly established to handle this situation. Except for the change in the locale of day care, parents were minimally inconvenienced by what was a rather radical disruption in the availability of day care services.

The child development council in our community also sees to it that families are made aware of programs that might prove useful to them. As an example, a newsletter sent to all parents with children in the FDC homes program frequently announces meetings of organizations such as Parents Without Partners. Because the day care network serves so many special or nontraditional families, it frequently functions as the conduit by which other community organizations or self-help groups make contact with families.

As we have seen in this section, many social forces and agencies can affect and be affected by day care, and such processes of influence can mediate the influence of supplementary care on child development. It is not sufficient, then, to speak just of day care and the family. To understand child development, day care and the family, the world of work, government policy, and child care agencies must be considered. As we hope the preceding, and subsequent speculative analyses demonstrate, we are still far from understanding this wider ecology of day care.

The Macrosystem.   We have already pointed out that ours is a culture that has traditionally viewed supplementary child care arrangements as inherently inferior to home rearing. This is most clearly reflected in the rise of day care primarily during times of national emergency (when, presumably, an inferior mode of child rearing could be tolerated), and in our acceptance of governmental support for day care only among disadvantaged and/or minority families (for whom we could presumably conscience an inferior type of child rearing).

As Peters (1979) has pointed out in criticizing child service policy in the United States, this differential availability of government-sponsored day care programs is partly a function of our cultural heritage of free enterprise, which emphasizes the individual's, and thus the individual family's responsibility for its own self-maintenance. From a more general perspective, Keniston (1977) observed that this idealized view of the American family as a self-sufficient, autonomous social unit has impeded the development of a coherent family policy in the United States. In countries with more socialized economies, this has not been the case and, not surprisingly, day care as well as other welfare programs are more universally available (Kammerman & Kahn, 1978). This relationship between political/economic philosophy and service provision underscores the role that the macrosystem plays in determining the quantity and quality of supplementary child care services available to families.

The development of the Women's Movement, with its ever-increasing influence on political, economic, and family life, demonstrates that prevailing ideologies are amenable to change. Most important, from the vantage point of this macrosystem analysis of day care, is the fact that such ideological change has direct consequences for the day-to-day experiences of children growing up in our society. Indeed, the change in the American family chronicled earlier, which we pointed to as being responsible for the rising demand for day care services, was stimulated largely by the emergent, nontraditional attitudes toward woman's role that have received wide acceptance in recent years.

Once the prevailing conception of woman as mother and housewife was amended, the kind of care provided children was bound to change. Our earlier review of the effects of day care indicates that the initial fears that such change raised among many concerned with the well-being of children have proved to be unfounded. It will be these noneffects of day care, and the widening influence of the Women's Movement, that we believe will ultimately lead to changes in prevailing attitudes and government policy toward day care. As more women work, and children in day care are recognized to be developing well, we can expect supplementary child care services to become more universally available.

We have suggested in the preceding analysis that cultural attitudes affect day care. A reciprocal process of influence also exists. Today, day care is more widely accepted as a viable child-rearing alternative or adjunct among middle-class families than it was 20 years ago, and the role that increased day care utilization and availability may play in sparking (or at least, abetting) ideological change is formidable. Day care provides families with alternatives, and those alternatives include women in the labor force and single parenthood. Indeed, it is the availability of day care, no doubt, that has influenced more fathers to take custody of their children following divorce. Such nontraditional families are today possible because day care is available as a family support, enabling fathers to work as well as to rear their children.

These influences of day care on society are unlikely to be viewed as positive by everyone. Whether such changes in American life prove to be in the interest of the nation, the community, the family, and the individual child, will depend, we believe, on the quality of care provided children. If day care is adopted as a quick fix to enable women to work and to enhance the viability of single-parent families, then short-term gains may result in long-term costs. It must not be overlooked that the conclusion that day care experience is not harmful to children is based on studies of children reared in high-quality programs. If such quality is not provided, there is no reason to assume that negative consequences of day care will not emerge.

CONCLUSIONS

Throughout this chapter we have referred to the elusive concept of quality day care but have not attempted to define it. Having concluded our analysis of the ecology of day care, it seem appropriate that we add substance to this often used, but rarely defined notion.

Basic to quality in day care programs is the provision of a stable caregiving milieu in which frequent changes are made neither in children's placements nor in staff providing care within a placement. We believe, as we expressed elsewhere in this chapter, that stability enables the young child to develop a sense of control over the world, a sense that is essential if the child is to thrive. Consequently, stable caregiving arrangements are considered a sine qua non of quality care.

Stability alone, though, does not assure quality, Recent research indicates that groups larger than 15–18 children undermine the potential for day care to provide growth-promoting experiences (Travers & Ruopp, 1978). We prefer groups that are modest (eight to 12 children), or even small in size (less than six), and mix children of various ages in order to promote cross-age learning. Contact with adults engaged in other than caregiving roles is also important, so that day care does not become an experience that, like school, isolates children from persons other than their peers and those responsible for their care. Opportunities to assume responsibilities and participate in what we refer to as practical life experiences need to be provided. Day care, especially full-time care, should not simply expose young children to an age-appropriate school experience that stresses play and the acquisition of formal academic skills. Being competent means understanding how the world functions and being able to accept responsibilities. Of course day care for preschoolers should not forgo play and school experiences; rather our point is that day care providers need to recognize that most of human learning occurs as part of the curriculum of everyday living. To the extent that day care serves to sequester children in schoollike environments for 8 to 10 hours a day, opportunities for informal learning are curtailed.

Most important to quality care are the care providers themselves. Formal education and training are of little importance if a caregiver is insensitive to the individual needs of a child, engages in few one-to-one contacts with his or her charges, and lacks the creativity to turn daily mundane events (e.g., folding the laundry, a trip to the store, cooking) into interesting learning experiences. Language is essential to the cognitive development of all children, so caregivers must be willing, and able, to engage in frequent and meaningful discourse with those in their care.

Ultimately, the people we select to rear the next generation must be concerned with the welfare of children and enjoy their involvement in caring for them. Rarely are day care workers well paid. Much of the return for their efforts must come in the form of intrinsic satisfaction. Even if the pay were better, money would not be sufficient. No society should entrust its most important responsibilities, and here we are referring to the care of its children, to persons seeking just a job. Commitment and concern, to children and their families, are also necessary prerequisites, then, of the caregiver capable of providing quality care.

Traditional analyses of quality day care stop here, with what in Bronfenbrenner's (1977, 1979) ecological model is the microsystem of day care. As adherents to an ecology of human development, we recognize though, that consideration of quality day care only begins with an analysis of the immediate context in which children are reared. Also essential is the systematic consideration of the wider ecology of day care.

At the level of the mesosystem, quality care entails frequent and informative communication between parents and care providers. But it is not enough for caregivers to tell parents what Johnny or Susan did all day. To be effective in their jobs, care providers must be kept informed of the child's experiences outside day care. Does the child expect to be scolded when he disobeys? Has he been having a difficult time with his siblings? Is his home life organized? The need for such information is sure to touch on some personal family concerns considered to be private. We contend, though, that because a once personal and private responsibility of the family (child rearing) is shared with others when a child is placed in day care, much of the information that has always been viewed as private by parents needs to be shared with the child's part-time, supplementary parents (i.e., the caregiver[s]).

When families make plans to share their rearing responsibilities, they must recognize that they are entering into a social contract that commits them to providing the child with a quality care experience. *We contend this is a right of the child.* But it must be recognized by all that the assurance of such quality is not the sole province of the provider. Families must realize that it is a responsibility they share jointly with the care provider(s). Indeed, it is a responsibility shared by each community and by society as well. If communication to assure quality care is to be a two-way street between home and day care, and if those sharing the rearing of the child are to be allowed to make reasonable demands on each other, then a variety of care arrangements must be available. Unless parents have a choice in making child care arrangements, it is difficult to envision how the demands for open communication between the two rearing contexts can be met. And without such open communication, quality care is jeopardized.

At the level of the exosystem, we are convinced that supervisory agencies— governed by parents, interested individuals in the community, and care providers, and responsible for overseeing the day care network—are essential to the assurance of quality day care. With the assistance of such supervisory agencies, we know it is possible to coordinate child care at the community level, efficiently train providers, provide materials inexpensively, and support caregivers in their most important roles. These agencies cannot be too large, because they cannot risk losing contact with those with whom they are most concerned—children, parents, and caregivers. Nor can they risk being isolated from other community services. In fact, we believe they must establish working, reciprocal relations with these other agencies. There is no reason that day care can not serve as the link for many families to the entire community service network. Indeed, day care needs to be conceptualized more broadly as a support system for families—one that services to assist parents, and thereby promote child development, in ways other than through the provision of supplementary care. A quality day care program, we contend, with the support and guidance of a supervisory agency, can function as a resource referral for families.

Quality day care also depends on the employment practices of industry and the concern the private sector shows for the families in its employ. Most important in this regard are flexible work hours that enable parents to care, as well as provide economic support for their children. Parents need to know that they will be able to arrange schedules to take care of their children themselves or maintain arrangements for supplementary care. If overtime or regular work shifts threaten the stability of child care arrangements, employers must be sensitive to such worker needs. Workers, though, must recognize that benefits provided by employers to assist in child care must be reciprocated, for example, in enhanced productivity or fewer unnecessary absences from the job. Again we see, then, that the provision of quality day care carries with it family obligations. So long as day care is construed as something given by another, it will be conceptualized as a welfare service. Such a conceptualization is the surest way we know to undermine quality, as it undermines the dignity of all involved in it.

Finally, at the level of the macrosystem, quality care is dependent on the maintenance of respect for the role of child rearer. It is unfortunate that in its most radical form, the Women's Movement has functioned to demean this role. Child care is considered by many today to be the province of the unskilled and unimportant. Too often we have heard reference made to parents who care for their children on a full-time basis as persons who are not doing anything important (Lott, 1973): "Is that *all* you are doing?" If this remains the "liberated" attitude of our society toward parenting, then the responsibilities of day care workers will never be seen in a much more positive light. Why should it be okay to care for the children of others, if it is not respectable to care for your own?

Children, their families, and the nation run a grave risk if attitudes and ideologies demeaning child care flourish in the minds of citizens and in the policies of government. Child care is a basic, and necessary, function of the human group, one that is essential for our survival. But more than just minimal care is required to maintain the quality of human existence. When we disregard the impact of our activities on this basic function, we open Pandora's box.

We know from the research summarized in this chapter on the effects of day care, that out-of-home care need not be deleterious to child development. In fact, in some instances, the data indicate that it can even be beneficial. Such effects cannot be taken for granted, however. Indeed, it is essential to recognize that the absence of findings revealing negative consequences of day care derives primarily from the fact that children in high-quality programs have been the primary subjects of study in day care research. Only if such quality is assured should we comfortably accept day care. Because we have no choice but to accept such supplementary care in American society today, we incur the responsibility of providing care of such quality.

ACKNOWLEDGMENT

We would like to express our appreciation to Douglas Powell of the Merrill–Palmer Institute for the constructive feedback he provided on an earlier draft of this chapter.

REFERENCES

Ainsworth, M. *Attachment: Retrospect and prospect.* Presidential address to the biennial meetings of the Society for Research in Child Development, San Francisco, March 1979.

Ainsworth, M., & Wittig, B. Attachment and exploratory behavior of one-year-olds in a strange situation. In B.M. Foss (Ed.), *Determinants of infant behavior IV.* London: Methuen and Co. Ltd., 1969.

Aldous, J. Family interaction patterns. *Annual Review of Sociology*, 1977, *3*, 105–135.

Ambron, S. Causal Models in early education research. In S. Kilmer (Ed.), *Advances in early education and day care* (Vol. 2). Greenwich, Conn.: JAI Press, 1980.

Arend, R., Gove, F., & Sroufe, L. Continuity in early adaptation: From attachment theory in infancy to resiliency and curiosity at age five. *Child Development*, 1979, *50*, 950–959.

Baumrind, D. Child care practices anteceding 3 patterns of pre-school behavior. *Genetic Psych Monographs*, 1967, *75*, 43–88.

Beller, E., Litwok, E., & Sullivan, K. *An observational study of interaction in day care*. Unpublished manuscript, Temple University, no date.

Belsky, J. Child maltreatment: An ecological integration. *American Psychologist*, 1980, *35*, 320–325. (a)

Belsky J. Future research in day care: An ecological analysis. *Child Care Quarterly*, 1980, *9*, 92–99. (b)

Belsky, J. Early human experience: A family perspective. *Developmental Psychology*, 1981, 17, 3–23.

Belsky, J., & Steinberg, L. The effects of day care: A critical review. *Child Development*, 1978, *49*, 929–949.

Belsky, J., Walker, A., & Anderson, P. *Comments on HEW day care regulations*. Unpublished paper, The Pennsylvania State University, September 1979.

Biemiller, A., Avis, C., & Lindsay, A. *Competence supporting aspects of day care environments—a preliminary study*. Paper presented at the Canadian Psychological Association Convention, Toronto, June 1976.

Blanchard, M., & Main, M. Avoidance of the attachment figure and social–emotional adjustment in day care infants. *Developmental Psychology*, 1979, *15*, 445–446.

Blehar, M. Anxious attachment and defensive reactions associated with day care. *Child Development* 1974, *45*, 683–692.

Bowlby, J. *Maternal care and mental health*. Geneva: World Health Organization, 1951.

Bronfenbrenner, U. *Is early intervention effective?* DHEW Publication No (OHD) 76–30025, Washington, D.C., 1974.

Bronfenbrenner, U. Reality and research in the ecology of human development. *Proceedings of the American Philosophical Society*, 1975, 119, 439–469.

Bronfenbrenner, U. Toward an experimental ecology of human development. *American Psychologist*, 1977, *32*, 513–531.

Bronfenbrenner, U. *The ecology of human development*. Cambridge, Mass.: Harvard University Press, 1979.

Carew, J. *Observation study of caregivers and children in day care homes: Preliminary results from home observations*. Paper presented at Biennial Meetings of the Society of Research in Child Development, San Francisco, April 1979.

Clarke-Stewart, A. *Assessing social development*. Paper presented at the Biennial Meeting of the Society for Research in Child Development, San Francisco, March 1979.

Clarke-Stewart, K. A. Observation and experiment: Complementary strategies for studying day care and social development. In S. Kilmer (Ed.), *Advances in early education and day care*. Greenwich, Conn.: JAI Press, Inc., 1980.

Cochran, M. A comparison of group day and family child-rearing patterns in Sweden. *Child Development*, 1977, *48*, 720–707.

Connell, D. B., Layzer, J. I., & Goodson, D. *National study of day care centers for infants: Findings and implications*. Unpublished manuscript, ABT Associates Inc., Cambridge, Mass., 1979.

Cummings, E. M. Caregiver stability and day care. *Developmental Psychology*, 1980, *16*, 31–37.

Doyle, A., & Somers, K. The effects of group and family day care on infant attachment behaviors. *Canadian Journal of Behavioral Science*, 1978, *10*, 38–45.

Emlen, A. *Family day care for children under three*. Paper presented for the International Symposium on the Ecology of Care and Education of Children under Three, February 1977.

Emlen, A., & Perry, J. Child care arrangements. In L. Hoffman & F. I. Nye (Eds.), *Working mothers*. Washington, D.C.: Jossey-Bass, 1974.

Falender, C., & Heber, R. *Mother-child interaction and participation in a longitudinal program*. Mimeographed. Rehabilitation Research and Training Center, Madison, Wisconsin, 1976.

Farran, D., & Haskins, R. Reciprocal influence in the social interactions of mothers and three-year-old children from different socioeconomic backgrounds. *Child Development*, 1980, 51, 780-791.

Farran, D., & Ramey, C. Social class differences in dyadic involvement during infancy. *Child Development*, 1980, *51*, 254-257.

Fein, G., & Clarke-Stewart, A. *Day care in context*. New York: Wiley, 1973.

Fosburg, S. *Design of the National Day Care Home Study*. Paper presented at the annual meeting of the American Educational Research Association, Boston, April 1980.

Fraiberg, S. *Every Child's birthright: In defense of mothering*. New York: Basic Books, 1977.

Goldfarb, W. The effects of early institutional care on adolescent personality. *Journal of Experimental Education*, 1943, *12*, 106-129.

Golden, M., Rosenbluth, L., Grossi, M. T., Policave, H. J., Freenan, H., Jr., & Brownlee, M. *The New York City Infant Day Care Study: A comparative study of licensed group and family day care programs and the effects of these programs on children and their families*. New York: Medical and Health Research Association of New York City, Inc., 1978.

Gunnarson, L. *Children in day care and family care in Sweden: A follow-up*. Bulletin No. 21, Department of Educational Research, University of Gothenburg, 1978.

Hall, A., & Weiner, S. *The supply of day care services in Denver and Seattle*. Menlo Park, Calif.: Stanford Research Institute, Center for the Study of Welfare Policy, 1977.

Hawkins, P., Wilcox, M., Gillis, G., Porter, A., & Carew, J. *Observation study of caregivers and children in day care homes*. Paper presented at the biennial meeting for the Society of Research in Child Development, San Francisco, March 1979.

Heinicke, C., Friedman, D., Prescott, E., Puncel, C., & Sale, J. The organization of day care: Considerations relating to the mental helath of child and family. *American Journal of Orthopsychiatry*, 1973, *43*, 8-22.

Hetherington, E. M. Children and divorce. In R. Henderson (Ed.), *Parent-child interaction: Theory, research, and prospect*. New York: Academic Press, 1980.

Hill, C. R. The child care market: A review of evidence and implications for federal policy. In *Policy Issues in Day Care: Summaries of 21 Papers*. Washington, D.C., Department of Health, Education, and Welfare, 1977.

Hill, C.R. Private demand for child care: Implications for public policy. *Evaluation Quarterly*, 1978, *2*, 523-545.

Hock, E. *Alternative approaches to child rearing and their effects on the mother-infant relationship*. Final reports, Washington, D.C.; Department of HEW, Office of Child Development, Grant No. OCD-490, 1976.

Hock, E. Working and nonworking mothers and their infants: A comparative study of maternal caregiving characteristics and infant social behavior. *Merrill-Palmer Quarterly of Behavior and Development*, 1979.

Hofferth, S. Day care in the next decade: 1980-1990. *Journal of Marriage and The Family*, 1979, 644-658.

Howes, C., & Rubenstein, J. *Influences on toddler peer behavior in two types of day care*. Unpublished manuscript, Harvard University, 1980. (a)

Howes, C. & Rubenstein, J. *Prediction of infant adaptation to day care*. Paper presented at the International Conference on Infant Studies, New Haven, Conn., March 1980. (b)

Howes, C., & Rubenstein, J. *Social experiences of toddlers at home and in two types of day care*. Unpublished manuscript, Harvard University, 1980. (c)

Joffee, C. *Friendly intruders: Child care professionals and family life*. Berkeley, Calif.: University of California Press, 1977.

Kamerman,   S., & Kahn, A. *Family policy: Government and families in fourteen countries*. New York: Columbia University Press, 1978.

Keniston, K. *All our children*. New York: Harcourt, Brace, & Jovanovich, 1977.

Kermoian, R. *Type and quality of care: Mediating factors in the effects of day care on infant responses to brief separation*. Paper presented at the International Conference on Infant Studies, New Haven, Conn., May 1980.

Kleinman, C. Industry steps up its day care output. *Day Care and Early Education*, 1973, *1*, 27–30.

Lally, R. *The family development research program: Progress report*. Unpublished paper, Syracuse University, 1973.

Lazar, I., Hubbell, U., Murray, H., Rosche, M., & Royce, J. *Summary report: The persistence of preschool effects*. Washington, D.C.: Summary of final report of the Administration of Children, Youth, and Families, Department of Health, Education, and Welfare, October 1977.

Lein, L. Male participation in home life: Impact of social supports and breadwinner responsiblity on the allocation of tasks. *The Family Coordinator*, 1979, 489–495.

Lieberman, A. F. Psychology and day care. *Social Research*, 1978, *45*, 416–451.

Lightfoot, S. Families and schools: Creative conflict or negative dissonance. *Journal of Research and Development in Education*, 1975, *9*, 34–44.

Lippit, R. Improving the socialization process. In J. Clausen (Ed.), *Socialization and society*. Boston: Little, Brown, 1968.

Lott, B. E. Who wants the children? Some relationships among attitudes toward children, parents, and the liberation of women. *American Psychologist*, 1973, *28*, 573–582.

Martensson, S. Childhood interaction and temporal organization. *Economic Geography*, 1977, *53*, 99–125.

Macrae, J. W., & Herbert-Jackson, E. Are behavioral effects of infant day care programs specific? *Developmental Psychology*, 1975, *12*, 269–270.

Matas, L., Arend, R., & Sroufe, L. Continuity in adaptation in the second year: The relationship between quality of attachment and later competence. *Child Development*, 1978, *49*, 547–556.

Moore, T. Exclusive early mothering and its alternatives: The outcome of adolescence. *Scandinavian Journal of Psychology*, 1975, *16*, 255–272.

Michelson, W. Spatial and temporal dimensions of child care. *Signs; Journal of Women in Culture and Society*, 1980, *5*, 242–247.

O'Connell, J., & Farran, D. *The effects of day care intervention on the use of intentional communicative behaviors in socioeconomically depressed infants*. Paper presented at the Sixth Biennial Southeastern Conference on Human Development Alexandria, Va., April 1980.

Office of Assistant for Planning and Evaluation. *The Appropriateness of the Federal Interagency Day Care Requirements (FIDCR): Report on Findings and Recommendations*. Washington, D.C.: United States Department of Health, Education, and Welfare, June 1978.

Papousek, H. Effects of group rearing conditions during the preschool years of life. In V. Denenberg (Ed.), *Education of the infant and young children*. New York: Academic Press, 1970.

Peters, D. *A summary of the Pennsylvania day care study*. University Park: Pennsylvania State University, 1973.

Peters, D. Social science and social policy and the care of young children: Head start and after. *Journal of Applied Developmental Psychology*, 1979, *1*, 7–27.

Portnoy, F., & Simmons, C. Day care and attachment. *Child Development*, 1978, *49*, 239–242.

Powell, D. R. *The interface between families and child care programs: A study of parent–caregiver relationships*. Detroit, Mich.: The Merrill–Palmer Institute, 1977.

Powell, D. R. Correlates of parent–teacher communication frequency and diversity. *The Journal of Educational Research*, 1978, *71*, 333–341. (a)

Powell, D. R. The interpersonal relationship between parents and caregivers in day care settings. *American Journal of Orthopsychiatry,* 1978, *48,* 680–689. (b)

Powell, D. R. Family–environment relations and early childrearing: The role of social networks and neighborhoods. *Journal of Research and Development in Education,* 1979, *13,* 1–11.

Powell, D. R. Toward a socioecological perspective of relations between parents and child-care programs. In S. Kilmer (Ed.), *Advances in early education and day care* (Vol. 1). Greenwich, Conn.: JAI Press, Inc., 1980.

Prescott, E. *A comparison of three types of day care and nursery school–home care.* Paper presented at the biennial meeting of the Society for Research in Child Development, Philadelphia, March 1973.

Prescott, E., & David, T. *The effects of the physical environment on day care.* Paper prepared for the Office of the Assistant for Planning and Evaluation, DHEW, July 1976.

Prescott, E., & Jones, E. Day care of children—assets and liabilities. *Children,* 1971, *18,* 54–58.

Prescott, E., Jones, E., & Kritchevsky, S. *Group day care as a child-rearing environment.* Final report to Children's Bureau. Pasadena, Calif.: Pacific Oaks College, 1967.

Ramey, C.T., & Campbell, F. A. Compensatory education for disadvantaged children. *Social Review,* 1979, *87,* 171–189 (a).

Ramey, C., & Campbell, F. Early childhood education for psychosocially disadvantaged children: The effects of psychological processes. *American Journal of Mental Deficiency,* 1979, *83,* 645–648 (b).

Ramey, C., Dorval, B., & Baker-Ward, L. Group day care and socially disadvantaged families: Effects on the child and the family. In S. Kilmer (Ed.), Advances in early education and day care. JAI Press, 1981.

Ramey, C.T., Farran, D. C., & Campbell, F. A. Predicting IQ from mother–infant interactions. *Child Development,* 1979, *50,* 804–814.

Ramey, C., & Haskins, R. Early education, intellectual development, and school performance: A reply to Arthur Jensen and J. McV. Hunt. *Intelligence,* 1981, in press.

Ramey, C., MacPhee, D., & Yeats, K. Preventing developmental retardation: A general systems model. In L. Bond and J. Joffee (Eds.), *Facilitating infant and early childhood development* (Vol. 6,) *Primary Prevention of Psychopathology.* Hanover, N.H.: University of New England, 1981.

Ramey, C., & Mills, J. *Mother–infant interaction patterns as a function of rearing conditions.* Paper presented at the meeting of the society for Research in Child Development, Denver, April 1975.

Ricciuti, H. *Effects of infant day care experience on behavior and development: Research and implication for social policy.* A report to the Department of HEW, Federal Interagency Day Care Required Policy Committee, Washington, D.C., 1976.

Rohe, W. & Patterson, A. The effects of varied levels of resources and density on behavior in a day care center. In D.H. Carson (Ed.), *Man–environment interactions.* EDRA, 1974.

Roopnarine, J. & Lamb, M. Peer and parent-child interaction before and after enrollment in nursery school. *Journal of Applied Developmental Psychology,* 1980, 1, 77–81.

Rubenstein, J. L., & Howes, C. *Caregiving and infant behavior in two natural environments.* Paper presented at the annual Convention of the American Psychological Association, Washington, D.C., September 1976.

Rubenstein, J. L., & Howes, C. Caregiving and infant behavior in day care and in homes. *Developmental Psychology,* 1979, *15,* 1–24.

Rubenstein, J. L., Howes, C., & Boyle, P. *A two-year follow-up of infants in community-based infant day care.* Paper presented at the biennial meeting of the Society for Research in Child Development, San Francisco, March 1979.

Rubenstein, J. L., Pedersen, F. A., & Yarrow, L. J. What happens when mother is away: A comparison of mothers and substitute caregivers, *Developmental Psychology,* 1977, *13,* 529–530.

Ruderman, F. *Child care and working mothers.* New York: Child Welfare League, 1968.

Saunders, M., & Keister, M. *Family day care: Some observations.* Unpublished manuscript, University of North Carolina at Greensboro, 1972.

Schwarz, J., Strickland, R., & Krolick, G. Infant day care: Behavioral effects at preschool age. *Developmental Psychology,* 1974, *10,* 502–506.

Sheehan, A. M., & Abbott, M. S. A descriptive study of day care characteristics. *Child Care Quarterly,* 1979, *8,* 206–219.

Sibbison, V. The influence of maternal role perceptions on attitudes toward and utilization of early child care services. In D. Peters (Ed.), *A summary of the Pennsylvania day care study.* University Park: Pennsylvania State University, 1973.

Spitz, R. A. Hospitalism: An inquiry into the genesis of psychiatric conditions in early childhood. *Psychoanalytic Study of the Child,* 1945, *1,* 53–74.

Sroufe, L. The coherence of individual development. *American Psychologist,* 1979, 34, 834–841.

Stallings, J., & Porter, A. *National Day Care Home Study: Observation component.* Draft final report to the Day Care Division, Administration for Children, Youth, and Families, DHEW, April 1980.

Steers, R., & Rhodes, S. Major influences on employee attendance: A process model. *Journal of Applied Psychology,* 1978, *63,* 391–407.

Steinberg, L., & Green, C. *How parents may mediate the effect of day care.* Paper presented at the biennial meeting of the Society for Research in Child Development, San Francisco, March 1979.

Steinberg, L., & Greenberger, E. Part-time employment of high-school students: An ecological perspective on research and policy. Unpublished manuscript, University of California at Irvine, September 1979.

Steiner, G. *The children's cause.* Washington, D.C.: The Brookings Institution, 1976.

Travers, J., & Ruopp, R. *National day care study: Preliminary findings and their implications: 31 January, 1978.* Cambridge, Mass.: Alot Assoicates, 1978.

Urban Institute. *The suble revolution: Women at work,* Washington, D.C.: The Urban Institute, 1980.

Vaughn, B., Gove, F., & Egeland, B. The relationship between out-of-home care and the quality of infant–mother attachment in an econimically disadvantaged population. *Child Dvelopment,* 1980, in press.

Waters, E., Wippman, J., & Sroufe, L. Attachment, positive affect, and competence in the peer group: Two studies in construct validation. *Child Development,* 1979, *50,* 821–829.

Westinghouse Learning Corporation & Westat Research, Inc. *Day care survey—1970: Summary report and basic analysis.* Washington, D.C.: Office of Economic Opportunity, 1971.

Wynn, R. L. *The effect of a playmate on day care and home-reared toddlers in a strange situation.* Paper presented at the biennial meeting of the Society for Research in Child development, San Francisco, March 1979.

5

Varying Degrees of Paternal Involvement in Infant Care: Attitudinal and Behavioral Correlates

Michael E. Lamb
University of Utah

Ann M. Frodi
University of Rochester

Carl-Philip Hwang
University of Göteborg

Majt Frodi
University of Göteborg

Like several other chapters in this volume (those by Sagi, Radin, and Russell), our focus here is on two-parent families in which fathers have an unusually extensive involvement in child care. Because child rearing is traditionally viewed as a maternal responsibility, families in which fathers share equally in or are primarily responsible for child care can justifiably be considered nontraditional. Why do some couples divide parental responsibilities in this nontraditional fashion and what effects does this have on the ways in which mothers and fathers behave in interaction with their young infants? These are the questions that we address in this chapter. Our discussion of these topics is based on the results of an ongoing longitudinal study of more than 50 Swedish couples and their firstborn infants. Most of the data presented here are drawn from three publications (Frodi, Lamb, Frodi, Hwang, Forström, & Corry, 1981; Lamb, Frodi, Hwang, Frodi, & Steinberg, 1982a, 1982b) reporting findings obtained in the first four phases of our longitudinal study—assessments that took place prenatally, and when the infants were 3, 5, and 8 months of age.

Our study was designed to take advantage of a unique national family policy adopted by the Swedish government during the last decade. Under the leadership of former Prime Minister Olöf Palme, the Swedes have embarked on a series of reforms designed to eliminate what they considered to be antiquated sex-role stereotypes. Like many of those concerned with the attainment of equal rights for women in the United States, Palme and his colleagues recognized that equal employment opportunities for men and women could not be ensured until men relieved women of some traditional responsibilities for home and child care. Among the reforms designed to promote the involvement of men in traditionally feminine activities was the establishment of a national parental leave program that was blind with respect to the parent's sex. Beginning in 1974, the government guaranteed the equivalent of paid sick leave (up to 90% of the individual's regular salary) for 9 months to any parent who remained away from work in order to care for a newborn child. The 9-month period could be divided between the two parents at their discretion. Both could work half-time for 9 months, one could take the first 3 months and the other the next 6, all 9 months could be taken by one parent, and so on. In addition to the 9 months of leave paid for by the National Health Insurance, employers were also required to allow new mothers and fathers 2 weeks of leave with full pay immediately after the child's birth. In order to encourage parents to take advantage of the national parental leave, the enabling legislation mandated employers to guarantee reemployment, without prejudice or loss of seniority, to any parent taking parental leave. (The reader is referred to a report by Lamb and Levine (in press) for further details about the policy and its utilization.)

Since the practice was initiated in 1974, a large number of Swedes have taken advantage of it. To the disappointment of the social reformers, however, the vast majority of the parents have been mothers. Suffice it to say that by 1979, less than 15% of the new fathers in Sweden took paid parental leave (other than the ''free'' 2-week period that most fathers took) and the majority of these took only about 1 month or less of leave. In the latter cases, the fathers tended to take leave at the same time as their wives, and the extent to which they became involved in child care, rather than simply vacationing at public expense, is not known.

Our longitudinal study was concerned with the small but growing number of men who took parental leave for more than a month, during which time they had primary responsibility for their infants' care. By comparing the behavior and attitudes of these men and their wives with the behavior and attitudes of traditional husbands and wives, we sought to determine: (1) whether the attitudes and values of traditional and nontraditional couples differed; (2) how stable these attitudes were over the transition to parenthood, and whether the differences between traditional and nontraditional couples were still evident after they became parents; (3) whether the attitudinal differences were related to differences in paternal involvement, parental satisfaction, and parental behavior; and (4) whether there were differences (both qualitative and quantitative) in the behavior of traditional and nontraditional parents during the first months of parenthood. In the pages that follow, we first introduce the sample and provide an overview of the longitudinal study. We then discuss attitudinal differences and stability over time, before discussing evidence concerning the behavior of traditional and non-traditional parents.

THE SWEDISH STUDY: GOALS AND PROCEDURE

By comparing families in which fathers were and were not expected to take parental leave in order to become seriously involved in infant care, we sought to determine why some couples chose to divide parental responsibilities in a nontraditional fashion. Demographic information indicated that highly involved fathers were disproportionately likely to be well educated and to come from middle-class backgrounds, but such statistics do not tell one much about the attitudes, values, and motivations of highly involved fathers and their wives. We explored these by means of interviews conducted both before and after the birth of the first child into 52 families, half of whom initially planned to divide parental responsibilities nontraditionally. The prenatal interviews allowed us to determine how the parents planned to divide parental responsibilities, how their family and friends felt about their plans, and how important parenthood and employment were to each of the parents. The postnatal interviews permitted us to determine how parental responsibilities were actually divided, to obtain reevaluations of the importance of parenthood and employment, and to assess each parent's satisfaction. We were thus able to explore the attitudinal correlates of both anticipated and actual paternal involvement, as well as the effects of childbirth on a set of attitudes pertaining to parenthood. In addition, we observed each parent interacting with his or her 3-month-old infant in order to assess the individual's responsiveness to the infants' signals as well as gender differences in the behavior of mothers and fathers. When the infants were 8 months old, we again observed them interacting with their parents. In these observations, too, we focused on gender differences in the styles of parental behavior as well as the differential treatment of sons and daughters.

Although we do not discuss these data here because they have yet to be analyzed, the parents and infants were observed again around the infants' first birthdays and when they were 16 months old. These observations permitted us to explore gender differences in parental behavior once again, as well as the security of infant–mother and infant–father attachment and the effects of degree of involvement in caretaking on the relative formative importance of the two infant–parent attachments.

The Subjects

Our sample consisted of 52 couples, all of whom lived in Göteborg (Sweden) and were expecting their first child. Participants were recruited through childbirth preparation classes. The men ranged in age from 22 to 51 years; the women from 21 to 35. We initially recruited 26 couples in which the father planned to stay home as primary caretaker for a month or more as well as 26 couples in which the father planned to take little more than the 2-weeks leave assured by his employer. These groups were called, respectively, the nontraditional and traditional families. The method of recruitment ensured that most of our subjects had middle-class backgrounds, occupations, and educations, although there was a fair range on these dimensions. On all demographic dimensions but one, the two groups did not differ. The nontraditional parents, however, were slightly better educated than the traditional parents.

Procedure

The first contact with the couples took place during the third trimester of pregnancy. At this point, the mothers- and fathers-to-be were independently interviewed in their homes concerning: (1) the way in which they planned to divide parental leave between them (this information was used both the classify the families and to rate them on a scale, anticipated degree of paternal involvement); (2) the attitudes of family and friends toward the planned division of caretaking responsibility (perceived support); (3) the value or importance of work to the interviewee; and (4) the value/importance of parenthood to the interviewee and to his or her spouse. All interviews were semistructured and were tape-recorded so that the responses could be rated later using previously developed 8-point scales (Lamb, Chase-Lansdale, & Owen, 1978). The ratings were made by at least two researchers working independently. Comparisons between the two independent ratings revealed high and consistent reliability on all scales (see Lamb et al., in press, for further details). The parents also completed Weinraub's Household Task Inventory (Weinraub & Leite, 1977) at this time. Responses to the inventory permitted us to assess the degree to which household labor was divided in a sex-typed manner.

Three months after the infants' births, they were observed twice in their own homes. On one occasion, mother and infant were observed for an hour, whereas the other observation involved only father and infant. During these observations, one of the investigators recorded a detailed account of the infant's and the parent's behavior, using a keyboard device that automatically encoded the time of every entry (Stephenson, 1979). Meanwhile, another researcher chatted to the parents so as to relieve any anxieties they felt about being observed. From the observational records, we created the following summary measures of parental behavior: vocalizations, contact behavior (the combined frequency of touch, tickle, tend, and kiss), functional behavior (the summed frequency of tending and changing), and play. All these measures were recorded with good interobserver reliability, as documented by Lamb et al. (1982a). We also attempted to assess the parents' responsiveness by creating two measures of behavioral contingency. In one, we computed the probability of a parental response within 5 seconds to an infant's fuss or cry, whereas in the other, we computed the probability of a parental response to any infant's signal or behavior. The parents also completed a Swedish translation of Bem's Sex Role Inventory (BSRI: Bem, 1974) shortly after the home observations. The responses were used to classify the parents as masculine, feminine, androgynous, or undifferentiated, depending on the pattern of scores on the masculinity and femininity dimensions of the BSRI.

Two months later (when the infants were 5 months old) the parents were again interviewed, separately and independently, in their homes. These interviews were longer than the prenatal ones (they averaged 90 to 120 minutes) and the questions were designed to elicit responses pertaining to: (1) the degree of paternal involvement in caretaking and in interaction with the child; (2) satisfaction with parenthood; (3) resentment of the infant; (4) the value/importance of work; and (5) the value/importance of parenthood. As before, all these constructs were tapped using a semistructured interview. Responses were tape-recorded and then rated independently by two researchers using predetermined 8-point rating scales (Lamb et al., 1978). Interrater reliability was again maintained at a high level.

Finally, when the infants were 8 months old, they were observed at home interacting with both of their parents for about 100 minutes. During this session, an observer used a keyboard-recorder device to encode details of parental and infant behavior, although in the analyses completed thus far, we have only considered the parental behavior. The observer noted the initiation and termination of bouts of play and physical contact (holding), as well as the occurence of smiles, vocalizations, affectionate behaviors (hugs, kisses), and caretaking behaviors ("tends"). When play occurred, the observer identified the type of play using the following seven categories: coordinate play, when the child and adult engaged in a reciprocal game in which each took turns; parallel play, in which the child and adult played side by side on similar activities with little direct interaction; stimulus play, which involved attempts by the parent to stimulate the infant and attract/hold its attention; minor physical play, which involved limited degrees of physical contact (e.g., tickling); physical play, which involved vigorous, robust stimulation (e.g., rough and tumble play); conventional play, which involved ritualized activities like peek-a-boo; and idiosyncratic play, which was coded when the other definitions were inappropriate. When holding occurred, the observers distinguished among seven reasons for holding the infant: Caretaking was scored when the infant was picked up to be placed on a changing table, in a high chair, etc.; discipline was scored when the child was moved from some forbidden site; play was scored when the child was picked up for social interaction; affection, when the child was picked up to cuddle, kiss, or hug it; soothing, when it was distressed and needed comforting; respondent, when the child clearly asked to be held; and other, when none of the other reasons applied. Unfortunately, measures of the duration of play and physical contact bouts were not reliable, so all our analyses were based on frequency measures. The categories of play and physical contact were based on those used by Lamb (1976, 1977c) to distinguish between maternal and paternal interactional styles.

Just before the infants' first birthdays, we recontacted the parents to ask how the parental leave had actually been divided. If the father had taken parental leave, we asked when and for how long. The families were then reclassified using this information. Seventeen of the fathers had taken more than 1 month of parental leave ($\bar{X} = 2.82$ months), 34 had taken 2 weeks or less ($\bar{X} = 0.24$ months), and one family was no longer available for study. Analyses of the 8-month observational data were based on the revised family classifications. We have yet to see whether differences on the early interview measures distinguish between those families who in fact adopted a nontraditional pattern and those who did not.

In the next two sections, we review our findings in the context of related research. We first discuss the interview measures and their interrelations and then discuss the evidence concerning parental behavior in traditional and nontraditional families.

PARENTAL ATTITUDES: PRENATAL AND POSTNATAL

The interviews were designed with two purposes in mind. First, they provided information about the parents' attitudes and thus allowed us to determine how traditional and nontraditional parents differed and why some parents chose a nontraditional child-rearing style whereas others did not. Second, they allowed us to determine whether differences in parental attitudes and the division of child-rearing responsibilities predict differences in the styles of parental behavior.

Few studies have directly addressed the issues of concern to us, and these few studies have not involved nontraditional families like those in our sample. However, many of the issues have been discussed in speculative chapters (Lamb, Chase-Lansdale, & Owen, 1979; Lamb & Easterbrooks, 1981; Lamb, Owen, & Chase-Lansdale, 1980), and some relevant data have recently been obtained by Owen, Chase-Lansdale, and Lamb (in preparation).

The major constructs explored in the prenatal interviews were the support provided by family and friends, the importance of work to the individual, the importance of parenthood to the individual and her or his spouse, and the degree of paternal involvement anticipated by both mothers- and fathers-to-be. In the postnatal interviews, which were conducted when the infants were 5 months old, we again assessed value of work and value of parenthood. In addition, we assessed satisfaction with parenthood, resentment of the infant, and (by way of a diary description of specific days) the degree of paternal involvement in interaction with the child as well as in direct child care activities.

Following the reasoning outlined in earlier chapters by Lamb and his coauthors, we expected that parental sensitivity, paternal involvement and paternal satisfaction would be greatest when parenthood was highly valued and when work was valued less. Similarly, we expected that the value of parenthood would be negatively, and the value of work positively related to resentment of the infant's intrusion. In comparisons of the traditional and nontraditional parents, we expected that nontraditional fathers (who planned to leave work temporarily in order to care for their infants) would value parenthood more and work less than the traditional fathers did. Predictions about their wives' attitudes were less clearcut. On the one hand, decisions about the division of child-rearing responsibilities are jointly made by both parents. Conceivably, therefore, nontraditional fathers aspire to a major role in child care not only becuase parenthood is unusually important to them, but also because it is less important to their wives than to them. On the other hand, Russell (1978) found in a study of highly involved Australian fathers that the fathers' sex roles, but not the mothers', were related to paternal involvement; involved fathers scored higher on Bem's (1974) femininity scale than the traditional fathers did. This would lead one to expect that fathers' attitudes alone would be related to the traditionality of the planned caretaking arrangement. Finally, we expected stability over time in the attitudes assessed both pre- and postnatally.

In their study of dual-earner American couples expecting their first child, Owen et al. (in preparation) obtained some support for these hypotheses. Owen et al. found that mothers who planned to return to paid employment within 6 months of their infants' births valued parenthood less and work more than did mothers who planned to stop paid work until their children were older. These differences were evident both pre- and postnatally as there was substantial attitudinal stability over time, especially among mothers. Although Owen et al. did not gather the observational data that would have allowed them to relate the value of parenthood and work to behavioral responsiveness, they did confirm that value of parenthood, degree of paternal involvement, and satisfaction were consistently and positively intercorrelated, as were resentment of the infant and value of work among mothers. Secure mother–infant attachments were more likely to develop when the mothers' value of parenthood was high. There was no significant and consistent relationship between the fathers' value of parenthood and the security of infant–father attachment.

Validity of Interview Measures

After years of disappointment with interview and questionnaire measures (Yarrow, Campbell, & Burton, 1968), psychologists have tended to avoid using interviews and self-report measures for more than a decade. In the last few years, however, several researchers have cautioned against the premature rejection of interviews as sources of information (Lamb, in press; Parke, 1978). Interviews may be poor ways of assessing how respondents or their children behave, but they are invaluable ways of determining why they behave in certain ways and what their attitudes and values are. Of course, the validity and reliability of

Table 5.1
Agreement Between Spouses

Dimension	All	Subjects	
		Traditional	Nontraditional
Prenatal:			
Sex-typed division			
of household chores	.72***	.75***	.59**
Anticipated paternal			
involvement	.56***	n.s.	.75***
Perceived support	.27⁺	n.s.	n.s.
Value of			
parenthood:			
F's value and			
M's perception	.42***	n.s.	.51**
M's value and			
F's perception	.54***	n.s.	.63***
5 months:			
Value of			
parenthood:			
F's value and			
M's perception	.63***	.62***	.72***
M's value and			
F's perception	.41**	.51**	n.s.
Perceived support	n.s.	n.s.	n.s.
Paternal caretaking	.43**	n.s.	.41*
Paternal involvement	.40**	n.s.	.59***

⁺ $p < .06$
* $p < .05$
** $p < .01$
*** $p < .001$

interview measures cannot be assumed; they must be assessed by convergent operations, that is, by examining patterns of correlation among independently assessed constructs.

In the Swedish study, we explored the validity of the interview measures by asking husbands and wives independently about the same constructs and then comparing their responses. Time constraints prevented us from employing this strategy with all constructs. In the prenatal interviews, both parents responded to questions about the division of household chores (Weinraub Inventory), anticipated paternal involvement, and the supportiveness of family and friends. In addition, each described the value of parenthood to himself or herself as well as to the spouse, so that we would compare the value of parenthood reported by each individual with the spouse's perception of this. In the 5-month postnatal interviews, we asked both parents about perceived support, degree of paternal caretaking, and degree of paternal involvement in interaction with the child (not just caretaking). We again asked them to evaluate the importance of parenthood to themselves as well as to their spouses.

The data presented in Table 5.1 reveal significant concordance between the spouses on all dimensions except perceived support. However, when the responses of traditional and nontraditional couples were considered separately, significant differences between the two family types emerged. There was substantial agreement between nontraditional spouses on all dimensions except perceived support[1] and mothers' postnatal value of parenthood, whereas there was much less agreement between the traditional husbands and their wives. The latter couples agreed only concerning the value of parenthood and the household division of labor. Either our measures were not valid within this group, or these couples communicated more poorly (with one another and/or with the interviewers) than the nontraditional couples did. In either case, our findings contrast sharply with those of Owen et al. (in preparation), who found substantial agreement between traditional American men and their wives on many of the same dimensions.

In sum, although there are doubts about the validity of the interview measures pertaining to the traditional families, most of the constructs assessed here seemed to be valid. In our opinion, we achieved valid self-report measures where others had reported difficulties by asking multiple questions pertaining to each construct, and later rating the responses on the appropriate dimension instead of allowing the respondents themselves to rate constructs as value laden as "value of parenthood" for example. In addition, we relied upon interviews rather than questionnaires, because the latter typically elicit brief, socially desirable responses that have little reliability or validity unless highly specific, factual information is desired. Although ours was a time-consuming procedure, we believe that it is a potentially useful procedure that others might want to employ.

Prenatal Interviews

Analyses of the prenatal interview data from the Swedish study revealed substantial and predictable differences between the traditional and nontraditional families (categorized on the basis of prenatal plans regarding paternal leave), despite the fact that the families were remarkably similar on background variables such as maternal and paternal age, education, and occupation (see Lamb et al., 1982a, for further details). An inspection of Table 5.2 reveals that the fathers-to-be in nontraditional families valued parenthood more and work less than their wives did. The reverse was true of the traditional families, in which the fathers-to-be valued work more and parenthood less than their spouses did. There was a significant interaction between parental gender and family type on both

---

[1]Because agreement regarding perceived support was so low, we eliminated this measure from further consideration.

TABLE 5.2
Sex of Parent and Family Type Interactions on Prenatal Parental
Attitudes

	Traditional		Nontraditional			
	Fathers	Mothers	Fathers	Mothers	F	p
Value of Parenthood (Range: 1–8)	4.03	5.42	5.38	4.85	6.11	.02
Value of Work (Range: 1–8)	5.74	4.71	5.26	6.16	6.64	.01
Anticipated Parental Leave (Range: 0–9 months)	0.60	8.24	2.39	6.44	35.41	.00001

value of parenthood and value of work. Judged by their evaluations of work and parenthood, the traditional Swedish families appeared very similar to the young American families studied by Owen et al. (in preparation). Meanwhile, the desire among nontraditional families for fathers to be unusually involved in child care is understandable. Indeed, given the relative importance of parenthood and work to these men and their wives, the way they planned to distribute responsibility for child care seemed to be ideal.

Interestingly, there were only significant interactions between parental gender and family types on the two principal measures; there were no significant main effects for either gender of family type. Overall, in other words, mothers and fathers valued work and parenthood equally, and the parents in traditional families valued work and parenthood as much as the nontraditional parents did. As would be expected, the nontraditional parents anticipated much greater paternal involvement in early child rearing than did the traditional parents. Standardized paper-and-pencil measures completed by the subjects—the Weinraub Household Task Inventory and the Bem Sex Role Inventory—indicated (predictably) that the nontraditional families distributed household tasks in a less sexstereotyped fashion than the traditional couples did, and that the husbands and wives themselves were less sex typed. All in all, then, the interview data suggested that the traditional and nontraditional families really did represent distinctly different groups of parents.

Five-Month Interviews

The 5-month interviews of the two parents served multiple purposes. First, because we questioned the parents again about the value of work and the value of parenthood, we were able to assess the temporal stability of these attitudes (and thus whether the infants' births affected the parents' attitudes). Because we expected (and verified in the prenatal interviews) parenthood to be more important to nontraditional fathers, we expected them to show more stability over time in the evaluation of parenthood. Second, once the infants were born, we were able to explore a number of issues pertaining to parenthood that could not be assessed during pregnancy (e.g., satisfaction with parenthood and resentment of the infants' intrusion) and could thus examine correlations among them as well as their correlations with the values assessed both prenatally and postnatally. Third, we asked both spouses prenatally to predict how involved the fathers would be and later asked them to indicate just how involved and active the fathers really were. Correlations with the attitudinal measures allowed us to assess the correlates of both actual and anticipated paternal involvement. We expected that fathers who valued parenthood more and those who enjoyed parenthood would be more actively involved, whereas those who resented the infants' intrusion would be less active. We expected fewer relationships between maternal attitudes and paternal involvement. Further details regarding these analyses and predictions are contained in a report by Frodi et al. (1981).

Both of the constructs assessed pre- and postnatally (value of work and value of parenthood) were stable over time, as indicated by the data presented in Table 5.3. In addition, prenatal assessments of the fathers' value of parenthood and of anticipated paternal involvement predicted paternal commitment to caretaking as perceived by the fathers at 5 months. (Table 5.3). Among fathers, prenatal value of work was modestly and negatively correlated with the importance attached to parenthood in the 5-month interview. Resentment of and satisfaction with parenthood 5 months postpartum were not correlated with any of the prenatal measures. However, at 5 months the value of parenthood to both mothers and fathers was negatively correlated with resentment and positively correlated with satisfaction with parenthood. Further, fathers' postnatal reports of the value of parenthood and of their satisfaction with parenthood were positively correlated with measures of paternal caretaking and paternal involvement. Mothers perceived their spouses to be more involved and to engage in more caretaking when mothers' value of work was higher. Mothers' value of work, measured at 5 months, was positively correlated with their resentment and negatively correlated with their reported satisfaction with parenthood.

Overall, therefore, the intercorrelations were predictable and meaningful. Unfortunately, however, although there was apparent stability over time on the measures that were assessed pre- and post-natally, the prenatal measures did not significantly relate to other postnatal measures, even when relationships were predictable.

The patterns of correlations within the subgroups composed of traditional and nontraditional mothers and fathers differed somewhat from the pattern reported previously and displayed in Table 5.3. Among traditional fathers, the 5-month appraisal of value of parenthood ($r = -.47$) and paternal caretaking ($r = -.40$) were both negatively correlated with prenatal value of work. Among nontradi-

TABLE 5.3
Intercorrelations Between Prenatal and Postnatal Measures

	PRENATAL		5 MONTHS			
	Value of Parenthood	Value of Work	Value of Parenthood	Value of Work	Paternal Caretaking	Paternal Involvement
FATHERS						
Prenatal:						
Anticipated paternal involvement in child care	.49***		.56***		.28*	
Value of parenthood			.40**		.28*	
Value of work			−.29*	.43**		
5 months:						
Resentment			−.52***		−.34**	
Satisfaction with parenthood			.72***		.68***	.46***
Value of parenthood					.52***	.37**
Value of work						
MOTHERS						
Prenatal:						
Anticipated paternal involvement in child care						
Value of parenthood			.37**			
Value of work				.49***		
5 months:						
Resentment			−.42**	.44**		
Satisfaction with parenthood			.67***	−.30*		
Value of parenthood						
Value of work					.33*	.30*

* $p < .05$
** $p < .01$
*** $p < .001$

tional fathers, however, resentment was negatively correlated with both paternal caretaking ($r = -.55$) and paternal involvement ($r = -.52$). The latter measures were positively correlated with the postnatal value of (r's $= .79$ and .59, respectively) and satisfaction with (r's $= .72$ and .56, respectively) parenthood. Among nontraditional mothers, there was a negative association between postnatal assessments of the value of work and the value of parenthood ($r = .34$), whereas there were no interpretable correlations among the traditional mothers. The traditional fathers thus resembled the nontraditional mothers to the extent that value of work and value of parenthood were negatively related.

The reader will recall that analyses of the prenatal attitudes revealed no significant main effects for Parental Gender or Family Type, but significant interactions between these two factors on the reported value of work and value of parenthood. By contrast, analyses of the 5-month interview data yielded no significant interactions. Instead, nontraditional parents valued both parenthood ($\bar{X} = 5.66$) and work ($\bar{X} = 5.97$) more than the traditional parents did ($\bar{X}$'s = 4.86, 5.11, respectively). Predictably, the nontraditional fathers reported more caretaking ($\bar{X} = 6.48$) and involvement ($\bar{X} - 6.10$) than traditional fathers did ($\bar{X}$'s = 4.34, 4.41, respectively), but there were no differences between traditional and nontraditional families in the mothers' reports of the fathers' caretaking and involvement. It is important to note that by the time of the 5-month interview, few of the fathers had assumed primary caretaking responsibility, and there was no difference between traditional and nontraditional families in the number of men who had done so or in the average amount of time the men had spent as primary caretakers.

On only one measure was there a significant effect for parental gender. Mothers ($\bar{X} = 5.70$) reported more satisfaction with parenthood than fathers did ($\bar{X} = 5.14$). Other analyses showed that androgynous parents were more satisfied with parenthood ($\bar{X} = 6.04$) and valued parenthood more ($\bar{X} = 5.88$) than those who were sex typed ($\bar{X}$'s = 5.20, 5.10, respectively). Paternal involvement and parental attitudes were unrelated to the infants' sex.

Summary

The construct assessed in this study appear to be both valid and reliable. The fact that the subjective value of parenthood and value of work remained stable over a 6- to 8-month period underscores the potential importance of these as characteristics of individuals. Meanwhile, the fact the spouses agreed on issued about which they were both questioned suggests that our ratings were valid. The attitudes—expecially the prenatal attitudes—of traditional and nontraditional parents differed in predictable ways, suggesting that the value of parenthood and value of work were important influences on (or correlates of) the anticipated division of parental responsibilities.

OBSERVATIONAL DATA: THREE AND EIGHT MONTHS

The interview data, as reviewed above, revealed the traditional and nontraditional couples to have substantially different values and to aspire to a very different division of child-rearing responsibilities. To what extent, one wonders, did these differences in parental ideology (particulary those espoused before the children were born) presage differences in parental behavior? As noted earlier, the nontraditional fathers did not spend substantially more time caring for their infants in the first few months, although some of them later took several months of paid leave in order to serve as primary caretakers. We are less concerned here, however, with the relative involvement of mothers and fathers than with the manner in which they interacted. By observing traditional and nontraditional parents interacting with their infants, we hoped to determine whether they provided their children with different social experiences.

Studies of traditional families have consistently reported stylistic differences between maternal and paternal behavior. Yogman, Dixon, Tronick, Als, and Brazelton (1979; see also Yogman, in press) reported that in the course of face-to-face interaction with 2- to 4-month-old infants, fathers emitted more repetitive tapping and physically stimulating behaviors, whereas mothers engaged in more rhythmic, "containing" behaviors. These maternal and paternal styles appeared similar to those reported by Lamb (1976, 1977c, 1980) on the basis of lengthy home observations of 7- to 13-month-olds. Lamb reported that fathers engaged in more physically stimulating and idiosyncratic types of play than mothers did. Mothers were in turn more likely to initiate conventional games (like pat-a-cake) and stimulus games involving toys. When mothers held their infants, it was usually for the purpose of caretaking or discipline, whereas when fathers held their infants, it was usually for play. The relative prominence of fathers in play (especially physically stimulating play) and mothers in caretaking activities has also been reported by Belsky (1979), Clarke-Stewart (1978), Power and Parke (1979), Rendina and Dickerscheid (1976) and Russell (chapter 6, this volume) among others.

To what can we attribute these distinctive behavioral styles? They may simply reflect the traditional role prescriptions for male and female parents (and thus be sociological in origin) or they may reflect more basic, innate gender differences and propensities (and thus be biological in origin). By studying the behavioral styles of nontraditional parents, we hoped to elucidate this issue. If nontraditional (caretaking) fathers behave more like traditional mothers than traditional fathers, it would suggest that the style differences have their basis in the differential socialization and distinctive role demands of adult men and women in traditional cultures. Field (1978) applied this logic in a recent study. She reported that, when engaged in face-to-face interaction with their 2–3-month-old infants, primary caretaking fathers resembled primary caretaking mothers more than noncaretaking fathers on several measures. However, each subject was viewed only for 3 minutes. Further, no secondary caretaking mothers were studied, so it was not possible to assess the effects of parental gender and caretaking roles in a factorial design. For these reasons, further study of this issue seemed necessary. Unfortunately, we were unable to recruit a sample of families in which fathers were primary (if not exclusive) caretakers from birth onward, and so we were unable to study comparable groups of primary and secondary caretaking mothers and fathers. Nevertheless, any observed differences between traditional and nontraditional families would indicate that the behavioral styles (whatever their origins) were at least amenable to social influence, whereas the absence of differences between the two types of families would suggest that the styles had their origins in early sex-role socialization or in biology.

We were also interested in the ways in which traditional and nontraditional parents treated sons and daughters. Previous research involving traditional families has revealed a general preference on the part of both men and women for sons (Arnold, Bulatao, Buripakdi, Chung, Fawcett, Iritani, Lee, & Wu, 1975). In addition, there is a tendency for mothers and fathers to interact preferentially with young infants of the same sex (Parke & O'Leary, 1976; Parke & Sawin, 1980). Such tendencies seem to lessen during the course of the first year, returning with renewed intensity around the time of the infants' first birthdays (Lamb, 1977a, 1977b). We wished to see whether comparable preference patterns were evident in nontraditional families, as the latter appear eager to dispose of many of the trappings of traditional sex-role sterotyping.

Three-Month Observations

The first of the observations designed to address these issues took place when the infants were 3 months old (see Lamb et al., 1982a, for further details). Somewhat to our surprise, there were very few main effects for family type and few significant interactions between the family type and parental gender factors. There was, however, a significant multivariate effect for parental gender, as well as one significant univariate main effect (see Table 5.4). Regardless of family type, mothers were more likely to engage in contact behaviors (touch, tickle, tend, kiss). There were no significant gender differences in the occurrence of play, although the frequency of maternal/paternal involvement in caretaking (changing, tending) varied depending on family type. A significant parent-gender-by-family-type interaction indicated that traditional fathers rarely

TABLE 5.4
Parental Behavior During 3-month Observations:
Effects of Parental Gender

	Mothers	Fathers	F	P
Parental Behavior				
Kiss[a]	9.11	4.20	14.42	.0003
Touch[a]	20.60	13.31	17.43	.0001
Contact[a]				
(Touch, Tend,				
Tickle)	47.69	35.24	10.63	.002
Responsiveness[b]	0.68	0.75	3.29	.07

[a]Frequency per hour.
[b]Probability of response within 5 seconds of infant fuss or cry.

changed their infants' diapers or tended to their infants' needs, whereas the nontraditional fathers did so as often as their wives did. All in all, however, there were sex differences in the style of parental behavior that continued to exist regardless of the parents' relative responsibility for child rearing. These results are somewhat similar to those reported by Field (1978), although in her report, Field emphasized those measures on which gender differences disappeared rather than those in which gender differences remained regardless of involvement in caretaking.

Nevertheless, it is important not to attribute too much significance to these findings because at the time of the 3-month observations *none* of the fathers—regardless of prenatal commitment—had assumed much responsibility for child care. All the infants initially were breast-fed by their mothers, and so the mothers were primary caretakers in all families. Stated differently, none of the fathers had yet assumed a major role in caretaking, as those who still wanted to do so planned to take paternal leave later in the year. This therefore increased the importance of the 8-month observations.

Analyses of the parental behavior during the 3-month observations also yielded two significant interactions between family type and the infants' gender. Traditional parents engaged in more functional behavior with sons ($\bar{X} = 16.6$) than with daughters ($\bar{X} = 13.8$), whereas the reverse was true in nontraditional families ($\bar{X}$'s = 12.3, 17.2, respectively). Likewise, traditional parents directed more distal bids (smiles, vocalizations) to sons than to daughters, whereas the reverse was true in nontraditional families.

Eight-Month Observations

Like the observations conducted when the infants were 3 months old, the 8-month observations were designed to determine whether the style of parental behavior was most closely related to parental gender or to caretaking role (see Lamb et al., 1982b, for further details). For the 8-month analyses, however, we were able to assess family type depending on whether the father actually did take parental leave and serve as primary caretaker for more than a month sometime prior to the observation. (The classification used for the 3-month analyses was based on prenatal declarations of anticipated involvement.) Seventeen of the 51 fathers spent more than a month as primary caretakers ($\bar{X} = 2.8$ months); these men and their wives constituted the nontraditional groups for the purposes of the 8-month observations.

The analyses of these observational data suggested conclusions similar to those based on the 3-month observations. As Table 5.5 shows, mothers were more likely to display affection, vocalize, smile, and tend to their infants than fathers were. Mothers were also more likely to hold the infants, especially for the purposes of discipline or soothing. There were no main effects for parental gender on any of the play measures, whereas these measures alone showed

TABLE 5.5
Effects of Parent's Gender and Family Type on Parental Behavior

Measure	Mother		Father		Parent Effect (F)	Family Type Effect (F)
	Trad	Nontrad	Trad	Nontrad		
Affectionate behavior	3.05	3.55	1.42	0.69	16.84***	—
Vocalize	34.34	39.93	23.59	21.10	10.47***	—
Smile	0.24	0.43	0.18	0.07	3.25+	—
Tend	1.18	1.58	0.74	0.62	6.90**	—
Play (total)	6.82	4.39	6.07	3.45	—	6.04*
Stimulus	5.04	2.58	4.05	2.19	—	6.95**
Parallel	0.04	0.22	0.19	0.13	—	—
Coordinate	0.21	0.10	0.38	0.03	—	5.51*
Minor Physical	0.65	0.96	0.83	0.83	—	—
Physical	0.15	0.27	0.55	0.29	2.73+	—
Conventional	0.73	0.27	0.47	0.27	—	5.10*
Idiosyncratic	0.07	0.	0.05	0.	—	3.73+
Hold (total)	3.29	3.63	2.38	2.46	12.06***	—
Caretaking	0.86	1.07	0.79	0.76	—	—
Play	1.06	1.31	1.01	1.06	—	—
Affection	0.56	0.78	0.44	0.77	—	2.86+
Discipline	0.59	0.74	0.41	0.18	3.34+	—
Soothing	0.71	0.64	0.37	0.40	3.65+	—
Respondent	0.03	0.03	0.	0.06	—	—
Other	0.58	0.75	0.83	0.90	—	—

+ $p < .10$
* $p < .05$
** $p < .01$
*** $p < .005$

Note: In all cases, d.f. = 1, 98; only significant or near significant F-values are shown. Means indicate rates per hour of observation.

family-type effects. Analyses of variance revealed that the traditional parents (both mothers and fathers) played with their infants more—especially those games classified as stimulus, coordinate, conventional, or idiosyncratic. (These main effects for family type were unexpected and uninterpretable.) Because the play measures did not yield significant family-type-by-parental-gender interactions (indeed there were only a chance number of such effects), furthermore, they do not help elucidate our central issue.

These effects excepted, the 8-month observational data, like the 3-month data, indicated that parental gender has an important influence on parental behavior—regardless of the parents' relative involvement in caretaking. This conclusion was also supported by an analysis of the relationship between parental sex role (assessed with the femininity scale on the BSRI) and parental behavior.

In his study of highly involved Australian fathers, Russell (1978) found that the fathers' sex role was related to degree of involvement, whereas the mothers' was not. Radin (1978, 1980) reported no relationship between either parents' sex role and his or her degree of involvement. Our results were more akin to Radin's. In our study, neither parents' sex role was related to more than a chance number of the behavioral measures listed in Table 5.5.

Summary

The behavioral observations conducted when the infants were 3 and 8 months old point toward a similar conclusion, even though different parents constituted the nontraditional and traditional groups at each age. In general, parental gender appeared to be a more important influence on style of parental behavior than was family type. This suggests that the maternal and paternal interactional styles revealed in many previous studies may be biological in origin. On the other hand, these differences may have their origins in the years of differential socialization to which the parents have been subjected, even if they are now eager to shake off the remaining trappings of sex stereotypy. Unfortunately, whereas it would have been comparatively easy to demonstrate the sociological and psychological origins of the parental style differences had there been many parental-gender-by-family-type interactions, the absence of such interactions is more difficult to interpret.

CONCLUSION

Overall, the results of this study suggest that the availability of paid paternal and maternal leave permits the couples to divide parental responsibilities in accordance with their personal preferences rather than simply in accordance with social expectations and pressures. Even though a substantial number of the fathers were not as involved as they had hoped to be, one-third of the fathers in the sample were able to take a major role in infant care. We hope in future analyses to determine what accounted for the discrepancy between prenatal plans and actual parental involvement on the part of many fathers.

Analyses based on our interview measures are especially impressive because we were successful in defining and assessing theoretically important constructs in a reliable and valid fashion. The two major constructs, value of parenthood and value of work, were stable over time and were meaningfully correlated with various interview measures of adjustment to and involvement in parenting. Further investigation of the antecedents and implications of the individual differences in these attitudes are warranted. It would also be valuable to determine why these constructs were harder to assess validly in traditional than in nontraditional parents.

The results of the observational analyses, by contrast, were somewhat surprising to us. Regardless of their family type, mothers and fathers behaved in characteristically different ways. Stated differently, degree of paternal involvement in child care did not change the way fathers behaved in interaction with their infants. These findings suggest that the differences between maternal and paternal behavioral styles are due either to biologically based differences between the sexes, or to well-socialized sex differences. Whatever their origins, the fact that mothers and fathers behave in a gender-differentiated fashion regardless of paternal involvement in child care should allay fears that the development of gender identity is adversely affected by increased paternal involvement in traditionally feminine activities. Of course, we need to assess these children as they grow older in order to determine what the effects of increased paternal involvement have been.

ACKNOWLEDGMENTS

The research described in this chapter was supported by the Riksbankens Jubileumsfond of Sweden. We are grateful to them for their generosity, and to Britta Forström, Tom Corry, and Jamie Steinberg for assistance in the collection and analysis of the data. Without the parents' gracious cooperation, of course, the research would not have been possible.

REFERENCES

Arnold, F., Bulatao, R. A., Buripakdi, C., Chung, B. J., Fawcett, J. T., Iritani, T., Lee, S-J., & Wu, T-S. *The value of children: A cross-national study* (Vol. 1). Honolulu: East-West Center, 1975.

Belsky, J. Mother-father-infant interaction: A naturalistic observational study. *Developmental Psychology,* 1979, *15,* 601-607.

Bem, S. The measurement of psychological androgyny. *Journal of Consulting and Clinical Psychology,* 1974, *42,* 155-162.

Clarke-Stewart, K. A. And daddy makes three: The father's impact on mother and young child. *Child Development,* 1978, *49,* 466-478.

Field, T. M. Interaction patterns of primary versus secondary caretaker fathers. *Developmental Psychology,* 1978, *14,* 183-184.

Frodi, A. M., Lamb, M. E., Frodi, M., Hwang, C-P., Forström, & Corry, T. Stability and change in parental attitudes following an infant's birth into traditional and nontraditional Swedish families. *Scandinavian Journal of Psychology,* 1981, in press.

Lamb, M. E. Interactions between eight-month-old children and their fathers and mothers. In M. E. Lamb (Ed.), *The role of the father in child development.* New York: Wiley, 1976.

Lamb, M. E. The development of mother-infant and father-infant attachments in the second year of life. *Developmental Psychology,* 1977, *13,* 637-648(a).

Lamb, M. E. The development of parental preferences in the first two years of life. *Sex Roles,* 1977, *3,* 495-497.(b)

Lamb, M. E. Father-infant and mother-infant interactions in the first year of life. *Child Development,* 1977, *48,* 167-181. (c)

Lamb, M. E. The development of parent–infant attachments in the first two years of life. In F. A. Pedersen (Ed.), *The father–infant relationship*. New York: Praeger Special Studies, 1980.

Lamb, M. E. On the familiar origins of personality and social style. In L. Laosa, & I. Sigel (Eds.), *The family as a learning environment*. New York: Plenum, in press.

Lamb, M. E., Chase-Lansdale, P., & Owen, M. T. *The effects of maternal employment on infant social development*. Grant proposal to the Spencer Foundation of Chicago, 1978.

Lamb, M. E., Chase-Lansdale, P., & Owen, M. T. The changing American family and its implications for infant social development: The sample case of maternal employment. In M. Lewis, & L. A. Rosenblum (Eds.), *The child and its family*. New York: Plenum, 1979.

Lamb, M. E., & Easterbrooks, M. A. Individual differences in parental sensitivity: Origins, components, and consequences. In M. E. Lamb, & L. R. Sherrod (Eds.), *Infant social cognition*. Hillsdale, N.J.: Lawrence Erlbaum Associates, 1981.

Lamb, M. E., Frodi, A. M., Hwang, C-P., Frodi, M., & Steinberg, J. Effects of gender and caretaking role on parent–infant interaction. In R. N. Emde, & R. J. Harmon (Eds.), *Attachment and affiliative systems*. New York: Plenum, 1982, in press. (a)

Lamb, M. E., Frodi, A. M., Hwang, C-P., Frodi, M., & Steinberg, J. Mother- and father-infant interaction involving play and holding in traditional and nontraditional Swedish families. *Developmental Psychology*, 1982, *18*, in press. (b)

Lamb, M. E., & Levine, J. A. The Swedish parental leave policy: Characteristics and utilization. In M. E. Lamb, & A. Sagi (Eds.), *Fatherhood and social policy*. Hillsdale, N.J.: Lawrence Erlbaum Associates, in press.

Lamb, M. E., Owen, M. T., & Chase-Lansdale, P. L. The working mother in the intact family: A process model. In R. R. Abidin (Ed.), *Parent education and intervention handbook*. Springfield, Ill.: C. C. Thomas, 1980.

Owen, M. T., Chase-Lansdale, P. L., & Lamb, M. E. *Mothers' and fathers' attitudes, maternal employment, and the security of infant–parent attachment*. Manuscript in preparation.

Parke, R. D. Parent–infant interaction: Progress, paradigms, and problems. In G. P. Sackett (Ed.), *Observing behavior* (Vol. 1). Baltimore: University Park Press, 1978.

Parke, R. D., & O'Leary, S. Father-mother-infant interaction in the newborn period: Some findings, some observations, and some unresolved issues. In K. Riegel, & J. Meacham (Eds.), *The developing individual in a changing world*. (Vol. 2), *Social and environmental issues*. The Hague: Mouton, 1976.

Parke, R. D., & Sawin, D. B. The family in early infancy: Social-interactional and attitudinal analyses. In F. A. Pedersen (Ed.), *The father–infant relationship*. New York: Praeger Special Studies, 1980.

Power, T. G., & Parke, R. D. *Toward a taxonomy of father–infant and mother–infant play patterns*. Paper presented to the Society for Research in Child Development, San Francisco, March 1979.

Radin, N. *Childrearing fathers in intact families with preschoolers*. Paper presented to the American Psychological Association, Toronto, September 1978.

Radin, N. *Childrearing fathers in intact families: An exploration of some antecedents and consequences*. Paper presented to a Conference on Fatherhood and Social Policy, Haifa (Israel), July 1980.

Rendina, I., & Dickerscheid, J. D. Father involvement with first-born infants. *Family Coordinator*, 1976, *25*, 373–379.

Russell, G. The father role and its relations to masculinity, femininity, and androgyny. *Child Development*, 1978, *49*, 1174–1181.

Stephenson, G. R. Plexyn: A computer-compatible grammar for coding complex social interactions. In M. E. Lamb, S. J. Suomi, & G. R. Stephenson (Eds.), *Social interaction analysis: Methodological issues*. Madison, Wis.: University of Wisconsin Press, 1979.

Weinraub, M., & Leite, J. *Knowledge of sex-role stereotypes and sextyped toy preference in two-year-old children*. Paper presented to the Eastern Psychological Association, Boston, April 1977.

Yarrow, M. R., Campbell, J. D., & Burton, R. V. *Childrearing*. San Francisco: Jossey-Bass, 1968.

Yogman, M. W. Development of the father-infant relationship. In H. Fitzgerald, B. Lester, & M. W. Yogman (Eds.), *Theory and research in behavioral pediatrics* (Vol. 1). New York: Plenum, in press.

Yogman, M. W., Dixon, S., Tronick, E., Als, H., & Brazelton, T. B. *The goals and structure of face-to-face interaction between infants and fathers*. Paper presented to the Society for Research in Child Development, New Orleans, March 1979.

6 Shared-Caregiving Families: An Australian Study

Graeme Russell
Macquarie University

INTRODUCTION

The traditional theoretical, professional, and cultural belief is that mothers *should* have the major responsibility for the care of children. This is the most fundamental of the beliefs on which current sex-role patterns are based. It is commonly assumed that: The mother–infant relationship is both unique and necessary; fathers do not have the same capacity for nurturance and are not as sensitive as mothers are to the needs of children; the father–infant relationship is not very important. These views are well captured in a statement by Bowlby (Tucker, 1976): "Mothers are specially prepared biologically; if mothers don't look after babies, then babies are not going to prosper."(p. 44) Fathers' relationships with, and influence over their infants are usually assumed to be indirect; they are thought to provide the economic and emotional support for mothers. This view is often expressed in the form of the advice that: "The most important thing a father can do for his children is to love their mother." If fathers are given any status as parents it is usually later in a child's life during adolescence (Russell, 1982) and more especially for sons.

Yet, although the majority of families with young children adopt life-styles that are consistent with these beliefs—mother as the full-time caregiver and father employed in the paid work force—a significant minority of families do not conform to this pattern. For example, in a quasi-random sample of 250 Australian two-parent families with at least one child under 10 years of age, a significant number of fathers (15%) were found to participate in *all* aspects of child rearing—diaper changing, bathing, feeding, play, providing affection and discipline—regardless of whether they had infant or older children (Russell,

139

1982). In several families fathers shared the tasks equally when both parents were at home, and in approximately 7% of the families surveyed, fathers had a significant *responsibility* for daily caregiving, (e.g., by caring for their children for some part of each day). Neither psychologists nor sociologists have paid much attention to these nontraditional families. Indeed, until recently the role of fathers as *primary caregivers* had been almost completely ignored (Levine, 1976).

The investigation of nontraditional families in which fathers have a major caregiving role, however is likely to be especially important for our understanding of: family patterns; parental roles; socialization practices; sex differences; and sex-role stereotypes. The study of fathers' caregiving behavior, for example, provides an excellent opportunity to explore the interaction of the several person and situation factors likely to influence the display and self-reporting of sex-role behavior and sex-role self-concepts (cf. previous studies that have been laboratory-based [e.g., Bem & Lenney, 1976]). A change to a nontraditional family life-style involving fathers as caregivers might also be viewed as a significant life event (Hultsch & Plemons, 1979), especially for fathers. It might be expected, then, that this life-style change will be associated with changes both in parents (e.g., in their personalities; in their marital relationships) and in their children (e.g., sex-role development). The study of such families, therefore, is especially important for the growing theoretical and empirical study of life-span development (Gutmann, 1975; Hill & Mattessich, 1979; Hultsch & Plemons, 1979).

The aim of the present chapter is to discuss findings from a study of Australian two-parent families in which fathers had the major or equal responsibility for the day-to-day care of their children—here termed shared-caregiving families. This is done within the context of three broad issues;

1. *Family Lifestyles*   The day-to-day life-styles and child-care patterns of shared-caregiving families are described and compared with those of traditional families in which mothers were not employed and fathers were employed. Of particular interest here are family-type differences in divisions of labor for child care, and the time spent on, and the content of parent–child interactions. This analysis, therefore, provides a framework within which to establish the extent of the nontraditional nature of a shared-caregiving family pattern.

2. *Explanations for a shared-caregiving family pattern*   The possible antecedents of a nontraditional caregiving pattern are examined. Discussion here focuses both on parents' explanations for adopting their life-styles, and how shared-caregiving families differ from traditional families. These latter analyses emphasize family-type differences in personal and family characteristics, parental employment characteristics, and differences in sex-role self-concepts and beliefs.

3. *Consequences of a shared-caregiving life-style* This section discusses questions concerning the impact that this life-style has and is likely to have on family relationships between these families and significant others. The focus here is on parents' assessments of their problems of adjustment, and their evaluations of the advantages and disadvantages of their shared-caregiving life-styles.

FAMILY LIFE-STYLES

The nontraditional families described in this chapter are defined by the extent to which fathers take responsibility for the day-to-day care of their children. They are two-parent families in which the mother and father share the caregiving or the father has the major responsibility, *and* in which the father has *sole responsibility* for his children for at least 15 of their waking hours each week—the average reported by parents was 26 hours/week. In 58% of the families mothers had the major responsibility for obtaining income, in 30% it was shared, and in only 12% did fathers have the major responsibility. The families were traditional in other respects, however (i.e., in most families the mother and father were legally married and lived in comparative social isolation with their own children).

The emphasis in this study was on fathers' caregiving behavior. The decision to define a sample in terms of fathers' caregiving responsibilities rather than in terms of parental employment structure was influenced by findings from the initial phase of this study. Analyses presented elsewhere (Russell, 1982) show that the number of hours fathers spend on paid employment is a poor predictor of their involvement in child care, regardless of whether the mother is employed or not. Furthermore, few differences were found in fathers' caregiving responsibilities between families in which fathers were employed (i.e., employment roles shared), and when they were not employed (i.e., employment roles reversed).

Data Collection

Families ($N = 50$) were recruited as part of a more extensive study of 300 Australian families (Russell, 1982). Ten were recruited by random sampling in shopping centers, 10 were families known to people who were recruited from shopping centers, and 30 were families who responded to advertisements placed on univeristy, community, and preschool notice boards.

Data were obtained from interviews conducted in parents' homes. There were two parts to the interview. *Part I:* Both mother and father were present. The primary aim was to collect information about family lifestyles and divisions of labour. A full description of the procedure adopted in this part of the interview is given in Russell (1978). *Part II:* Mothers and fathers were interviewed separately. Here, questions were unstructured and open-ended. They covered the following areas: beliefs about parental roles; beliefs about child development; child-rearing values and aspirations; and several questions specifically related to their current life-styles (e.g., their reasons for adopting this life-style, problems of adjustment, reactions of significant others, perceptions of changes in family relationships). Parents in 33 families (of 50) also completed the Bem (1974) Sex Role Inventory (see also Russell, Antill, & Cunningham, 1978).

Family Characteristics

The mean age of fathers was 31 and mothers 29. Couples had been married for an average of 7.5 years. In comparison to traditional families (Russell, 1982) shared-caregiving families had fewer children [average 1.7 versus 2.3; $t(193) = 2.5$, $p < .02$] and older children [mean age of youngest child: 3.5 versus 2.3 years; $t(193) = 2.4$, $p < .02$]. Shared-caregiving parents were more highly educated (percentage completed university: *fathers:* shared—36; traditional—22 [$X^2(1) = 3.73$, $p < .10$]; *mothers:* shared—42; traditional—16 [$X^2(1) = 13.05$, $p < .01$], and the mean occupational status of mothers (Congalton, 1969) was higher [4.0 versus 4.7; $t(193) = 2.2$, $p < .05$]. They were not simply an educated professional middle class, however, A striking feature of this sample was the diversity of fathers' present or previous occupations. Whereas 36% had occupations that were professional in nature, 34% had occupations that could be classified as either semiskilled or unskilled (Congalton, 1969).

Employment Patterns

There were four different patterns of employment represented in the sample: (1) mother employed full-time and father unemployed (32%); (2) both mother and father employed full-time (30%); (3) mother employed full-time and father employed part-time (26%); (4) mother employed part-time and father employed full-time (12%). Mothers on the average, were outside the home for employment purposes for 40 hours/week and fathers for 28 hours/week. Families had been in their nontraditional patterns for an average of 26 months.

All families had one aspect of employment in common—flexibility in work hours. At least *one* parent was employed in a job for which either: (1) there was potential to work part-time or to select working hours to suit a different type of family organization; or (2) the hours of the person employed full-time were less than 9:00 to 5:00 (e.g., mother employed as a school teacher). Nevertheless, in 30% of the families some significant accommodation of work to family (Bailyn, 1978) had taken place (i.e., people had either changed their jobs or had selected work hours to enable them to change caregiving patterns).

Parental Responsibilities and Availability

The normative pattern in traditional families is for mothers to have the sole responsibility for children for a major part of the week—on the average 40 waking hours/week, with fathers very rarely taking sole responsibility—on the average 2 hours/week (Russell, 1982). Sole responsibility is defined as when one parent is with the children and the other parent is out of the home or engaged in some activity from which it is agreed the parent cannot be interrupted. In shared-caregiving families patterns of responsibility were very different. Fathers were found to have sole responsibility for 26 hours/week; mothers for 15 hours each week.

Differences between the two family types were also evident for the amount of time parents were available to their children. In shared-caregiving families fathers reported being available for an average of 54 hours/week and mothers 49 hours/week. The corresponding figures in traditional families were: fathers—33 hours; mothers—76 hours. It is worth noting, however, that the total time for which *both* parents were available to their children was comparable in the two family types: shared—103 hours/week; traditional—109 hours/week. This is not surprising when it is considered that in neither family type were children cared for for any significant period of time either by other people or in an institution. Indeed, the majority of shared-caregiving families were very strong in their view that child care was *their* responsibility.

Quantity of Parent–Child Interaction

Two types of estimates were made here. First, the amount of time each parent spent in day-to-day caregiving activities (DC) such as feeding, changing diapers, bathing, and dressing. Second, the amount of time spent in play and other significant interactions (PI) such as parent helping with homework, child helping a parent prepare a meal, clean the house, do the garden, etc. To be included in this latter category, an activity had to be carried out jointly and be engaged in on a regular basis. These estimates, as was noted earlier, were based on data obtained from a *joint* family interview (Russell, 1978).

The amount of time spent each week on DC activities by shared-caregiving fathers was 9 hours, and by mothers 11 hours. For traditional fathers this figure was 2 hours/week, and for traditional mothers 20 hours. A similar pattern emerged for PI estimates. Fathers in shared-caregiving families reported spending 18 hours and mothers 16 hours on PI activities, whereas in traditional families fathers spent an average of 10 hours and mothers 23 hours. Although there were these major differences between the two family types in terms of the relative amounts of time spent by mothers and fathers, with this split being very close to 50/50 in shared-caregiving families, the two family types were again comparable for the absolute amount of time spent by *both parents combined.* Total parent–child interaction in shared-caregiving families was 53 hours/week, and in traditional families it was 56 hours/week.

Types of Play Activities

Differences in the specific types of play activities engaged in by parents were examined in two ways. First, a comparison was made between indoor (ID) and outdoor (OD) activities, and second, between activities that were defined as cognitive and creative (CC), and those that were more physical, fun, and amusement oriented (FA). Previous observational (Lamb, 1976) and interview (Russell, 1979b) analyses have shown that in traditional families mothers are more likely to be involved in indoor, conventional, cognitive, and toy-oriented play, whereas fathers are more likely to be involved in outdoor and physical and rough and tumble play. The present analysis supports these findings for traditional families. Fathers in traditional families were more likely to be involved in outdoor than indoor play (64% OD, 36% ID), and for mothers it was the reverse (34% OD, 66% ID). These mother–father differences are highly significant [$X^2(1) = 25.2$, $p < .001$]. Differences between mothers and fathers in shared-caregiving families were considerably reduced: fathers: OD—55%, ID—45%; mothers: OD—43%, ID—57% [$X^2(1) = 1.1$ $p > .05$]. This pattern of mother–father differences was also evident in the second play analysis. The figures for traditional families were: fathers: CC—35%, FA—65%; mothers: CC—55%, FA—45%; [$X^2(1) = 11.7$, $p < .001$] and for shared-caregiving families: fathers: CC—44%, FA—56%; mothers: CC—45%, FA—55% [$X^2(1)$ < 1, $p > .05$]. It seems, therefore, that compared to traditional parents, mothers and fathers in shared-caregiving families are much more similar in terms of the types of play activities they engage in with their children.

Summary

The day-to-day life-styles of the group of shared-caregiving families reported on here were very different from those of traditional families. Greater similarity in the roles of shared-caregiving parents were evident at all levels of analysis: responsibility for child care; amount of time each parent was available to his or her children; time spent in significant interactions (care and play); and the content of play activities. Despite the greater similarity in the roles of mothers and fathers, however, the *absolute* amount of parent–child interaction in shared-caregiving and traditional families was almost exactly the same.

It is also clear that in absolute terms fathers in these families have a heavy commitment to daily caregiving. It is difficult to determine, however, exactly how these fathers compare with those described in two other similar studies (De Frain, 1979; Radin, 1980). Both De Frain and Radin report their figures for caregiving responsibilities in relative rather than absolute terms. De Frain, for example, reported that fathers in his sample performed 46% of child-care duties, but did not report how much *time* fathers actually spent on these tasks. Radin (1980) has suggested that the families in the present study are most likely comparable to her 'intermediate group', and not as committed to caregiving as her 'primary group'. Although this seems to be the case when the *relative involvement* of mothers and fathers is considered, there is some doubt about it when other factors are considered. Radin's sample of father as prime care-giver included only one father who was not employed in some way, whereas the present sample includes 16 such fathers. Furthermore, given that in Radin's sample the children were attending a preschool or child-care center for an average of 17 hours each week (compared with 6 hours/week here), it might be expected that the fathers reported on here are spending more time in care giving and, therefore, are more committed to this role. Additional data from the other two studies, giving more specific details of the time spent by fathers on care giving, is needed to resolve this question.

ADOPTING A SHARED-CAREGIVING LIFE-STYLE

Given the paucity of research on nontraditional families and especially those in which fathers are the primary caregivers, there is little basis on which to generate hypotheses for testing or to begin to develop a general explanatory model. Writings in other areas, nevertheless, suggest some useful starting points.

At one level a broad distinction could be made between *person and situation* variables. The maternal employment literature (Hoffman & Nye, 1974; see chapter 3, this volume) suggests that situational factors associated with family finances (e.g., father's occupational status and income) and family characteristics (e.g., number and ages of children) might be important. Hypotheses about person variables can be generated from the recent literature on sex roles. Laboratory studies have shown that there is a relationship between the display of nurturance and sex-role classification; specifically, that traditionally masculine males are less likely to display nurturance towards a baby (Bem & Lenney, 1976; Bem, Martyna, & Watson, 1976). It may be that this relationship extends to parenting behavior, especially the behavior of fathers. It might be expected, therefore, that shared-caregiving fathers will describe themselves in a less traditionally masculine way than traditional fathers.

It is highly likely, however, that there are variables associated with this type of family that are not to be found in other literature. As such, the present discussion covers a wide range of variables and begins with an analysis of parents' own explanations for their particular life-styles. The aim here is not to provide a definitive explanation for this type of life-style, but to provide a basis for the generation of hypotheses and further research.

Parental Explanations

Parents were asked what their main reasons were for adopting their life-style and whether they felt that one parent had been more influential than the other in making the decision to change life-styles. There were four major types of explanations:

1. *Inability of fathers to gain employment* (6 families): Either the father was in poor health or he was unable to get a job he was happy with.
2. *Financial benefits* (19): Parents explained that they needed or wanted the extra income resulting from having both parents employed.
3. *Career factors* (12): The majority of families in this category were those in which a change in life-style was associated with the desire of the mother to pursue her career; a smaller group ($N = 3$) consisted of families in which fathers were "at home" studying in order that they might advance their careers in the future.
4. *Beliefs about child-care responsibilities* (13): These were people who were ideologically committed to shared child care; they felt very strongly that *both* parents should be involved in child care. Three fathers in this group were also very strong in their rejection of traditional career values and offered this as an additional explanation.

Parents who offered the first two types of explanation saw their change of life-styles as being *necessary,* whereas parents in the latter two categories saw their change as being a matter of *choice*. In 39% of families it was agreed that the mother was more influential in making the decision; 22% said that it was mainly the father's decision; and 39% of families saw it as a joint decision. A relationship was found between the reasons given for changing life-styles and the person seen as more influential in the decision. When the change was seen as being a financial necessity, the mother was perceived as being more influential in 64% of these families; and when the change was by choice, 79% saw the father as being the most influential.

In developing an explanatory model, therefore, emphasis might need to be placed on: family financial situation; the nature of parental employment, especially mothers' employment; beliefs about parental roles. Nevertheless, it seems important to go beyond these explanations. Given a certain set of family financial or employment conditions, there may be several possible alternatives for family change. For example, if a family is in financial difficulty possible alternatives might be: Father take a second job; both mother and father work and children be cared for by another person; both parents work, but in jobs that permit them to organize their hours of work so that they share the care of their children. Are there any particular reasons why these families chose the alternative of father taking on caregiving responsibilities? It seems there are; several factors appear to mediate this change.

Possible Mediating Variables

1. Family Characteristics   It could be argued that a nontraditional life-style involving a radical change in caregiving patterns is more likely to eventuate when the demands of caregiving are reduced and when there is less conflict with cultural beliefs about the needs of children and the roles of mothers (e.g. breast-feeding, maternal–infant bonding). As such it might be hypothesised that shared-caregiving families will be more likely to have fewer and older children than those families who adopt a traditional caregiving pattern. Data presented in the previous section comparing shared-caregiving and traditional families on these two variables support this hypothesis. Furthermore, there were only nine of the shared-caregiving families in which there was a child under 6 months of age.

2. Employment: Potential for and Type of   A decision for fathers to assume a caregiving role and for mothers to be employed appears more likely when the mothers' potential for employment is higher—that is, her training and back-ground are such that she can gain employment readily and/or she has a higher earning capacity. The latter hypothesis is supported here; as was reported earlier, mothers in shared-caregiving families were found to have occupations of higher status than mothers in traditional families. Shared child care would also be more likely to occur when parents have flexibility in their hours of employment, enabling them to organize their employment around family needs. Again, data presented earlier support this hypothesis; in all families in the present sample at least one parent had some flexibility in hours of employment, *or* the hours at his or her place of employment were less than 35 hours/week. This latter employ-ment characteristic was especially common for mothers. Indeed, there were only two mothers in the entire sample who had hours of employment and job demands (travel, overtime, etc.) comparable to what is commonly found for men in traditional families (Russell, 1982).

3. Prior Experiences   It might be that there is a link between these fathers' and mothers' adoption of a nontraditional life-style and their own parents (e.g., a father whose own father was very involved is more likely to become involved). Although this type of information was not collected here, both Radin (1980; chapter 7, this volume) in her United States study and Sagi (Chapter 8, this volume) in his Israeli study report data that support such a hypothesis. Of particular impor-tance, it seems, is having had a mother who was employed (Radin, 1980), and a father who was himself highly involved (Sagi, Chapter 8). Another possibility is that a father's more recent experiences, especially with his own children, might affect his willingness to adopt the caregiving role. For this hypothesis then, it would be expected that fathers who have more knowledge about and are more competent in child care, and have had more contact and experience and therefore are more self-confident with their children, will be more likely to assume this role. Support was found for this hypothesis in the present study.

Fathers in shared-caregiving compared to fathers in traditional families were more likely to have attended prenatal classes [$X^2(1) = 3.57$, $p < .10$], and more likely to have attended the birth of their children [$X^2(1) = 4.63$, $p < .05$]. There was also a nonsignificant trend for caregiving fathers to have read more books on child care or child rearing. These findings are probably of even greater significance than this analysis might first imply. There has been a recent shift in cultural and hospital attitudes towards having fathers more involved in the birth process. The shared-caregiving families studied here, however, tended to have older children and therefore would be expected to have been subjected to these shifts to a lesser degree. These findings suggest then that caregiving fathers might have been more committed fathers before their change in life-style, and that this prior commitment could have mediated their change in life-style.

4. Beliefs About Parental Roles   It has been argued by Parke (1978) that parental behavior might be mediated by parental beliefs, for example, about their roles or their perceptions of their children. Bem (1979), in like manner, has suggested that differences in sex-role behavior might be a consequence of differences in beliefs about the two sexes. Thus, it may be that parents' decisions to adopt a nontraditional life-style are linked to their *beliefs* about the underlying bases of the differences in parental roles, and that it is this cognitive component that mediates the change.

Following this line of argument, it was hypothesised that parents in nontraditional families would be: less likely to believe that there are fundamental biological differences between mothers and fathers; more likely to believe that mothers and fathers have equal abilities to be caregivers; and more likely to attribute current sex differences in parental roles to social factors. Parents were asked two questions in this context, one focused on their beliefs about the notion of a maternal instinct, and the other on their beliefs about the ability of fathers to be caregivers.

Responses to the first question on whether or not differences in the roles of mothers and fathers can be explained by the existence of a maternal instinct or a fundamental difference between males and females, could be coded into two broad categories: Agree or not agree. Of the parents who didn't agree, 60% said they felt mothers were socialized into their role. The percentages of each type of response for fathers and mothers in the two family types are presented in Table 6.1. As can be seen from this table, there is a high percentage of parents who believe that there is a fundamental biological difference between mothers and fathers that enables mothers to be better at caring for children. The percentage of

TABLE 6.1

Percentages of Fathers and Mothers in Shared-Caregiving and
Traditional Families Who Agree and Don't Agree That There Is a
Maternal Instinct

	Shared-Caregiving		Traditional	
	Mothers	Fathers	Mothers	Fathers
Agree	51	53	66	78
Don't Agree	49	47	34	22

parents who believe in a maternal instinct, however, is much higher in traditional families, and more particularly among traditional fathers. Significant differences in responses were found between fathers and mothers in traditional families ($X^2(1) = 4.24$, $p < .05$), and between traditional and nontraditional fathers, ($X^2(1) = 6.2$, $p < .01$). No differences were found between mothers and fathers in nontraditional families.

Additional chi-square analyses were performed to determine whether these family differences in beliefs could be explained by other specific differences in family characteristics noted earlier (i.e., mother's and father's education levels, occupational status, and age of child). None of the analyses carried out on these variables was significant ($p > .10$).

Responses to the question about the ability of fathers to be caregivers were coded into three categories: agreement that fathers do have the ability—that differences currently existing are attributable to differences in societal expectations and socialization practices; uncertain (e.g., a belief that most couldn't but a special few possibly could); and disagreement. The percentages of responses falling into each of these categories are shown in Table 6.2. As for the previous question, significant mother/father differences were found only for parents from traditional families ($X^2(2) = 15.03$, $p < .001$); fathers in this type of family were significantly less likely to believe that fathers could be successful caregivers.

TABLE 6.2

Percentage of Shared-Caregiving and Traditional Parents Who Agree,
Disagree, and Who Are Uncertain That Fathers Have the Ability to
Care for Children

	Shared-Caregiving		Traditional	
	Mothers	Fathers	Mothers	Fathers
Agree	90	82	65	49
Disagree	0	6	22	35
Uncertain	10	12	13	16

Significant family-type differences were found for fathers ($X^2(2) = 11.2$, $p <$ .005); fathers in shared-caregiving families were more likely to believe that fathers are capable of performing the caregiving role equally as well as mothers. No differences were found between mothers and fathers in shared-caregiving families.

Chi-square analyses were again carried out for occupation and education levels, and age of youngest child. The only variable for which there was a significant chi-square was father's occupation. Fathers with high occupational rankings (Congalton, 1969) were found to be significantly *less likely* to believe that fathers could take on the caregiving role ($X^2(6) = 16.5$, $p < .01$).

Responses to this question are also relevant to the issue of the competency of fathers in the caregiving role. Competence is difficult to assess at the best of times, and is impossible to assess using the methods employed in this study. Nevertheless, given that not one of the mothers and only 10% of the fathers in shared-caregiving families thought that fathers do not have the ability to be caregivers, there is a strong argument to be made that these fathers were perceived as being competent.

It is obvious from these analyses that there are significant family-type differences in beliefs about parental roles in line with the hypotheses outlined above. Indeed, the differences between caregiving and traditional fathers are especially marked; caregiving fathers are very similar to mothers in their emphasis on social explanations for role differences. It is impossible to say, of course, whether the nontraditional life-style changed the beliefs or whether the life-style was a consequence of the beliefs. Clearly, further research is needed to examine this hypothesis in a more systematic manner.

Parental Roles and Masculinity, Femininity, and Androgyny

The hypothesis that there is likely to be a relationship between sex-role orientation and father involvement in child care represented the beginning of the current research program. It was argued (Russell, 1978) that involvement in child care—changing diapers, feeding, etc.—and the display of nurturant behavior are not associated with concepts of masculinity in western cultures (cf. Pleck & Sawyer, 1974). Support was found for this hypothesis in a study of traditional fathers: Fathers classified as androgynous on the Bem (1974) Sex-Role Inventory (BSRI) were found to be more involved in day-to-day care activities and play with their children than those classified as masculine. No relationships were found between mothers' sex-role classifications and their involvement in child care, or between sex-role and social class variables.

Similar findings might be expected for fathers in the present study, fathers who describe themselves in a less traditionally masculine way should be more likely to feel comfortable in a child-care role. The findings for mothers, however, might be expected to be different from those found previously in traditional families (Russell, 1978). Mothers in the shared-caregiving families are all employed and therefore are taking on a traditional male role. It might be expected, therefore, that these mothers, in comparison to traditional mothers, will be more likely to be androgynous and to score higher on the BSRI *masculinity* scale. The argument here about a relationship between sex-role orientation and family life-styles, of course, presents the same problem as those encountered in the previous section (i.e., it is difficult to ascertain what is causing what, whether the life-style is a consequence of sex-role orientation or, as Abrahams, Feldman, & Nash (1978) have argued, sex-role scores are a consequence of family life-styles). I will return to this issue again later.

1. A Comparison Between Shared-Caregiving and Traditional Families. Mean BSRI masculinity and femininity scores for parents in shared-caregiving and traditional families are shown in Table 6.3. Differences between the two groups of families are greatest for fathers' femininity and mothers' masculinity; both are higher in shared-caregiving families. T-tests revealed that the family-type difference in fathers' femininity scores is significant [$t(193) = 3.37, p < .01$], and the difference between mothers' masculinity approaches significance [$t(193) = 1.59, p < .10$].

Distribution of sex-role classifications for the two groups of families is presented in Table 6.4. The sex-role classifications: androgynous (high masculinity, high femininity); feminine (low masculinity, high femininity); masculine (high masculinity, low femininity); and undifferentiated (low masculinity, low femininity) were defined using the same medians as those employed by Russell et al. (1978). Compared to traditional families, significantly more mothers and fathers in the shared-caregiving group are androgynous (mothers: $Z = 4.7, p < .01$; fathers: $Z = 1.98, p < .05$), fewer mothers are feminine ($z = 4.8, p < .01$), and fewer fathers are masculine ($Z = 4.05, p < .01$). Furthermore, there were only *two* families in the shared-caregiving group for which there was a feminine

TABLE 6.3
Mean Masculinity and Femininity Scores for Shared-Caregiving
and Traditional Families

	Shared-Caregiving		Traditional	
	Mothers	*Fathers*	*Mothers*	*Fathers*
Masculinity	4.54	4.89	4.32	4.99
Femininity	5.01	4.75	4.92	4.46

TABLE 6.4
Sex-role Classifications for Shared-caregiving and Traditional Families

	Shared-caregiving		Traditional	
	Mothers	Fathers	Mothers	Fathers
Androgynous	44%	41%	23%	31%
Feminine	25%	16%	49%	12%
Masculine	16%	21%	9%	37%
Undifferentiated	15%	22%	18%	19%

mother/masculine father combination. Even so, 43% of shared-caregiving fathers were *not* high on the femininity scale, and 40% of shared-caregiving mothers were *not* high on the masculinity scale.

In my earlier study (Russell, 1978), fathers low on femininity married to women high on masculinity were found to participate more in child care than low-femininity fathers married to women low on masculinity. This relationship between mothers' masculinity and fathers' femininity might also be important here. It may be, for example, that given family financial difficulties, a sufficient mediational condition for a change in life-style might be that *either* parent be high on the opposite-sex sex-role scale. Table 6.5 shows the within-family relationship between mothers' masculinity scores and fathers' femininity scores (expressed as high and low in relation to the median). A chi-square test was carried out on these figures but was not significant ($X^2(2) = 1.93, p > .10$). Nevertheless, in 82% of families either the mother was high on masculinity or the father was high on femininity or both were high on the opposite-sex scale. Only in 18% of the families was *neither* parent high on the opposite-sex scale. These data obviously show a trend in the direction of there being a relationship between mothers' and fathers' scores, in agreement with the hypothesis outlined previously. Exploration of this hypothesis in future studies therefore appears necessary. Moreover, there is an urgent need for the development of conceptual models and analytical techniques to examine more closely *within*-family relationships like the one discussed here.

2. Sex-Role Differences Within Shared-Caregiving Families.   As was noted earlier, explanations given by parents for their changed life-styles could be grouped according to whether the change was seen as being *necessary,* or as being a matter of *choice.* Analyses were carried out to examine whether these two groups differed in their sex-role scores. It was predicted that those mothers and fathers who had chosen to change would score higher on the opposite-sex BSRI scales than those who hadn't chosen to change. Although not statistically significant, differences were evident, but not entirely in the predicted direction. Fathers who were caregivers by choice scored higher on the femininity scale

TABLE 6.5
Family Dyad Classifications for Fathers High and Low on Femininity
and Mothers High and Low on Masculinity

Mother's Masculinity	Father's Femininity	
	High	Low
High	42%	18%
Low	22%	18%

[4.93 versus 4.50; $t(31) = 1.66$, $p < .10$], as expected. The trend for mothers, however, was in the opposite direction from that predicted; when the change was by choice, mothers scored lower on the masculinity scale [4.39 versus 4.74; $t(31) = 1.4$, $p < .20$]. Despite being somewhat at variance with the predictions, these findings are consistent with data presented earlier showing that when the change was seen as being necessary mothers were more responsible for, or influential in the decision, and when parents said they had chosen their life-style, fathers were more influential. Thus, it may be that the critical factor in this analysis is whether or not the *person* had chosen to become involved in a radically different life-style. This possibility was examined and the data are presented in Table 6.6. This table shows a breakdown of scores on opposite-sex BSRI scales as a function of the person as being most influential in the decision to change. As can be seen from the table, the fathers' femininity is highest when he is the most influential, and the mothers' masculinity is highest when she is seen as the most influential. Although one-way analyses of variances did not show these differences to be significant (both F-values were approximately equal to 1.5) a trend is evident that warrants further investigation.

3. Limitations of Sex-Role Findings and Explanations.   Findings presented here are in apparent agreement with the initial hypothesis—mothers and fathers in shared-caregiving families scored higher than traditional parents on the

TABLE 6.6
Mean Femininity Scores for Fathers and Mean Masculinity Scores for
Mothers as a Function of the Person Perceived as Being Most
Influential in the Decision to Change Life-styles

	Person Most Influential in Decision to Change		
	Mother	Father	Joint
Father's femininity	4.53	4.91	4.89
Mother's masculinity	4.77	4.55	4.30

opposite-sex scales of the BSRI (i.e., fathers scored higher on femininity and mothers higher on masculinity). Despite this relatively strong support for the hypothesis that sex-role self-concepts mediate the change in family life-styles, there are several problems with this rather simplistic interpretation.

First, it was also found here that there is a complex interaction between sex roles, reasons given for change (especially family financial/employment situation), and the person seen as having more influence over the decision to change. It is unclear from the present analysis whether one of these variables should be given more status than another.

A second, related problem concerns the effect that life-styles might have on sex-role scores. The hypothesis put forward at the outset was that sex-role variables are antecedents of the change in life-styles; that the high levels of masculinity in mothers and femininity in fathers are instrumental in the decision to change. An alternative hypothesis, of course, is that life experiences *influence* sex-role self-concepts (Abrahams et al., 1978) and that any differences found in masculinity and femininity scores between family types simply reflect the different behaviors they perform on a day-to-day basis; that is, fathers are performing a more expressive role and mothers are performing a more instrumental role, and their sex-role self-concepts have changed as a consequence of this experience. Doubt is cast on this general explanation by the finding in the present study that the correlation between length of time in this life-style and fathers' femininity is minus .20—a relationship that is in the opposite direction from that that would be predicted from the life-experience hypothesis. It may be, however, that this type of analysis is too crude to provide an adequate test. Indeed, it is possible that changes in sex-role scores might be mediated by several factors: length of the experience; the degree of influence the person had in the decision to change; and the person's satisfaction with his or her new role. For example, a father who sees himself as being forced into the change in life-style and who is dissatisfied with the caregiving role might react in the opposite direction and overemphasize his "masculinity." Lack of adequate data prevented the exploration of this hypothesis here, but obviously it is one needing further investigation.

Perhaps further caution should be expressed about a simple sex-role interpretation of a shared-caregiving life-style when the present findings are compared with those of De Frain (1979) and Radin (1980). De Frain, in contrast to the present study, did not find any differences between the sex-role scores of his shared-role and random fathers. He did find, however, that shared-role mothers were significantly less feminine than a random sample of mothers. Even so, it is difficult to compare findings, as De Frain used a sex-role difference score. It is uncertain, therefore, whether his mothers were less feminine because of a lower femininity score or, in agreement with the present study, because their masculinity scores were higher.

Radin, in contrast with both the present study and De Frain's, did not find any differences in mothers' sex-role scores between her three family types—

mother-prime, intermediate, father-prime. In agreement with the present study, however, she did find differences in fathers' femininity scores. Fathers in traditional families (mother-prime) were found by Radin to score significantly lower on the femininity scale than fathers in her intermediate group in which fathers performed 41% of child-care tasks. Fathers in her primary caregiving group, however, did not score higher on the femininity scale; their scores were very similar to those of fathers in traditional families. Such a pattern of findings is difficult to explain, although it may be that an explanation can be found in the way that Radin has defined her groups. Although her father-prime group was performing relatively more of the child-care tasks, it may still be that in absolute terms, they are doing less than the intermediate group. Moreover, as was pointed out earlier, more precise data from both Radin's and De Frain's studies about the amount of time fathers spend on caregiving are needed before the present findings can be compared with theirs with any degree of certainty.

Summary

It seems there are many paths to the adoption of a family life-style in which fathers are caregivers. Factors found to be important were: family financial situation; the employment potential of parents, but more especially of mothers; flexibility in hours of employment; family characteristics; prior experiences with their children and knowledge about child care; beliefs about the roles of parents; and the sex-role self-concepts of parents. A complex interaction was also found among sex roles, family financial situation, and the person seen as being more influential in the decision to change family life-styles.

No simple explanation emerged here, and perhaps a single simple explanation is not possible given the diversity of the sample. It may be that in some families financial problems override all other factors; for others, financial problems might be a necessary precondition for change, but the change might be mediated by sex-role self-concepts and beliefs; for still others, beliefs about parental roles might provide the necessary and sufficient conditions for change (even to the extent of being critical in the decision to have only one or two children). Furthermore, the evidence reported here suggests that these variables might combine in different ways *within* families. Given a poor financial situation, for example, having *one* parent who rejects traditional beliefs about parental roles might be sufficient for change to occur.

The list of possible antecedents and mediators presented in this section is by no means complete. One major omission concerns the impact that the life-style itself has. It is possible that people might begin a life-style for one reason, but then continue in it for very different reasons. Indeed, several parents made this comment during their interview. One father, for example, said that they changed life-styles for financial reasons, but had continued beyond the point of financial necessity mainly because of the value they now placed on their shared-caregiving pattern and the improvement that had resulted in the father–child relationship. For others, continuing in the life-style might be dependent on the support they get from significant others and from social institutions. These issues concerning the impact of the nontraditional life-style are considered in the next section.

POSSIBLE CONSEQUENCES

One factor that emerged very strongly indeed from this study was the impact that changes in family patterns appeared to have on mothers and fathers, and on their relationships with significant others. This is not surprising, given that this life-style, and particularly the public involvement of men in the day-to-day care of children, represents a radical change in the culturally accepted family pattern. A shared-caregiving life-style, therefore, appears to have the characteristics of what has been termed a significant life event in the life-span development literature (Hultsch & Plemons, 1979). The aim of this section is to examine the impact of the nontraditional life-style through an analysis of mothers' and fathers' reactions and the reactions of significant others. This might be seen as a first step in defining the attributes of this particular event (Hultsch & Plemons, 1979) and form a basis for further investigation of the more precise impact that this life-style has on family development. Certainly, the data presented here can only be seen as exploratory and hypothesis generating.

Initial Reactions and Problems of Adjustment

The change in life-styles is likely to involve several different types of reactions and problems of adjustment. Especially salient for fathers might be: (1) their reaction to the physical aspects of the caregiving role—similar perhaps to that experienced by most mothers in their initial adjustment to the caregiving role; and (2) their own and others' reactions to the radical nature of their role change (i.e., reactions to a *male* taking on a role that is a rigidly defined female role).

The possible negative aspects of changing life-styles were assessed by asking parents a general question on what they disliked about their current life-style, and then what specific difficulties they felt had been experienced by fathers, mothers, and children.

   1. General Dislikes.   By far the commonest response by both fathers (42%) and mothers (48%) was that there was nothing that they really disliked about their life-style. Pressures on the husband–wife relationship was the next most common response, being reported by 20% of fathers and 18% of mothers. Two further major response categories emerged: loss of status and problems concerned with the father taking on the caregiving role (fathers: 28%; mothers: 6%); and mothers' loss of contact with their children (fathers: 6%; mothers: 30%). These general difficulties were also reflected in the specific difficulties reported by parents. Overall, however, parents appeared to experience more difficulties with their changed life-style than their children did.

2. Mothers. The most common difficulties experienced by mothers were: (1) lack of time and the rushed life-style—60% of mothers reported this, and 48% of fathers said they felt mothers experienced this difficulty; and (2) guilt feelings about leaving their children (mothers: 28%; fathers: 26%). Twenty-six percent of both mothers and fathers said that mothers had not experienced any major difficulties. Mothers and fathers, therefore, were in close agreement in indicating that mothers' difficulties were mainly associated with the physical and time demands of their role—or dual role as the case was in a significant number of families.

3. Fathers. Difficulties experienced by fathers centered on: (1) the demands—the constancy and boredom—associated with their full-time caregiving role (reported by 48% of fathers, and 50% of mothers reported fathers had experienced this difficulty); (2) lack of adult company (fathers: 14%; mothers: 10%); (3) coping with the exhaustion and emotional problems of the mother (fathers: 12%; mothers: 10%); (4) pressure from male peer group about their role change (fathers: 12%; mothers: 12%); and (5) tension related to financial matters (fathers: 10%; mothers: 4%). Twenty-eight percent of both mothers and fathers reported that fathers did not have any major difficulties with their role change.

4. Children. Seventy-six percent of fathers and 64% of mothers said that their children had not experienced any major problems with the change in family life-styles. A common response from parents was: "That suprised us," as most seemed to have expected some reaction from their children. Twenty-four percent of fathers and 20% of mothers said that their children experienced some minor difficulties in the initial stages (e.g., anxiety about mother leaving), and 6% of mothers felt that their children resented their change in life-style.

5. Families. In families in which both parents were employed, mothers and fathers experienced some problems that seemed to be peculiar to their life-styles. In these families, both parents had dual roles, and in many the return of one person from employment coincided with the others leaving. Parents especially felt the rush and constant demands on their time, the lack of time they had with each other, and the lack of personal free time.

Analyses were also carried out to investigate the hypothesis that fathers' and mothers' experiences of difficulties would be related to reasons given for changing life-styles and fathers' femininity and mothers' masculinity. A relationship was found with reasons for changing, but not with sex roles. Of the mothers and fathers who said they hadn't experienced any major difficulties, 80% and 78%, respectively, were from families in which the change was reportedly of their own choosing. In comparison, of those who said they had experienced difficulties, only 44% of both mothers and fathers had reported that the change was of their own choosing. This relationship between experienced difficulties and reasons for changing was statistically significant for mothers [$X^2(1) = 4.5$, $p < .05$], and approached significance for fathers [$X^2(1) = 3.2$, $p < .10$].

In terms of previous sex-role findings, it was predicted that those parents who experienced less difficulty with their role changes would also be more likely to score higher on the opposite-sex scale of the BSRI. Support was not found for this hypothesis. The mean femininity score for fathers who hadn't experienced any difficulty was 4.75, and the mean masculinity score for mothers in this group was 4.54, the same means as those for the group who had experienced difficulties. It may be, however, that there is a relationship between these variables, but that the present analysis, using a broad distinction between difficulties experienced versus not experienced, is too crude. Future analyses might examine the relationship between sex-role variables and the *degree of difficulty* experienced.

Perceived Advantages

Although the change in life-styles brought with it many problems, the majority of parents were also very positive about it. Parents' perceptions of the advantages of their life-styles were assessed by a general question asking what they liked about their current life-style, and by a series of specific questions asking about the advantages for parents and children.

1. General Advantages.   The most common response to this question was that the life-style change had meant a strengthening of family relationships (fathers: 40%; mothers: 40%). Both parents also felt that they had gained considerably at the personal level (fathers: 28%; mothers: 44%). This type of response was especially strong for mothers who felt very positive about the changes in self-esteem brought about by their returning to employment. Other major response categories were: financial gains (fathers: 36%; mothers: 24%) and greater equality in marital and parental roles (fathers: 12%; mothers: 16%).

2. Mothers.   The major advantages seen for mothers were: increased mental stimulation as a result of participating in work outside the home (reported by 44% of mothers and 28% of fathers); greater independence (mothers: 38%; fathers: 36%); job satisfaction (mothers: 40%; fathers: 30%); increased self-esteem (mothers: 22%; fathers: 20%); and satisfaction derived from a career (mothers: 18%; fathers: 18%).

3. Fathers.   An improved father–child relationship was by far the most commonly mentioned advantage—this was reported by 70% of fathers and 60% of mothers. Other major responses were: greater understanding of children and what is involved in bringing them up (fathers: 26%; mothers: 24%); greater awareness of mother/housewife role (fathers: 20%; mothers: 20%); and freedom from career pressures (fathers: 26%; mothers: 20%).

4. Children.   Both mothers and fathers saw the advantages for children as either a closer father–child relationship (fathers: 64%; mothers: 60%) or an improved relationship with both parents (fathers: 34%; mothers: 30%).

Changes in Family Relationships

1. Husband–Wife.   Changes in marital relationships were seen as occurring on four dimensions: less interaction/less time together (fathers: 38%; mothers: 34%); increased tension and conflict (fathers: 20%; mothers: 18%); an overall improvement in relations brought about primarily by the greater awareness each parent now had of the demands of employment and caregiving roles (fathers: 22%; mothers: 28%); and a greater equality in husband–wife relations (fathers: 16%; mothers: 18%). Another significant response noted here involved the process of adjustment in the marital relationship. Many ($N = 26$) couples reported that they experienced a period of heightened conflict during the first few months, but that these issues were gradually resolved. Most of these conflicts revolved around the question of who would do what, or criticisms of the way in which one person carried out tasks that were previously the domain of the other person (e.g., mothers criticising fathers' standards of housework).

2. Father–Child.   These responses paralleled those mentioned in the foregoing; the most significant change was an improvement in father–child relationships. Seventy-four percent of fathers and 66% of mothers felt that fathers had become much closer to their children and that they now had a very strong bond with them. The next most common response (fathers: 32%; mothers: 22%) was that fathers had a more realistic relationship with their children, that children now saw both sides of *both* parents. Finally, there was a view that fathers had a better understanding of children and their day-to-day needs (fathers: 28%; mothers: 26%). *All* fathers said their relationship had changed in some way and most were very enthusiastic about this change.

3. Mother–Child.   The most common response was that there was no change in mother–child relationships (mothers: 26%; fathers: 34%). On the other hand, many parents felt that the mother–child relationship was not as close as it had been (mothers: 28%; fathers: 28%). Other responses were: Mother had become more tolerant (mothers: 32%; fathers: 26%); and that some mothers tried to overcompensate, because of the guilt they felt about leaving their children (mothers: 10%; fathers: 4%).

Reactions of Significant Others

The degree of support given by significant others might play a critical role in the maintenance of this type of alternative life-style. The support that parents felt they had was assessed by a series of questions concerning the reactions of others in general; and those of relatives, close friends, neighbors, and the people parents worked with. There were few differences in responses between mothers and fathers and so their responses have been combined.

1. General Reactions.   Forty-two percent of parents felt that reactions by and large had been positive, and 34% felt that reactions had been primarily negative. Thirty percent of families also felt that there had been a specific positive response directed towards fathers, an ''Oh, isn't he marvelous—my husband wouldn't do that,'' type of reaction, and 18% of families thought that people had difficulty understanding their life-styles and why they would want to do it (incomprehension and disbelief).

2. Relatives.   It seems that most relatives did not exactly approve of a shared-caregiving life-style. Mainly negative reactions were reported by 42% of families, mainly positive reactions by 34%, and the remaining 24% reported both positive and negative reactions (e.g., they felt the mothers' relatives were supportive but the fathers' weren't). The most commonly expressed negative reactions from relatives concerned the children and the mother; some felt that it was not good for the children to have their father and not their mother care for them, whereas some felt that the mother was not a 'good mother', that she should not leave her children to go out to work.

3. Close Friends, Neighbors, and Workmates.   An inspection of these responses revealed that the sex of the neighbor or friend was an important factor, and so responses were divided into male and female reactions. Female friends and neighbors seemed more supportive than male friends and neighbors. In 72% of families it was reported that female friends were generally positive, but only 48% felt that male friends were positive in their reactions. The same kind of sex breakdown occurred in the reported reactions of people the parents worked with. Female workmates were reported to be positive by 74% of families, whereas only 42% of male workmates were. Men especially felt the negative reactions of other men who saw them as being a ''bit funny,'' ''a bit of a woman,'' ''under the thumb,'' and also as being ''bludgers'' (not doing an honest day's work). Some of the fathers were also sceptical about how deep womens' positive reactions were. One father reported being described as a ''good baby-sitter,'' which he felt did not really accord him equal status with the child's mother. Others reported that they felt some women were threatened and were not accepting of them in social groups in the neighborhood or at school, playgrounds, etc., and two fathers reported that some mothers were reluctant to allow their children to play with their own children when they were at home. The feeling here was that the mothers thought the fathers were incompetent, that they couldn't trust their children in the care of a man. Such a reaction is consistent with many fears that people expressed about men's involvement in child care. The most extreme of these have been that fathers, because of their increase contact with children and their involvement in diaper changing and the like, will be more likely to abuse their babies, commit incest with their daughters, and produce homosexual sons (Russell, 1982).

Summary

A shared-caregiving life-style appeared to have considerable impact on families and their relationships with others. Fathers especially felt the demands of their child-care role, the negative reactions of significant others, especially their male peers, and the quite marked change—generally positive—in their relationships with their children. Mothers, on the other hand, appeared affected by the demands of their two roles—family and employment, the loss of contact with their children, the negative reactions of relatives, the positive reactions of their female friends, and the improvement in their personal well-being and satisfaction derived from their employment. Parents also experienced problems with their marital relationship, particularly in the early months.

Children appeared to be the least affected by the change. They were reported to have few problems and had the advantage of a closer relationship with their father. Most parents were surprised by the lack of reaction from their children—parents who were ideologically committed to their change, as well as parents who felt they were forced into changing life-styles.

At all levels of analysis then, both advantages and disadvantages were evident. Given the parents' mixed reactions and the varying degrees of support given by significant others, it might be expected that this type of life-style is somewhat fragile and that people are unlikely to continue in it for an extended period of time. The next section takes up this question of the possible fragility of the life-style by reporting on a follow-up study of part of the present sample.

CONTINUING IN A NONTRADITIONAL LIFE-STYLE: A TWO-YEAR FOLLOW-UP

Data collection for this study was carried out in two phases. The first involved an initial sample of 23 families recruited as part of a larger study of Australian families (Russell, 1982). The second phase has involved the recruitment of additional families (still ongoing) and a 2-year follow-up of the initial sample. The long-term goal of the study is to follow up all families 2 and 5 years after their initial interviews.

After having spent considerable time studying traditional families in which fathers had very little commitment to child care, my enthusiasm (personal, political, and academic) for finding a group of shared-caregiving families was difficult to disguise (Russell, 1979a). The 2-year follow-up, however, brought a sobering reality back to the project. Certainly, the initial study had shown that changing roles was not all plain sailing; most families had encountered one difficulty or another. But then, a high proportion were very strong in their view about the value of their life-styles and were very committed to them. A finding that many had reverted back to a more traditional life-style, therefore, was somewhat unexpected.

Family Patterns Two Years Later

Eighteen of the initial sample of 23 families were located and reinterviewed. Nine of these families had since changed back to a traditional life-style (although three mothers were in part-time or casual employment); in four families all children were now at school and both parents were employed full-time—mothers, however, were carrying out the majority of child-care tasks; one couple had separated—the mother took the children; and in *only four* families was the family pattern the same as when the first interview had been conducted. Of the families who had changed back to a traditional life-style, five said they did so for employment or economic reasons (e.g., father had found a job [3 families], father changed to a job that was more highly paid), one because of a pregnancy, and three because the father was dissatisfied—he had had enough. In the original interview, six of the nine families had given economic necessity as their major reason for adopting a nontraditional life-style. Two of the nine, however, had said that they changed because of their strong beliefs about sharing child-care responsibilities. Indeed, these were two of the most committed families! Both, though, were better off financially *after* they returned to a traditional life-style. Thus, financial considerations appear to be very important both in the decision to change to a nontraditional pattern *and* the decision to revert to a traditional one. A final note on these nine families: They were all families who had said previously that they experienced problems with shared caregiving.

Fathers' femininity and mothers' masculinity scores (as assessed during the initial interview) were also examined for those who had changed back, to explore the hypothesis that it is the more traditional masculine fathers and feminine mothers who are more likely to revert to a traditional family life-style. The mean fathers' femininity score was 4.55 and the mean mothers' masculinity score was 4.57. The differences between these means and those for the other 14 in the sample did not approach significance. Subject numbers are small, however, and further studies are needed to examine more closely the hypothesis that sex-role variables mediate changes back to a traditional family pattern.

The number of families who continued in the life-style, of course, is too small for any meaningful conclusions to be drawn. Two were professional families and two were traditional working class. The former two had chosen to adopt their life-style, whereas, the latter two had adopted their life-style for financial reasons. Three of the fathers were very committed to their caregiving role whereas one wasn't. An understanding of why these families and not others continue is crucial to the question of the antecedents and consequences of this life-style. Do these families, for example, have stronger support from significant others, or is it the change in father–child relationships that maintains this pattern? These and other questions will be taken up in future stages of this project when other families are followed up.

A Retrospective View of a Nontraditional Life-style

Parents who were reinterviewed were again asked questions about their perceptions of the advantages and disadvantages of fathers being caregivers, and about the impact they felt their nontraditional life-style had had. Although the responses were generally consistent with those noted earlier, parents, and more especially mothers, who had changed back were less convinced now about the advantages.

The overwhelming majority of parents in the once nontraditional families (93%) still saw the major benefit for fathers and children as being improved father–child relationship. Fathers thought they had also gained personally through their increased understanding of the role of caregiver and the demands of children, and that this had had an impact on their personal development. Five of the nine recidivists were strong in their views that family relationships were better now in comparison to their memories of life before adopting a nontraditional life-style. Fathers were reported to "help out" more too, compared to the period prior to their adopting a shared-caregiving lifestyle.

Fathers' increased understanding of the caregiving role was also seen as a major gain for mothers; they felt this helped them to cope with the demands of the role and had brought a greater equality to their relationships. The other major advantages mothers thought were: their increased self-esteem and fulfillment derived from their employment; and their reduced child-care load. Mothers who had changed back, however, did not seem to be as positive about their previous life-styles. Although four said they would prefer the traditional life-style, they also said their experience had been valuable and that they wouldn't trade it. The other five said that there weren't any significant advantages for them at all. A common response from these was that their current life-style was better for mothers because it was less rushed and more relaxed, and that the mother–child relationship was now stronger. All these mothers came from families in which the initial change was related to economic necessity, so it may be that this type of response is not typical of shared-caregiving families. The study of additional families who have changed back should shed further light on the exact nature of the family characteristics and/or employment patterns that might mediate responses of this type.

The major disadvantages fathers saw for their nontraditional life-style centered on the nature of the caregiving role—the constancy, boredom, and lack of adult company; and the lack of support and criticism they received from significant others. For three fathers constant questioning by their male peers about their lack of employment seemed to be a significant factor in their decision to change back. It is also interesting to note here that fathers who were in a career framework, and who returned to employment, said that their period out of employment hadn't had a noticeable effect on employment—something they had worried about.

SUMMARY AND CONCLUSIONS

The present study is best interpreted as a *first* attempt at describing and defining some of the possible antecedents and consequences of one type of nontraditional two-parent family pattern—a pattern that involves fathers and mothers sharing the care of their children. The aim of this section is to draw out the limitations of the study and discuss possible directions for future research.

Defining a Nontraditional Life-Style

If the consequences of nontraditional family patterns involving fathers as caregivers are to be fully understood then more precise data are needed on the day-to-day life-styles of such families. It seems insufficient simply to classify them in terms of the relative amounts of caregiving performed by each parent (De Frain, 1979: Radin, 1980), or their employment structure. Findings presented here and elsewhere (Russell, 1982) show that regardless of what the father does when the mother is not at work (i.e., whether he is employed or not), most mothers "take over" when they are at home. It is uncertain, however, whether mothers also take over other domestic tasks (e.g., cooking), as data were not collected on divisions of labor for all household work. Future studies will need to look at general domestic tasks as well as caregiving tasks to ascertain the full extent of changes in divisions of labor for family work.

Although rejected as an important variable in this first exploratory study, employment patterns might be critical for out understanding of some aspects of this type of lifestyle, in particular, why some people continue and others don't. It may be, for example, that a shared-caregiving life-style based on dual employment is more likely to be maintained than one based on the reversal of employment roles. This latter type of life-style represents a more radical change in family roles than the former, and therefore the personal and social pressures experienced by parents in these families might be greater.

Future studies could also attempt to seek out families in which the change in caregiving roles is more extreme. In five families in the present sample, fathers performed 65% of caregiving tasks, and all were unemployed and very committed to the caregiving role. It may be that this is a special group similar to those described by Levine (1976), and quite distinct from the rest of the sample. And, perhaps it is only these families who will differ significantly from nontraditional families on child development variables.

Antecedents

Although several possible antecedents and mediating variables emerged, it is difficult at this stage of the research to sort out the relative importance of each of them. If stretched, perhaps an economic argument could be used to explain all the changes in life-styles. All but eight of the families were better off financially after their change, and in the follow-up study economic factors were again found to be important in those families who had changed back to a traditional life-style. It is difficult to decide, however, just how much emphasis should be placed on this economic gain. All two-parent families would realize a substantial gain if both parents were employed. Despite this, there are, at least in Australia, few families with preschool-aged children in which both parents are employed (approximately 25%), and even fewer still in which fathers take on a significant caregiving role when both parents are employed. To what extent this is due to people not really having a choice because of the structure of society (e.g., rigidity of employment structure), or to personal characteristics of the people involved, is difficult to untangle here. Although most of the families in this sample had a degree of job flexibility, it was also the case that many had changed their jobs or work hours or had modified their career aspirations to accommodate their present family life-style. Nevertheless, it does seem clear that greater availability of job flexibility would at least enable more people to exercise choice. Whether or not those with job flexibility do choose to share child-care responsibilities, however, is a question that needs to be investigated.

Other variables that seemed important here were: parental explanations of their changed life-styles, especially whether the change was seen as an economic necessity or whether it was considered to be a personal choice—this is probably the most critical of the variables isolated here and one that needs to be explored in more depth in future studies; family characteristics; previous experiences with their children; beliefs about the roles of mothers and fathers; and sex-role variables.

The finding that these families have fewer and older children is consistent with previous studies that have found that families in which mothers are employed are smaller and have older children (Hoffman & Nye, 1974). Thus, as was suggested earlier alternative child-care arrangements are most likely to occur when child-care demands are reduced, and when there is less conflict with cultural beliefs such as: "breast-feeding is important" and "young babies need their mothers."

Whether or not there are specific personal characteristics that mediate the change in life-styles, however, is a very open question, and one for which it will be difficult to find an answer given the diverse nature of this particular sample. Some support was found for the hypothesis that prior experiences are important—this group of families had a higher proportion of fathers who had attended the birth. With changing attitudes to childbirth and more fathers now attending it may be that this relationship will not emerge as clearly in future studies. If the importance of this variable is to be examined further, therefore, it will be necessary to collect specific information about a fathers' *degree of involvement* in the birth process and the early care of his child, as well as data on his competence and confidence in performing caregiving tasks. The collection of such data, however, presents other problems. Given that this family pattern is rare, and that it usually only begins to emerge when children are older, it is most likely that these data will have to be retrospective, thus presenting serious problems of interpretation. Moreover, it may be that involvement at this early stage is not in itself a cause of father involvement, but simply an indication of a father's commitment to his role.

Many of the problems of interpretation, of course, would be solved if it were possible to obtain measures on critical variables *before* (cf. Lamb, Frodi, Hwang, & Frodi, Chapter 5, this volume), and at various times *after* people have changed their life-styles. Data of this type would be especially helpful in trying to sort out the importance of beliefs about parental roles and sex-role variables. In the present study, it is these two variables in particular for which it was impossible to decide whether they were antecedents or consequences. Data collected at various times before and after the change would also help to interpret the complex interaction found here among sex-role variables, explanations parents gave for changing life-styles, and the person seen as being the most influential in the decision to change. Hopefully, with the expansion of the present sample and the planned 2- and 5-year follow-ups, some progress will be made on these questions.

The study of shared-caregiving families, therefore, while providing a more realistic framework for the study of sex-role behavior, raises more questions than it answers. Although this line of research does not lend itself easily to investigation under highly controlled laboratory conditions, it illustrates very vividly the complexity of sex-role behavior, a complexity that has been ignored in most psychological studies.

Consequences

One of the major limitations of the present study is its emphasis on self-report and open-ended questions. Although it can be argued that such an approach is necessary in the early stages of the investigation of a previously unstudied phenomenon, it does limit quite severely the conclusions that can be drawn. Nevertheless, several directions for future research have emerged from parents' descriptions of the impact that this life-style has.

All of the families studied here had at one time conformed to traditional family roles, with fathers being employed and mothers at home. Their behavior as currently reported, involved a dramatically different set of experiences. As a consequence of these experiences mothers and fathers reported changes in themselves (e.g., mothers' increased self-esteem); attitudes (e.g., fathers' attitudes to the caregiving role); relationships within the family (e.g., fathers' reportedly improved relationships with their children); and their relationships with significant others (e.g., lack of support given to fathers by members of their male peer group). The long-term effects these changes might have on personal and family development, their subsequent life experiences, and their reactions to other life situations, should prove fruitful areas for future research. Support is given to this proposal by the findings from the 2-year follow-up of families who had returned to a traditional life-style. It was reported that the shared-caregiving experience had especially affected fathers' understanding of, and involvement in child-care tasks, and their relationship with their children.

Given the consistency and strength of the report of a change in the father–child relationship, it seems especially important to investigate this in a more direct way. Studies would need to focus both on the child's attachment to the father, and the father's attachment to the child. It was this latter aspect of the relationship that emerged so strongly here. Fathers reported they felt a much closer bond with their children. Many marvelled at this, saying that they could never have anticipated how important this would become to them. Studies to investigate this possible effect, of course, are difficult to design. Again, there are quite severe problems in obtaining before and after measures. Designs, therefore, will have to rely on comparisons between caregiving fathers, traditional fathers, traditional mothers, and employed mothers (cf. Lamb et al., Chapter 5).

Because the focus of this investigation has been on reported behavior, very little can be concluded about styles of parent–child interaction. Even so, there are several points that can be made. The first concerns the content of play. Fathers in shared-caregiving families, in comparison to fathers in traditional families, were more involved in indoor, conventional, cognitive, and creative play. These data, then, like the observational data of Field (1978) on fathers who are primary caregivers, suggest that fathers who have a major caregiving role adopt a style of interaction that is more similar to that found for mothers in traditional families. What is needed now are observational data to investigate further this finding and to explore in more depth the hypothesis that style of parent–child interaction has a strong situational component. Data are also needed to investigate whether this change in roles also results in a greater similarity between mothers and fathers in their socialization practices, and whether in turn this has an effect on the development of boys and girls in these families in comparison with children in traditional families.

The second point is that in contrast with traditional families, children in shared-caregiving families have much more contact alone with their fathers. Data from recent father studies (Clarke-Stewart, 1978; Lamb, 1979) suggest that parent–child interactions differ according to whether the parents are observed together or separately. We might expect, therefore, that patterns of parent–child interaction and socialization practices in these shared-caregiving families will be very different from those in traditional families where the normative pattern is one of children mainly experiencing mothers alone and mothers and fathers together. Furthermore, this also means there are quite marked differences between the two family types in terms of the day-to-day parental role models experienced by the children. Observational studies are needed to explore these hypotheses in a more systematic way.

Children's spending more time alone with their fathers might also have an indirect effect on socialization. Given the negative reactions by others to this lifestyle, it may be that caregiving fathers do not engage in social interaction outside the home as frequently as mothers normally do. And, perhaps they do not develop social networks with other parents—mainly mothers—in their neighborhood, meaning that there would be a reduction in their child's interactions with other adults and other children (Cochran & Brassard, 1979).

The more extreme cultural reaction in Australia to changing child-care roles to have fathers more involved includes the possible adverse effects on the child, specifically, child abuse, incest between fathers and daughters, and an increase in homosexuality. Clearly, data are not available to address these reactions apart from Radin's (1980) finding that children in families in which the father is the primary caregiver were no different in their sex-role identities from children in traditional families. In addition, as has already been noted, parents in the present study—both those who were very strongly committed to shared child-care roles and those who had changed for economic reasons—were surprised by the lack of reaction from their children. Furthermore, many appeared disconcerted by the absence of a reaction. Indeed, given the multiplicity of factors that contribute to a child's development, and the *combination of roles* by both parents in this sample, major differences in child development outcomes perhaps should not be expected.

Summary

Although the overwhelming majority of Australian fathers do not share caregiving responsibilities, a small minority do. The present interview study involved 50 two-parent families in which fathers had the major or equal responsibility for the day-to-day care of their children. Mothers were employed in all families; fathers were employed in two-thirds of them. Half of the families said they had adopted their life-styles because of economic necessity and half because they wanted to. In comparison to traditional families, these families were more likely to have:

mothers and fathers with higher education levels; mothers with higher status occupations; fewer and older children; one parent who had some flexibility in employment; mothers who were higher on the masculine subscale and fathers higher on the feminine subscale of Bem's (1974) Sex Role Inventory. Differences were also found between the two family types for the quantity and content of parent–child interactions.

This study also investigated parents' assessments of the impact that their life-styles had on themselves and others. The most commonly reported difficulties were: mothers—the physical demands of the life-style, particularly the rush and exhaustion, and their guilt about leaving their children, fathers—adjusting to the constant demands of the caregiving role, and the criticisms of their male peer group. Overall, however, nearly 30% of parents did not report any difficulties for themselves, and 70% said that their children hadn't experienced any difficulties either. The major advantages reported were: mothers—increased independence, mental stimulation, self-esteem, and job satisfaction; fathers and children—the greatly improved father–child relationship. Changes were also reported in: husband–wife relationships—less time spent together, more tension, and greater equality; mother–child relationships—not as close, and greater tolerance. Only 30% of relatives, close friends, and neighbors were seen by parents as being totally supportive of their nontraditional life-styles. Overall, however, women were seen as being more supportive than men.

A 2-year follow-up of 18 of these families revealed that nine had since adopted a traditional family life-style and that in only four families were the life-styles the same as when they were first interviewed. Those who had reverted to a traditional life-style were less convinced now about the advantages of their previous life-styles, particularly for mothers. The major benefits they now saw were for the father–child relationship (much closer) and the husband–wife relationship (fathers were now more likely to 'help out').

Future research is especially needed to investigate the possible antecedents of these life-styles, focusing on factors associated with family finances, employment, and the personal characteristics of the parent—in particular, their previous experiences, their beliefs about parental roles, sex-role variables and other personality variables. Research is also needed to examine the possible consequences of the life-style, especially changes in the father–child relationship, the personal effects on fathers and mothers and their development, socialization practices, and developmental outcomes for the children.

ACKNOWLEDGMENTS

This study was supported by grants from Macquarie University and the Australian Research Grants Commission. The author wishes to acknowledge the assistance of Sue Tindale and Judy French in the collection and analysis of data.

REFERENCES

Abrahams, B., Feldman, S. S., & Nash, S. C. Sex-role self-concept and sex-role attitudes: Enduring personality characteristics, or adaptations to changing life situations? *Developmental Psychology,* 1978, *14,* 393-400.

Bailyn, L. Accommodation of work to family. In R. Rapoport & R. N. Rapoport (Eds.) *Working Couples.* St. Lucia, Australia: Queensland University Press, 1978.

Bem, S. L. The measurement of psychological androgyny. *Journal of Consulting and Clinical Psychology,* 1974, *42,* 155-162.

Bem, S. L. Theory and measurement of androgyny: A reply to the Pedhazur-Tetenbaum and Locksley-Colton critiques. *Journal of Personality and Social Psychology,* 1979, *37,* 1047-1054.

Bem, S. L., & Lenney, E. Sex typing and the avoidance of cross-sex behavior. *Journal of Personality and Social Psychology,* 1976, *33,* 48-54.

Bem, S. L., Martyna, W., & Watson, C. Sex typing and androgyny: Further explorations of the expressive domain. *Journal of Personality and Social Psychology,* 1976, *34,* 1016-1023.

Clarke-Stewart, K. A. And daddy makes three: The father's impact on mother and young child. *Child Development,* 1978, *49,* 466-478.

Cochran, M. M., & Brassard, J. A. Child development and personal social networks. *Child Development,* 1979, *50,* 601-616.

Congalton, A. A. *Status and prestige in Australia—studies of Australian society.* Melbourne: Cheshire, 1969.

De Frain, J. Androgynous parents tell who they are and what they need. *The Family Co-ordinator,* 1979, 237-243.

Field, T. Interaction behaviours of primary versus secondary caretaker fathers. *Developmental Psychology.* 1978, *14,* 183-184.

Gutmann, D. Parenthood: A key to the comparative study of the life cycle. In N. Datan & L. H. Ginsberg (Eds.), *Life-span developmental psychology: Normative life crisis.* New York: Academic Press, 1975.

Hill, R., & Mattessich, P. Family development theory and life-span development. In P. B. Baltes & O. G. Brim, Jr. (Eds.), *Life-span development and behavior* (Vol. 2) New York: Academic Press, 1979.

Hoffman, L. W., & Nye, F. I. (Eds.). *Working mothers.* San Francisco: Jossey-Bass, 1974.

Hultsch, D. F., & Plemons, J. K. Life events and life-span development. In P. B. Baltes & O. G. Brim (Eds.), *Life-span development and behaviour* (Vol. 2), New York: Academic Press, 1979.

Lamb, M. E. Interactions between 8-month-old children and their fathers and mothers. In M. E. Lamb (Ed.), *The Role of the father in child development.* New York: Wiley, 1976.

Lamb, M. E. The effects of the social context on dyadic social interaction. In M. E. Lamb, S. J. Suomi, & G. R. Stephenson (Eds.), *Social interaction analysis.* Madison, Wis.: University of Wisconsin Press, 1979.

Levine, J. A. *Who will raise the children? New options for fathers (and mothers).* New York: Bantam, 1976.

Parke, R. D. Parent–infant interaction: Progress, paradigms, and problems. In G. P. Sackett & H. C. Haywood (Eds.), *Application of observational–ethological methods to the study of mental retardation.* Baltimore: University Park, 1978.

Pleck, J., & Sawyer, J. (Eds.). *Men and masculinity.* Englewood Cliffs, N.J.: Prentice-Hall, 1974.

Radin, N. *Childrearing fathers in intact families: An exploration of some antecedents and consequences.* Paper presented to a study group on "The role of the father in child development, social policy, and the law," University of Haifa, Haifa, Israel, July 1980.

Russell, G. The father role and its relation to masculinity, femininity, and androgyny. *Child Development,* 1978, *49,* 1174-1181.

Russell, G. *Fathers as caregivers: "They could . . . if they had to."* Paper presented to the 49th Congress of ANZAAS, Auckland, New Zealand, 1979. (a)

Russell, G. *The role of fathers in child development—An Australian perspective.* Paper presented to the 15th National Conference of the Australian Preschool Association, Sydney, 1979. (b)

Russell, G. *The changing role of fathers.* St. Lucia, Australia: Queensland University Press, 1982.

Russell, G., Antill, J., & Cunningham, J. The measurement of masculinity, femininity, and androgyny: A reply to Rowland (1977). *Australian Psychologist,* 1978, *13,* 41-50.

Tucker, N. John Bowlby on latchkey kids. *Psychology Today,* 1976, *2*(11), 37-41.

7

Primary Caregiving and Role-Sharing Fathers

Norma Radin
The University of Michigan

Fathers who are primary caregivers in intact families are rare. Although ample literature testifies to the fact that fathers are becoming increasingly involved in childrearing in the United States (Glick, 1978; Pleck, 1979; Smith & Reid, 1980), and an increasing number of men are rearing children as single parents through the awarding of custody or the death or desertion of the wife (Gersick, 1979; Glick, 1979; Mendes, 1976; Santrock & Warshak, 1979), there is virtually no evidence that an increasing number of men have chosen to become primary caregivers of youngsters while their wives work or attend school, nor are there clues about the number of such families. As Parke and Sawin (1980) have observed, in spite of trends supporting new roles for mothers and fathers, parental roles are still most commonly allocated in a traditional fashion. Published studies of such families are as rare as the men themselves, although there have been a few in recent years (Field, 1978; Levine, 1976; Russell, 1978). This is unfortunate, because fathers who serve as primary caregivers in two-parent families are invaluable to researchers. They provide the opportunity to test whether it is the male gender or the male role that accounts for the unique effects of fathers on children and for men's differential behavior with boys and girls. There has been much speculation about what would happen in such situations by researchers such as Hoffman (1977) and Lamb and Bronson (1980), but little hard data has been presented. The study reported here was undertaken in 1978 to shed some light on what does indeed occur to fathers, mothers, sons, and daughters when fathers take on the responsibility for washing, bathing, feeding, and caring for preschoolers while mothers leave home to work or attend school. In addition, I attempted to examine some of the personal characteristics and socialization experiences of the mothers and fathers that might have led them to adopt this nontraditional pattern of child rearing. The antecedents and conse-quences of paternal child rearing in two-parent families are not only significant for child development researchers and role theorists, as has been suggested, but also for members of the helping professions who are called upon to counsel couples considering or presently engaged in partial role reversal.

In spite of the scarcity of empirical data about paternal child rearing in intact families, various theories and concepts do provide a foundation for generating predictions about possible antecedents and consequences of this form of child care. Regarding antecedents, investigations focused on young adults' perceptions of their parents have suggested some socialization variables that might be rele-vant. Reuter and Biller (1973) concluded after such a study that males who have adequate opportunities to observe nurturant fathers will imitate their behaviors; nonnurturant or unavailable fathers may be inadequate models. These views are consonant with numerous investigations linking paternal warmth and the son's identification with his father (Kagan, 1958; Payne & Mussen, 1956; Radin, 1972; Sears, 1953). Other studies (Biller, 1969; Biller & Borstelman, 1967; Hetherington, 1965; Hetherington & Frankie, 1967; Mussen & Rutherford, 1963) have stressed the relationship between filial masculinity and the father's role as decision maker and dominant member of the family. Based on the aforementioned literature, I hypothesized that men who chose to reject their traditional fathers as models would have fathers who were less available, less loving, and less powerful in decision making in the family than men playing the traditional paternal role. There is some slight support for this proposition. In a study of nontraditional families who were raising children in communes or in a social contract arrangement without marriage, it was found that "alternative life-stylers" viewed their early childhood as more unhappy than the control group of traditional parents (Eiduson & Weisner, 1976). More recently, a study of androgynous parents was conducted by De Frain (1979) who asked these mothers and fathers about the factors in their childhood or adult life that prepared them for role sharing. The most important factor proved to be role models, both positive and negative, in the home. Because the majority of the men and women described their parents as traditional, the inference can be drawn that most of their parents provided negative models. The one specific example cited by De Frain was an androgynous parent who attributed the current life-style to "father chauvinistic antics." Finally, a study of men who sought custody of their chil-dren concluded that these men were disappointed with their own fathers' emo-tional distance from them when they were children and intended to act differently in their own father–child relationships (Gersick, 1979).

As far as mothers are concerned, the literature, as reviewed by Hoffman (1977), strongly indicates that girls whose mothers were employed tended to be more nontraditional in their own views about sex roles. Social learning theory would also predict that employed mothers would tend to have daughters who worked while in the mother role. Thus, it could be hypothesized that more nontraditional than traditional wives would have mothers who worked while their children were young.

It is unclear whether sex-role orientations propel men or women into roles antithetical to the traditional stereotypes. Russell (1978, 1980, this volume), who found role-sharing fathers more effeminate than their traditional peers, suggested that sex-role self-concepts, as reflected in the Bem Sex Role Inventory, influences lifestyle. Abrahams, Feldman, and Nash (1978), on the other hand, concluded that sex-role orientations change as individuals move through the life cycle; specifically, that discrete life situations call for more or less stereotypical masculine and feminine behavior and that the attributions people make about their own sex-role self-concepts tend to converge with these role demands. Hyde and Phillis (1979), focusing on androgyny scores, agreed that sex-role orientations change in keeping with sex-relevant life experiences as individuals age from 13 to 86, but the direction of the change was different from that suggested by Abrahams et al. Thus, the sex-role orientations of parents who partially reverse child-care roles may be expected to differ from those of traditional parents, but whether these orientations can be viewed as antecedents of the family pattern is questionable.

Regarding the effects of nontraditional child rearing on youngsters, socialization theory suggests that the child's sex-role identification would be among the characteristics most likely to be influenced by parental role reversal. Predictions are difficult, however, because some perspectives suggest that there may be no effects on this aspect of development. Mussen and Distler (1960) and Kagan (1958), from a social learning perspective, have postulated that for a boy to adopt a masculine identity (defined stereotypically), his father must be nurturant and powerful. Because traditional female tasks are popularly considered to have low status, the boy may not take on the typical male orientation when his father is the prime caregiver. Further, Bronfenbrenner (1958) and Biller and Borstelman (1967) suggested that paternal engagement in housewives' tasks fosters a feminine identification in sons. However, Maccoby and Jacklin (1974) and Kohlberg (1966), with a more cognitive orientation, concluded that the young child is a self-socializer in the area of sex identity; parental behavior appears to be relatively unimportant in the process. Money and Ehrhardt's research (Pleck, 1975) similarly suggests that nontraditional parental roles will have little effect. These researchers found that the variable most influential in establishing a youngster's gender identity is the parents' perception of the child's sex. This will determine whether they respond to the youngster as a male or female, which in turn will determine, in most cases by 2 years of age, whether the child has a masculine or feminine gender orientation. This has been referred to as the "closed gate" phenomenon (Money & Tucker, 1975). In view of these contradictory predictions, no hypothesis seems warranted.

Theoretical support for the view that paternal child rearing will affect the child's locus of control is indirect. Aldous' (1974) theory of role makers suggests certain personality predispositions that might be expected of individuals creating new roles in families. These include flexibility, interpersonal sensitivity, and some sense of controlling their own destiny. According to Aldous, creators of new roles must possess these qualities because role makers have to improvise their behaviors in the absence of normative guidelines. Empirical support for this proposition was found in a study of college women who were role innovators in the occupational domain. It was found that these students were more autonomous and more motivated by internally imposed demands than noninnovators (Tangri, 1972, p. 177). Similarly, nontraditional views of sex roles were found to be linked to internal locus of control in a study of women experiencing marital dissolution (Brown, Perry, & Harberg, 1977).

In view of the foregoing, it can be anticipated that role-making fathers who have some sense of controlling their own destiny will value autonomy, will model and reinforce evidence of internality in their children, and will allow the youngsters some control over their own destiny. The empirical literature indicates that parents who are nondirective and allow early independence have children with an internal locus of control (Loeb, 1975; Wichern & Nowicki, 1976). Thus, it can be hypothesized on several bases that children reared in nontraditional families will manifest more internality than their peers in traditional homes.

One can also speculate that fathers who become primary caregivers will seek to promote the cognitive growth of their daughters as well as their sons and aspire for careers for both sexes. Hoffman (1977) indicated that there were arguments that could be used both for and against the proposal. Men in general treat sons and daughters differentially, rearing sons for careers and advanced education, and girls for maternal and homemaking roles. Thus, the more fathers are involved in child care, the more differential treatment daughters may experience. Conversely, men who do become involved in child care may be different and/or may be changed by the experience in such a way that they do not treat sons and daughters differently. We cannot predict how child-rearing fathers will behave with girls, although Hoffman has predicted that they will differentiate less than normal. It is also possible that men who are primary caregivers may be less masculine in sex role orientation and aspire for careers and advanced education for neither sons nor daughters. Thus, no hypothesis regarding child-rearing fathers' efforts to stimulate the cognitive growth of their children can be generated with confidence.

Concerning perceptions of parental roles by children in families where fathers are primary caregivers, social learning theory suggests that youngsters will adopt the perceptions modeled in their homes. However, perceptions of paternal and maternal roles may be so closely linked to the child's sex-role identity that self-socialization or a fixed gender identity may be the more powerful variable involved, overriding the influence of parental behavior. Further, it has been suggested (Kohlberg, 1966; Meyer, 1980; Pleck, 1975), that preschool children have rather rigid stereotypic views of parental roles. In the light of the opposing theories, no predictions seem justified in this area.

As far as interpersonal sensitivity or empathy are concerned, although some Piagetians (Chandler & Greenspan, 1972) might disagree, it is likely that the empathetic model provided by a father sensitive to the child's needs will foster the preschooler's ability to decenter emotionally, particularly if the father also reinforces manifestations of this tendency in the child. On this basis, social learning theory (Bandura, 1972; Gewirtz & Stingle, 1968) suggests that children of nontraditional fathers would be more empathetic than those of traditional fathers. Because children tend to model the parent whom they most resemble (Kagan, 1958; Mischel, 1970), and there is evidence that girls model their mother's empathy (Barnett, King, Howard, & Dino, 1980), it is probable that the differences in empathy between traditional and nontraditional offspring will be more evident in boys than in girls.

Finally, to expand our limited knowledge of two-parent families in which men are the primary caregivers, the interrelationships among the various aspects of child care as performed by fathers, as well as parents' views of the disadvantages of the current arrangement and the reason for the wife's employment were explored. In addition, the relationship between some variables pertaining to the mothers' fathers and measures of paternal involvement in child rearing were examined.

SAMPLE

To control for as many extraneous variables as possible, the sample was restricted with respect to social class, age of child, and race. The sample consisted of 59 intact, middle-class families, 58 white and one Asian, with a child 3 to 6 years of age, except for one family with a child 32 months of age. There were 32 boys and 27 girls in the study and the parents all approved of the father's involvement in child care under the current arrangement. The family's social class was assessed using Hollingshead's (1970) Four-Factor Index of Social Status, which rates the employed father's education and occupation and the employed mother's occupation and education. The scores of the father and mother are averaged if both parents are working to obtain a family score but if only one member is working, the score of that individual constitutes the family score.

The average child's age was 54 months, the average father's age was 34 years, the length of time the average family had the current child-care arrangement was 35 months, and the average Hollingshead score for the fathers and families put both within the top classes in the Hollingshead schema. The children spent an average of 17 hours per week in a nursery, day-care center, or kindergarten. The average masculine and feminine scores for fathers on the Bem Sex Role Inventory (Bem, 1974) were within one standard deviation of the scores cited by Abrahams et al. (1978) in their investigation of traditional fathers. In addition, the average Bem *t*-score, reflecting essentially the difference between the feminine and masculine average scores, was within the "near masculine" range, as delineated by Bem and Watson (1976).

Participant families were sought through local newspaper articles, radio announcements, flyers left at nurseries and day-care centers, and notices posted at student housing centers asking for fathers involved in child care. The traditional families were recruited through contacts of project staff and friends of the contacts. The strategy resembled that used by Santrock and Warshak (1979), who studied children in the custody of their fathers. The sample, most of whom lived within 50 miles of Ann Arbor, was clearly self-selected. In the vast majority of cases, one of the parents phoned the project as a result of having heard about it. Families in which mothers were the primary caregivers and also worked more than 10 hours per week were excluded, as that population was to be investigated in the doctoral dissertation of a staff member of the project (Carlson, 1980).

PROCEDURE

Three appointments with the family were made. In the first, conducted in the home, the father was interviewed for approximately 1 hour in the child's presence with no one else present. The entire interview was audiotape-recorded. In the second interview, mothers were asked the same questions, either at home or at their place of employment, with no one else present. In the third session, again in the home, a series of tasks was administered to the child.

The measures administered to the child were: (1) Stanford Preschool Internal-External Scale (SPIES) (Mischel, Zeiss, & Zeiss, 1974), a measure of locus of control involving a choice between two responses; (2) the Stephens-Delys Test of Internality (Stephens & Delys, 1973), a locus-of-control test with open-ended questions for preschoolers; (3) The revised *It*-Scale (Biller, 1969; Brown, 1956), which assesses the child's sex-role orientation; (4) the Parent Role Perception Test (PRPT), a modification of the *It*-Scale developed for this project, which assesses the child's concept of the parent role. In this test, pictures of various household objects are shown, such as a washing machine, and the child is asked which parent uses each item; (5) a shortened version of The Kagan Parent Role Test, which asks questions such as "Who spanks the most, mothers or fathers?" to determine the qualities associated with each parent. It was developed by Kagan and Lemkin (1960); (6) Borke's Empathy Test (Borke, 1971), which assesses empathy in children through a series of short stories; (7) the Peabody Picture Vocabulary Test, a verbal test of intelligence, employed to be certain the child-rearing groups were equated for the children's intellectual abilities; and (8) the Ravens Coloured Progressive Matrices Test, a nonverbal intelligence test, also employed to be certain the groups were comparable with respect to children's cognitive abilities.

The parental interviews included some open-ended and some closed-ended questions designed to tap, among other things: (1) the parents' perceptions of their fathers' nurturance and availability (modification of the scale developed by Reuter and Biller (1973) was used to assess these perceptions); (2) the parents' perceptions of the power their fathers had relative to their mothers in decision making. The questions used to assess the dominance of the preschooler's grandfather were adapted from the items used by Price-Bonham (1976) and Blood and Wolfe (1960) to assess decision making and family power outcomes; (3) the parents' perceptions of their fathers' role in their socialization and physical care when they were under 10. (The items were adapted from those used by Gecas, 1976); (4) The parents' sex role orientation, which was assessed by the Bem Sex Role Inventory (Bem, 1974), which asks the respondents to indicate, on a 7-point scale, how well each of 60 adjectives, (e.g., sympathetic, ambitious) describes them. One-third of the items are masculine, one-third feminine, and one-third neutral; (5) the parents' long-term educational and career expectations for their preschooler and efforts to stimulate the child's intellectual growth. These were assessed by a shortened Cognitive Home Environment Scale (Radin & Sonquist, 1968), from which is obtained a total score and three factor scores (Educational Materials in the Home, Direct Teaching, and Future Expectations).

Initially, an effort was made to use the parent's own descriptions of their child-rearing practices to classify families into groups differing in the degree of paternal involvement, but it was found that many parents were uncertain to which category they belonged and it was clear that the parents, even those with much paternal involvement, did not classify themselves into mother-primary and father-primary caregiver groups. There were many gradations. It was therefore decided to divide the sample into thirds, so that high, medium, and low paternal involvement groups would be formed. In order to divide the sample in a meaningful way, a global index of father involvement in child rearing was computed a priori, on the basis of included responses to questions in five areas: (1) statements of father involvement in child care (e.g., rating on a 5-point scale); (2) father's responsibility for physical child care (e.g., feeding the children); (3) father's responsibility for socialization of the child (e.g., setting limits for the children's behavior); (4) father's involvement in decision making regarding the child (e.g., when the child should be disciplined); and (5) father's availability to the child (e.g., frequency with which the father was home during the week for lunch). The responses to these five components were totaled and labeled the Paternal Involvement in Child Care Index. The father's total involvement score was added to the mother's total involvement score for a grand total involvement score that formed a continuous variable. The top one-third (with 20 families) and bottom one-third (with 20 families) were labeled the Father Primary Caregiver Group and the Mother Primary Caregiver Group, respectively. The middle scores formed a group of 19 families labeled the Intermediate Group. The overall mean for the total father score was 40.6 and for the total mother score, 40.3, remarkably close in view of the fact that neither parent knew how the other had responded, nor how we were scoring their replies. There were 10 boys and 10 girls in the father-prime and mother-prime groups. In the intermediate group there were 12 boys and 7 girls. The groups formed were closely associated with both mothers' and father's global estimates of the percentage of time the father had primary responsibility for the children. For the father primary caregiver group, the mean percentage cited by the fathers was 58% and by mothers 56%. For the mother primary caregiver group, the mean percentage cited by fathers was 22% and by mother 23%. For the intermediate group it was 40.3% for fathers and 41.4% for mothers. Thus, the grand total involvement score seemed to be a valid measure on which to base the group assignment. It should be noted that the group labeled "intermediate" here resembles De Fain's (1979) androgynous families, in which fathers performed 46% of the child-caring tasks.

The same questions and scoring procedure used with parents were used to determine the parents' perceptions of their own fathers' role in child rearing when they were young, with one exception. The component "Statement of Involvement," when referring to the fathers in the sample, contained two components, a 5-point rating of the degree of paternal involvement and a global estimate of the respondent's view of the percentage of time the father had primary responsibility for the child when the youngster was not in a day-care facility, with a sitter, or asleep. For the fathers of the fathers and mothers in the study, only the former item was included. The variables pertaining to the grandfathers of the preschoolers will be referred to as "grandfather variables" in the rest of the chapter. The instrument and scoring procedures are described in greater detail elsewhere (Carlson, 1980; Radin, 1978).

To be certain there were no confounding differences between the father-primary caregiver group and mother-primary caregiver group, t-tests were employed to examine possible differences on the following variables: child's age, father's age, child's scores on the Peabody Picture Vocabulary Test, Total Score on the Ravens Coloured Progressive Matrices test, Hollingshead Family Score, Hollingshead Father Score, and the number of hours per week the child was in a nursery, day-care center, or school. In no case were there significant differences. In addition, there was no difference among groups in the percentage of children who had older male siblings. In the father-primary caregiver group, all the mothers worked or attended school on a full-time basis and all the fathers but one had some type of part-time job or attended school; in the mother-primary caregiver group none of the mothers worked more than 10 hours per week and all the fathers were employed full time. In the intermediate group, 13 of the mothers were employed full time, three half time, and three were unemployed, and all the fathers were employed or attending school on a full-time basis. Of the 17 fathers who were primary caregivers and employed (two were full-time students), three were teaching at the university level, two were sales representatives, two were writers, and one individual held each of the following positions: a public school teacher, a part-time research assistant, a part-time computer programmer in public relations, a rabbi, a doctor, a self-employed businessman, an engineer, a toolmaker's apprentice, and a child-care worker in a psychiatric hospital. Their wives were employed in occupations such as university faculty member, nurse, social worker, and teacher. Two wives were full-time students.

In families where the wives were primary caregivers, the husbands held positions such as engineer, manager, university faculty member, psychologist, and accountant. One was a student.

DATA ANALYSIS

Two-way analyses of variance were computed for the father primary caregiver and mother primary caregiver groups, using sex of child and degree of paternal involvement in child care as the independent variables and scores on the various child and relevant parent and grandfather measures as the dependent variables. Pearson product moment correlations were also computed for the entire sample of 59 and for boys and girls separately, interrelating the child and parent variables, the measures of fathers' involvement in child care, and selected grandfather variables. To score the Bem Sex Role Inventory, the responses to the masculine items were averaged for a masculinity score and the responses to the feminine items averaged for a femininity score. In addition, the Bem t-score was computed, as recent research (Abrahams et al., 1978; Hyde & Phillis, 1979; Jones, Chernovetz, & Hansson, 1978) indicates that the Bem t-test is a valid method of scoring the instrument. The t-score reflects the difference between the feminine and masculine scores of each respondent and provides a rough estimate of position on the masculine–androgynous–feminine dimension.

RESULTS

Parents' Perceptions of Father's Role in Child Rearing.   The correlations among the fathers' reports of paternal involvement, the grand total, or composite of mother and father totals, and social class variables appear in Table 7.1, as do the intercorrelation of the same variables for mothers. It can be seen that for fathers all the components of the total father involvement score, except one, correlated significantly with one another and with the grand total score. The exception was the component "decision making about childcare." It consists of two items, "Who in your family generally makes decisions concerning when the children should be disciplined?" and "Who in your family generally makes decisions concerning when children are old enough to try new things?" In addition, the Hollingshead index for fathers was negatively associated with the socialization factor, statement of involvement, and total father scores; in contrast, the Hollingshead family score was not significantly associated with any measure of

TABLE 7.1

Intercorrelations Among Selected Parental Measures for the Total Sample

	1	2	3	4	5	6	7	8	9
1 Total paternal involvement score	X	.87***	.76***	.68***	.64***	.13	.91***	−.36**	−.16
2 Statement of involvement	.72***	X	.61**	.39**	.44***	.07	.76***	−.32*	−.13
3 Child care	.63***	.61***	X	.48**	.34*	−.12	.68***	−.13	−.12
4 Socialization	.57***	.50***	.36**	X	.47***	−.06	.62***	−.27*	−.13
5 Availability	.69**	.48***	.32*	.40**	X	−.01	.59***	−.24	−.16
6 Decision making	.24	.29*	.05	.39**	.35**	X	.21	−.10	.09
7 Grand total paternal involvement	.91***	.83***	.70***	.65***	.62***	.39**	X	−.34**	−.16
8 Hollingshead Index—father	−.26*	−.30*	−.11	−.20	−.16	−.27*	−.34**	X	.62***
9 Hollingshead Index—family	−.13	−.25	−.16	−.09	−.08	−.07	−.16	.62**	X

Mothers

Fathers

Note. $N = 59$ for all variables except Hollingshead Index where $N = 58$. Where $N = 58$. Where $N = 59$; d.f. $= 57$, where $N = 58$, d.f. $= 56$.

*$p < .05$
**$p < .01$
***$p < .001$

paternal involvement as reported by fathers. The intercorrelations among mothers' reports of paternal involvement were as closely related as those of father measures. The overall mean of the correlations was .31 for father measures and .38 for mother measures. However, mothers' estimates of father involvement in decision making were significantly correlated with other maternal reports of paternal child-rearing, suggesting that paternal decision making concerning children was not unrelated to other aspects of the fathers involvement, as the father reports would suggest.   Also resembling the paternal data were the correlations between indices of paternal involvement and social class. None of the involvement measures were significantly associated with the Hollingshead index for the family, but three involvement measures were negatively linked to measures of the father's social class. As with fathers, two of these measures were total score and statement of involvement. Further, as was true for fathers, even the nonsignificant correlations were negative.

Table 7.2 indicates that there was generally high agreement between mothers' and fathers' views of the fathers' role in child care in the total sample and for boys, except concerning the fathers' role in decision making. However, even in this area the correlation was significant. For girls, there was more consensus regarding the fathers' decision-making power than about some other components, three of which were not significantly related. In spite of this there was relatively high agreement between the total scores based on mothers' and fathers' reports, indicating that there was high agreement between mothers' and fathers' scores across categories if not in the same categories. As evidence of this, mothers' views of fathers' involvement in child care correlated significantly with fathers' statements of their involvement ($r = .51$, $p < .001$) and mothers' statements of fathers' involvement were significantly associated with the fathers' perception of their role in child care ($r = .56$, $p < .0001$). In sum, there is substantial evidence that

TABLE 7.2
Correlations Between Mothers' and Fathers' Responses to Paternal
Involvement Measures

Measure	Total Sample ($N = 59$)	Boys ($N = 32$)	Girls ($N = 27$)
Statement of father's involvement	.66***	.68***	.18
Father's role in child care	.71***	.75***	−.19
Father's role in socialization	.60***	.61***	.08
Father's role in decision making	.32*	.37*	.47*
Father's availability	.55***	.51**	.59**
Total score of father's involvement	.68***	.66***	.75***

Note. Where $N = 59$, d.f. = 57; where $N = 32$, d.f. = 30; where $N = 27$, d.f. = 25.
*$p < .05$
**$p < .01$
***$p < .001$

mothers and fathers tend to agree in their perceptions of the fathers' role in child care and that all the components of child rearing assessed were closely associated except for the father's role in decision making. The data also suggest that greater paternal involvement in child rearing is linked with lower socioeconomic status for fathers but not for the family as a whole.

Potential Antecedents. The significant correlations in the total sample between potential antecedents and maternal and paternal reports of paternal involvement appear in Table 7.3. Entered into the correlation matrix as potential precursors were five measures of each parent's perception of his or her father's behavior while under 10 years of age: his availability; decision-making power; total involvement in child care; nurturance; and the parent's feelings about father's involvement as another measure of his nurturance. In addition, entered into the matrix as possible antecedents are two measures of each parent's sex-role identity, masculinity, and femininity. Five aspects of paternal involvement for each parent plus the total paternal involvement index for each parent and the grand total of paternal involvement were entered into the matrix as measures of paternal involvement in child care.

TABLE 7.3
Significant Correlations Between Potential Antecedents and
Measures of Paternal Involvement in Child Care for the Total Sample

Potential Antecedent	Paternal Child-rearing Measure	Coefficient of Correlation
Mother variables		
Her father's availability	Father: Decision making	−.31*
	Mother: Decision making	−.30*
	Mother: Child care	.34*
Her past feelings re: her father's involvement	Father: Statement of involvement	.28*
	Father: Child care	.41**
	Father: Total score	.27*
Father variables		
Bem masculinity	Mother: Statement of involvement	−.28*
	Mother: Child care	−.28*
	Father: Child care	−.29*
	Father: Decision making	.37*
Bem femininity	Father: Decision making	−.27*
His father's decision making	Mother: Decision making	.42**

Note. The N for the total sample is 59; however, because of some missing data, the N's ranged from 53 to 59. D.f. $= N - 2$.
*$p < .05$
**$p < .01$

A fairly clear pattern emerges: mothers who perceived their fathers as having had less involvement in child care when they were growing up had husbands who were heavily involved in child rearing. Further, mothers who had very positive feelings concerning their fathers' involvement when they were young had husbands who were involved in rearing their children. Mothers' masculine and feminine Bem scores were unrelated to any measures of paternal child care, but fathers' Bem masculinity scores are negatively associated with their involvement in the physical care of the children and with mothers' overall estimates of their child-rearing activities. Conversely, fathers' Bem masculinity scores are positively related to fathers' views of their involvement in decision making. One variable pertaining to the fathers' views of their fathers linked to paternal involvement in the child care and that relationship was positive.

In Table 7.4 appear the correlations between potential antecedents of paternal child rearing and measures of that variable for boys and girls. For girls, a similar pattern holds as appeared in the total sample. Again, the less involved the mothers' fathers were, the more likely their husbands were to be heavily involved in the rearing of their children. Fathers' masculinity is again negatively associated with their involvement in child care and positively associated with their decision-making power; their femininity was also negatively associated with decision making.

For boys, the pattern that emerged was similar to that observed for the total sample and for girls except that no paternal variables were significant. In general, paternal involvement in child care was positively linked to the wives' feelings about their own fathers' involvement and negatively associated with the amount of paternal involvement they experienced as children. There was an exception in the case of paternal involvement in decision making. Here the more positively the wives felt about their fathers' role in child care, the less power and influence their husband had in making decisions about their sons.

In Table 7.5 appear the significant correlations between potential antecedents and measures of paternal involvement in the father primary caregiver group and the mother primary caregiver group. In the latter group, more paternal involvement was again associated with less involvement by mothers' fathers and with mothers' positive feelings about their fathers; physical care of the children was an exception to this pattern. In the father primary caregiving group the same set of associations was found and again physical care of the child was the exception. Unexpectedly, in this group there was a significant positive association between the fathers' Bem masculinity score and the mothers' total score for fathers' involvement in child care, as well as a negative correlation between mothers' Bem masculinity and total scores for paternal involvement.

In sum, although there were exceptions, it appears that the more mothers perceive their own fathers' involvement in child care to have been gratifying but limited, the greater their husbands' involvement in caring for their children. The mothers' sex-role orientation for the most part seems to be irrelevant. In contrast, the father variables linked to degree of paternal involvement do not pertain to perceptions of their own fathers but to their sex-role orientation, and here their

TABLE 7.4
Significant Correlations Between Potential Antecedents and
Measures of Paternal Involvement in Child Care by Sex of Child

Potential Antecedent	Paternal Child-rearing Measure		Coefficient of Correlation
Girls			
Mother variables			
Her father's availability	Mother:	Decision making	−.57**
	Mother:	Availability	−.39*
	Father:	Socialization	−.40*
	Father:	Decision making	−.40*
Her past feelings re: her father's involvement	Mother:	Availability	.40*
Father variables			
Bem masculinity	Mother:	Child care	−.40*
	Father:	Decision making	.41*
Bem femininity	Mother:	Decision making	−.41*
Boys			
Mother variables			
Total score for her father's involvement	Father:	Statement of involvement	−.48*
Her past feelings re: her father's involvement	Mother:	Decision making	−.45*
	Mother:	Child care	.53*
	Father:	Child care	.58***
	Father:	Decision making	−.38*
	Father:	Total score	.43*
	Mother:	Statement of involvement	.36*
	Father:	Statement of involvement	.43*

Note. The N for girls is 27 and 32 for boys; however, because of missing data the N's varied from 25 to 27 for girls and from 26 to 32 for boys. For boys, none of the father variables correlated significantly with paternal child-rearing measures. D.f. = $N - 2$.

*$p < .05$
**$p < .01$

masculinity related to child-care activities in divergent ways. For example, the more masculine their orientation, the greater their involvement in decision making and the less their involvement in physically caring for the children. In general, more maternal variables than paternal variables were associated with measures of paternal involvement in child rearing.

Potential Consequences for Children. In Table 7.6 appear the significant correlations for the total sample between paternal child-rearing measures and measures of the children's characteristics. Entered into the computation were 13 parental measures (six measures of paternal involvement for each parent plus the grand total score) and 15 child measures. The child scores included three measures related to Stanford Preschool Internal–External Scale (the total score for internality, the score for internality concerning positive consequences, and the score for internality concerning negative consequences); the Stephens–Delys Internality Score; two scores obtained from the Parent Role Perception Test (paternal and maternal role stereotyping scores); five measures obtained from the Kagan Parent Role Test (paternal punitiveness, paternal nurturance, maternal nurturance, and total number of father responses); the score for empathy obtained from the Borke

TABLE 7.5

Significant Correlations Between Potential Antecedents and
Measures of Paternal Involvement in Child Care by
Father-Involvement Group

Potential Antecedent	Paternal Childrearing Measure		Coefficient of Correlation
Mother Primary Caregiver Group			
Mother variables			
Total score for her father's involvement	Father:	Socialization	−.69**
Her father's availability	Father:	Socialization	−.48*
	Mother:	Decision making	−.50*
	Mother:	Child care	.50*
Her father's decision making	Father:	Socialization	−.57*
Her total score for her father's nurturance	Father:	Socialization	.52*
	Mother:	Socialization	.53*
Father Primary Caregiver Group			
Mother variables			
Total score for her father's involvement	Father:	Statement of involvement	−.61**
	Father:	Child care	.60*
Her father's availability	Father:	Decision making	−.47*
	Mother:	Socialization	−.47*
Her past feelings re: her father's involvement	Mother:	Availability	.48*
Bem masculinity	Mother:	Total score	−.54*
	Mother:	Grand total score of father's involvement	−.55*
Father variables			
Bem masculinity	Mother:	Total score	.49*

Note. The N for each group is 20; however, because of missing data the N's ranged from 17 to 20. D.f. = $N − 2$. For Mother Primary Caregiver Group, no father variables were significantly correlated with paternal child-rearing measures.

*$p < .05$
**$p < .01$

TABLE 7.6
Significant Correlations Between Child Measures and
Paternal Involvement Variables for the Total Sample

Paternal Child-Rearing Measure	Child Measures	r
Combined parent responses		
Grand total	SPIES total internal score	.42***
	SPIES total internal score for negative outcomes	.36**
	Kagan total father responses	.27*
	Kagan maternal punitiveness	−.27*
Father responses		
Total score	SPIES total internal score	.33**
	SPIES total for negative outcomes	.28*
	PRPT paternal-role stereotyping	−.28*
	Kagan maternal punitiveness	−.30*
Child care	PRPT paternal-role stereotyping	−.32*
	Kagan maternal punitiveness	−.29*
Decision making	SPIES total internal score	.32*
	Kagan paternal punitiveness	.27*
Statement of involvement	PPVT percentile	.27*
Mother responses		
Total score	Kagan paternal punitiveness	.30
	Kagan total father responses	.28*
	SPIES total internal score	.44***
	SPIES total for negative outcomes	.38**
Statement of involvement	SPIES total internal score	.32*
	Kagan total father responses	.31*
Socialization	SPIES total internal score	.27*
Child care	SPIES total internal score	.32*
	SPIES total for negative outcomes	.29*
	Kagan maternal punitiveness	−.32*

Note. The N's varied between 54 and 59 because of missing data on some child measures.
D.f. $= N - 2$.
   *$p < .05$
   **$p < .01$
   ***$p < .001$

scale; the It-Scale score; and two measures of the child's intellectual ability (the Peabody Picture Vocabulary Test mental age percentile and the percentile of the total score on the Ravens Coloured Progressive Matrices Test).

Several major themes are evident in Table 7.6. Fathers' involvement in child care was positively related to the internality of their children, and especially to feelings of responsibility for negative outcomes. There were also indications emerging from the Kagan Parent Role Test, which focuses on personality traits, that mothers were perceived as less punitive and fathers as more punitive when paternal involvement was high. However, when considering sex-related activities of parents, it appears from Table 7.6 that there was a reduction in children's stereotyped perception of fathers when the men played an important role in child rearing. Even with, and perhaps because of this reduction in paternal stereotyping, the fathers emerged as salient figures when they were involved in child care, for

TABLE 7.7
Significant Correlations Between Child Measures and
Paternal-Involvement Variables for Girls

Parent Variable	Child Measures	r
Combined parent responses		
Grand total	SPIES total internal score	.53**
	SPIES internal score for negative outcomes	.49**
	Kagan paternal punitiveness	.48*
Father responses		
Total score	SPIES internal score for negative outcomes	.42*
Statement of involvement	PPVT percentile	.47*
Decision making	PRPT maternal-role stereotyping	.49*
Mother responses		
Total score	SPIES total internal score	.56**
	SPIES internal score for positive outcomes	.39*
	SPIES internal score for negative outcomes	.50**
	Kagan paternal punitiveness	.52**
	Kagan total father responses	.38*
Statement of involvement	SPIES total internal score	.57**
	SPIES internal score for positive outcomes	.40*
	SPIES internal score for negative outcomes	.51**
	Kagan paternal punititveness	.52**
	Kagan total father responses	.44*
Availability	Stephens–Delys total internality	−.38*
Socialization	SPIES total internal score	.53*
	SPIES internal score for positive outcomes	.40*
	SPIES internal score for negative outcomes	.45*
	Kagan paternal punitiveness	.46*
Decision making	SPIES total internal score	.55**
	SPIES internal score for positive outcomes	.56**

Note. Because of missing child data, the *N*'s for boys varied between 30 and 32 and for girls between 26 and 27.

  *p < .05
 **p < .01

there was a positive association between the total number of responses of "Father" on the Kagan scale and measure of paternal involvement. There was also a positive relationship between paternal involvement and the verbal ability of children.

Table 7.7 contains the significant association between paternal child-rearing measures and potential consequences in the subsample of girls. There was again strong evidence of a relationship between paternal involvement in child care and the youngsters' internality, in this case for both positive and negative outcomes. For girls, as for the total sample, greater involvement by fathers in child care was associated with perceptions that fathers were more punitive and more salient. There was some evidence that girls' stereotyped thinking of the mother's role is enhanced with greater father power in decision making. Finally, one of the indices of father involvement in child care was positively associated with verbal ability in girls.

In Table 7.8 there appear the significant correlations between paternal involvement and boys' measures. There are considerably fewer relationships than there were for daughters, nine as opposed to 23 for girls. Once again, the children's internality was related to paternal involvement in child care; in this case, the effects were evident on both locus-of-control instruments. In addition, the fathers' involvement in child care was associated with a decrease in stereotyping of the paternal role where activities were concerned and an increase where traits were involved. For mothers the results were less clear because mothers were perceived as less punitive as well as less nurturant. Again, the score for the

TABLE 7.8
Significant Correlations Between Child Measures and
Paternal-Involvement Variables for Boys

Parent Variable	Child Measures	r
Combined parent responses		
Grand total	SPIES total internal score	.37*
Father responses		
Child care	Kagan total maternal punitiveness	−.36*
Decision making	PPVT percentile	.37*
Socialization	Kagan paternal nurturance	−.42*
Mother responses		
Total score	SPIES total internal score	.40*
	Stephens–Delys total internality	.38*
Socialization	PRPT paternal role stereotype	−.51**
	Kagan maternal nurturance	−.35*
Child care	Kagan maternal punitiveness	−.48**

Note. Because of missing child data the N's varied between 30 and 32.
*$p < .05$
**$p < .01$

TABLE 7.9
Significant Correlations Between Paternal-Involvement
Measures and Scores on the Cognitive Home Environment
Scale for the Total Sample and Boys and Girls

Group	Paternal Involvement Measure	Cognitive Home Environment Scale	Coefficient of Correlation
Total	Grand total	Father: Direct teaching	.29*
sample	Father scores		
	Statement of	Mother: Direct teaching	−.30*
	involvement	Father: Direct teaching	.28*
	Child care	Father: Direct teaching	.38*
	Total score	Father: Direct teaching	.33*
	Mother scores		
	Statement of	Mother: Educational	.33*
	involvement	material in home	
Girls	Mother scores		
	Statement of	Mother: Educational	.51***
	involvement	material in home	
		Mother: Direct teaching	−.42*
	Socialization	Mother: Total score	−.45*
	Child care	Mother: Total score	−.49*
	Decision making	Mother: Direct teaching	−.44*
Boys	Grand total	Father: Direct teaching	.41*
	Father scores		
	Decision making	Father: Direct teaching	.47**
	Mother scores		
	Total score	Father: Direct teaching	.39*

Note: The N's for the total sample varied between 54 and 59; the N's for the girls varied between 26 and 27; the N's for the boys varied between 30 and 32. D.f. $= N - 2$.
*$p < .05$
**$p < .01$

children's verbal intelligence was positively associated with a measure of paternal involvement, in this case with paternal involvement in decision making. It appears that high paternal involvement in child care was associated with greater internality for both sons and daughters. In addition, there was evidence of a strengthening of the children's stereotypic thinking of parents in relation to personality traits and a weakening of stereotypic thinking in relation to parental activities in the home.

Potential Consequences for Parents.   In Table 7.9 appear the correlations between paternal involvement indices and four scores on the Cognitive Home Environment Scale for each parent: total score, and scores for the three factors, Direct Teaching, Education Materials in the Home, and Future Expectations. It can be seen that with an increase in paternal involvement in child care, there is an increase in paternal engagement in direct teaching activities (e.g., teaching children to count) for the sample as a whole. An examination of gender subgroups revealed that the direct teaching increased only in the fathers of boys. For daughters, maternal involvement in direct teaching and other cognitively stimulating activities was reduced with no accompanying increase in father activities. The one stimulating aspect that was enhanced for girls when mothers were away working or in school and fathers were caregivers was an increase in the number of educational materials in the home.

Additional Data on Potential Consequences. Table 7.10 contains the significant F-scores obtained in the analyses of variance performed with the sex of the child and father involvement in childcare (high versus low) as the independent variables. The dependent variables based on parent data were five measures pertaining to the fathers' perceptions of their own fathers, three Bem scores for each parent, and for scores derived from the Cognitive Home Environment Scale for each parent: the total score and three factor scores (Educational Materials in the Home, Direct Teaching, and Future Expectations). Children's measures used as dependent variables were: the two cognitive scores, the *It*-Scale score, the Borke Empathy scale scores, three scores pertaining to the SPIES, four scores pertaining to the Kagan Parent Role Test, and two scores obtained from the Parent Role Perception Test. Significant differences between the high and low parental involvement groups emerged for 5 variables. The mean was higher for the father-involved group for the SPIES total internal score, the father's Cognitive Home Environment Scale total score, and the mother's score for Educational Materials in the Home. The mean was lower for the high father-involved group for maternal punitiveness on the Kagan Parent Role Test, and for the mother's score for Direct Teaching.

There was one significant sex-of-child effect: boys obtained higher (i.e., more masculine scores on the *It* scale than girls did. Finally, there were two interaction effects and they involved the fathers' and mothers' total scores on the Cognitive Home Environment Scale. The rank orderings of the means were mirror images of one another. Fathers with daughters in the high father-involved group ranked highest and fathers with daughters in the low father-involved group ranked lowest. For mothers the pattern was exactly reversed. Mothers in the low father-involved group with daughters obtained the highest scores and mothers in the high father-involved group with daughters obtained the lowest scores.

In general, analyses-of-variance both supported and complemented the findings that emerged in the correlational computations. Confirmed were the findings that children of more heavily involved fathers were more internal and had stronger stereotypes regarding parental characteristics, but children's own sex-role orientations appeared to be unaffected by the degree of paternal involvement in child rearing. Also supported was the suggestion that increased paternal efforts to stimulate the intellectual growth of the preschoolers accompanied greater paternal involvement in child care. Complementing the correlational data pertaining to

TABLE 7.10
Two-Way Analyses of Variance with Significant F-Values

Dependent Variable	D.F.	F-Value for Sex Effect	F-Value for Father-Involvement Effect	F-Value for Interaction Effect
SPIES total internal score	38	3.35	10.75**[b]	0.23
It Scale	39	9.63*[a]	0.18	1.25
Kagan Maternal Punitiveness	39	0.52	5.68*[d]	0.52
Father's Cognitive Home Environment Scale—total score	39	.00	4.55*[b]	6.05*[c]
Mother's Cognitive Home Environment Scale—educational materials in the home	36	.00	4.50*[b]	.00
Mother's Cognitive Home Environment Scale—direct teaching	31	.092	4.24*[d]	1.58
Mother's Cognitive Home Environment Scale—total score	35	.07	2.52	6.34*[e]

[a]The mean is higher for boys.
[b]Mean of High Father Involvement group higher than mean of Low Father Involvement group.
[c]Rank order, highest to lowest:
    1. Girls in High Father-Involvement Group
    2. Boys in Low Father-Involvement Group
    3. Boys in High Father-Involvement Group
    4. Girls in Low Father-Involvement Group
[d]Mean of High Father-Involvement Group lower than mean of Low Father-Involvement Group
[e]Rank order, highest to lowest:
    1. Girls in Low Father-Involvement Group
    2. Boys in High Father-Involvement Group
    3. Boys in Low Father-Involvement Group
    4. Girls in High Father-Involvement Group
*$p < .05$
**$p < .01$

direct teaching efforts were the findings that, overall, the parents who were primary caregivers made greater efforts to foster the cognitive growth of daughters.

Additional Data on Potential Antecedents.   To explore the parents' sex-role orientations and the influence of the work experience of the mothers' mothers and the fathers' mothers, several additional computations were performed. Although there was no significant difference in the fathers' Bem masculinity or femininity scores when primary caregiving and traditional fathers were compared, there was a significant difference between the intermediate and mother-prime childrearing groups in paternal Bem Femininity scores, with the score being greater in the intermediate group ($t_{30} = 2.88$, $p < .05$). It was also found that there was a significant difference between the father primary caregiving group and each of the other two groups in the number of families in which the mothers of both parents worked outside the home before the parents were 10 years of age. For the father primary caregiver group the figure was 25%; for the other two groups it was 0%. This difference was significant ($\chi^2 = 5.71$ $p < .05$).

Wives' Employment.   The reasons offered by mothers and fathers for the wives' employment in the father primary caregiver group were also explored and the following results obtained:

Reason for Wife's working	Fathers ($N = 19$)	Mothers ($N = 18$)
Had to	16%	17%
Wanted to	21%	22%
Both Factors Involved	58%	61%

The N's were less than 20 because one wife was a full-time student and not working and the question was skipped in error in one mother's interview (not the spouse of a man who said his wife had to work). It is noteworthy that only two couples agreed that the wife had to work; in both cases the wives indicated they would prefer part-time rather than full-time employment. One woman added that she would like to have the same allocation of tasks even if she were to work half time.

The feelings concerning maternal employment in the father primary caregiver group can be contrasted with the views of the wives who were primary caregivers. When asked about the disadvantages of the current child-care arrangement, 10 of the 20 women in the latter group mentioned being housebound and lacking stimulation, but only one expressed a desire to return to work.

When parents in the father primary caregiver group were asked their feelings about the father's role in child care, the following answers were obtained: 100% of the mothers and 80% of the fathers "Liked it a lot"; 20% of the fathers "liked it." None of the mothers or fathers selected the categories of "neutral," "dislike it," or "dislike it a lot" in their replies.

A question was also asked about the parents' satisfaction with the current arrangement. In the father primary caregiver group, 17 fathers were satisfied and three were not, but none of the dissatisfied men were fathers who said their wives had to work. Of the three men who were dissatisfied, one was discontented because his wife was working out of town, another preferred that his wife be available to care for the children during the day when they were sick and be at home during the weekday evenings, and the third preferred that his wife not work evenings and that he not have to work at all.

Of the 20 wives involved, 18 were satisfied with the current arrangement and two were not—the two who said they were working because they had to and whose husbands concurred. One indicated she would prefer to work part time and felt guilty about being away from home so much. The second said she would prefer to have more weekends with the family. Thus it appears that in families where the father was the primary caregiver the men did not object to their wives working and the women felt they were working because they wished to do so. Further, both parents approve of the fathers' current role in child care.

Advantages and Disadvantages of Current Arrangements.   Finally, the parents were queried about personal advantages and disadvantages of the current child-care arrangements. They were asked to elaborate if they indicated there were disadvantages, and many parents volunteered information about the advantages as well. Nineteen of the 20 fathers who were primary caregivers said there were advantages and one said there were none. Seven of the fathers described the advantages in terms of being closer to the children. Two said they enjoyed being with the youngsters, and two said they knew their children well. One father stated he had "moved from reluctance to looking forward to kids," suggesting that the original reason for the child-care arrangement may not have been the same as the reason for maintaining it.

Six of the 20 primary caregiver fathers said the current arrangement had no disadvantages, while 14 stated there were disadvantages. Eight of the 14, or 40% of the total group, perceived the disadvantages in terms of interference with their jobs. One said he had made a choice not to be so competitive by choosing to spend so much time with his children. Another stated there was not enough time for career expansion. A third said it was harder to put energy into his professional work. Three of the 14 fathers who saw personal disadvantages referred to the demands in terms of time and energy. One father said, "Children take time;" another said it was hard to get children ready for school.

When the 20 wives of child-rearing fathers were asked the same question about advantages and disadvantages of the current arrangement, 19 said there were advantages and one felt she could not answer. The advantages cited included the reduction of pressure and guilt. For example, one mother said, "It relieves me;" another felt it helped her to relax; and a third indicated she felt less guilty because the children were being taken care of and she was "not gypping them." Three of the mothers felt there were no personal disadvantages to the current arrangement, but 17 did see problems. Twelve of these women (or 60%

of the total group) expressed regret at not having enough time to be with the children. For example, one mother said she missed a lot of her daughter's growing up, the things she did during the day; another said she didn't see the children enough during the daytime and couldn't help them with some of the problems that came up; a third stated she was not as close to the child as she would have liked to be; and a fourth said her husband was able "to do the fun stuff with the kids" and she couldn't participate.

Other disadvantages cited by a few mothers were the difficulty of sharing child-care tasks and the limited time for husband and wife to be together; one mother felt the child was confused by their arrangement for sharing child-care tasks. In sum, the data in general suggested that men heavily involved in child care enjoyed being with their youngsters but felt their careers might be suffering. Their spouses felt good about their husband's role in child rearing but missed having close contact with their children.

DISCUSSION

The purpose of this study was to explore some possible antecedents and consequences of paternal child rearing in middle-class, intact, primarily white families. Because only concurrent measures were employed, any attributions concerning direction of influence are, of course, highly speculative. However, efforts were made to obtain specific information about the parents' childhood experiences with their own fathers and about their feelings about those experiences at the time. Thus, it is hoped that some tentative conclusions can be drawn about the impact of childhood experiences on parental behavior. Similarly, by obtaining personality and cognitive measures of young children, and information concerning their perceptions of their parents' roles, it appeared reasonable to make some tentative statements about the influence of paternal child rearing on the preschoolers' functioning. It is possible that the adults distorted their memories of their fathers in the light of their current roles, and that the parents selected family roles on the basis of their preschoolers' attributes and/or their desire to stimulate the children's cognitive growth. This seems the more unlikely direction of influence, however, particularly as the parents had maintained the current arrangement for an average of 35 months. However, until longitudinal studies are conducted, any conclusions about the causes or effects of paternal child rearing in two-parent families must be stated with great caution.

Antecedents

With the foregoing proviso, some tentative conclusions can be drawn about antecedents of paternal child rearing in two-parent families. It appears that among the factors that predict partial parental role exchange are the mothers' perceptions that their own fathers' involvement was gratifying but limited. It is not difficult to understand why this combination would motivate mothers to attempt to create a less frustrating experience for their children. It had been hypothesized that the employment of the mothers' mothers would precede mothers' and fathers' agreement to have the fathers play the major role in child rearing, but this single variable apparently was not sufficient; the decision appeared to be influenced only when both husbands and wives grew up in a home with working mothers. This too is understandable, for a husband unaccustomed to a mother leaving children to seek employment, particularly in middle-class families, might well be reluctant to collaborate in a partial reversed-role arrangement. The notion that the fathers of child-rearing men would be unloving, unavailable, and powerless was unsupported. There were no differences between the mother primary caregiving group and the father primary caregiving group in any assessment of these characteristics, and only one significant relationship was obtained between any of these assessments and measures of paternal involvement in child care. Unloving, unavailable, and powerless fathers may influence their sons in many ways but apparently not toward becoming primary child rearers in intact families.

The data concerning the sex-role orientation of the fathers who chose to become heavily involved in child care was unexpected. It was believed that such fathers would be more effeminate and/or less masculine than traditional fathers; however, no significant differences were found between primary caregiving fathers and the husbands of primary caregiving wives on the Bem masculinity scores, Bem femininity scores, or Bem t-scores. Furthermore, the different components of caregiving related to the Bem masculinity scores in divergent ways. For some components, the father's Bem masculinity was linked with more involvement, for some with less masculinity, and for other aspects of child rearing there was no relationship with the father's sex-role orientation. Clearly the issue of person–role fit is not simple when paternal child rearing is considered. On the other hand, in father-primary caregiver families, the less masculine the mothers and the more masculine the fathers, the greater the paternal involvement in child care. These data may suggest that child-rearing fathers and their wives are "overcompensating" or protesting too much about their masculinity, but another explanation is more likely, one that Lamb and Bronson (1980) alluded to in discussing possible effects on children of fathers who take on the child-care role. Lamb and Bronson suggested that it is the individual whose gender identity is secure who can comfortably deviate from traditional role prescriptions. Those with insecure identities are more likely to conform rigidly to traditional role structures. It is possible that fathers in this study who openly violated family sex-role expectations and enjoyed the experience were indeed those most comfortable with their own masculinity and most secure in their gender identity. The finding that men have higher femininity scores than traditional fathers when they have a large role in child care (but not the major role) is provocative. Perhaps there is a curvilinear relationship between paternal involvement in child care and the father's femininity or androgyny. Hopefully more data will become available soon to clarify the issue.

It has been suggested by Russell (1980), who studied families from divergent social classes, that an important factor influencing the decision by parents to have the father play the role of primary caregiver is economic necessity, the need for the mother to work. Presumably women can obtain jobs more readily than men. In this study of middle-class families, economic need was not a major factor in the parents' decision to move to a modified reversed-role structure. In only two of the 20 families did mother and father agree that the mother was working because she had to, and those two mothers were the only women who expressed this view. Even in these cases the mothers indicated that if given a choice they would work part time rather than full time. The conclusion that can be drawn from these data is that choice entered into virtually all the decisions to engage in paternal child rearing; the families were not forced into the arrangement. Rather, it appears that one of the antecedents of paternal caregiving is the mothers' desire to work. Eighteen of the 20 women whose husbands were primary caregivers were working at least partially because they wished to and the other two wished only to reduce the hours of employment. In contrast, only one of the primary caregiver mothers expressed a desire for employment. Thus, although it had not been predicted, it appears that the mother's desire for employment is an important factor propelling a family into a paternal child-rearing pattern.

As far as feelings about the current child-rearing arrangements are concerned, all the parents in the father primary caregiver group approved of the fathers' involvement in child care. In addition, 85% and 90% of the fathers and mothers respectively were satisfied and wished no modification in the families' child-rearing pattern. This does not mean that there were no costs to these men and women. Seventy percent of the fathers and 85% of the mothers perceived that there were disadvantages; the majority of the men described the costs in terms of their impeded careers and the majority of the women described the costs in terms of their loss of close involvement with their children. Thus, it appears that even when parents choose to violate sex-role expectations, there are still internal pressures to fulfill the tasks for which they were socialized. The problem seems to stem from internal rather than external forces. None of these middle-class parents cited peer pressure as a factor in their dissatisfaction with the current plan. It was the gap in the fulfillment of their own needs that caused discontent. Perhaps the absence of pressure from friends and associates to comply with traditional sex-role expectations may be related to the type of community in which this study was conducted. Those who live in Ann Arbor or work in Ann Arbor and live nearby are influenced by the norms of the students and faculty of the University of Michigan. One of the more powerful norms today is denigration of traditional sex-role stereotypes and another is the expectation that women fulfill their potential through school or employment.

It has been suggested that job flexibility in Australia is an important precurser of paternal child rearing in intact families (Russell, 1980). This appears to be true in the United States as well, although the variety of positions held by child-rearing fathers in this study suggests that flexibility is not an unusual employment condition or one difficult to obtain in a location where there are many profession-als, students, academics, and self-employed individuals. The data also suggest that inflexible hours can be tolerated in a paternal child-rearing arrangement if the job is part-time or allows the father to be with the child in the afternoon and early evening.

In sum, given an abundance of jobs permitting fathers to be heavily involved in child care, and an environment that supports deviation from traditional sex-role stereotypes, it appears that the factors influencing a couple's decision to select the father primary caregiver model are best sought at the individual and family level of analysis, not at the meso- or macrolevels. This investigation suggested that the mothers' attitudes toward their own fathers and toward employ-ment, and the prior experience of both parents with working mothers in their families of origin, were the most important factors. The parents' sex-role orienta-tion and the fathers' attitudes toward their own fathers appear to exert little, if any influence in this matter. The husbands' willingness to impede their own career advancement may also be involved.

Consequences

Because the father's sex-role orientation was the same in father primary caregiv-ing families and mother primary caregiving families, it was not surprising that the children's sex-role orientation did not differ across groups. This finding suggests that the activities fathers engage in, per se, need not influence the children's perception of their own masculinity or femininity; both social learning and cognitive development theories could explain the results, the former in terms of parent models with traditional sex-role orientations and the latter in terms of intellectual growth and rigid stereotyped thinking outweighing the influence of non-sex-typed activities observed in the home. There was some support for the modeling interpretation as the sex-role orientation scores of fathers and children were significantly correlated (Radin, 1978).

The finding that preschoolers of both sexes show greater internality when fathers are heavily involved in child care supports our hypothesis, as does the finding that within the total sample, the youngsters' internal locus of control in-creased in association with paternal involvement. This study did not directly assess the internality of the fathers or mothers. It was assumed that creators of new roles, particularly those defying societal norms, would perceive themselves as masters of the major outcomes in their lives. Whether such family role makers do possess and model greater internality than traditional parents remains to be investigated. Furthermore, whether family role makers differentially reinforce behaviors of their preschoolers indicative of internality (e.g., accepting responsibility for misdeeds) is an independent issue that warrants examination. The finding that children's internality concerning negative outcomes is related to paternal involvement suggests that this may occur. Because internality has been consistently linked to school success in young children (Bridge & Moock, 1979; Coleman, Campbell, Hobson, McPartland, Mood, Weinfeld, & York, 1966), the findings regarding locus of control hold much promise for families that adopt paternal child-rearing practices.

It was anticipated that parents who had partially reversed child-care roles would have preschoolers with nonstereotyped parental perceptions or with perceptions no different from those of their peers in traditional families. It was surprising to see an accentuation of stereotypes in the area of parental traits. The explanation may lie in the finding that fathers who spent a good deal of time with their children had as masculine an orientation (e.g., assertive, forceful) as men whose wives were the child rearers; in addition, they were more salient to their children than traditional fathers. The net effect may be that a vivid example of a "manly" father is ever present, so that the children's stereotyped perceptions of fathers as punitive and mothers as nonpunitive are thereby enhanced. Some support for the proposition that child-rearing men are more punitive than mothers and/or as punitive as traditional fathers emerged in Russell's (1980) study of child-rearing fathers in intact families. According to Russell: "Fathers in these families were seen by both parents to have higher standards for child behavior and as being stricter [p. 11]."

The indication that paternal involvement in child care is negatively related to children's sex-role stereotyped perceptions concerning the use of household items suggests that the two types of parental perceptions, those concerning personal characteristics and activities, are not isomorphic. Children in families where fathers are caregivers appear to see their fathers as using washing machines and brooms but perceive them as forceful nevertheless. Bronfenbrenner's (1958) suggestion that men associated with household items would be perceived by their children as less masculine was not supported by our data.

The finding that child-rearing fathers tend to provide more stimulation in the cognitive area for their daughters and hold higher career aspirations for them than do traditional fathers was not predicted but is in keeping with theories and data suggesting that traditional fathers foster differential development in sons and daughters, with greater emphasis placed on achievement in boys (Hoffman, 1977, Radin, 1976). For example, it has been found (Aberle & Naegele, 1952) that middle-class fathers want their sons to do well in school and have desirable careers but their major aspiration for their daughters is that they marry well and be good wives. Thus, it is not too surprising that men who have chosen to forego career advancement in favor of child care, as suggested by their lower social-class index and their own statements, and who have wives who have focused on an occupational role, would differ in this regard. They may well try to develop their daughters' intellectual abilities, perhaps to combat sexist influences they will experience in the larger society. Not as readily explained is the finding that more stimulation is provided for both boys and girls when fathers are the primary caregivers. Perhaps the desire of middle-class men to foster sons' career development is present in nontraditional as well as traditional families, but men who are rearing their children have more time to operationalize that wish.

The data on the Cognitive Home Environment Scale also shed some light on the question of whether child-rearing fathers continue to behave differently toward sons and daughters. The answer appears to be affirmative, although they do not behave like traditional fathers. The findings suggest that men heavily involved in raising their preschoolers will spend more time in efforts to stimulate the children's cognitive growth, particularly with their daughters. However, their direct teaching activities still appear to be focused on sons, not daughters. One is left with the conclusion that primary caregiving fathers make greater efforts than traditional fathers to foster their daughters' intellectual growth, possibly indirectly through exposing the child to educational materials, but paternal behavior still differs by the sex of the child. Accompanying the increase in paternal efforts to stimulate children in paternal child-rearing families is a decrease in mothers' efforts, with the activities of one parent complementing the activities of the other. When one parent's efforts are great, the other parent's efforts are minimal. We can only speculate about the long-term effects of this pattern, particularly for girls in paternal child-rearing families. The fact that verbal intelligence test scores of both boys and girls are positively correlated with the degree of paternal involvement in child care gives reason to predict beneficial outcomes.

The study also supported previous research suggesting that fathers are more confused about their interactions with their daughters than with their sons (Radin, 1976). The higher correlations between mothers' and fathers' perceptions of paternal behavior with boys than with girls may be due to mothers' confusion, but it is more likely that paternal confusion was involved. The issue warrants further investigation.

In conclusion, it appears that middle-class white, two-parent families, living in communities surrounding a large university, are most likely to have fathers heavily involved in child care when: both parents grew up in homes with working mothers; the wives wish to work; and the wives had fathers who are recalled in very positive terms but were uninvolved in child rearing. Once such an arrangement gets under way, and the parents are satisfied with the exchange, the fathers, who have maintained their masculine identity, appear to increase their efforts to stimulate their children's cognitive growth, particularly their daughters', and become involved in direct teaching of their sons; the mothers, still feminine in orientation, reduce such activities. With their sexual identities unaffected, the children's internality and intellectual abilities appear to flourish. As a whole, the evidence should not discourage other families from considering this alternative family style.

ACKNOWLEDGEMENTS

The research described in this chapter was supported by a grant from The University of Michigan Rackham School of Graduate Studies. I wish to express my deep appreciation to the students and volunteers who were involved in numerous aspects of this investigation, especially Bonnie Carlson, Bennet Wolper, Zona Scheiner, and Kathleen Faller, and to the parents who generously donated their time to this project.

REFERENCES

Aberle, D. F., & Naegele, K. D. Middle-class fathers' occupational role and attitudes toward children. *American Journal of Orthopsychiatry,* 1952, *22,* 336–378.

Abrahams, B., Feldman, S. S., & Nash, S. C. Sex role self-concept and sex role attitudes: Enduring personality characteristics or adaptations to changing life situations? *Developmental Psychology,* 1978, *14,* 393–400.

Aldous, J. The making of family roles and family change. *The Family Coordinator,* 1974, *23,* 231–235.

Bandura, A. The role of modeling processes in personality development. In C. S. Lavatelli & F. Stendler (Eds.), *Readings in child behavior and development* (3rd ed.). New York: Harcourt Brace Jovanovich, 1972.

Barnett, M. A., King, L. M., Howard, J. A., & Dino, G. A. Empathy in young children: Relation to parents' empathy, affection, and emphasis on feelings of others. *Developmental Psychology,* 1980, *16,* 243–244.

Bem, S. L. The measurement of psychological androgyny. *Journal of Consulting and Clinical Psychology,* 1974, *42,* 155–162.

Bem, S. L., & Watson, C. *Scoring packet: Bem Sex-Role Inventory.* Stanford, Calif.: Stanford University, 1976.

Biller, H. B. Father dominance and sex-role development in kindergarten-age boys. *Developmental Psychology,* 1969, *1,* 87–94.

Biller, H. B., & Borstelmann, L. J. Masculine development: An integrative review. *Merrill–Palmer Quarterly,* 1967, *13,* 253–294.

Blood, R. O., Jr., & Wolfe, D. M. *Husbands and wives.* New York: The Free Press, 1960.

Borke, H. Interpersonal perception of young children: Egocentrism or empathy? *Developmental Psychology,* 1971, *5,* 263–269.

Bridge, R. G., & Moock, P. R. *The determinants of educational outcomes: The impact of families peers, teachers and schools.* N.Y.: Ballinger Publishing Co., 1979.

Bronfenbrenner, U. The study of identification through interpersonal perception. In R. Tagiuri & L. Petrillo (Eds.), *Personal-perception and interpersonal behavior.* Stanford, Calif.: Stanford University Press, 1958.

Brown, D. G. Sex-role preference in children. *Psychological Monographs,* 1956, *70* (14, Serial No. 287).

Brown, P., Perry, L., & Harberg, E. Sex role attitudes and psychological outcomes for black and white women experiencing marital dissolution. *Journal of Marriage and the Family,* 1977, *39,* 519-561.

Carlson, B. E. *Shared vs. primarily maternal childrearing: Effects of dual careers on families with young children.* Unpublished doctoral dissertation, University of Michigan, 1980.

Chandler, M. J., & Greenspan, S. Ersatz egocentrism: A reply to H. Borke. *Developmental Psychology,* 1972, *7,* 104-106.

Coleman, J. S., Campbell, E. A., Hobson, C. J., McPartland, J., Mood, A. M., Weinfeld, F. D., & York, R. L. *Equality of educational opportunity.* Washington, D.C.: Department of Health, Education, and Welfare, Office of Education, 1966.

De Frain, J. Androgynous parents tell who they are and what they need. *The Family Coordinator,* 1979, *28,* 237-243.

Eiduson, B. T., & Weisner, T. S. *Alternative socialization settings for infants and young children.* Paper presented at the Western Meeting of the Society for Research in Child Development, Emeryville, Calif., April 2, 1976.

Field, T. Interaction behaviors of primary versus secondary caretaker fathers. *Developmental Psychology,* 1978, *14,* 183-184.

Gersick, K. E. Fathers by choice: Divorced men who receive custody of their children. In A. Levinger & O. C. Moles (Eds.), *Divorce and separation.* New York: Basic Books, 1979.

Gewirtz, J. L., & Stingle, K. G. Learning of generalized imitation as the basis for identification. *Psychological Review,* 1968, *75,* 374-397.

Glick, P. C. Social change and the American family. In *The Social Welfare Forum, 1977.* New York: Columbia University Press, 1978, 43-62.

Glick, P. C. Children of divorced parents in demographic perspective. *Journal of Social Issues,* 1979, *35,* 170-182.

Gecas, V. The socialization and child care roles. In F. I. Nye (Ed.), *Role structure and analysis of the family.* Beverly Hills, Calif.: Sage Publications, 1976.

Hetherington, E. M. A developmental study of the effects of the sex and dominant parent in sex role preference, identification, and imitation in children. *Journal of Personality and Social Psychology,* 1965, *2,* 188-194.

Hetherington, E. M., & Frankie, G. Effects of parental dominance, warmth, and conflict on imitation in children. *Journal of Personality and Social Psychology,* 1967, *6,* 119-125.

Hoffman, L. W. Changes in family roles, socialization and sex differences. *American Psychologist,* 1977, *32,* 644-658.

Hollingshead, A. B. *Four-factor index of social status.* Unpublished manuscript, 1970. (Available from Department of Sociology, Yale University, New Haven, Conn.)

Hyde, J. S., & Phillis, D. E. Androgyny across the life span. *Developmental Psychology,* 1979, *15,* 334-336.

Jones, W. H., Chernovetz, M., & Hansson, R. O. The enigma of androgyny: Differential implications for males and females. *Journal of Consulting and Clinical Psychology,* 1978, *46,* 298-313.

Kagan, J. The concept of identification. *Psychological Review.* 1958, *65,* 296-305.

Kagan, J., & Lemkin, J. The child's differential perception of parental attributes. *Journal of Abnormal Social Psychology,* 1960, *61,* 440-447.

Kohlberg, L. A cognitive developmental analysis of children's sex-role concepts and attitudes. In E. E. Maccoby (Ed.), *The development of sex differences.* Stanford, Calif.: Stanford University Press, 1966.

Lamb, M. E., & Bronson, S. K. Fathers in the context of family influences: Past, present, and future. *School Psychology Digest,* 1980, *9,* 336-353.

Levine, J. A. *Who will raise the children: New options for fathers and mothers.* New York: Lippincott, 1976.

Loeb, R. C. Concomitants of boys' locus of control examined in parent–child interactions. *Developmental Psychology,* 1975, *11,* 353-358.

Maccoby, E. E., & Jacklin, E. N. *The psychology of sex differences.* Stanford, Calif.: Stanford University Press, 1974.

Mendes, H. A. Single fatherhood. *Social Work,* 1976, *21,* 308–312.

Meyer, B. The development of girls' sex-role attitudes. *Child Development,* 1980, *51,* 508–514.

Mischel, W. Sex-typing and socialization. In P. H. Mussen (Ed.), *Carmichael's manual of child psychology* (Vol. 2, 3rd ed.). New York: John Wiley & Sons, 1970.

Mischel, W., Zeiss, R., & Zeiss, A. Internal–external control and persistence: Validation and implications of the Stanford Preschool Internal–External Scale. *Journal of Personality and Social Psychology,* 1974, *19,* 265–278.

Money, J., & Tucker, P. *Sexual signatures.* Boston: Little, Brown & Co., 1975.

Mussen, P. H., & Rutherford, E. Parent–child relationships and parental personality in relation to young children's sex-role preferences. *Child Development,* 1963, *34,* 589–607.

Parke, R. D., & Sawin, D. B. The family in early infancy: Social interactional and attitudinal analyses. In F. A. Pederson (Ed.), *The father–infant relationship: Observational studies in a family context.* New York: Praeger, 1980. 44–70.

Pleck, J. H. Masculinity–femininity: Current and alternative paradigms. *Sex Roles,* 1975, *1,* 161–178.

Pleck, J. H. Men's family work: Three perspectives and some new data. *The Family Coordinator,* 1979, *28,* 481–488.

Price-Bonham, S. A comparison of weighted and unweighted decision-making scores. *Journal of Marriage and the Family,* 1976, *38,* 629–640.

Radin, N. Father–child interaction and the intellectual functioning of four-year-old boys. *Developmental Psychology,* 1972, *6,* 353–361.

Radin, N. The role of the father in cognitive/academic and intellectual development. In M. E. Lamb (Ed.), *The role of the father in child development.* New York: John Wiley & Sons, Inc., 1976.

Radin, N. *Childrearing fathers in intact families with preschoolers.* Paper presented at the Annual Meeting of the American Psychological Association, Toronto, September 1978.

Radin, N., & Sonquist, H. *The Gale preschool program: Final report.* Ypsilanti, Mich.: Ypsilanti Public Schools, March 12, 1968.

Reuter, M. W., & Biller, H. B. Perceived paternal nurturance-availability and personality adjustment among college males. *Journal of Consulting and Clinical Psychology,* 1973, *40,* 339–342.

Payne, D. E. & Mussen, P. H. Parent-child relations and father identification among adolescent boys. *Journal of Abnormal and Social Psychology,* 1956, *52,* 358–362.

Russell, G. The father role and its relation to masculinity, femininity and androgyny. *Child Development,* 1978, *49,* 1174–1181.

Russell, G. *Fathers as caregivers: Possible antecedents and consequences.* Paper presented to the study group on "The role of the father in child development: Theory, social policy, and the law." University of Haifa, Haifa, Israel, July 15–17, 1980.

Santrock, J. W., & Warshak, R. A. Father custody and social development in boys and girls. *Journal of Social Issues,* 1979, *35,* 4, 112–125.

Sears, P. S. Childrearing factors related to the playing of sex-type roles. *American Psychologist,* 1953, *8,* 432 (Abstract).

Smith, A. D., & Reid, W. J. *The family role revolution.* Paper presented at the Annual Program Meeting of the Council on Social Work Education, Los Angeles, March 1980.

Stephens, M., & Delys, P. A locus of control measure for preschool children. *Developmental Psychology,* 1973, *9,* 1, 55–65.

Tangri, S. S. Determinants of occupational role innovation among college women. *Journal of Social Issues,* 1972, *28,* 177–199.

Wichern, F., & Nowicki, S., Jr. Independence training practices and locus of control orientation in children and adolescents. *Developmental Psychology,* 1976, *12,* 77.

8

Antecedents and Consequences of Various Degrees of Paternal Involvement in Child Rearing: The Israeli Project

Abraham Sagi
University of Haifa, Israel

Honor your father and your mother
Exodus 20:12

Scholars commonly assume—without the necessary empirical support—that the mother is the only important influence on child development (Lamb, 1975, 1976, 1981a). In a thorough synthesis and review of the literature regarding the role of the father, Lamb and Goldberg (in press) concluded that there is no empirical support for the notion that mothers are biologically better prepared for nurturance and parenthood, and the claim that mothers alone can provide affectionate parenting appears untrue. Fathers can be as sensitive and responsive as mothers (Frodi, Lamb, Leavitt, & Donovan, 1978; Parke & Sawin, 1980), even if they usually do not actualize this potential.

By studying what usually is the case (i.e., traditional families) we cannot elucidate the potential and capacity of fathers to be nurturant caretakers because there are circumstances preventing the actualization of this potential. Furthermore, fathers' involvement and the desire of men to be involved in child care appears to be increasing in recent years, as evidenced by studies on single fatherhood (Gasser & Taylor, 1976; Levine, 1976; Mendes, 1976; Orthner, Brown & Ferguson, 1976), divorced fathers (Hetherington, Cox & Cox, 1976), paternal and joint custody (Freed, 1980; Greif, 1979), maternal employment (L. Hoffman, 1977), alternative life styles such as families with social contracts and families living in communes (Eiduson & Alexander, 1978), and nontraditional families in Sweden (Lamb, Frodi, Hwang, Frodi, & Steinberg, in press).

Consequently, it is important to study intact families with various degrees of paternal involvement in child care, including in the sample highly involved fathers (i.e., nontraditional fathers). This will advance our understanding of fathers' potential and capacity for effective nurturant parenthood.

DEFINITION OF NONTRADITIONAL FATHERS

There are several ways of defining nontraditional fathers. It is easiest to define nontraditional fathers in the context of nonintact families. Widowed, divorced, and adoptive fathers function in family situations that form the basis for non-traditionality. Although much can be learned about the fathers' potential for child rearing from studies of these types of nontraditional patterns, it is important to consider the aspects of nontraditionality exhibited in intact families as well. Because their nontraditionality does not derive from the objective circumstances that affect single fathers, it appears to be harder to define nontraditional fathers in intact families.

In considering the intact family, it is common to perceive the mother as playing the expressive role and the father the instrumental role (Parsons & Bales, 1955). Scholars studying nontraditional families generally use this typology as a baseline, marking deviations from it as "nontraditional." Although this typology may facilitate the definition of nontraditionality to some extent, it does not constitute an adequate definition. Is it satisfactory to assess the father's involvement in child care only in comparison to that of the mother? According to this system of evaluation, paternal nontraditionality is determined by quantitatively comparing mothers' and fathers' involvement in a given set of child-care activities. It is possible to determine nontraditionality on different dimensions of comparison as well. The fathers' activities can be compared to those of other fathers, or can be assessed independently, by determining the ratio of expressive and instrumental activities undertaken by the same father. Moreover, one may assess the extent of historical change in paternal child-care by comparing each father to his own father, and then use the rate of change as an index on nontraditionality.

Whatever alternative is selected, the definition of nontraditionality cannot be complete without taking into consideration the cultural context. For example, the role of the father, his background, and his impact on his children and family may be different in a kibbutz where children sleep in a central arrangement than in a kibbutz where children stay overnight with their parents.

However we define nontraditionality, recent findings (Levine, 1980) show that fathers who are more involved than the traditional norm are still less involved than the average mother. Incidentally, working mothers appear to be less involved than their husbands in their jobs. Thus, the deviation from the stereotypic parental behavior does not yet show a genuine role reversal, nor a state of equal role sharing, and one must be careful not to equate "nontraditional" with "role-reversing" or even "role-sharing" families. Levine (1980) suggested that we should not talk about the men who become "mothers" or about a new image for fathers, but rather about a new image for the family, with various degrees of paternal involvement considered. Even if these different degrees of involvement do not reflect drastic role shifting, they are sufficient to justify using the term "non–traditional" family.

Examining degrees of paternal involvement raises additional questions: can we compare nontraditional and traditional fathers, using one continuum of conceptualization and operation? Is the Parsonian typology relevant at all? Are the theoretical and empirical bases behind the Parsonian assumption valid for generating hypotheses? The answer is probably no. In other words, once paternal involvement is not defined in terms of the conventional conceptualization, the entire family system must be considered both more flexible and more complex. Lamb and Frodi (1980) also maintain that nontraditional fathers should be considered in different terms than traditional fathers, and they point out that nontraditional fathers may use different strategies for fostering psychological development than traditional fathers do.

It should be emphasized that these different strategies may occur in both nontraditional families that are markedly "deviant" and in those in which fathers are only slightly more involved than the average father. Whether the original basis for the deviation is intrinsic motivation or is due to circumstance, the change in paternal involvement interacts with and produces new circumstances for the father and his family, circumstances that in their turn may react upon the father and cause him to change and accommodate his strategy for exerting influence. This changing and accommodating process may change the ways in which fathers influence their children.

In order to examine more directly the ways in which fathers influence their children, a number of questions are addressed in this chapter. These questions form the basis of the sections that follow.

First, I consider the components of paternal involvement. In the initial section, I discuss the degree to which different aspects of paternal involvement covary, analyze the characteristics of involved and uninvolved fathers, and examine the levels of satisfaction of fathers who are differentially involved.

In the second section, I discuss factors affecting the degree of paternal involvement. The major focus here is on the fathers' recollections of their own fathers' involvement. The explanatory power of two hypotheses is examined: that fathers imitate their own fathers' behavior and that they attempt to compensate for the perceived uninvolvement of their fathers.

In the third section, I examine the effects on children of varying degrees of paternal involvement. This issue is addressed using data gathered from both the fathers and their children. The focus is on empathy, sex role, locus of control, and achievement.

Finally, I present preliminary data on the components and determinants of paternal involvement in subgroups (the Druze and the kibbutznikim) other than the urban Jews who are the focus of most of this research.

The Israeli project includes various segments of the Israeli population, representing different sociocultural styles. Three major populations have been investigated: urban families (Jews), rural Druze families, and kibbutz families. A complete set of data is available for the urban population, but only partial data are available for the other two groups at this time. Therefore, the core of the discussion is based on data regarding urban Jews. However, the data from the other population groups are also discussed where relevant.

DESCRIPTION OF THE STUDY WITH URBAN FAMILIES

In a large middle-class suburb of Haifa, all intact families with two children, one of whom, the subject, was between 3 and 6 years of age, were approached in the initial stage of recruitment. The parents completed a short questionnaire requesting each parent to rank independently the amount of time she or he was involved with the child in comparison to the spouse. Only those families in which both parents agreed on the father's involvement in child care were considered for inclusion in the study. In about 15 of the families there was agreement that the father was more involved than the mother; twenty of 150 agreed that mothers and fathers took equal responsibility in child rearing. These 35 were included in the study. In 115 of the 150 families there was agreement that the mothers were the primary caretakers. Twenty-five of these were selected randomly. Thus, there were altogether 60 families included in the final sample. This recruitment process maximized the possibility of arriving at a sample that contained sufficient variation in paternal involvement. It should be noted that, for the purposes of the analyses reported later, level of involvement was determined by an intensive questionnaire administered to the 60 subjects who were selected on the basis of the aforementioned process.

A structured questionnaire similar to the one used by Radin (1978, 1980) in the United States was completed by the fathers in this project. The fathers were asked to indicate the extent of their involvement in child care as well as their fathers' involvement in child rearing when they were children. The questionnaire assessed the following: (1) *involvement* (i.e., to what extent the father judged that he was involved in child rearing; (2) *responsibility for physical child care* (e.g., bathing, feeding); (3) *responsibility for the socialization process* (e.g., disciplining); (4) *decision making* in areas related to the child (e.g., what to buy for the child); (5) father's *availability* to his child (e.g., having lunch together); (6) amount of *nurturance* and *warmth* conveyed to the child (e.g., kissing and hugging). Each of these six aspects had a scoring range of 0–12 with a total score of 0–72 on what Radin labeled the Paternal Involvement in Child Care Index (PICCI). According to this index, the higher score indicates the greater involvement in child rearing.

The 60 PICCI scores were divided into three categories. The highest 20 scores formed the category of fathers with *high involvement;* the next 20 scores formed the *intermediate* group; the lowest 20 scores the group of fathers with *low involvement.*

Satisfaction is an important factor in evaluating paternal involvement. Therefore, the fathers were asked to rank their satisfaction with the various components of involvement in child care. They were also asked to indicate their satisfaction with *their* fathers' involvement in two ways: (1) from their current viewpoint as adults; and (2) from their recollections of how they felt as children.

The effects of paternal involvement on the child were examined by testing the following domains of child development: empathy, independence, achievement, locus of control, gender development, and children's perception of their fathers.

COMPONENTS OF PATERNAL INVOLVEMENT

Reviewing the research, Lamb (1981) indicated that in traditional families, paternal involvement is more intense with sons than with daughters, and that father–child interaction is characterized by a stereotypic relationship, whereby the father encourages expressive behavior in the daughter and instrumental behavior in the son. This characterization is typical in traditional families, but it is unclear whether the same stereotypic differentiation exists in less traditional ones. It is possible that these patterns may not be characteristic of nontraditional families.

To better understand the nature of the highly involved fathers, therefore, I have looked at: (1) the relationships between the various domains of his involvement, and (2) the father's feelings about his involvement. It is important to analyze the relationships among the various domains because this may help us understand the meaning of paternal involvement. Furthermore, by examining the subjective evaluations of paternal involvement—particularly satisfaction—one may better understand the factors affecting paternal motivation and involvement.

The correlations among the various components of paternal involvement in child care (Table 8.1) represent a coherent pattern, where the different components are in congruence with one another, despite the fact that some components

TABLE 8.1
Intercorrelations Among Paternal Measures

	Physical care	Socialization	Nurturance	Availability	Decision Making	PICCI Total
Involvement	.72	.70	.83	.68	.72	.92
Physical care		.77	.83	.57	.64	.86
Socialization			.80	.53	.60	.83
Nurturance				.67	.66	.93
Availability					.74	.80
Decision making						.83

All correlations are significant at $p < .001$.
$N = 60$.

represent expressiveness and others instrumentality. In other words, expressiveness seems to co-occur with instrumentality without the stereotypic division. It bears out what has already been proposed (Lamb & Frodi, 1980), that masculinity is not necessarily contradictory to interpersonal warmth. This is also the case when observing the interrelations among components of involvement according to sex of the child (Table 8.2).

The results concerning the relationship between satisfaction with various components of involvement in child care are presented in Table 8.3. These correlations clearly show that highly involved fathers are more pleased with nearly all aspects of involvement than less involved fathers are. This pattern clearly contradicts the traditional assumption that men feel uncomfortable when involved with their children more than the norm.

With regard to the children's satisfaction with paternal involvement, it will be recalled that fathers were asked to indicate their satisfaction with their fathers' involvement from their current viewpoint as adults, and from their recollections of how they felt as children. Fathers' involvement ($M = 35.45$) was higher than that reported for their fathers ($M = 27.06$). Paternal satisfaction with involvement was also higher ($M = 3.63$) than that reported for their fathers [$M = 3.07$, $t_{(51)} = 2.95$, $p < .005$]. Moreover, the fathers expressed greater satisfaction with their own paternal involvement ($M = 3.7$) than they felt regarding their fathers' involvement [$M = 3.06$, $t_{(49)} = 3.47$, p $< .001$]. These results imply that the fathers are more satisfied with what they do than with what they feel their fathers did for them, which is consistent with the fact that fathers' involvement is greater than that reported for fathers' fathers. Thus the tendency is both toward increased perceived paternal involvement and toward developing more positive attitudes about it. It seems likely that the increased amount of satisfaction heightens involvement.

TABLE 8.2
Intercorrelations Among Paternal Measures According to Sex

	Physical care	Socialization	Nurturance	Availability	Decision Making
Involvement—Boys	.70	.67	.89	.66	.73
Involvement—Girls	.73	.75	.79	.69	.70
Physical care—Boys		.74	.82	.45	.62
Physical care—Girls		.80	.83	.67	.65
Socialization—Boys			.75	.50	.60
Socialization—Girls			.84	.57	.62
Nurturance—Boys				.52	.73
Nurturance—Girls				.79	.61
Availability—Boys					.80
Availability—Girls					.68

Note: All correlations are significant at $p < .001$.
$N = 60$.

TABLE 8.3
Correlations between Paternal Measures and Satisfaction

	Involvement	Physical Care	Socialization	Decision Making	Nurturance	Availability
Satisfaction	.40**	.46***	.32*	.30*	.53***	.24

*p < .05.
**p < .01.
***p < .001.
N = 55.

The relationship between involvement and satisfaction was further analyzed by considering those fathers who were dissatisfied ($N = 13$). Only one of these 13 fathers claimed that his dissatisfaction arose from being overly involved in child rearing. All the others stated that their dissatisfaction came from not being sufficiently involved. To examine these 12 subjects more closely, their PICCI scores were related to the median, yielding 10 dissatisfied fathers with scores below the median. This difference was found to be significant (a goodness-of-fit text; $\chi^2 = 5.33$, $p < .05$), implying that dissatisfaction was more characteristic of traditional fathers.

In sum, a pattern emerged whereby fathers who are highly involved in child rearing manifested a capacity to integrate expressive and instrumental activities and thereby model less stereotypically masculine behavior than traditional fathers do. The fathers' satisfaction with this style of paternal behavior may positively affect their children's development.

DETERMINANTS OF PATERNAL INVOLVEMENT

When examining the determinants of paternal involvement, many different factors must be considered. These include: the behavior of the fathers and parents (especially their fathers' involvement); the fathers' personality; the families' socioeconomic circumstances; and cultural norms or expectations.

To elucidate processes associated with various degrees of paternal involvement, the present section focuses on the relationship between the fathers' involvement in child care and their reports of their fathers' involvement when they were children. This discussion is based on data from the Israeli project as well as from previous studies.

Two major hypotheses can be generated with regard to the father–father's father relationship. The "compensatory" hypothesis suggests that high paternal involvement is a function of the involved fathers themselves having had fathers who were unavailable and not affectively supportive, so that the current high involvement is an attempt to compensate for lack of intense contact with the subjects' fathers. Alternatively, the "modeling" hypothesis suggests that high paternal involvement in child care is associated with fathers whose own fathers were also highly involved in child care. According to the "modeling" hypothesis, current nontraditional involvement is a result of a father imitating his own involved, available, and supportive father. Some empirical data pertaining to these hypotheses are available.

The following studies relate to the compensatory hypothesis. Mendes (1976) identified a subgroup of single fathers as "aggressive seekers," namely, fathers who acted forcefully to obtain custody of their children, with complete disregard for the mothers' wishes and desires. Mendes found these fathers to be motivated by competing interpersonal forces, some of which seemed to stem from traumatic childhood experiences. In other words, their strong desire for custody arose from compensatory needs resulting from their own childhood.

Further apparent support for the compensatory hypothesis is found in Eiduson and Alexanders (1978) study of "alternative families" (in which the parents were unmarried). The fathers in "alternative families" viewed their childhood as unhappy, whereas a comparison group of traditional fathers perceived their childhood as happy; also, traditional mothers were found to have had a better relationship with their mothers than "alternative mothers" had.

Considering intact families, De Frain (1979) defined parents who claimed to share child-care and career responsibilities relatively equally as "androgynous." Most "androgynous" parents rated their parents as traditional, at least in terms of sex-role orientation. Therefore, this too lends support to the compensatory hypothesis.

However, when Radin (1980) tried to verify the compensatory hypothesis in intact families, she found that child-rearing fathers did not necessarily have unloving, unavailable, and powerless fathers. Therefore, she concluded that there was not a direct relationship in her sample between uninvolved fathers' behavior and the way their sons acted when they became fathers themselves.

In sum, the few available studies do not conclusively support the compensatory hypothesis. Although studies of single fathers or "alternative families" do lend support to the compensatory hypothesis, studies on nontraditional fathers in the intact family do not. Moreover, the compensatory hypothesis denies the potential for positive modeling.

Concerning the modeling hypothesis, Manion (1977) found that fathers who were more involved in child care recalled their own fathers as being more nurturant; whereas less involved fathers recalled their fathers as being less nurturant. This study provides some evidence for the modeling hypothesis, although more thorough investigation is necessary.

In the Israeli project, the involvement of fathers in child care was correlated with the perceived involvement of their fathers ($r = .49$) indicating a moderate linear relationship between the two variables. As can be seen in Table 8.4, most of the PICCI components of the father correlated significantly with those of the father's father. The general trend supports the modeling hypothesis.

TABLE 8.4
Correlations between Fathers' PICCI Scores and Fathers' Fathers' PICCI Scores

Father's father	Involvement	Physical Care	Socialization	Decision Making	Nurturance	Availability	Total
Involvement	.47**	.33**	.42***	.39***	.43***	.51***	.49***
Physical care	.36**	.43***	.41***	.32**	.36**	.39***	.43***
Socialization	.33**	.35**	.46***	.36**	.34**	.31**	.40***
Decision making	.50***	.36**	.40***	.38***	.39***	.45***	.48***
Nurturance	.24*	.22*	.15	.17	.26*	.22*	.25*
Availability	.30**	.25*	.16	.25*	.29*	.52***	.34**
Total	.46***	.39***	.41***	.38***	.43***	.50***	.49***

*$p < .05$.
*$p < .01$.
***$p < .001$.
$N = 60$.

The internal consistency of the fathers' PICCI has been shown before (Table 8.1), and the relevant correlations among paternal reports of the fathers' fathers are presented in Table 8.5. The internal consistency for fathers' fathers is evident as well (i.e., the various paternal measures are highly correlated).

This internal consistency and the correlations supporting the modeling hypothesis seem to indicate that highly involved fathers (with higher PICCI scores) can incorporate both "expressive" (e.g. nurturance) and "instrumental" (e.g. decision making, some aspects of socialization) activities into one coherent whole. In other words, fathers can act instrumentally while simultaneously being available, warm, supportive, and nurturant with their children. These paternal characteristics are then imitated and reinforced when the son becomes a father, even if the pattern of fatherhood consists of both "masculine" and "feminine" activities.

The data can also be evaluated by noting the direction of change occurring in paternal involvement in child rearing. This kind of change can be examined by subtracting the father's PICCI from the PICCI reported for his father, assessing whether this difference is significant, and regarding its direction (positive or negative). The difference between the mean scores of each PICCI component for the fathers versus that of the fathers' fathers were compared by means of t-tests. The means and relevant significance value are presented in Table 8.6.

Table 8.6 indicates that fathers of this generation say they are becoming more involved than their fathers in child rearing. Therefore, in addition to claiming imitation of their fathers, the fathers go beyond their own fathers' involvement. This intensification of paternal involvement is further evident in that the correlations for the fathers' fathers were lower than those for the fathers (Tables 8.1, 8.5).

Taking into consideration both the Israeli data, which supported the modeling hypothesis, and the other findings reviewed previously, it appears reasonable not to treat the compensatory and modeling hypotheses in "all or none" terms. The two curves representing the relationship between the father and his son are not mutually exclusive, and either process is possible depending on the circumstances.

TABLE 8.5
Intercorrelations Among Fathers' Fathers' Measures

	Physical Care	Socialization	Nurturance	Availability	Decision Making	PICCI Total
Involvement	.73	.56	.64	.66	.72	.91
Physical care		.71	.57	.49	.59	.83
Socialization			.38	.42	.59	.72
Nurturance				.59	.50	.78
Availability					.58	.77
Decision Making						.83

All correlations are significant at $p < .001$.
$N = 60$.

TABLE 8.6
Mean Scores of PICCI Components for Fathers and Fathers' Fathers

	Fathers	Fathers' Fathers	t	p
Involvement	8.08	5.68	4.80	.001
Physical care	2.93	2.26	2.20	.04
Socialization	3.30	3.16	0.54	NS
Decision Making	5.28	3.97	3.66	.001
Nurturance	8.05	5.40	5.36	.001
Availability	7.82	6.58	4.44	.001
PICCI Total	35.45	27.06	4.88	.001

$N = 60$.

That is, above a given level of involvement by his father, the son tends to imitate and even strengthen the paternal behavior when he himself becomes a father. Below a certain level of involvement by his father, the son may compensate for the perceived unavailability of his father by becoming highly involved when he is a father. The fact that both processes operate may account for the few negative correlations Radin (1978, 1980) found between the involvement of the fathers and that of their fathers.

Apparently, processes of compensation and imitation stimulate the actualization of the tendency for involvement. On the basis of the available research, it is unclear what minimum amount of paternal involvement is necessary for the father to be perceived as a model to imitate rather than a model to reject.

Independently of the father's father's-involvement in child care and its potential effect on his child's developing paternal role, there are other variables that are related to the development of a more involved father.

In this connection, Russell (1979, 1980), in his Australian study, performed the most thorough analysis of the characteristics of nontraditional fathers. The following variables were found to be associated with high paternal involvement in caregiving: high education of wives; fathers who work fewer hours than uninvolved fathers; fathers who attended delivery; fathers who had high femininity scores and mothers who had high masculinity scores in Bem's (1974) test; and families with one child. All these variables, however, were not examined in the Israeli project.

Another central variable related to paternal involvement is maternal employment. Hoffman (1979) and Lamb (1981) concluded that in families where the mothers work, the fathers are somewhat more involved in child care. L. Hoffman (1977, 1979) suggested further that maternal employment is associated with less traditional role division at home. The Israeli project examined this variable and the findings are presented in Table 8.7. As can be seen, 38% of the mothers in this sample worked. In 91% of the families with working mothers, the fathers were in the groups of fathers with either intermediate or high involvement.

TABLE 8.7
The Number of Working and Nonworking Mothers in the
Three Groups of Paternal Involvement

	Fathers with Low Involvement	Fathers with Intermediate Involvement	Fathers with High Involvement
Mothers work	2	11	10
Mothers do not work	18	9	10

$\chi^2_{(2)} = 10.29$, $p < .01$.

Moreover, of the 10 families with highly involved fathers, seven mothers had full-time employment (about 40 hours per week). In seven of the 11 families with intermediate involvement, the mothers had part-time positions (about 20 hours per week). Although the intermediate category has been defined as a type of nontraditional style, it can be seen that the nature of maternal employment in this category differs from that in families with highly involved fathers.

Based on previous studies and the Israeli data, it is unclear to what extent one can associate the relationship between maternal employment and paternal involvement to circumstantial or motivational factors. The Israeli data show that full-time employment of the mother was associated with more parental involvement. However, the association between the number of hours the mothers worked and the degree of paternal involvement in child rearing does not necessarily support one explanation or another. Although paternal involvement may be an incidental outcome of maternal employment, it is equally possible that the mother's decision to work full time or part time is based on a variety of considerations. Thus where parents have decided to share childcare to a moderate extent, mothers may decide to work part-time, whereas others may choose high paternal involvement so that mothers can pursue self-actualization in full-time employment. As can be seen, the current set of data do not provide a basis for any clear-cut conclusions regarding the motivation versus circumstances issue.

Another aspect of maternal employment is the mother's satisfaction with her role as a working mother. Hoffman (1974, 1979) suggested that the mother's satisfaction with her role increases her effectiveness as a parent. In this respect, Schubert, Bradley-Johnson, and Nuttal (1980) also reported that the quality of mother–infant interaction among working mothers was not inferior to that of nonworking mothers.

The Israeli project assessed the couple's satisfaction with maternal employment, but because 91% of the working mothers had husbands who were highly involved in child care, the differential satisfaction associated with families with high versus low paternal involvement could not be assessed. The data show that most husbands of working mothers managed very well in their situation and seemed satisfied with it (91%), and that their wives were satisfied as well (100%). Thus, it appears that the changing pattern, where mothers work, either as a result of self-motivation or of circumstances, is well accepted by both the mother and the father, thereby contributing to effective parenthood. In sum, these findings indicate that paternal involvement is significantly affected by the patterns of behavior modeled by the fathers' own fathers. The results also show that fathers are able to integrate instrumental and expressive characteristics into their paternal behavior. Both mothers and fathers seem happy with increased paternal involvement and the enhanced opportunities for maternal employment.

CONSEQUENCES FOR CHILDREN

Rationale.   In this section, the effects on children of increased paternal involvement are discussed. When considering effects of paternal involvement on children, one must be careful not to generate hypotheses derived from the traditional conceptualization of fatherhood. It has been suggested previously that the dynamics and strategy of exerting influence may be different in nontraditional families.

The following discussion aims to show that the directions of influence in traditional and nontraditional fathers are not necessarily different. For example, if a traditional father encourages masculinity in his son, it would be incorrect to hypothesize that nontraditional fathers would do the opposite. In other words, nontraditional fathers may not exert opposite influences on their children; it would be more appropriate to speak of differences in configurations of influence.

As we have seen, the effects of traditional fathers are usually categorized in conventional terms such as the expressive–instrumental division. For this reason, the focus here is both on constructs that are associated with instrumental and expressive dimensions and on constructs that have been studied extensively in investigations of traditional families. The traditional family encourages such characteristics as empathy, interpersonal affective communication, sensitivity, and dependency in girls, whereas boys are directed toward more independence, internal locus of control, and achievement, with less emphasis on expressive skills. Regarding the development of gender role, many theories have been proposed (Bronfenbrenner, 1960; Kohlberg, 1966; Mischel, 1970; Mussen, 1969; Sears, 1965), and whatever their different views, most attempt to explain why girls acquire feminine, and boys masculine roles.

When considering deviations from the traditional family, one may note that the entire system of dynamics changes. Aldous (1974) suggested that when a person assumes a role within the family that deviates from the norm (''role maker''), he or she needs to maintain a high level of self-esteem, independence, and ability to control his or her situation. Furthermore, this person should be sufficiently sensitive to interpret properly signals conveyed by others in different situations. These abilities facilitate personal and interpersonal growth and development.

According to Aldous, the complexity of influences changes and the directions of influence broaden during the "role-making" process. Because role makers are capable of assimilating seemingly contradictory skills (e.g., being masculine-career oriented and at the same time taking care of children), they can exert influences in seemingly opposite directions (e.g., causing the child to be career oriented as well as developing his expressiveness). This fits perfectly with Lamb and Frodi's (1980) notion that interpersonal warmth is not necessarily inconsistent with masculinity.

Considering the complexity of influences, one must take into consideration the feelings of the fathers. It has been shown previously that the highly involved father is pleased with his situation, and it is of interest to see to what extent this paternal satisfaction affects his development and that of the child.

Heath (1978) conducted a longitudinal investigation of students in their twenties and early thirties and found, in support of Erikson's hypothesis, that fatherhood may enhance a man's maturity, his self-awareness, his familial relationships, and the acceptance and integration of his emotional needs. From an Eriksonian point of view, it can be argued that the positive contribution to the father himself forms a basis for tolerance with his children, for self-control, and for communication of emotions.

In Russell's Australian study (1980), fathers reported that involvement in child care added another dimension to their lives and they were pleased with it. The positive feeling that change evoked in the father may be seen as a mediating mechanism enriching the influence exerted on the child. A similar pattern was found among single fathers (Orthner et al., 1976), who stressed their capability as fathers and expressed satisfaction with their parenthood.

Thus, the available evidence and Lamb's (1982) recent analysis show that satisfaction with parenthood may cause the father to be more responsive and sensitive with his children. His potential influence on his children is therefore broader, and nontraditional fathers are likely to influence their children in expressive as well as instrumental skills. They increase the likelihood of identification with them as well. This broad potential influence stems from either an intrinsic integrative capacity or from a capacity acquired through experience. Moreover, the complex, integrative skills of the nontraditional fathers and their less stereotypic paternal behavior are likely to reduce, directly or indirectly, sex differences in various aspects of the development of their children.

In this regard, the Israeli project tested the following domains of child development: empathy, independence, achievement, and locus of control. Empathy can be conceived as an expressive skill, and the remaining domains as instrumental. Gender development and children's perception of their fathers were also examined.

Empathy.   This concept has been extensively described by M. Hoffman (1978), who proposed a developmental theory of empathy. In his discussion of the socialization processes affecting empathy, Hoffman did not direct attention to the differential role of fathers and mothers but reported (M. Hoffman, 1977) that girls show earlier and greater development in the domain of empathy. In tracing the reason for the sex differences in empathic development, it is important to examine who influences the development. Because girls are assumed to identify most closely with their mothers, we may infer that the girls' development in empathy stems from a situation where it is the mothers who transmit empathic skill in the socialization process.

A recent study (Barnett, King, Howard, & Dino, 1980), focusing on the relationship between parenthood and empathy, found the mother in the traditional family to be the major contributor to the children's empathic skills. Whether the development of empathy is a mere function of female effects, or due to the simple fact that it is mothers who spend most of their time with their children, is an open question, and some of the answers may be provided by examining fathers who are more involved with their children.

A few studies (Rutherford & Mussen, 1968; Speece, 1967) indicate that when traditional fathers are nurturant, their children develop greater generosity and altruism than the children of less nurturant fathers. Moreover, Hoffman (1970) found that more involved fathers cause a higher level of moral internalization in their children. Because it has been established that altruism and moral internalization are integrally related to empathy (Hoffman, 1976), it can be argued on the basis of this indirect evidence that empathy is not a sex-differentiated characteristic. It is the supportive and nurturant involvement in child rearing, rather than femininity, that is necessary for the development of empathy. Lamb (1981) concluded that warm and sensitive fathers help lay the basis for social competence in the child and establish a better capability for interpersonal relationships.

The Israeli project considered empathy as a type of social competence and used Borke's (1971) Empathy Test as a measure.[1] The results were as follows: Children of high-involved fathers scored highest ($M = 11.70$); next was the intermediate group ($M = 10.30$); and last were the low-involved fathers ($M = 9.15$). The differences were found to be significant $F_{2,54} = 14.64$, $p < .001$).

It can be concluded that fathers contribute to the development of empathy and that their influence increases in accordance with their involvement. Perhaps the potential for interpersonal skills in children is not fully materialized in traditional families because of insufficient paternal involvement.

Locus of Control, Achievement, and Independence.   The constructs of locus of control, achievement, and independence are interrelated because they all represent the instrumental domain. Therefore, for the present purposes they are

---

[1]A more thorough discussion on the controversy concerning this measure—whether it represents empathic capacity or cognitive role taking—is beyond the scope of this chapter.

discussed together, because hypotheses can be generated on similar logical grounds.

Traditional fathers expect boys to exhibit more internal locus of control, achievement, and independence, and they expect girls to be more dependent and less achievement oriented. This stereotypic division was discussed recently by Block (1978), who also maintained that fathers pay less attention to their daughters. However, Lamb, Owen, and Chase-Lansdale (1979) suggest that fathers not only pay less attention to their daughters, but also provide a different kind of attention, where they encourage more expressiveness and less instrumentality. Furthermore, Lamb et al. stated that more strict and less nurturant fathers tend to increase their daughters' independence. This does not mean that the way to enhance independence should include rejection, but it does mean that fathers should reduce "infantilizing nurturance" (Lamb et al., 1979) in their attitude toward their daughters.

The question that arises is what happens when we consider families that deviate from the traditional structure, where fathers are capable of incorporating instrumental and expressive approaches simultaneously. For example, it can be seen (Gasser & Taylor, 1976; Schlesinger & Todres, 1976) that single fathers encourage participation of their children in various roles in the home; rather than using external assistance they prefer to rely on their children and themselves to share problems and chores. This sharing is accompanied by emotional support and loving and nurturant behavior. These fathers encourage their children to develop independence and a sense of control of the situation, but this does not come at the expense of providing nurturance and warmth. Lozoff (1974) further supports the notion that enhancement of instrumentality is not necessarily at the expense of expressiveness. In her study, women who performed well both in intellectual skills and achievement as well as in interpersonal communication reported that they had supportive fathers with whom they were able to identify. Lamb (1981) concurred with these findings and maintained that fathers who model instrumental competence while providing emotional support encourage more successful professional development in their daughters.

Because paternal involvement in child rearing does not necessarily indicate a lack of instrumental skills, but perhaps a complementary capacity for expressiveness, we may hypothesize that the expressiveness of highly involved fathers facilitates their children's acquisition of such skills as internal locus of control, achievement, and independence. The Israeli project examined these three constructs.

Locus of control was assessed by direct testing of the child, whereas information regarding independence and achievement was gathered by examining the expectations of the fathers. The Stanford Preschool Internal-External Scale [(SPIES); Mischel, Zeiss, & Zeiss, 1974] was completed by the children, and the Torgoff Developmental Timetable (Torgoff, 1967) by the fathers.

Children of fathers with intermediate and high involvement exhibited significantly ($F_{2,54} = 12.01$, $p < .001$) more internal locus of control ($M = 7.35$ and

$M = 8.25$ respectively) than children of fathers with low involvement ($M = 5.70$). This applied to both boys and girls. Moreover, fathers with intermediate and high involvement reported that they encouraged achievement ($M_{\text{intermediate}} = 60.75$ and $M_{\text{high}} = 57.47$) and independence ($M_{\text{intermediate}} = 60.52$ and $M_{\text{high}} = 57.60$) in their sons and daughters earlier ($F_{2,54} = 34.48$, $p < .001$ for achievement; $F_{2,54} = 30.43$, $p < .001$ for independence) than did fathers with low involvement ($M_{\text{achievement}} = 83.57$ and $M_{\text{independence}} = 81.92$). The findings consistently showed that highly involved fathers had high expectations of their children on instrumental measures and that they encouraged development in this direction.

The Child's Gender Development and Perception of the Father.   As before, we must be careful to generate differential hypotheses for traditional and nontraditional families. In a synthesis of the literature, focusing mainly on the traditional family, Lamb (1981) concluded that girls do not imitate their fathers with regard to gender development, whereas boys do identify with their fathers (Payne & Mussen, 1956) and do so more readily when fathers are supportive and nurturant.

When we consider families where paternal involvement is greater than the norm, it is still unclear what latitude is available for daughters to imitate their fathers and for boys to do so more intensively than in traditional families. Paternal warmth and nurturance are necessary in order for boys to identify successfully with their fathers even in traditional families, so that increased warmth and nurturance in "deviant" families may not leave much latitude for change in this respect. Nevertheless, De Frain's (1979) findings show that "androgynous" parents generate in their children a broader perspective of sex role than do traditional parents. Lamb and Bronson (1980) also maintain that fathers who are involved in child rearing need not exhibit a lack of masculinity, nor do they influence their children in a nonmasculine direction, but quite the contrary; men who are secure with their masculinity can "afford" to be less stereotypic.

Regarding sex role, the Israeli project dealt with two major areas of inquiry. First, the children's gender orientation was examined by employing the It-scale. The hypothesis was that highly involved fathers would have more influence, particularly on their daughters, so that these girls should score higher than daughters of less involved fathers on the masculine dimension of the It-scale. With regard to boys, even children in traditional families, who follow a normal identification process, tend to have high scores of masculinity on the It-scale. Therefore, not much latitude is left while using this test to reflect the increased masculinity expected in the sons of nontraditional fathers.

Second, we examined the children's perceptions of their fathers. Comparing children of highly involved fathers with those of less involved fathers, we investigated the differences in the children's perception of their fathers in terms of their nurturance, punitiveness, and dominance. The Kagan Parent Role Test (Kagan & Lemkin, 1960), which includes items relevant to these three categories, was administered to the children. Unlike the gender orientation, in the case of the children's perception of their fathers, more ''degrees of freedom'' may be available for influence by highly involved fathers not only on daughters but also on sons. The hypothesis here was that sons and daughters of highly involved fathers would perceive their fathers as more nurturant and dominant and as less punitive than children of less involved fathers.

The findings show that paternal involvement did influence the It-scale scores. Children in the groups with intermediate and high paternal involvement scored higher in masculinity ($F_{2,54} = 9.74$, $p < .001$) than children in the groups of low paternal involvement ($Ms = 51.00$; 47.30; 38.3 respectively). There were sex differences ($F_{1,54} = 197.63$, $p < .001$), not surprisingly, with girls scoring as less ($M = 33.00$) and boys as more masculine ($M = 58.07$). In other words, despite the differential effects of the fathers, the children's gender development proceeded normally, with the boys continuing to exhibit male-oriented and the girls female-oriented scores. Moreover, a significant interaction ($F_{2,54} = 4.24$, $p < .05$) was found to support the hypothesis regarding sex-role orientation: an effect for paternal involvement was found only for girls, whereby daughters of fathers with intermediate and high involvement scored higher on the masculinity aspect than did the daughters of low-involved fathers ($Ms = 41.20$; 37.00; 20.80 respectively). At the same time, the scores of all the girls were within the femininity range. Boys in all three paternal groups scored equally ($M_{high} = 57.60$; $M_{intermediate} = 60.8$; $M_{low} = 55.8$). The explanation of the ''ceiling effect'' on the It-scale provided previously for boys is applicable here as well. Based on these data, it can be seen that involved fathers do not eliminate the feminine tendencies of their daughters, but add to the sex-role orientation a masculine perspective as well.

Concerning children's perceptions of their fathers, it can be seen in Table 8.8 that children (sons and daughters) of fathers with intermediate and high involvement perceived them as more nurturant, more dominant, and less punitive than children of fathers with low involvement.

These findings indicate that the father can be perceived as being both powerful and nurturant, and that the child makes a distinction between power and punitiveness. The less stereotypic models at home enabled the children to perceive

TABLE 8.8
Summary of Means and F-Values for Kagan Parent Role Test
According to Paternal Involvement

	Low Paternal Involvement	Intermediate Paternal Involvement	High Paternal Involvement	F-Value
Punitiveness	5.75	4.70	4.35	5.98*
Nurturance	1.25	2.85	4.10	34.80*
Dominance	9.30	12.30	14.95	35.36*

*$p < .001$.

their fathers as maintaining dominance while being capable of reflecting love and warmth at the same time.

In sum, we have seen that more involved fathers expect their children to be more independent and achievement oriented than do less involved fathers. Involved fathers also believe that they provide their children with more cognitive stimulation than less involved fathers do. In addition, increased paternal involvement directly affects the development of empathy, internal locus of control, sex-role orientation, and perception of fathers on the part of young children.

FATHERS IN OTHER ISRAELI SUBCULTURES

West and Konner (1976) first analyzed the role of fathers in a cross-cultural context and concluded that styles of fathers vary in relation to family structure and the work activities of adult men and women. In order to examine populations with varying family patterns and work activities, the Israeli project included, in addition to urban communities, families from kibbutzim and from the Druze community.

The Druze. The Druze are an independent religious and ethnic group in Israel. They regard themselves as "Sons of Ma'aruf," namely, "sons of grace," and they are very proud of their uniqueness. The Druze usually settle on mountains, and they reside mainly in the Lebanese mountains, the Druze Mountains (Syria), the Golan Heights, and Israel. In Israel, there are 46,000 Druze (8% of the non-Jews in Israel), and they are centered in the Western Galilee and Mount Carmel. Although they are not Arabs, their language is Arabic. They have an independent legal–religious status, maintaining their own religious justice system, which is supposed to conform to and reinforce Druze tradition. The Druze marry at a very young age: females in late adolescence (median age is 18.7), and males in their early twenties (median age is 22.1) (Dela-Pargola, 1980). Usually the marriages are prearranged by the extended family system.

The birthrate among the Druze is very high (average of 6.9 children per family) and, because of early marriage and the very conservative family system, the duration of marriage is very long, with a minimal number of separations or divorce. The level of education is relatively low, particularly in the female population. The division of roles within the family is traditional, with females doing all the housework and child rearing, while the fathers are responsible for breadwinning. Due to the significant gap in education between most men and women, the men in some families have begun to assume more responsibility for their children's education. For example, it is the fathers who possess the capacity to assist in the acquisition of writing and reading skills, as most mothers are illiterate.

The current project is taking place in the village of Isafia, located on Mt. Carmel, close to metropolitan Haifa. Although the women lead a fairly sheltered existence, the men are exposed to city life and serve in the Israeli Defense Forces. The family system as a whole is very traditional, but we have a unique situation, where women are highly religious and maintain their traditionality, whereas the men are less religious, some not at all, and more exposed to other practices and beliefs.

The fathers and children in the project were administered tests similar to those given to the other population groups, with relevant language and cultural adjustments. The scoring system was somewhat different from that used for urban Jews, with the PICCI scores ranging from 432 to 2160. Although this difference can be treated by a statistical transformation, there were some internal changes in structuring the items, mainly due to cultural adjustments, that make the PICCI scores in the different populations statistically noncomparable. The number of children in the family was not controlled for. The level of education for females was no more than primary school and that of males was an average of 10 years. The current data are limited to 36 fathers.

The correlation between PICCI for fathers versus fathers' fathers is $r = .34$, $p < .05$, which suggests that modeling affects paternal behavior. Examining this relationship more closely, we found that it was specifically nurturance ($r = .36$, $p < .05$) and physical care ($r = .58$, $p < .001$) that were likely to be modeled. Thus, we can see that even in a society as traditional as that of the Druze, these linear patterns appear, especially for expressive functions.

Moreover, as was the case with urban Jews, Druze fathers tended to perceive themselves as more expressively involved with their children, so that whereas the PICCI mean score of the fathers' fathers was 1122.47, that of the fathers was 1259.56, and the difference was found to be significant [$t_{(35)} = 2.74$, $p < .01$]. If we use the midpoint (i.e., 1296) of the possible range (i.e., 432—2160) as the cutoff, the father's score is lower than this cutoff ($Z = -1.73$, $p < .05$) and falls within the range of fathers with low involvement among urban Jews. Nevertheless, we can see the trend, as perceived by the fathers, for a change toward more paternal involvement in child care. Fathers exceed their fathers' involvement mainly in the areas of nurturance [$t_{(34)} = 5.34$, $p < .001$] and physical care [$t_{(34)} = 4.51$, $p < .001$].

The correlations found between PICCI scores of fathers and their fathers, as well as the increased paternal involvement, suggest a pattern similar to that of urban Jews (i.e., that sons tend to imitate their nurturant and involved fathers, and to intensify this involvement when they become fathers themselves). These trends could be the outcome of "intrinsic motivation" or of circumstances, such as the ones deriving from the fact that fathers of this generation are more educated than their wives and their fathers, and have been subject to the influence of the city, thereby recognizing their potential for positive contribution to their children. Whatever the motivation for change, a change toward more paternal involvement is definitely taking place. This change is likely to have positive effects on the aspects of child development described previously for the Jewish sample. This area is being further investigated at the present time.

Druze fathers were also found to exhibit satisfaction with their paternal involvement in childrearing ($r = .52$, $p < .001$). Examining the differences between their satisfaction with their involvement in child rearing versus their satisfaction with their fathers' involvement based on childhood recollections ($M = 3.26$) and current adult perceptions ($M - 3.11$) revealed significant differences [$t_{(34)} = 3.14$, $p < .005$; $t_{(34)} = 3.19$, $p < .005$]. Thus even in such a traditional culture, Druze fathers can be seen to enjoy their paternal role more than they enjoyed that of their fathers, and this increased satisfaction is associated with their perceived increased paternal involvement, particularly on the expressive level.

As with the Jewish sample, those fathers who scored 3 or less on the satisfaction scale were asked to explain their dissatisfaction. Of nine dissatisfied fathers, six felt that they were not sufficiently involved in child rearing; three felt that they were overly involved. Although the N is too small to warrant any statistical test, "eyeballing" the data suggests that dissatisfaction is more highly associated with feelings of insufficient involvement. Although they are traditional in many respects, the Druze seem to feel, as do other fathers, more comfortable with increased involvement in child rearing, despite informal reports by interviewees indicating that for the father to show physical contact and affection in public is shameful. The Druze's inhibition of their affectionate and nurturant behavior toward their children is probably a function of unsupportive traditional norms rather than lack of skills or desire for such behavior.

Fathers in Kibbutzim. The kibbutz is no longer a new phenomenon in sociological and psychological research, and its use as a natural laboratory has been discussed recently by Beit-Hallahmi and Rabin (1977). Each kibbutz is a cooperative community having an average of about 100 families. Kibbutz members, both men and women, work in agriculture and industry belonging to the kibbutz. The profits belong to the kibbutz as a system, and members are provided on an equal basis with residence facilities, food, clothing, and other necessary services. During the day, children are cared for, physically and educationally, by child caretakers (metapelet—singular; metaplot—plural) and teachers. Some kibbutzim still maintain the traditional style of sleeping arrangements, where the children sleep in a children's house together with other children their age rather than with their parents. Other kibbutzim have been shifting to a familial arrangement, whereby children join their parents in the afternoon and stay with them overnight.

The kibbutz ideology places little emphasis on sex differences, but as Tiger and Shepher (1975) pointed out, use of the Hebrew language (which is heavily loaded with gender marks) and the exposure to the city makes the erasure of sex differences impossible. Tiger and Shepher also noted that most of the time children spend with their parents is devoted to nurturant interactions, whereas education and socialization are taken care of by the collective system. The children's centers in the kibbutz differ in several ways from urban day-care centers. Because the kibbutz metaplot are members of the kibbutz, they feel more attached to the children and seem to be warmer and more nurturant with the children than are teachers in urban day-care centers, who do their jobs for money. The size of the group in the kibbutz is smaller and there is a higher ration of metaplot per child, than in urban arrangements. Moreover, the children's center is located inside the kibbutz (i.e., the children's home environment), which makes the parents more available and accessible. Therefore, in addition to nurturance by the parents, the socialization and educational processes are heavily loaded with sincere warmth and nurturance by the caretakers and educators. The kibbutz arrangement for children coincides with Etaugh's (1980) suggestions for a good solution to the problem of supplementary care (i.e., a family day-care setting). Furthermore, it should be noted that family life is of crucial importance in the kibbutz. Tiger and Shepher (1975) stressed that couples usually make sure to have their meals together in the central dining room and are intensively involved in cultural activities together, take their vacations together, and in many cases serve together during the night shifts (baby-sitting, etc.). Also, family parties are heavily emphasized and parents take any opportunity—sabbaths, holidays, and other occasions—to be with their children. There is an emphasis on what Tiger and Shepher refer to as "familism." Tiger and Shepher's findings indicated that it was the women (70%) who more strongly support the familial sleeping arrangement, whereas only about 50% of the men did so. This figure is sufficient to indicate that many fathers want more involvement in the family.

The project examined two types of kibbutzim: those with a collective system and those with a familial system. Data are currently available for 28 fathers from the collective system and 25 fathers from the familial system. All fathers had at least high school education, and the kibbutzim included in the study (like most kibbutzim) are considered middle to upper middle class.

In both kibbutz systems, the correlations between the PICCI scores of fathers and those of their fathers were found to be insignificant. Based on these findings, neither the modeling nor the compensatory hypotheses were supported. However, fathers in both the familial system ($M = 1328.80$) and the collective system ($M = 1357.99$) scored higher than their fathers ($Ms = 1116.90$ and 1187.50 respectively), and pairwise tests revealed significant differences [$t_{(23)} = 2.52$, $p < .02$; $t_{(27)} = 2.47$, $p < .02$]. Furthermore, the findings showed, as was the case with the Druze, that the nurturant component contributed significantly to the change in paternal involvement. In the collective system, the mean nurturance score for the fathers was 313.80 and that for their fathers was 254.50 [$t_{(26)} = 3.97$, $p < .001$]. The mean score for the fathers in the familial system was 300.60 and that for their fathers was 230.70 [$t_{(22)} = 3.62$, $p < .002$]. The difference in the physical care component was also significant in the collective system, with fathers scoring 188.00 and their fathers 143.10 [$t_{(26)} = 3.97$, $p < .001$]. Fathers in the familial system were found to be significantly more available ($M = 279.40$) than their fathers reportedly had been [$M = 223.40$; $t_{(22)} = 2.58$, $p < .02$].

Thus, on the one hand, the findings show no relationship between paternal behavior of fathers and their fathers and, on the other hand, a change toward more paternal involvement in this generation, as perceived by the fathers, particularly with regard to nurturance, physical care, and availability. This may indicate that the changes are not an outcome of modeling or compensatory processes within the family, but rather a result of a change in the members' perception of the kibbutz. In other words, it is possible that fathers and mothers today do not agree with the original kibbutz system and that they desire to reinforce the family unit. This is in line with Tiger and Shepher's (1975) findings that the kibbutz today places more emphasis on the need for a strong family system than it did formerly.

The change in the status of the family unit, its impact on the educational system, and the amount of nurturance provided today by both the parents and other socialization agents in the kibbutz in consistent with the findings of Avgar, Bronfenbrenner, and Henderson (1977) that kibbutz children today perceive their environment as being more supportive and nurturant than that of city children.

Regarding satisfaction with paternal role, the fathers in the collective system reported greater satisfaction ($M = 4.67$) with their roles than with their fathers' roles as perceived from current recollections of their own childhood [$M = 3.63$, $t_{(26)} = 3.12$, $p < .005$] and from their adult viewpoints [$M = 3.93$, $t_{(26)} = 2.43$, $p < .05$].

Fathers in the familial system exhibited a similar pattern; their mean score of satisfaction with paternal role was 4.26 higher [$t_{(22)} = 2.45$, $p < .05$] than that of their satisfaction with their fathers' involvement from childhood recollections ($M = 3.13$). The number of dissatisfied fathers (a score of 3 or below) in the familial system was zero, and in the collective system was six, four of whom explained their dissatisfaction as due to insufficient involvement. Again, the N is too small to warrant a statistical analysis. However, regarding dissatisfaction with their fathers' roles, all 12 dissatisfied subjects from the familial system and all 10 dissatisfied subjects from the collective system indicated that their dissatisfaction was due to insufficient involvement by their fathers when they were children.

The correlation between the level of satisfaction of fathers in the familial system with the level of paternal involvement was also significant ($r = .39$, $p < .05$). The reason for the lack of significant correlation between these variables in the collective system is unclear. Perhaps the fact that the fathers in the collective system scored highest on the PICCI and on the satisfaction scale, with a relatively small variance, reduced the likelihood of finding significant statistical relationships. The fathers may have felt that they were sufficiently involved, because the supportive system for children in the kibbutz is more than satisfactory, thus reducing individual differences in level of satisfaction. This is consistent with the previously mentioned advantage of family day-care centers (Etaugh, 1980).

In sum, the tentative findings for the kibbutz fit within the general framework suggested repeatedly throughout this chapter. That is, regardless of the sleeping arrangement in the kibbutz, the fathers tend to be quite involved in child rearing and they are very satisfied with this involvement. Although the fathers in the familial system responded differently than those in the collective system in a few dimensions, we still have sufficient basis to indicate that the kibbutz system today, whether it has familial or collective arrangements, has very high quality socioenvironmental conditions, which cause fathers (and probably mothers) to be more satisfied with their situation. The extent to which this has direct effects on the child has been noted by Avgar et al. (1977) and remains to be better understood when further data from this project and others are available.

Summary. Despite ecological differences—especially in family structure and roles—between the urban Jewish population and the two subgroups considered in this section, there are striking similarities between them on the dimensions considered here. Among the Druze (but not among the kibbutz fathers), paternal involvement appeared to be motivated by imitation of the fathers' own fathers, just as it seemed to be among the urban Jews. In both subgroups, as among the urban Jews, there was a tendency for fathers to believe themselves to be more involved and more nurturant than their own fathers, and in every case, increased involvement was associated with enhanced satisfaction. Further research is needed to determine whether increased paternal involvement has the same effects on Druze and kibbutz children as on urban Jewish children.

CONCLUSION

In this chapter, I have attempted to examine the validity of the notion that mothers alone can be effective parents, and to show that fathers also possess significant potential, which can be materialized if the necessary environmental conditions are established.

The complete urban sample, combined with the still-incomplete samples of Druze and kibbutz fathers, provided sufficient evidence to conclude that fathers perceive themselves as more involved than their own fathers. This perceived increase in involvement in child care of the more recent generation of fathers is not necessarily at the expense of instrumental activity, and it has been shown that expressive and instrumental elements may co-occur. Furthermore, it has been shown that increased paternal involvement in child care correlated with a higher level of paternal satisfaction, whereas a lower level of involvement was associated with paternal dissatisfaction. Therefore, the general pattern contradicts the stereotypic attitude that men feel uncomfortable when they are involved in child care more than the norm. The fact that the same processes take place even in a community as traditional as that of the Druze, lends preliminary support to the possibility that there exists a universal tendency for fathers to seek greater involvement in childcare. Further research in other subcultures will permit an examination of the validity of such a generalization.

With regard to the fathers' background, it appears that the compensatory versus modeling controversy cannot be resolved unequivocally. Some studies, in particular those dealing with nonnormative families (single parents, etc.), support the compensatory approach, whereby the fathers' high involvement in child care is a result of and an attempt to compensate for insufficient paternal care they themselves had received as children. The Israeli study, and very few others, examined intact families within the context of normative family life. The study showed that a modeling process takes place (i.e., fathers who are highly involved in child care reported that their fathers were involved as well).

It can be seen that in different cultural and circumstantial contexts and at different times, both processes of compensation and of modeling may take place. Both processes imply that fathers are "predisposed" for paternal involvement and both processes are apt to stimulate fathers toward greater involvement in child care. Furthermore, in all subcultures investigated, because we have seen a general trend for greater paternal involvement associated with an increased feeling of satisfaction, it is likely that in time more fathers will become increasingly involved in child care, in which case these changes will be due largely to a modeling process.

It was argued that a higher paternal involvement in intact families is not necessarily in conflict with the fathers' instrumental skills and hence the potential impact of highly involved fathers is broader in its spectrum because it includes both the instrumental and the expressive elements. This positive effect is probably reinforced by the feeling of satisfaction associated with paternal involvement. The potential impact of fathers on children has been demonstrated with the urban sample in a variety of domains, such as empathy, independence, achievement, locus of control, sex-role orientation, and perception of the paternal role by children. The data showed that high paternal involvement is associated with a better development in all of these domains, which represent both instrumental and expressive skills. These data support Lamb and colleagues' (in press) assertion that men with nontraditional attitudes are likely to enhance positive development in their children. The influence of involved fathers is a combination of the positive aspects of traditional femininity and masculinity.

Based on the current data, it is unclear to what extent the effect of paternal involvement is of direct or mediating nature. The fathers' nurturance and involvement may mediate such variables as sex-role orientation, independence, achievement, and locus of control. Alternatively, it may be argued that paternal involvement has not only indirect effects, but direct effects as well. For example, Russell (1979, 1980) indicated that involved fathers may exhibit more empathy toward their children and thereby directly affect the children who imitate them. Such direct effect implies that the influence of more involved fathers on their children stems from a configuration of paternal characteristics representing a father who is a "role maker," with a high level of self-actualization. This area must be further investigated, but whether direct or indirect, paternal involvement has been shown to have positive effects on children. Also, more data is needed from the Druze and kibbutz samples and from other cultures before definite generalizations can be made. Multivariate and cross-cultural approaches should facilitate arriving at a better understanding of many aspects pertaining to paternal involvement in child rearing, particularly with regard to the father's role in the context of the family.

REFERENCES

Aldous, J. The making of family roles and family change. *The Family Coordinator*, 1974, *23* 231–235.

Avgar, A., Bronfenbrenner, V., & Henderson, C. R., Jr. Socialization practices of parents, teachers, and peers in Israeli kibbutz, moshav, and city. *Child Development*, 1977, *48*, 1219–1227.

Barnett, M. A., King, L. M., Howard, J. A., & Dino, G. A. Empathy in young children: Relation to parents' empathy, affection, and emphasis on the feelings of others. *Developmental Psychology*, 1980, *16*, 243–244.

Beit-Hallahmi, B., & Rabin, A. I. The kibbutz as a social experiment and as a child-rearing laboratory. *American Psychologist*, 1977, *32*, 532–541.

Bem, S. L. The measurement of psychological androgyny. *Journal of Consulting and Clinical Psychology*, 1974, *42*, 155–162.

Block, J. Another look at sex differentiation in the socialization behaviors of mothers and fathers. In F. Denmark (Ed.), *Psychology of women: Future directions of research*. New York: Psychological Dimensions, 1978.

Borke, H. Interpersonal perceptions of young children: Egocentrism or empathy? *Developmental Psychology*, 1971, *5*, 263–269.

Bronfenbrenner, U. Freudian theories of identification and their derivatives. *Child Development*, 1960, *31*, 15–40.

De Frain, J. Androgynous parents tell who they are and what they need. *The Family Coordinator*, 1979, *28*, 237–243.

Dela-Pargola, S. *Population*. A publication of the State of Israel Information Center, Jerusalem, 1980. (in Hebrew).

Eiduson, B. T., & Alexander, J. W. The role of children in alternative family styles. *Journal of Social Issues*, 1978, *34*, 149–167.

Etaugh, C. Effects of nonmaternal care on children: Research evidence and popular views. *American Psychologist*, 1980, *35*, 309–319.

Freed, D. *The changing role of the father as to child custody in American jurisdiction*. Paper presented at a study group on "The role of the father in child development: Theory, social policy and the law," sponsored by the Society for Research in Child Development, Haifa, Israel, July 1980.

Frodi, A. M., Lamb, M. E., Leavitt, L. A., & Donovan, W. L. Fathers' and mothers' responses to infant smiles and cries. *Infant Behavior and Development*, 1978, *1*, 187-198.

Gasser, R. D., & Taylor, C. M. Role adjustment of single-parent fathers with dependent children. *The Family Coordinator*, 1976, *25*, 397-401.

Greif, J. B. Fathers, children, and joint custody. *American Journal of Orthopsychiatry*, 1979, *49*, 311-319.

Heath, D. H. What meaning and effects does fatherhood have for the maturing of professional men? *Merrill-Palmer Quarterly*, 1978, *24*, 265-278.

Hetherington, E. M., Cox, M., & Cox, R. Divorced fathers. *The Family Coordinator*, 1976, *25*, 417-428.

Hoffman, L. W. Effects of maternal employment on the child—a review of the research. *Developmental Psychology*, 1974, *10*, 204-228.

Hoffman, L. W. Changes in family roles, socialization, and sex differences. *American Psychologist*, 1977, *32*, 644-658.

Hoffman, L. W. Maternal employment: 1979. *American Psychologist*, 1979, *34*, 859-865.

Hoffman, M. L. Moral development. In P. H. Mussen (Ed.), *Carmichael's manual of child psychology* (Vol.2). New York: Wiley, 1970.

Hoffman, M. L. Empathy, role-taking, guilt, and development of atruistic motives. In T. Lickona (Ed.), *Moral development and behavior: Theory, research and social issues*. New York: Holt, Rinehart, & Winston, 1976.

Hoffman, M. L. Sex differences in empathy and related behaviors. *Psychological Bulletin*, 1977, *84*, 712-722.

Hoffman, M. L. Empathy, its development and prosocial implications. In C. B. Keasey (Ed.), *Nebraska Symposium on Motivation* (Vol. 26). Lincoln: University of Nebraska Press, 1978.

Kagan, J., & Lemkin, J. The child's differential perception of parental attributes. *Journal of Abnormal and Social Psychology*, 1960, *61*, 440-447.

Kohlberg, L. A cognitive–developmental analysis of children's sex-role concepts and attitudes. In E. E. Maccoby (Ed.), *The development of sex differences*. Stanford, Calif.: Stanford University Press, 1966.

Lamb, M. E. Fathers: Forgotten contributors to child development. *Human Development*, 1975, *18*, 245-266.

Lamb, M. E. The role of the father: An overview. In M. E. Lamb (Ed.), *The role of the father in child development*. New York: Wiley, 1976.

Lamb, M. E. Fathers and child development: An integrative overview. In M. E. Lamb (Ed.), *The role of the father in child development* (Rev. ed.). New York: Wiley, 1981.

Lamb, M. E. On the familial origins of personality and social style. In L. Laosa & I. Sigel (Eds.), *The family as a learning environment* (Vol. 1). New York: Plenum, 1982.

Lamb, M. E., & Bronson, S. K. Fathers in the context of family influences: Past, present and future. *The School Review*, 1980, *9*, 336-353.

Lamb, M. E., & Frodi, A. M. The role of the father in child development. In R. R. Abidin (Ed.), *Handbook of parent education*. Springfield, Ill.: Charles C. Thomas Publishers, 1980.

Lamb, M. E., Frodi, A. M., Hwang, P., Frodi, M., & Steinberg, J. Attitudes and behavior of traditional and nontraditional parents in Sweden. In R. Emde & R. Harmon (Eds.), *Attachment and affiliative systems: Neurobiological and psychobiological aspects*. New York: Plenum, in press.

Lamb, M. E., & Goldberg, W. A. The father–child relationship: A synthesis of biological, evolutionary and social perspectives. In L. W. Hoffman, R. J. Gandelman, & H. R. Schiffman (Eds.), *Parenting: Its causes and consequences*. Hillsdale, N.J.: Lawrence Erlbaum Associates, 1982.

Lamb, M. E., Owen, M. T., & Chase-Lansdale, L. The father–daughter relationship: Past, present and future. In C. B. Kopp & M. Kirkpatrick (Eds.), *Becoming female*. New York: Plenum, 1979.

Levine, J. *Who will raise the children? New options for fathers (and mothers)*. New York: Lippincott, 1976.

Levine, J. *Images of the new fatherhood*. Paper presented at a study group on "The role of the father in child development: Theory, social policy and the law," sponsored by the Society for Research in Child Development, Haifa, Israel, July 1980.

Lozoff, M. M. Fathers and autonomy in women. In R. B. Kundsin (Ed.), *Women and success*. New York: Morrow, 1974.

Manion, J. A study of fathers and infant caretaking. *Birth and the Family Journal*, 1977, *4*, 174–179.

Mendes, H. Single fatherhood. *Social Work*, 1976, *21*, 308–312.

Mischel, W. Sex-typing and socialization. In P. H. Mussen (Ed.), *Carmichael's manual of child psychology*. New York: Wiley, 1970.

Mischel, W., Zeiss, R., & Zeiss, A. Internal–external control and persistence: Validation and implications of the Stanford Preschool Internal–External Scale. *Journal of Personality and Social Psychology*, 1974, *29*, 265–278.

Mussen, P. H. Early sex-role development. In D. A. Goslin (Ed.), *Handbook of socialization theory and research*. Chicago: Rand McNally, 1969.

Orthner, D. K., Brown, T., & Ferguson, D. Single-parent fatherhood: An emerging family style. *The Family Coordinator*, 1976, *25*, 429–437.

Parke, R. D., & Sawin, D. B. The family in early infancy: Social interactional and attitudinal analyses. In F. A. Pedersen (Ed.), *The father–infant relationship: Observational studies in a family context*. New York: Praeger, 1980.

Parsons, T., & Bales, R. F. *Family, socialization, and interaction process*. Glencoe, Ill.: Free Press, 1955.

Payne, D. E., & Mussen, P. H. Parent–child relationships and father identification among adolescent boys. *Journal of Abnormal and Social Psychology*, 1956, *52*, 358–362.

Radin, N. *Childrearing fathers in intact families with preschoolers*. Paper presented at the Annual Meeting of the American Psychological Association, Toronto, September 1978.

Radin, N. *Childrearing fathers in intact families: An exploration of some antecedents and consequences*. Paper presented at a study group on "The role of the father in child development: Theory, social policy and the law," sponsored by the Society for Research in Child Development, Haifa, Israel, July 1980.

Russell, G. *Fathers as caregivers: 'They could. . . if they had to'*. A paper presented at the 49th Congress of ANZAAS, Auckland, New Zealand, January 1979.

Russell, G. *Fathers as caregivers: Possible antecedents and consequences*. Paper presented at a study group on "The role of the father in child development: Theory, social policy and the law," sponsored by the Society for Research in Child Development, Haifa, Israel, July 1980.

Rutherford, E. E., & Mussen, P. H. Generosity in nursery school boys. *Child Development*, 1968, *39*, 755–765.

Schlesinger, B., & Todres, R. Motherless families: An increasing social pattern. *Child Welfare*, 1976, *35*, 553–558.

Schubert, J. B., Bradley-Johnson, S., & Nuttal, J. Mother–infant communication and maternal employment. *Child Development*, 1980, *51*, 246–249.

Sears, R. R. Development of gender role. In F. A. Beach (Ed.), *Sex and behavior*. New York: Wiley, 1965.

Tiger, L., & Shepher, J. *Women in the kibbutz*. New York: Harcourt Brace Jovanovich, 1975.

Torgoff, I. *Parents' differential sex-typing control attitudes and family structure*. Paper presented at the biennial meeting of the Society for Research in Child Development. New York City. 1967.

West, M. M., & Konner, M. J. The role of the father: An anthropological perspective. In M. E. Lamb (Ed.), *The role of the father in child development*. New York: Wiley, 1976.

9 Effects of Divorce on Parents and Children

E. Mavis Hetherington, Martha Cox, and Roger Cox
University of Virginia

The divorce rate in the United States has shown a marked increase over the past 20 years, with a notable acceleration in the past decade. The country's divorce rate has more than doubled since 1965. It is estimated that more than 40% of the current marriages of young adults will terminate in divorce. In addition, parents are no longer staying together for the sake of the children; over 60% of divorcing couples have children. After a divorce most children live with a custodial mother and see their fathers intermittently or not at all. Although the proportion of children living with a divorced father has tripled since 1960, only one tenth of children reside with their fathers following divorce, and this is more likely to be found with school-aged than with preschool children (Glick & Norton, 1978). Marital disruptions and rearrangements in nuclear family ties are increasingly common experiences in the lives of many parents and their children.

It has been noted by Bane (1977) that: "a high rate of divorce per se is not a matter for concern in a society that values individual choice, even though some of the consequences of divorce may warrant societal attention. A divorce rate of zero might, in fact, be very worrisome, if it meant that unhappy, destructive marriages could not be dissolved [p. 14]."

In spite of the fact that divorce may be a positive solution to destructive family functioning and the eventual outcome may be a constructive one, for many family members the transition period following separation and divorce is stressful (Hetherington, 1981; Wallerstein & Kelly, 1980; Weiss, 1975, 1976). Divorce can be viewed as a critical experience that affects the entire family system, and the functioning and interactions of the members within that system.

233

Two things must be kept in mind in attempting to appraise the effects of divorce on families.

The first is that the outcomes of divorce will differ for different members of the family. Stresses, support systems, and successful coping strategies associated with divorce vary for husbands and wives, parents and children, and even among children in the same family. The means and ability for solving problems will diverge greatly in parents and children and in children of different ages. In addition, the needs and adaptive strategies of children and parents are not always compatible. The pathway to well-being for one family member may lead to a disastrous outcome for another.

The second important consideration is that divorce cannot be viewed as an event occurring at a single point in time; it represents an extended transition in the lives of parents and children. The point at which we tap into the course of divorce will to a large extent determine our evaluation of the effects of divorce. Some sequelae of divorce emerge rapidly following separation, some increase over the first year following divorce and then abate, and still others show a delayed emergence (Hetherington, 1981; Wallerstein & Kelly, 1980).

In conceptualizing the short-term effects of divorce, a crisis model of divorce may be most appropriate. In the period during and immediately following divorce, family members may be resounding to changes in their life experiences. In this period, stresses associated with conflict, loss, change, and uncertainty may be the salient factors. Research findings suggest that most family members can adapt to the crisis of divorce within a few years if it is not compounded by multiple stresses and continued adversity. The longer term adjustment of family members is related to the more sustained or concurrent economic, environmental, social, and emotional conditions that persist or are concomitants of life in a one-parent household.

In this chapter we report the results of the Virginia Longitudinal Study of Divorce, in which the impact of divorce on families and the development of children in the 2 years following divorce were examined. Parts of this study have been reported elsewhere (Hetherington, Cox, & Cox, 1978, 1979a, 1979b); however, this is the first attempt to bring together the main findings of the project. The first goal of the study was to examine responses to the family crisis of divorce and patterns of reorganization and alterations in functioning of the family over the 2-year period following divorce. It was assumed that the family system would go through a period of disorganization immediately after the divorce, followed by recovery, reorganization, and eventual attainment of a new pattern of equilibrium. The second goal was to examine stresses, support systems, and patterns of family functioning that were associated with positive and negative outcomes for members of divorced families. The third goal was to compare the stresses, support systems, family functioning, and developmental status of children in divorced and nondivorced families.

METHOD

Subjects

The original sample was composed of 72 white, middle-class children (36 boys, 36 girls) and their divorced parents from homes in which custody had been granted to the mother, and the same number of children and parents from nondivorced families. The mean ages of the divorced mothers and fathers, and of nondivorced mothers and fathers were 27.2, 29.6, 27.4, and 30.1, respectively. All parents were high school graduates and the large majority of the parents had some college education or advanced training beyond high school. Divorced parents were identified and contacted through court records and lawyers. Only families with a child attending nursery school, who served as the target child, were included in the study. The nondivorced families were a sample selected on the basis of having a child of the same sex, age, and birth order in the same nursery school as a child from a divorced family. In addition, an attempt was made to match parents on age, education, and length of marriage. Only first-born and second-born children were used in the study. At 2 years after divorce there were 102 families on which complete sets of measures were available that were used in the comparative analyses of nondivorced and divorced nonremarried families.[1] Sample attrition was due largely to remarriage in the divorced families (19 men, 10 women), separation or divorce in the intact sample (five families), relocation of a family or parent, lack of cooperation by schools, which made important measures on the child unavailable, and eight families who no longer wished to participate in the study. Because one of the interests in the investigation was to determine how mothers and children functioned in father-absent homes and how their functioning might be related to deviant or nondeviant behavior in children, families with stepparents were excluded from this study but remained in a stepparent study.

When a reduction in sample size occurs, bias in the final sample immediately becomes a concern. On demographic characteristics such as age, religion, education, income, occupation, family size, and maternal employment there were no differences between subjects who dropped out or were excluded from the sample and those who remained. When a family was no longer included in the study, a comparative analysis was done of their interaction patterns and those of the continuing families. Some differences in these groups are subsequently noted. In general, there were few differences in parent–child interactions in families who did or did not remain in the study. However, there were some differences in the

---

[1]In some of the earlier papers six families were randomly dropped to yield a sample of 96 families, 24 in each group. This was done because some of these early papers were based on presentations to audiences who were not sophisticated in statistics and became confused by analyses of unequal groups. The results are basically the same for both sets of analyses.

characteristics of parents who remarried and how they viewed themselves and their lives.

Procedure

The study used a multimethod, multimeasure approach to the investigation of family interaction. The measures used in the study included interviews, structured diary records of the parents, observations of the parents and child interacting in the laboratory and home, behavior checklists of child behavior, parent rating of the child's behavior, and a battery of personality scales on the parents. In addition, observations of the child were conducted in nursery schools, peer nomination and teacher ratings of the child's behavior were obtained, and measures of the child's sex-role typing, cognitive performance, and social development also were obtained. The parents and children were administered these measures at 2 months, 1 year, and 2 years following divorce.

A 6-year follow-up study that had not been planned as part of the original study was also conducted, using a greatly abbreviated set of measures. Although analysis of this follow-up study is not completed it will occasionally be referred to where relevant findings are available.

Parent Interview.   Parents were interviewed separately on a structured parent interview schedule designed to assess discipline practices and the parent–child relationship; support systems outside the family household system; social, emotional, and heterosexual relationships; quality of the relationship with the spouse; economic stress; family disorganization; satisfaction and happiness; and attitudes toward themselves. The interviews were tape-recorded. Each of the categories listed in Table 9.1 were rated on scales by two judges. In some cases the category involved the rating of only a single 5- or 7-point scale. In others it represented a composite score of several ratings on a group of subscales. Interjudge reliabilities ranged from .69 to .95 with a mean of .82. The interviews were derived and modified from those of Baumrind (1967, 1971), Sears, Rau, and Alpert (1965), Martin and Hetherington (1971), and others.

Parent Personality Inventories.   The parent personality measures include the Personal Adjustment Scale of the Adjective Checklist (Gough & Heilbrun, 1965), the Socialization Scale and Masculinity–Femininity Scale of the California Personality Inventory (Gough, 1969), Rotter's I–E Scale (Rotter, 1966), and the Speilberger's State–Trait Anxiety Scale (Speilberger, Gorsuch, & Lushene, 1970).

Structured Diary Record.   Each parent was asked to complete a structured diary record for 3 days (1 weekday, Saturday, and Sunday). Fathers were asked

TABLE 9.1

Control of child	Problems in running household
Maturity demands of child	Relationship with spouse
Communication with child	Emotional support in personal matters
Nurturance of child	Immediate support system
Permissiveness–restrictiveness with child	Social life and activities
Negative sanctions with child	Contact with adults
Positive sanctions with child	Intimate relations
Reinforcement of child for sex-typed behaviors	Sexuality
Paternal availability	Number of dates
Maternal availability	Happiness and satisfaction
Paternal face-to-face interaction with child	Competence as a parent
Maternal face-to-face interaction with child	Competence as a male/female
Quality of spouse's relationship with the child	Self-esteem
Agreement in treatment of the child	Satisfaction with employment
Emotional support in child rearing from spouse	Conflict
Economic stress	Tension in divorce
Family disorganization	

to include at least 1 day when they were both with their children. The diary record form was divided into half-hour units and contained a checklist of activities, situations, people, and five 7-point bipolar mood-ratings scales. The dimensions on the mood rating scales included: (1) anxious–relaxed; (2) hostile, angry–friendly, loving; (3) unhappy, depressed–happy; (4) helpless–competent, in control; and (5) unloved, rejected–loved. Each 30-minute unit was subdivided into three 10-minute units. If very different events had occurred in a 30-minute period, the subject was encouraged to record these separately and sequentially. For example, if a father had a fight with his boss and a phone call from his girl friend in the same half hour, these were recorded sequentially in separate columns. However, the parent was asked to note which was the most salient event in each 30-minute unit. The parent was instructed to check off what he or she was doing, where he or she was, with whom, and how he or she was feeling on the mood scales in each 30-minute unit from the time of getting up in the morning until going to sleep at night. The record sheet also left space for any additional comments the parent might care to make. Although the parents were encouraged to record at the end of each 30-minute period, the situations in which they found themselves sometimes made this impossible. When retrospective recording was done, it was noted, and the time at which the entry was made was also recorded. In the first session, a series of standardized scales dealing with affect, stress, and guilt had been included in the battery of parent measures; however, because the diary mood-rating scales were found to be better predictors of behavior than these more time-consuming tests, the standardized scales were subsequently dropped from the study.

TABLE 9.2
Interaction Coding

Parent Behavior	Child Behavior
Command (positive)	Opposition
Command (negative)	Aversive opposition
Question (positive)	Compliance
Question (negative)	Dependency
Nonverbal intrusion	Negative demands (whining,
Ignore	complaining, angry tone)
Affiliate (interact)	Aggression (tantrum, destruc-
Positive sanctions	tiveness)
Negative sanctions	Requests
Reasoning and explanation	Affiliate
Encourages	Self-manipulation
Dependency	Sustained play
Indulgence	Ignore
Opposition	Cry
Compliance	
Encourages independence	

Parent–Child Laboratory Interaction.   Each parent was observed separately interacting with the child in the laboratory in a half-hour free-play situation and in a half-hour structured situation involving puzzles, block building, bead stringing, and sorting tasks. The interaction sessions with each parent were scheduled on different days, separated by a period of about a month. Half of the children interacted with the mother first and half with the father first. All sessions were videotaped in order to permit the use of multiple coding of behavior. Behavior was coded in the categories in Table 9.2. The coding procedure was similar to that used by Patterson and his colleagues (Patterson et al., 1969), where the observation period was divided into 30-second intervals, and an average of approximately five behavior sequences of interactions between the subject and other family members was coded in the 30-second interval. However, in order to improve reliability, a tone sounded every 6 seconds during the recording interval. Two raters rated all sessions; interjudge agreement on individual responses averaged .83%.

Checklist of Child Behavior.   Although at least 3 hours of observations of the parent and child interacting in the home situation were collected at each of the three time points, this was not a sufficient time period to obtain an adequate sample of the children's behavior in which we were interested and that occurred relatively infrequently. Parents were given a behavior checklist and a recording form divided into half-hour units and were asked to record whether a given child's behavior had occurred in a particular half-hour period. Three hours of recording were available for fathers, but 24 hours were available for mothers. These behaviors included both acts regarded as noxious by parents, such as yelling, crying, whining, destructiveness, noncompliance, and so on, and those regarded as desirable, such as helping, sharing, cooperative activities, compliance, sustained play, or independent activities.

Parent Rating Scales of Child Behavior.   A parent rating scale of child behavior was constructed and standardized on a group of 100 mothers and fathers. Items used in previous observation questionnaires and rating scales or that seemed relevant to the interests of this study were included in an initial pool of 96 items. The parents were asked to rate their children on these items using a 5-point scale ranging from 1 (never occurs, occurs less often than in most children) to 5 (frequently occurs, occurs more often than in most children). Items that correlated with each other, that seemed conceptually related, or that had been found to load on the same factor in previous studies, were clustered in seven scales containing a total of 49 items. Only items that correlated with the total score in the scales were retained. Items were phrased to describe very specific behavior because many of these same items were also used on the Checklist of Child Behaviors previously described. The seven scales were aggression, inhibition, distractibility, task orientation, prosocial behavior, habit disturbance, and self-control. Divorced parents were asked to rate each item on the basis of the child's current behavior.

Children's Cognitive Measures.   All children took the Wechsler Preschool and Primary Scale of Intelligence (WPPSI), the Matching Familiar Figures Test (MFF), a measure of impulsivity and reflectivity, and the Embedded Figures Test.

Children's Sex Typing and Sex-Role Measures.   The measures of sex-role typing included a measure of sex-role preference for activities, toys, or vocations that had been previously identified by another group of children as being more appropriate for males or females; and the Draw a Person Test as a measure of sex-role orientation. In our sex-role preference measure children were not confined to making a choice between a masculine or a feminine alternative. We wanted their preferences to be independent in order to look at androgyny in children. On our measures of sex-role preferences of activities, toys, and vocations, children sorted the card demonstrating the activity, toy, or vocation into a "like very much" box, a "neutral" box or a "dislike very much" box. One of the problems with this task is that its reliability as assessed at a 4-week interval on a group of other children in the schools is much lower for younger than older children. The reliability at age 4 is .62, at age 5 is .73, and at age 6 is .80. It could be argued that sex-role typing is changing more rapidly at the earlier age but it nevertheless presents a problem in interpretation of results and more confidence should probably be given to the sex-role preference results in the last test session.

The measures of sex-role adoption included: teacher and parent ratings of the child's masculine or feminine behaviors; observations of the amount of time spent in playing with same- or opposite-sexed peers; and in participating in activities and social behaviors or using toys that had been determined through observation as being significantly more often used by one sex or the other.

Free-Play Observation in the School. Each child was observed in free-play situations in the classroom and playground for 6 half-hour sessions at 2 months, 1 year, and 2 years after divorce (a total of 9 hours). Observers recorded type of play, participants involved, affect being experienced, and the initiation or termination of play sequences every 10 seconds. For imaginative play, imaginative processes and themes were also recorded. Observer pairings were systematically rotated among eight observers to avoid observer drift in pairs of observers (Reid, 1970). Cohen's kappas were always significantly above chance levels of agreement. Reliability based on agreement for each category within each 10-second unit ranged from 85% to 100% across categories and averaged 92% over all codes. Play episodes were classified both in terms of Parten's (Parten, 1932) six social-play categories (unoccupied, solitary, onlooker, parallel, associative, cooperative) and in terms of a modification of Smilansky's (1968) four cognitive categories (functional, constructive, dramatic, games). The four cognitive categories were coded within Parten's social-play categories of solitary, parallel, associative, and cooperative play. The only cognitive category in which onlooker behavior could be coded was in functional play and this rarely occurred. Unoccupied behavior was not coded in cognitive categories.

Each play unit was also scored in one of 11 affect categories: (1) lively–excited; (2) happy, ebullient (characterized by smiling, laughter, or glee); (3) loving, affectionate; (4) angry, hostile, threatening; (5) proud–satisfied; (6) unhappy, sad, depressed; (7) anxious, fearful; (8) guilty, ashamed, embarrassed; (9) involved, task–oriented concentration; (10) apathy, distractible; (11) other.

The children involved in the play, changes in play, and who initiated and terminated play were also recorded. Duration of play and the age, sex, and number of other children involved in the play could be obtained from the record.

In addition, because of the theoretical significance of imaginative play, dramatic–imaginative play was further classified in terms of 15 types of imaginative transformations and processes and eight types of themes involved in the fantasy play (see Table 9.3). Each imaginative play episode was also coded according to whether the child was the initiator or recipient of each thematic behavior and affect unit.

Social Interaction Observations in School. Each child was observed in the classroom and playground for 18 10-minute sessions sampled: (1) in free play; (2) in small-group activities in the classroom where children would interact and move around the classroom; and (3) in teacher-controlled activities such as story

TABLE 9.3
Categories of Imaginative Processes and Themes in
Fantasy Play

Imaginative Processes

---

1. Object-related function: Playful use of toys or articles directly related or appropriate to the identity of the toy or article (e.g., feeding a doll with a toy spoon).
2. Functional change in objects: Use of an object in a manner not dictated by the identity of the object itself. Use of a stick as a spoon to feed a doll. Flying a toy couch around the room.
3. Reidentification of object or situation—giving a new identity to an object or situation. Building vertically with blocks and stating "This is the highest building in the world," or "This ball is the moon," "This room is the fort at the Alamo," "This chair is the castle of the wicked witch of the West." Reidentification frequently is accompanied by functional change in objects.
4. Object-related animation: Attributing appropriate lifelike qualities or roles to such things as dolls or animals. "This cow is going to go out and eat grass," "These soldiers are fighting" (pointing to a toy soldier).
5. Divergent animation of objects or toys representing living creatures: If an object representing a living creature such as a doll or an animal is endowed with unusual lifelike qualities such as an animal talking.
6. Divergent animation of objects or toys—not representing living creatures: Child lines up a row of blocks and says that these are soldiers looking for the enemy.
7. Attribution of presence, or involvement with use of imaginary objects: Child swings an imaginary sword.
8. Interaction with or presence of imaginary people: Child duels with an imaginary opponent.
9. Reference to situations or events with no objective representation in the reality situation: "I must rest before the battle tomorrow."
10. Self plays a role with minor transformation.
11. Role and attribution transformation of self—self plays role with major transformations: "I am the prettiest girl at the ball," but maintains the "I" identification.
12. Identity transformation of self. "I'm R_2—D_2," "I'll be Batman."
13. Other ascribed or minor transformations.
14. Assigns or ascribes role and attribute major transformations of others: (e.g., "You have just won an Olympic gold medal" still calls other by own name).
15. Ascribes or assigns identity transformation of others: (e.g., "You be the father").

Themes

---

1. Aggression and threat.
2. Exploration, discovery, adventure, curiosity.
3. Achievement, skill, mastery.
4. Fame power, aggrandizement, adulation by others, superiority.
5. Active prosocial behavior including caring for others, affection, helping, sharing, and sympathy.
6. Social interaction including talking, doing mutual task together (e.g., doing the dishes), playing, etc.
7. Separation, loss, isolation, rejection.
8. Other (when other was used the observer wrote in what the theme was).

TABLE 9.4
Categories of Social Behavior

Hostile physical aggression	Aversive opposition
Instrumental physical aggression	Comply
Fantasy physical aggression	Instruct, demonstrate, teach
Hostile verbal aggression	Reassurance and explanation
Instrumental verbal aggression	Question
Fantasy verbal aggression	Positive initiation
Help seeking	Negative initiation
Seeking praise, affection, or attention	Positive termination
Proximity maintenance or seeking	Negative termination
Negative physical or nonverbal (clinging, pouting, frowning)	Affiliate (interact)
Positive physical or nonverbal—smiling, patting, hugging	Ignore
Sharing or giving	Alone active
Helping	Alone inactive
Sympathy	Active attending
Verbal positive (praise, affection)	Inattention and distractibility
Verbal negative (cry, whine, complain, criticize)	Destructive
	High rate
Negative request or command	
Positive request or command	Noisy
Opposition	Activity change

telling, demonstrations, or directed questions and answer games or tasks. The situation and type of activity and people involved in any interaction were recorded. The child's behavior and the behavior of the person with whom the child was interacting were recorded every 6 seconds. Six seconds seems to be the minimum amount of time necessary to code an interaction reliably with this code; therefore, the coding represents a running sequential record of the child's behavior. The coding categories are presented in Table 9.4. Again reliabilities were high and all Cohen's kappas were significantly above chance levels of agreement.

Teacher Ratings.   Two teachers in each class rated the children on a series of 35 7-point scales adapted from the Kohn Social Competence Scale and the Kohn Symptom Checklist (Kohn & Rosman, 1972), the Schaefer and Aaronson Classroom Behavior Inventory (Schaefer & Aaronson, 1966), and Baumrind's Child Behavior Rating Scale (Baumrind, 1971). The 35 scales were clustered into five factors; (1) task oriented, purposive versus aimless, impulsive, distractible; (2) tractable–cooperative versus defiant–resistive; (3) hostile, aggressive, angry; (4) withdrawn, anxious, dependent; (5) socially constructive, friendly, helpful, interpersonally sensitive. Interteacher reliabilities across the factors ranged from .76 to .89 with a mean of .82.

Peer Nomination. A peer nomination inventory was constructed using a "Guess Who" format to measure the same five dimensions measured in the teaching rating scales. Each child received a different set of seven photographs including a subject and a random set of three boys and three girls. The child was asked to name the child in each photograph and was prompted if he or she had difficulty. The child was then asked to Guess Who "Always does what the teacher asks," "Got angry and called another child a bad name," "Helped a child who was crying," and so on. The total number of nominations on each scale for each child was recorded.

Sociometric Measure. Each child was also given an array of the photographs of all the children in the class and asked to pick which child he or she liked the very best, the next best, and the next best.

Observations and Ratings of Teachers. In addition to the observation of the child in the school, observations and ratings of five clusters of teacher behaviors were made. These teacher behaviors were: (1) assignment of responsibility and maturity demands; (2) structure and predictability—this included structuring of teaching episodes, defining roles, routines, and the organization and sequence of events; (3) responsiveness or what has been called "with-it-ness," which included attending, appropriate reinforcement, discussion of feelings, explanation, maintaining interest and involvement of the child, changing pace; (4) control—this involves following through on rules, resisting coercion, intervening effectively; (5) affective ambience—this cluster of behaviors described affection, good humor, quiet sensitive reprimands, high rates of praise versus hostile, negative, irritable, sour, rejecting, pessemistic, sarcastic, guilt inducing, loud, hard reprimands.

Measures of the Physical Setting in the School. These measures included number and sex of children, room size, density, number of teachers in the classroom, ratio of teachers to children, separation of classroom areas, amount and type of equipment, accessibility of equipment, and room decoration.

Data Analysis

The basic analysis was a repeated measures multivariate analysis of variance involving test session (2 months, 1 year, 2 years), sex of child, sex of parent, and family composition (divorced versus nondivorced). Sequential lag analyses and conditional probabilities were used to examine social interchanges in the observational studies. Structured equations, multiple regression and analyses, and cross-lagged panel correlations were calculated for selected parent and child variables in an attempt to identify functional and causal relationships contributing to changes in the behavior of family members across time.

The results of the study are not presented separately for each procedure used. Instead, the combined findings of the different procedures are used to discuss alterations in life-style, stresses and coping by family members, family functioning, children's behavior in the home and at school, and how these factors change in the 2 years following divorce.

CHANGE, STRESS, AND COPING IN DIVORCE

How does the life of a single parent differ from that of married parents? In changing to a new single life-style, what kind of stresses and satisfactions are experienced by members of a divorced couple? How might these be related to parent–child relations? The main areas in which change and stress were experienced were, first, those related to practical problems of living such as economic and occupational problems and problems in running a household; second, those associated with emotional distress and changes in self-concept and identity; and third, interpersonal problems in maintaining a social life, in the development of intimate relationships, and in interactions with the ex-spouse and child.

Practical Problems

The main practical problems of living encountered by divorced parents were those related to household maintenance, economic stress, and occupational difficulties. Many divorced men, particularly those from marriages in which conventional sex roles had been maintained and in which the wife had not been employed, initially experienced considerable difficulty in maintaining a household routine and reported distress associated with what one termed "a chaotic lifestyle." Mothers complained of task overload. When one parent is attempting to carry out the household and child-rearing tasks usually assumed by two parents the burden may be overwhelming. It should be noted that other investigators have reported that custodial fathers also are likely to complain of task overload although they usually have more assistance and are more economically secure than are custodial mothers (Ferri, 1973; George & Wilding, 1972; Spanier & Castro, 1979). This task overload was often associated with family disorganization. Family disorganization refers to the degree of structure in prescribed household roles, problems in coping with routine household tasks, and the regulating and scheduling of events. The households of the divorced mothers and fathers were more disorganized than those of intact families, although this disorganization was most marked in the first year following divorce and had significantly decreased by the second year. Members of separated households were more likely to get pickup meals at irregular times. Divorced mothers and their children were less likely to eat dinner together. Bedtimes were more erratic and the children were read to less before bedtime, there was less prolonged playfulness by mothers in caretaking routines, and children were more likely to arrive at school late.

Divorced fathers also had problems. Divorced men were less likely to eat at home than were married men. They slept less, had more erratic sleep patterns, and had difficulty with shopping, cooking, laundry, and cleaning. Some relief from stress associated with housework occurred with six of the fathers when female friends or an employed cleaning woman participated in household tasks.

Eleven of the divorced fathers reported little difficulty in household maintenance and said they enjoyed having full responsibility for ordering their lives. Most of these men had participated actively in household tasks and child care during their marriages, and following divorce were more likely to assist their ex-wives in maintenance of her home than were fathers who previously had difficulty in coping with such tasks.

Greater economic stress in divorced couples as opposed to married couples was apparent in our sample. Although the average combined income of the divorced families was equal to that of the nondivorced families, the economic problems associated with maintaining two households led to more financial concerns and limitations in purchasing practices of divorced couples. Significantly, more of the divorced women were employed by the end of the 2-year period. Divorced fathers were more likely than married fathers to increase their workload in an attempt to raise their income. This created some duress in the first year following divorce, when many fathers reported feeling immobilized by emotional problems and unable to work effectively. In addition, financial conflicts were one of the main sources of disagreement between divorced couples.

It had been suggested by Herzog and Sudia (1973) that many of the deleterious effects on children of a father's absence could be eliminated if economic stability were provided for mothers with no husband in the home. However, in our study the number of significant correlations was not above chance between income or reported feelings of economic stress, and parents' reported or observed interactions with their children or with behavior of the child in nursery school. This was true whether we use the total income for divorced husbands and wives, or the separate income for each of the households of the divorced spouses in the analyses. It may be that in our middle-class sample with an average combined maternal and paternal income of about $22,000, the range is not great enough to detect the effects of economic stress. In a lower-class sample, the greater extremes of economic duress might be associated with variations in parent–child interaction or the development of the child.

Changes in Self-Concepts and Emotional Adjustment of Parents

Interview findings, diary mood ratings, and parents' personality tests showed many differences between the self-concepts and emotional adjustments of parents in divorced and intact families. Many of these differences diminished over the 2-year period following divorce, with a marked drop occurring between 1 year and 2 years following divorce. In the first year following divorce, divorced mothers and fathers felt more anxious, depressed, angry, rejected, and incompetent. The effects were more sustained for divorced mothers, particularly for divorced mothers of boys, who at the end of 2 years were still feeling less competent, more anxious, more angry, and more externally controlled as measured by the I–E Scale than were married mothers or divorced mothers of girls. The diary record indicated that these negative feelings were most likely to occur in episodes involving interactions with their sons. This finding should be noted because the position is later advanced that the mother–son relationship is particularly problematic in mother-custody homes.

Divorced parents also scored lower on the Socialization Scale of the California Personality Inventory and Personal Adjustment Scale of the Adjective Checklist throughout the three sets of measures. Does this mean that divorced people were less well-adjusted than married couples, or that an adverse response to the stresses associated with a conflictual marriage and divorce endured over the 2-year postdivorce period? This can't be answered definitely from our data. The five couples in the larger intact sample who subsequently divorced within the 2-year period scored lower on these scales than the nondivorcing couples and as more external on the I–E Scale only in the period immediately preceeding the divorce, which suggests that these scales may be affected by the conflict associated with an unsatisfying marriage and with divorce.

Perhaps because he left the home and suffered the trauma of separation from his children, the divorced father seemed to undergo greater initial changes in self-concept than did the mother, although the effects were longer lasting in the mother. The continued presence of children and a familiar home setting gave mothers a sense of continuity that fathers lacked. Mothers complained most often of feeling physically unattractive, having lost the identity and status associated with being a married woman, and of a general feeling of helplessness. Fathers complained of not knowing who they were, of being rootless, and of having no structure or home in their lives. The separation induced great feelings of loss, previously unrecognized dependency needs, guilt, anxiety, and depression. Changes in self-concept and identity problems were greatest in parents who were older or who had been married longest. Although at 2 months following divorce about one-third of the fathers and one-quarter of the mothers reported an ebullient sense of freedom, which alternated with apprehension and depression, by 1 year the elation had been largely replaced by depression, anxiety, or apathy. These negative feelings markedly decreased by 2 years.

A pervasive concern of the fathers was the sense of loss of their children. For most this declined with time, but for many it remained a continued concern. Eight fathers who had initially been highly involved, attached, and affectionate parents reported that they could not endure the pain of seeing their children only intermittently, and by 2 years after divorce had coped with this stress by seeing their children infrequently although they continued to experience a great sense of loss and depression. However, it should not be thought that all divorced fathers felt less satisfied with their fathering roles following divorce. Ten of the fathers reported that their relationships with their child had improved, and that they were enjoying their interchanges more. Most of these fathers came from marriages in which there had been a high degree of husband–wife conflict.

One of the most marked changes in divorced parents in the first year following divorce was a decline in feelings of competence. They felt they had failed as parents and spouses, and they expressed doubts about their ability to adjust well in any future marriages. They reported that they functioned less well in social situations and were less competent in heterosexual relationships. Nine of the divorced fathers reported an increased rate of sexual dysfunction. In addition to these feelings specifically related to marriage, 36 of the divorced fathers reported that they felt they were coping less well at work.

The flurry of social activity and self-improvement that occurred during the first year following divorce, particularly in divorced fathers, seemed to be an attempt to resolve some of the identity and loss of self-esteem problems experienced by the divorced parents. We noticed that a substantial number of our men who initially appeared fairly conservative showed some striking changes over the first year following divorce. Facial flora began to sprout—beards, mustaches, and longer, more stylish haircuts were common. The former men in the grey flannel suits started to dress in a mod fashion. Jeans, leather jackets, boots, and shirts open to the waist with medallions on hairy chests appeared. In addition, our divorced fathers showed an increased incidence of purchasing motorcycles and sports cars. We called this the Hip, Honda, and Hirsute Syndrome. To some extent, this was paralleled in a less marked way in women. Divorced women showed changes in appearance, with some women becoming neglectful of their appearance and others becoming extremely concerned with concommitant changes in hairstyles and color, makeup, and manner of dress. Weight losses and gains of over 15 pounds were more common in our divorced women in the first year following divorce than in our nondivorced women. One divorced man commented that he had followed a beautiful, slender woman down the street for several blocks before he recognized her as his ex-wife who had lost 40 pounds. "Why didn't she do it 2 years ago?" he complained; "Her overeating and obesity were a continuing source of conflict during our marriage."

One year after the divorce fathers were in a frenzy of activity. Although at this time contacts with old friends had declined, dating and casual social encounters at bars, clubs, cocktail parties, and other social gatherings had increased. In this period, many of the divorced men and women were also involved in programs of self-improvement. Twenty-eight of the divorced fathers, in contrast to 13 of the unseparated fathers, and 20 of the divorced mothers, in contrast to 14 married mothers, were engaged in activities such as night school courses in photography, languages, pottery, jewelry making, modern dance, and creative writing, structured physical fitness programs, tennis, golf, or sailing lessons. However, by 2 years following divorce, both social life in divorced fathers and self-improvement programs for both divorced parents had declined. It should be noted that although these activities kept the parents busy and were associated with more positive emotional ratings, the most important factor in changing the self-concept 2 years after divorce was the establishment of a satisfying, intimate, heterosexual relationship. Only one father became involved in a homosexual relationship. He happened to have low ratings of self-esteem and happiness. It is obvious that on the basis of this finding, no conclusion can be drawn about the relative satisfaction of homosexual or heterosexual relationships.

Interpersonal Problems, Social Life, and Intimate Relations

Areas in which stresses are experienced by most divorced couples are in social life and in establishing meaningful, intimate interpersonal relationships. Almost all the divorced adults in this study complained that socializing in our culture is organized around couples and that being a single adult, particularly a single woman with children, limits recreational opportunities. Both the interview findings and the diary records kept by parents indicated that social life was more restricted in the divorced couples in the 2 years following divorce and that this effect initially was most marked for women. Divorced parents reported that at 2 months following divorce, married friends were supportive, and diary records indicated that considerable time was spent with them. However, these contacts rapidly declined. The dissociation from married friends was greater for women than for men, who were more often included in social activities and sometimes participated in joint family outings on visitation days. Shared interests and concerns led to more frequent contact with other divorced, separated, or single persons. Divorced mothers reported having significantly less contact with adults than did married parents, and often commented on their sense of being locked into a child's world. Several described themselves as prisoners and used terms like being "walled in" or "trapped" in a child's world. One woman commented that she felt she had been divorced only to marry Captain Kangaroo because he was the man she saw most of lately. Another divorced mother remarked "There's no 'time-outs' in the parenting game in one-parent families." This sense of isolation was less true of working than nonworking mothers. Many nonworking mothers complained that most of their social contacts had been made through professional associates of the husband, and that with divorce these associations terminated. In contrast, the employed mothers had contact with their co-workers and these relations often extended into after-hours social events. Although the employed women complained that it was difficult to get household chores done and of their concern about getting adequate care for their children, most felt the gratifications associated with employment outweighed the problems.

Maternal employment was an example of a situation that had a positive outcome for mothers but not necessarily for children. If the mother had always worked or did not begin to work until about 2 years after the divorce, there appeared to be no deleterious effects on the children. If mothers began to work around the time of separation and divorce, this was associated with a high incidence of behavior problems in children, especially in boys. It was as if the children had gone through a double loss of the mother and the father, which compounded their stress.

Social life for our total sample of divorced women increased over the 2-year period; however, it always remained lower than that of married women.

Divorced men had a restricted social life 2 months after divorce, followed by a surge of activity at 1 year, and a decline in activity to the wife's level by 2 years. In contrast to divorced women, who felt trapped, divorced men complained of feeling shut out, rootless, and at loose ends, and of a need to engage in social activities even if often they were not pleasurable. Divorced men and women who had not remarried in the 2 years following divorce repeatedly spoke of their intense feelings of loneliness.

Heterosexual relations played a particularly important role in the happiness and attitudes toward the self of both married and divorced adults. Happiness, self-esteem, and feelings of competence in heterosexual behavior increased steadily over the 2-year period for divorced males and females, but they were not as high even in the second year as those for married couples. It should be noted, however, that the subjects who later remarried and were shifted from this study of divorce and father absence to a stepparent study scored as high on happiness, although lower on self-esteem and feelings of competence, as did parents in intact families. Frequency of sexual intercourse was lower for divorced parents than married couples at 2 months, higher at 1 year for males, and about the same at 2 years. Divorced males particularly seemed to show a peak of sexual activity and a pattern of dating a variety of women in the first year following divorce. However, the stereotyped image of the happy, swinging single life was not altogether accurate. One of our sets of interview ratings attempted to measure intimacy in relationships. Intimacy referred to love in the sense of valuing the welfare of the other as much as one's own, of a deep concern and willingness to make sacrifices for the other, and a strong attachment and desire to be near the other person. It should be understood that this use of the term *intimacy* is not synonomous with sexual intimacy although, of course, the two frequently occur together. Intimacy in relationships showed strong positive correlations with happiness, self-esteem, and feelings of competence in heterosexual relations for both divorced and married men and women. Table 9.5 shows that in the divorced sample, but not in the married sample, if subjects were divided into those above and below the median in terms of intimacy in relationships, happiness correlated negatively with frequency of intercourse in the low-intimacy group and positively in the high-intimacy group. The same pattern held for self-esteem. This was true for both divorced males and females. The only nonsignificant correlation was for low-intimacy males immediately following divorce. Many males but few females were pleased at the increased opportunity for sexual experiences

TABLE 9.5
Correlations Between Frequency of Sexual Intercourse and
Happiness in High- and Low-Intimacy Divorced Groups

	High Intimacy		Low Intimacy	
	Male (N = 24)	Female (N = 24)	Male (N = 24)	Female (N = 24)
Two months	+.40*	+.43*	−.09 (n.s.)	−.42*
One year	+.40**	+.47**	−.41*	−.46*
Two years	+.54**	+.52**	−.48**	−.57**

*$p < .05$
**$p < .01$.

with a variety of partners immediately following divorce. However, by the end of the first year both divorced men and women were expressing a want for intimacy and a lack of satisfaction in casual sexual encounters. Women expressed particularly intense feelings about frequent casual sexual encounters, often talking of feelings of desperation, overwhelming depression, and low self-esteem following such exchanges. A pervasive want for intimacy that was not satisfied by casual encounters characterized most of our divorced parents, and the formation of an intimate relationship seemed to be a powerful factor in the development of happiness and satisfaction.

Relationships Between Divorced Partners

At 2 months following divorce, relations with the ex-spouse and children remained the most salient and preoccupying concern for divorced parents. Most (66%) of the exchanges between divorced couples in this period involved conflicts. The most common areas of conflict were those dealing with finances and support, visitation and child rearing, and intimate relations with others. In spite of the fact that the relationship between all but four of our divorced couples was characterized by acrimony, anger, feelings of desertion, resentment, and memories of painful conflicts, this was tempered by considerable ambivalence. Attachments persisted, and in some cases increased, following the escape from daily confrontations. Six of the couples had sexual intercourse in the 2 months following divorce. Thirty-four of the mothers and 29 of the fathers reported that in the case of a crisis the ex-spouse would be the first person they would call. Eight of the fathers continued to help the mother with home maintenance and four baby-sat when she went out on dates. With time both conflict and attachment decreased, although anger and resentment were sustained longer in mothers than fathers. The establishment of new intimate relations and remarriage were particularly powerful factors in attenuating the intensity of the divorced couples' relationship.

At 1 year after divorce, which seemed to be the most stressful period for both parents, 29 of the fathers and 35 of the mothers reported that they thought the divorce might have been a mistake, and that they should have tried harder to resolve their conflicts; the alternative life-styles available to them were not satisfying. By the end of the second year, only 12 of the mothers and 9 of the fathers felt this way. However, although most of the divorced partners did not regret the divorce by 2 years after the divorce, in the 6-year follow-up, even after remarriage, about 40% of the women and 25% of the men said that at times they were aware of continued emotional involvement with their former mates.

FAMILY FUNCTIONING

Thus far we have been focusing mainly on changes in the divorced partners in the 2 years following divorce and have seen that they encounter and cope with many stresses. We now compare family functioning and parent–child interactions in nondivorced and divorced families.

Parent–Child Relations

There were many differences between the interaction patterns in the divorced and nondivorced families. The differences were greatest during the first year, whereas a process of reequilibration in the divorced families seemed to be taking place by the end of the second year, particularly in mother–child relationships. However, even at the end of the second year, on many dimensions parent–child relations in divorced and intact families still differed. It is noteworthy that although there were still many stresses in the parent–child interactions of divorced parents at the end of 2 years, almost one-quarter of the fathers and one-half of the mothers reported that their relationships with their children had improved over the time during the marriage when parental conflict and tensions had detrimental effects.

Some of the findings for fathers must be interpreted in view of the fact that divorced fathers became increasingly less available to their children and ex-spouse over the course of the 2-year period. Although at 2 months divorced fathers were having almost as much face-to-face interaction with their children as were fathers in intact homes, who are often highly unavailable to their children (Blanchard & Biller, 1971), this interaction declined rapidly. At 2 months about one-quarter of the divorced parents even reported that fathers, in their eagerness to maximize visitation rights and maintain contact with their children, were having more face-to-face contact with their children than they had before the divorce. This contact was motivated by a variety of factors in the divorced fathers. Sometimes it was based on a deep attachment to the child or continuing attachment to the wife; sometimes it was based on feelings of duty or attempts to assuage guilt; often it was an attempt to maintain a sense of continuity in their lives; unfortunately, it was frequently at least partly motivated by a desire to annoy, compete with, or retaliate against the spouse. By 2 years after divorce, 19 of the divorced fathers were seeing their children once a week or more, 14 fathers saw them every 2 weeks, 7 every 3 weeks, 8 once a month or less. The frequency and duration of paternal visits was greater with sons than with daughters.

The results of the diary record, of the interview findings, and of observations relating to the parent–child interaction are presented in a simplified fashion and wherever possible, presented together. The patterns of parent–child interaction showed considerable congruence across these measures.

Divorced parents made fewer maturity demands of their children, communicated less well with their children, tended to be less affectionate with their children, and showed marked inconsistency in discipline and lack of control over their children in comparison to still married parents. Poor parenting was most apparent when divorced parents, particularly the divorced mothers, were interacting with their sons. Divorced parents communicated less, were less consistent, and used more negative sanctions with their sons than with their daughters. Additionally, divorced mothers exhibited fewer positive behaviors such as positive sanctions and affiliation, and more negative behaviors such as negative commands, negative sanctions, and opposition to requests of the child, with sons than with daughters. Sons of divorced parents seemed to be having a hard time of it, and this may in part explain why, as we shall see shortly, the adverse effects of divorce are more severe and enduring for boys than for girls.

Fortunately, people, even parents, learn to adapt to problem situations, and by 2 years after divorce the parenting practices of divorced mothers had improved. Poor parenting seemed most marked, particularly for divorced mothers, 1 year after divorce, which was a peak of stress in parent–child relations. Two years following the divorce, mothers were demanding more autonomous mature behavior of their children, communicated better, and used more explanation and reasoning. They were more nurturant and consistent and were better able to control their children than they had been before. A similar pattern occurred for divorced fathers in maturity demands, communication, and consistency, but they became less nurturant and more detached from their children with time. In the laboratory and home observations, divorced fathers were ignoring their children more and showing less affection.

The interviews and observations showed that the lack of control divorced parents had over their children was associated with very different patterns of relating to the child for mothers and fathers. The divorced mother tried to control her child by being more restrictive and giving more commands, which the child ignored or resisted. The divorced father wanted his contacts with his child to be as happy as possible. He began by being initially extremely permissive and indulgent with his children and becoming increasingly restrictive over the 2-year period, although he was never as restrictive as fathers in intact homes. The divorced mother used more negative sanctions than the divorced father did, or than parents in intact families do. However, by the second year her use of negative sanctions was declining as the divorced father's was increasing. In a parallel fashion, the divorced mother's use of positive sanctions increased after the first year as the divorced father's decreased. The "every day is Christmas" behavior of the divorced father declined with time. The divorced mother decreased her futile attempts at authoritarian control and became more effective in dealing with her child over the 2-year period.

The lack of control that divorced parents had over their children, particularly 1 year following divorce, was apparent in both home and laboratory observations. The observed frequency of a child's compliance with parents' regulations, commands, or requests could be regarded as a measure either of parental control or resistant child behavior. A clearer understanding of functional relationships in parent–child interaction may be obtained by examining the effectiveness of various types of parental responses in leading to compliance by the child, and the parents' responses to the child following compliance or noncompliance. Conditional probabilities were calculated on the differential compliance rates reported in Table 9.6. It can be seen that boys were less compliant than girls and that

TABLE 9.6
Children's Compliance to Three Types of Parental Commands

| | Nondivorced | | | | Divorced | | | |
| | Girl | | Boy | | Girl | | Boy | |
	Father	Mother	Father	Mother	Father	Mother	Father	Mother
Percentage of Compliance to Parental Commands (Positive)								
Two months	60.2	54.6	51.3	42.6	51.3	40.6	39.9	29.3
One year	63.4	56.7	54.9	44.8	43.9	31.8	32.6	21.5
Two years	64.5	59.3	57.7	45.3	52.1	44.2	43.7	37.1
Percentage of Compliance to Parental Commands (Negative)								
Two months	55.7	49.3	47.5	36.4	47.0	34.8	35.6	23.4
One year	59.2	51.5	50.3	38.8	39.1	27.2	28.3	17.2
Two years	60.5	54.6	53.6	39.0	49.9	39.7	39.7	31.8
Percentage of Compliance to Parental Reasoning and Explanation								
Two months	49.1	43.3	41.0	31.1	41.3	29.2	29.6	18.4
One year	55.4	48.0	46.2	34.5	26.3	23.1	24.5	14.1
Two years	62.3	58.1	58.1	47.6	50.3	42.5	41.4	36.9

fathers were more effective than mothers in obtaining compliance from children. This may be based at least partly on the fact that mothers gave over twice as many commands as did fathers, and that divorced mothers gave significantly more commands than did divorced fathers, or mothers and fathers in intact families. The pattern with the least effectiveness of any type of parental behavior occurring at 1 year and a marked increase in control over the child by 2 years was again apparent, although the divorced mothers and fathers never gained as much control as their married counterparts. Because developmental psychologists traditionally have regarded reasoning and explanation as the font of good discipline from which all virtues flow, the results relating to type of parental demands were unexpected. Negative commands were less effective than positive commands and, somewhat surprisingly, in the 2-months and 1-year groups, reasoning and explanation were less effective than either positive or negative commands. By the last test session, the effectiveness of reasoning and explanation had increased significantly over reasoning in the previous sessions. Two things are noteworthy about the pattern of change in reasoning. First, it should be remembered that subjects were almost 2 years older at the final session. The mean age at the 2-month session was 3.92 years, at the 1-year's session was 4.79, and at the final session was 5.81 years. It may be that, as children become more cognitively and linguistically mature, reasoning and explanation is more effective because the child can understand it and has a longer attention span. It may be also that internalization and role taking are increasing, and that explanations that involve appeals to the rights or feelings of others become more effective. Some support for the position that younger children may not fully comprehend or attend to explanations is found in a point biserial correlational post hoc analysis between the number of words in explanations and compliance or noncompliance of children. On going back over videotapes to see what was happening in cases where there was high use of reasoning and explanation and low compliance, it was observed that the parents often were using long-winded, conceptually complicated explanations and that the child seemed rapidly to become inattentive, distractible, and bored. Thereupon, the child either continued or resumed his or her previous activity or ignored and made no response to the parent. The average point biserial correlation between noncompliance and number of words across group was $-.58$ for two months, $-.44$ for one year, and $-.13$ for two years. "Short and sweet" would seem to be an effective maxim in instructing young children. The same type of analysis was performed on the home observations that had been recorded with audio- but not videotape, and the same pattern of results was obtained. Long explanations were associated with noncompliance to parents in younger children.

The second thing to be noted about these findings is that the superiority of reasoning over negative parental commands in obtaining compliance is true for boys, with the exception of sons interacting with their divorced fathers, but is not found for girls. Why should reasoning be relatively more effective in gaining compliance in boys? Barclay Martin (1975), in his review of research on parent–child interactions, suggested that coercive parental responses were more likely to be related to oversocialization and inhibition in girls but to aggression in boys. It may be that the greater aggressiveness frequently observed in preschool boys and greater assertiveness in the culturally prescribed male role necessitates the use of reasoning and explanation to develop the cognitive mediators necessary for self-control in boys. Some support for this was found in a greater number, significantly larger, and more consistent correlations for boys than for girls between the communication scale on the parent interview and also frequency of observed parental reasoning and explanation, with parent's ratings of their children's prosocial behavior, self-control, and aggression. A similar pattern of correlations was obtained between those parental measures and the frequency of negative and positive behavior on the behavior checklist. In contrast, high use of negative commands was positively related to aggression in boys but not in girls. In summary: Although reasoning and explanation were not clearly superior to other commands in gaining short-term compliance, in the long-term development of self-control, inhibition of aggression, and prosocial behavior in boys, they were more effective.

We can extend our analysis of compliance one step further and examine how parents responded to compliance or noncompliance by children. Developmental psychologists and behavior modifiers have emphasized the role of contingent reinforcement in effective parenting. Parental responses to compliance are presented in Table 9.7 and to noncompliance in Table 9.8. Again, conditional probabilities were calculated for these responses. Only the most frequently occurring responses are included in the tables. Only the most significant effects will be noted. First, it can be seen that in less than half the time that children complied did they get positive reinforcement. Not a very lavish reinforcement schedule for good behavior. Second, boys received less positive reinforcement than girls following compliance and more commands both positive and negative, and even negative sanctions such as "You didn't do that very fast," or "You'd better shape up if you know what's good for you." Boys were not as appropriately reinforced for compliance as were girls. This seemed to be the case particularly for divorced mothers and sons across all ages, although it can be seen that divorced mothers became significantly more appropriate in responding to compliance from their children from 1 year to 2 years after divorce. In contrast, divorced fathers were becoming less reinforcing and attentive to positive behaviors in their children in this period.

How did parents respond when children failed to obey their commands? In most cases they gave another command and sometimes used negative sanctions. Parents in intact families, especially mothers, were also likely to reason with the child in dealing with noncompliance. Sometimes parents, notably fathers, intruded physically by moving the child or objects around the child. There was much less ignoring of noncompliance than of compliance, especially by fathers

TABLE 9.7
Percentage of Parents Consequent Behaviors to Childrens' Compliance

	Positive Sanctions or Affiliate, Encourages							
	Nondivorced				Divorced			
	Girl		Boy		Girl		Boy	
	Fa.	Mo.	Fa.	Mo.	Fa.	Mo.	Fa.	Mo.
Two months	39.0	51.1	34.6	49.8	46.6	37.0	44.2	31.8
One year	42.6	49.7	37.2	45.6	47.4	32.5	42.4	28.8
Two years	44.4	49.4	39.8	48.1	36.8	41.6	34.7	37.3
	Ignore or No Response							
	Nondivorced				Divorced			
	Girl		Boy		Girl		Boy	
	Fa.	Mo.	Fa.	Mo.	Fa.	Mo.	Fa.	Mo.
Two months	21.4	15.8	18.7	16.3	19.2	28.9	17.6	27.9
One year	23.9	16.2	20.9	17.8	20.4	30.0	17.1	30.3
Two years	22.6	14.9	19.5	16.4	30.2	19.8	25.1	20.0
	Command Positive							
	Nondivorced				Divorced			
	Girl		Boy		Girl		Boy	
	Fa.	Mo.	Fa.	Mo.	Fa.	Mo.	Fa.	Mo.
Two months	11.6	16.2	15.1	20.3	6.2	18.8	10.0	20.4
One year	12.3	15.3	14.9	18.6	6.6	20.7	8.3	21.1
Two years	10.9	14.7	15.5	19.9	8.3	17.0	13.5	20.0
	Command Negative or Negative Sanctions							
	Nondivorced				Divorced			
	Girl		Boy		Girl		Boy	
	Fa.	Mo.	Fa.	Mo.	Fa.	Mo.	Fa.	Mo.
Two months	8.6	4.3	10.5	7.6	2.4	8.2	5.0	13.4
One year	6.7	5.1	9.7	6.6	4.2	10.3	8.1	14.9
Two years	6.9	4.8	9.9	6.9	7.6	5.6	9.3	10.5

in nondivorced families. If the parental ignoring responses are examined, it can be seen that one way divorced parents coped with noncompliance was by pretending it didn't happen. The chains of noncompliance by children followed by ignoring were of longer duration in divorced families than intact families, especially in the interactions of divorced mothers and their sons.

Divorced mothers increased dramatically in their use of reasoning and explanation in response to noncompliance in the second year following divorce, whereas divorced fathers became less communicative and more negative in their responses.

After reviewing the interview and observational findings, one might be prone to state that disruptions in children's behavior following divorce are attributable to emotional disturbance in the divorced parents and to poor parenting, especially by mothers of boys. However, before we point a condemning finger and say "fie" on these parents, especially on the divorced mothers who face the day-to-day problems of child rearing, let us look at their children. The findings on the behavior checklist, recording the occurrence of positive and negative behaviors in the home in 30-minute units, showed not only that children of divorced parents

TABLE 9.8
Percentage of Parents' Behaviors to Children's Noncompliance

	Command Positive							
	Nondivorced				Divorced			
	Girls		Boys		Girls		Boys	
	Fa.	Mo.	Fa.	Mo.	Fa.	Mo.	Fa.	Mo.
Two months	26.3	27.9	24.2	29.3	23.6	20.6	22.0	23.9
One year	24.8	23.6	25.7	27.5	20.5	16.9	20.0	15.3
Two years	25.1	26.8	26.0	27.9	19.1	23.0	18.0	20.6
	Reasoning and Explanation and Encourages Positive Questions							
	Nondivorced				Divorced			
	Girls		Boys		Girls		Boys	
	Fa.	Mo.	Fa.	Mo.	Fa.	Mo.	Fa.	Mo.
Two months	20.1	25.6	17.9	22.7	18.9	20.1	15.0	16.5
One year	22.7	25.3	20.1	23.2	18.1	16.3	16.9	11.9
Two years	26.8	30.4	24.3	28.5	14.0	27.4	13.2	22.7
	Command Negative and Negative Sanctions, Negative Questions							
	Nondivorced				Divorced			
	Girls		Boys		Girls		Boys	
	Fa.	Mo.	Fa.	Mo.	Fa.	Mo.	Fa.	Mo.
Two months	18.5	14.0	20.0	18.3	9.0	24.0	12.0	26.2
One year	20.4	15.7	22.5	17.0	9.9	26.8	13.1	28.1
Two years	22.2	17.5	26.8	17.5	19.8	20.2	22.2	21.7
	Ignore or No Response							
	Nondivorced				Divorced			
	Girls		Boys		Girls		Boys	
	Fa.	Mo.	Fa.	Mo.	Fa.	Mo.	Fa.	Mo.
Two months	5.3	8.1	4.1	9.9	13.5	15.8	14.3	16.0
One year	4.8	6.7	3.9	7.3	16.7	17.9	18.1	19.3
Two years	4.0	4.9	3.0	5.8	18.1	11.6	21.6	10.2
	Physical Intrusion							
	Nondivorced				Divorced			
	Girls		Boys		Girls		Boys	
	Fa.	Mo.	Fa.	Mo.	Fa.	Mo.	Fa.	Mo.
Two months	10.8	6.9	9.5	5.8	11.2	8.3	9.3	8.0
One year	8.6	5.7	8.7	5.4	9.1	8.2	8.4	7.5
Two years	7.2	5.8	6.9	5.0	8.1	6.0	7.3	5.9

exhibited more negative behavior than did children in nondivorced families, but also that these behaviors were most marked in boys and had largely disappeared in girls by 2 years after divorce. They were then also significantly declining in the boys. Children exhibited more negative behavior in the presence of their mothers than their fathers; this was especially true with sons of divorced parents.

These checklist results were corroborated by the home and laboratory observations and by parent ratings of their children's behavior. Divorced mothers may give their children a hard time, but mothers, especially divorced mothers, got rough treatment from their children. As previously remarked, children were more likely to exhibit oppositional behavior to mothers and comply to fathers. They also made negative complaining demands of the mother more frequently. Boys were more oppositional and aggressive; girls were more whining, complaining, and compliant. Children of divorced parents showed an increase in dependency over time, and exhibited less sustained play than children of nondivorced parents. The divorced mother was harassed by her children, particularly her sons. In comparison with fathers and mothers of intact families, her children in the first year didn't obey, affiliate, or attend to her. They nagged and whined, made more dependency demands, and were more likely to ignore her. The aggression of boys with divorced mothers peaked at 1 year, then dropped significantly, but was still higher than that of boys in intact families at 2 years. Some divorced mothers described their relationship with their child 1 year after divorce as "declared war," a "struggle for survival," "the old Chinese water torture," or "like getting bitten to death by ducks." As was found in the divorced parents' behavior, 1 year following divorce seemed to be the period of maximum negative behaviors for children and great improvement occurred by 2 years, although the negative behaviors were more sustained in boys than in girls. The second year appeared to be a period of marked recovery and constructive adaptation for divorced mothers and children.

Who is doing what to whom? It has been proposed, most recently by Gerald Patterson in a monograph entitled "Mothers: The Unacknowledged Victims" (1981), that the maternal role is not a very rewarding or satisfying one. Patterson demonstrated that the maternal role, particularly with mothers of problem children, demands high rates of responding at very low levels of positive reinforcement for the mothers. He assumes that mothers and their aggressive children become involved in a vicious circle of coercion. The lack of management skills of the mothers accelerates the child's aversive behavior for which she is the main instigator and target. This is reciprocated by increased coercion in the mother's parenting behavior, and feelings of helplessness, depression, anger, and self-doubt. In his study Patterson showed that decreases in the noxious behaviors of aggressive children through treatment procedures aimed at improving parenting skills were associated with decreases of maternal scores on a number of clinical scales on the MMPI, with a decrease in anxiety on the Taylor manifest anxiety scale, and with improvement on several other measures of maternal adjustment.

Patterson's model may be particularly applicable to the divorced mothers and children in our study.

We attempted to use cross-legged panel correlations and structural equations between selected parent and child measures at Times 1 and 2, and Times 2 and 3, to identify casual effects in these interactions.

High synchronous correlations between reported and observed poor parenting in divorced mothers, and reported and observed negative behavior in children occurred at each time period. The greater use of poor maternal parenting practices and higher frequency of undesirable behaviors in children from divorced families, even in the first sessions with mothers and sons, suggests that the coercive cycle was already underway when we first encountered our families 2 months after divorce. Stresses and conflicts preceeding or accompanying the divorce may have initiated the cycle. High rates and durations of negative exchanges between divorced mothers and their sons were apparent throughout the study. Sequence analyses of the home and laboratory observations showed that divorced mothers of boys were not only more likely than other parents to trigger noxious behavior, but also were less able to control or terminate this behavior once it occurred.

Causal direction for poor parenting practices and noxious child behavior could not be identified consistently by the panel correlations. However, the observational measures and child checklist measures, but not the interview and rating measures, indicated that poor parenting by divorced mothers at 2 months causes problem behaviors in children at 1 year. These effects are similar but not significant between 1 year and 2 years.

A striking finding was that self-esteem, feelings of parental competence as measured by the interview, state anxiety as measured by the Speilburger State–Trait Anxiety Scale, and the divorced mother's mood ratings of competence, depression, and anxiety on the Structured Diary Record not only showed significant synchronous correlations with ratings of children's aggression and checklist frequency of noxious behaviors, but also yielded significant cross-lagged panel correlations, which suggested that the child's behavior, particularly that of the son, was causing the emotional responses of the mother. The findings were similar but less consistent for mothers in nondivorced families. Mothers from both divorced and nondivorced families showed more state and trait anxiety, feelings of external control and incompetence, and depression than did fathers. This suggests that the feminine maternal role is not as gratifying as the paternal role, regardless of whether the family is intact or divorced. The more marked findings in divorced women seem in accord with Patterson's view that mothers of problem children are trapped in a coercive cycle that leads to debilitating attitudes towards themselves, adverse emotional responses, and feelings of helplessness.

In Patterson's study and others comparing parents of problem and nonproblem children, fathers were found to be much less affected by a problem child than were mothers. Fathers, particularly divorced fathers, spend less time with their children than do mothers, thereby escaping some of the stresses imposed by a coercive child and obtaining more gratification in activities outside the family. In addition, fathers seem less likely to get involved in such a coercive vicious cycle because children exhibit less deviant behavior in the presence of their fathers; furthermore, fathers are more able to control deviant behavior in their children once it occurs, as is shown in fathers' ratings of their child's behavior, frequencies of behavior on the checklist, and in observations in the laboratory and home.

The cross-lagged panel correlations showed a larger proportion of effects going in the direction of fathers causing children's behavior than in children causing fathers' behavior relative to the number found in mother–child interactions. Children's behavior showed few effects on the state anxiety, mood ratings, or self-esteem of fathers, especially divorced fathers. In addition, in intact families, negative child behaviors at 1 and 2 years following divorce seemed to be caused partially by poor control, low nurturance, and high use of negative sanctions by fathers in the earlier time period.

Family Conflict and Social Development in Children

The point is often made that children in single-parent families function more adequately than children in conflict-ridden nondivorced families. In attempting to examine this issue we utilized a variety of measures of children's behavior in the home and in the school. The home measures included the proportion of the child's problem behaviors and the proportion of desirable positive behaviors relative to total behaviors as recorded on a behavior checklist by mother and fathers; parents' ratings of the child's behavior; and finally, observational measures of the child's behavior when interacting with his or her mother or father on visitation days or in the home. Measures from the school included teacher ratings, peer ratings, and measures of social interaction based on direct observation of the child in the school situation.

Both the nondivorced and divorced families were divided into families who were rated on the basis of the interview or on observations as having intense continuing conflict or low or moderate levels of conflict. Separate repeated measure multivariate analyses of variance were performed involving test sessions (2 months, 1 year, 2 years), sex of child, family group, and level of conflict for the set of measures from each data source.

A distinction was made between parent–child conflict, husband–wife conflict, and encapsulated conflict. Encapsulated conflict refers to discord that is concealed from the children. Couples characterized by encapsulated conflict expressed extreme dissatisfaction with their relationship and quarreled frequently when alone but did not battle in front of the children. The following discussion refers to the findings dealing with overt parent–child or husband–wife conflict. These two types of conflict impacted in a similar adverse fashion on the children.

In contrast, encapsulated conflict to which children were not directly exposed had no apparent negative outcomes.

How does marital conflict impact on the child? Do children in one-parent households function better than those in nondivorced families characterized by marital discord? Two things are clear in the results. The first is that the pattern of differences between groups changes markedly over the course of the 2 year period following divorce. The second is that boys appear to be more vulnerable to the effects of both marital discord and divorce than are girls.

In the first year following divorce, children in the divorced families were functioning less well than those in the high-discord nondivorced families, who in turn showed more problems than children in the low-discord nondivorced families. In this period, children from both groups of divorced families were more oppositional, aggressive, lacking in self-control, distractible, and demanding of help and attention in both the home and school than were children in nondivorced families with high rates of marital discord.

By 2 years following divorce the pattern of differences between children from stressed nondivorced and low-conflict divorced families was reversed, although this effect differed somewhat for boys and girls. At 2 years, more acting-out aggressive behavior and less prosocial behavior such as helping, sharing, and cooperation was found in boys from conflictual nuclear families than in low-conflict divorced families. Although the behavior of boys from divorced families had improved greatly over the 2-year period following divorce and was less disrupted than that of boys in stressful nuclear homes it should be noted that they were still functioning less well than children in the low-stress nondivorced families. The boys from high-conflict divorced families showed more problems than any of the other groups of children at all three time periods. In the home there was still considerable conflict in the mother–son dyad and at school they were more socially isolated, verbally aggressive, immature, and less constructive in play.

The impact of both discord and divorce seems more pervasive and long lasting for boys than for girls. Differences between the social and emotional development of girls from divorced and nondivorced families with low conflict had largely disappeared by 2 years after divorce. In addition the effects of marital discord were less for girls than boys and certainly decreased in the 2-year period of the study. That is, the relation between marital discord and adjustment in girls was greater when they were 4 years old than when they were 6. At 6, the most notable differences between girls in high- and low-conflict families were in greater attention seeking, whining, and demandingness in the former group, both in the home and at school.

We have noted often in this chapter that the first year following divorce appears to be a particularly difficult period of transition and coping for divorced parents and their children. Members of divorced families exhibit more disrupted psychological and social functioning and emotional distress at 1 year after divorce than at 2 months after divorce. This is followed by a dramatic improvement in coping, and in psychological well-being and social adjustment during the second year following divorce. However things do seem to get worse before they get better.

These findings suggest that in the long run it is not a good idea for parents to remain in a conflicted marriage for the sake of the children if the alternative is a stable nonconflicted one-parent household. In the long run, marital discord may be associated with more adverse outcomes for children than is divorce. However the short-run picture appears to be quite different. In the transition period of family disequilibrium and reorganization in the first year following divorce, children's problems may be exacerbated before they begin to decline. The question that usually is asked about whether it is better to stay together, presumably in an acrimonious home, or to get a divorce seems to assume that marital conflict ceases at the time of divorce. For many families this clearly is not the case. In our study, and in the study by Wallerstein and Kelly (1980), a substantial proportion of the families remained as turbulent and conflicted following the divorce as during the marriage or actually increased in their marital discord. Wallerstein and Kelly report that in the main, bitterness and conflict between divorcing parents escalated rather than diminished following separation. In addition, in the early postseparation period many parents tried to involve their children actively in forming hostile alliances against the other parent, which precipitated feelings of confusion, conflict, guilt, and hostility in the children. It is the current conflict rather than the past conflict that is associated with most emotional and behavioral problems in children. Children who found themselves in a stable, conflict-free situation recovered within a 2-year period from the hostility and dissension associated with the separation and divorce. However, if intense conflict continued after divorce, particularly for boys, the effects were more deleterious than when it occurred in nondivorced families. Why should this be the case? The explanation seems to lie in the role of protective parental buffering, which we now discuss not only in its relationship to conflict but also as it relates to parental warmth or rejection and personal adjustment in parents.

Protective Parental Buffering

It has been found that in nuclear families a positive relationship with one parent can to some extent reduce the impact of an adverse relationship with the other (Rutter, 1977). This is less likely to be the case in single-parent households where the child sees the noncustodial parent intermittently or not at all, and where the noncustodial parent is not present to mitigate any deleterious behaviors of the custodial parent in day-to-day living experiences. This suggests that in the single-parent mother-headed family, the adjustment of the mother and the quality of mother–child relationship will be more directly reflected in the adjustment of the child than in nondivorced families.

Let us go back to our discussion of the role of marital conflict in the adjustment of children. We divided parents into those who had a positive, neutral, or negative relationship with their children. Further analyses revealed that under conditions of marital disharmony children in nuclear families who had a good relationship with one parent were less likely to develop behavior problems than children who had a poor relationship with both parents or a poor relationship with one and only a neutral relationship with the other. However even with positive relations with both parents there were some adverse effects of marital conflict, particularly for boys. In contrast, in single-parent families only a positive relation with the mother served to mitigate partially the effects of conflict between the parents. By 2 years after divorce there was no buffering effect if there was a good father–child relationship.

When we looked at the effects of configurations of high, moderate, or low levels of mothers', and fathers' adjustment as measured on the Socialization Scale of the California Personality Inventory, the Personal Adjustment Scale of the Adjective Checklist, or parent–child conflict or warmth or rejection of parents a similar effect occurred. In nondivorced families when both parents were poorly adjusted or had conflictual or rejecting relations with the child, the child showed more behavior problems than in families with one well-adjusted parent or one good parent–child relationship. In divorced families the good adjustment or positive relation with the father could not counter the adverse effects of an immature or rejecting mother. But again a well-functioning, warm mother counteracted the effects of negative parental attributes and behavior in the divorced families. This lack of effective protective buffering by the father in divorced families increased over time and was particularly apparent 2 years after divorce. In addition, the buffering effects countering a negative parental relationship with one parent, which we have described, occurred only when the other parent had a very good relationship with the child. If the relationship was classed as moderate or neutral, thus as not being unusually positive or negative, the frequency of adjustment problems was the same as if both parents had negative relations. It takes an exceptionally good relationship to buffer the effects of an exceptionally poor relationship with a parent.

THE CHILD IN SCHOOL[2]

It might be expected that the impact of divorce will be manifested not only in interpersonal relations within the family system but also in relations external to the family. Patterns of play and relations with peers have been found to be areas

---

[2]For more details on play and social interaction in the school see Hetherington, E. M., Cox, M., & Cox, R. Play and social interaction in children following divorce, *Journal of Social Issues, 1979, 35*, 26–49.

in which stress and difficuities in coping are often reflected. Age-inappropriate play, disruptions in play, and unpopularity with peers consistently have been found to be related to anxiety and emotional disturbance in children (Hartup, 1976; Roff, Sells, & Golden, 1972; Singer, 1977). In addition, children's play and interactions with peers not only provide critical opportunities to acquire certain social competencies but also play an important role for children in working through or modifying their problem behavior (Hartup, 1976, 1977a, 1977b; Singer & Singer, 1976; Sutton-Smith, 1971).

Over the course of the preschool years, children's play becomes more social and cooperative and involves more fantasy, dramatic play, and games (Parten, 1932; Piaget, 1962; Smilansky, 1968).

Disruptions and rigidity in the fantasy-play patterns of emotionally disturbed children have frequently been noted (Singer, 1977; Singer & Singer, 1976). Processes in imaginative play seem to be particularly vulnerable to the effects of psychological stress. It has been suggested that the failure to develop imaginative play is indicative of serious pathology, particularly of an acting out, impulsive type in children (Gould, 1972). Imaginativeness in play has been found to be associated not only with self-control, low impulsivity, and low aggression (Singer & Singer, 1976) but also with sharing, cooperation, independence (Singer, 1977), and social maturity (Rubin et al., 1976). In addition, children who show spontaneous imaginativeness in play are likely to show a broader range of emotions and more positive affect than less imaginative children. They are more likely to smile, be curious and interested in new experiences, and express joy in making believe and in peer relations (Singer, 1977). Singer states that: "imaginative play can be viewed as a major resource by which children can cope immediately with the cognitive, affective and social demands of growing up. It is more than a reactive behavior, however, for it provides a practice ground for organizing new schema and for transforming and storing material for more effective later expression in plans, actions or verbalization [p. 10].

Sutton-Smith (1971) has also emphasized the important role that imaginative play provides in allowing the child to experiment with and gain some sense of competence in and control over situations with which, in reality, the child would be unable to cope. Exploring a variety of possible experiences, courses of action, roles, and outcomes in fantasy play is an important aspect of cognitive and social development.

Free-Play Behaviors

Do the play patterns of children following divorce differ from those in nuclear families? Do these patterns change over time as the children grow older and as the children in divorced families begin coping with their new status in a single-parent family? Are the patterns different for boys and girls?

As the children aged, their play behavior became more task oriented, structured and imaginative, and involved more social interchanges with peers. With increasing age there was an increase in solitary-constructive, solitary-imaginative, associative-constructive, associative-imaginative, cooperative-constructive, and cooperative-imaginative play and in games. There was a decrease in functional play (play involving simple repetitive movements with or without objects, e.g., rocking, thumping) within all of the social-play categories. Parallel-functional and parallel-constructive play declined as children were becoming more involved in associative and cooperative play. Although the frequently reported shift from lone activities to social play was occurring, within solitary play it was only functional solitary play that declined with age, whereas constructive and imaginative solitary play increased over the 2-year period. In addition, both unoccupied and onlooker behavior decreased. Very little time was spent in games by the younger child but this too increased with age.

There were few sex differences in play and most of those obtained were involved in higher order interactions with time and family status. Girls showed more solitary functional and less solitary constructive play than did boys. Boys spent less time in parallel constructive play and were more involved in imaginative associative play than were girls.

At 2 months after divorce, boys and girls from divorced families were showing more functional play and less imaginative play in all categories than were their counterparts in nondivorced families. In addition, they were showing less associative and cooperative-constructive play. Children of both sexes from divorced families also were showing more unoccupied and onlooker behavior than were children from nondivorced families. Finally, the play episodes of children from divorced families were shorter.

These patterns of differences changed over time. By 1 year following divorce, girls in divorced families differed from those in nondivorced families only in showing less associative-imaginative and cooperative-imaginative play and in more onlooker behavior. By 2 years after divorce, even these differences had disappeared. In contrast, although boys from divorced families showed the most disruption in play at 1 year after divorce and more mature play patterns at 2 years following divorce, they still differed from boys in nondivorced families in a number of ways. In all three time periods boys from divorced families showed more solitary and parallel-functional play and less cooperative, constructive, imaginative, or game play than did boys in nondivorced families. In addition, they showed more onlooker behavior and shorter duration of play episodes at all three points in time. Finally, boys from divorced families spent an increasing amount of time playing with younger children and with girls rather than showing the more characteristic developmental pattern of a marked and increasing preponderance of time in play with same-sex peers. In classes in which there were mixed age groups, boys from divorced families also were spending more time with younger peers at 1 year and 2 years after divorce.

If these differences in play patterns between children in divorced families and those in nondivorced families can be viewed as responses to stresses and to the transition in family relationships following divorce, it appears that both boys and girls experience some disruptions in play immediately following divorce but that the effects are more sustained in boys. The play patterns of children from divorced families were less socially and cognitively mature when measured shortly after divorce. This might be due either to regression following the divorce or to a conflict-laden home situation preceding the divorce that had already retarded play development. Disturbances in play were also reflected in differences in the expression of affect. Angry, hostile, threatening affect and excitement were found more frequently in boys than in girls in both divorced and nondivorced families. At 2 months after divorce, both boys and girls in divorced families showed less happy, affectionate, and task-involved affect and more depressed, anxious, guilty, and apathetic affect than did children in nondivorced families. At 1 year after divorce, girls in divorced families were still less happy and more anxious than girls in nondivorced families, but again these differences were gone by 2 years following divorce. Negative types of emotion were more frequent and long lasting in boys following divorce. Boys from divorced families showed more hostile affect in the first year following divorce and were still less happy and more anxious 2 years after the divorce.

Let us now examine the fantasy play of the children from divorced and nondivorced families. We noted earlier that there was less imaginative play by children in divorced families and that differences among children from divorced and nondivorced families in the amount of fantasy persisted for boys but not for girls. In addition, when children from divorced families became involved in fantasy play in the first year following divorce, it was more likely to have been instigated by a peer than to have been self-initiated.

What differences were there among our groups of children in the types of imaginative processes involved in play? At all ages boys were more likely than girls to use imaginative processes involving objects that were present, and girls were more likely than boys to use fantasy processes involving imaginary objects, people, or situations. With increasing age, both boys and girls were less reliant on the presence of objects in their environment in initiating fantasy play and more often utilized fantasied objects, people, and events, and role and identity transformations. At 2 months following divorce, children from divorced families spent a larger proportion of their imaginative playtime in fantasy processes involving object-related functions, functional change in objects, and object-related animation than did children from nondivorced families. In addition, in this period they spent less of their time interacting with imaginary people. There were no fantasy process differences between girls from divorced and nondivorced families at 1 year and 2 years following divorce, but some differences for boys remained. In all three periods boys from divorced families less often made transformations of the self than did boys from nondivorced families. They seemed to have great difficulty in moving from "I" to the assumption of another's role in fantasy play. Gould (1972) has remarked that the transition from the consistent use of "I" in play to play in which the child is able to assume or alternate in playing another's role occurs between the ages of 3½ and 4. She noted that continued focusing on the ''I'' in fantasy play in children beyond this age tends to be associated with a preoccupation with aggression and an inability to assume the role of providing or caring for others in imaginative play. Some support for this is found in our data, as children from divorced families were more involved with themes in which they were the recipients or agents of aggressive behavior, and boys from divorced families had a smaller percentage of prosocial themes dealing with caring for others, affection, helping, sharing and, sympathy. In both divorced and nondivorced families, boys more often utilized aggressive themes and themes of aggrandizement and girls more often used prosocial caretaking or providing themes. These were the only significant thematic differences.

A certain rigidity and narrowness was also reflected in the fantasy play of both boys and girls from divorced families at 2 months after divorce and for a more sustained period for boys. At 2 months after divorce, boys and girls from divorced families had fewer different characters involved in their fantasies, less frequently made different uses of the same object in play, and showed less diversity in either themes or affect in play. Except for less variation in themes and affect, these differences had disappeared for girls by 1 year after divorce and even the variability differences were gone by 2 years after divorce. However, these indicators of thematic and affective narrowness persisted for boys from divorced families.

Social Interactions

When we looked at the social behavior of children across a broad range of situations in the school, we again found evidence of disrupted functioning in children immediately following divorce. Again these had largely disappeared for girls by 2 years after divorce and were decreasing but still lingering in boys.

At 2 months following divorce both boys and girls showed a pattern of greater fantasy aggression, opposition, and seeking help, attention, and proximity. In schools in which there were male adults, boys from divorced families made particularly strong attempts at maintaining contact and getting attention by following, touching, and seeking praise or affection from male adults. At 2 months after divorce children from divorced families shared and helped less than children in nondivorced families. They showed less positive nonverbal behavior (such as smiling or hugging) and more negative nonverbal behavior (such as pouting, clinging, and scowling), more crying, whining, and complaining, and more inattention, activity changes, and inactivity. We found higher fantasy aggression, more seeking of attention and affection, and more positive and negative physical contact with adults for girls from divorced families, compared to those in nondivorced families at all ages. In addition, in the first year following divorce, boys from divorced families were more likely than those from nondivorced families to make negative initiation bids and negative terminations of social interactions. Immediately following divorce, these boys showed a great deal of aversive opposition and negative commands toward both peers and adults, particularly female adults. This high rate of aversive opposition and negative demands toward female adults by boys from divorced families continued over the 2 years following divorce. They were also higher than boys from nondivorced families in physical and verbal hostile and instrumental aggression toward peers at both 2 months and 1 year after divorce. However, by 2 years after divorce, boys from divorced families, in comparison to those from nondivorced families, were showing low physical aggression and high verbal aggression, a pattern more frequently found in girls. The verbal and physical aggression displayed by girls from divorced families at 2 months, and by boys at 2 months and at 1 year, tended to be immature, unprovoked, and ineffective. They were seldom successful in gaining their ends through instrumental aggression. Their aggression was often accompanied by or followed by crying, dependency bids, or appeals to the teacher. One of the observers described them as incompetent bullies. Competent bullies are sometimes popular in the preschool set but it seems incompetent bullies rarely are.

By 2 years following divorce, boys also still were showing less helping behavior and less time affiliating or playing with people. It should be emphasized that, although the boys in the divorced families were still showing more noxious behaviors than boys from nondivorced families, their social behaviors had greatly improved. They were exhibiting less coercive behavior, less physical aggression, less aversive opposition, and fewer negative demands than they had at 1 year. However, rather than becoming more accepted, they appeared to be becoming more socially isolated relative to their male peers.

Reactions of Others

Perhaps by examining peer and teacher responses we can gain some understanding of what processes may be associated with these changes. The high rate of aversive behaviors in boys from single-parent homes in the first year following divorce was reacted to by male peers with high ignoring, opposition, aversive opposition, negative nonverbal responses, hostile physical aggression, hostile verbal aggression, and negative termination of interactions. By 2 years following divorce, although the negative oppositional and aggressive behavior by peers had gone, there was still more ignoring of boys from divorced families, fewer positive initiations, and more positive and negative terminations of interactions by male peers. There were few differences in the behavior of female peers when they were interacting with boys from divorced versus nondivorced families except that they spent more time playing with boys from mother-headed one-parent households.

A closer examination of initiations to peers may help clarify some of these findings. In the first two observation sessions, boys from divorced families were making many initiations toward peers. They wanted to interact. However, many of these initiations were negative, and the subsequent interactions were aversive, involving a combination of negative demands, physical and verbal aggression, dependency demands, crying, whining, and complaining. By 2 years after divorce the sons from divorced families were spending less time interacting with peers and were making fewer initiations, but a larger proportion of their initiations were positive. In fact, the proportion of positive to negative initiations is equivalent to that of boys in nondivorced families. At 2 months after divorce the boys from divorced families might attempt to initiate interactions by kicking over another child's sand castle or by standing silently staring and looming over the other child. By 2 years the boys from divorced families might say "I like building sand castles too," or "What a great sand castle," or might bring a twig with a leaf on it for a flag on the castle tower. However, their peers were neither accepting these initiations nor making initiations toward them. Perhaps they had learned to avoid them. A sequence analysis showed that males gave a high rate of opposition and ignoring responses to the initiations of these boys. Consequently, a significantly larger proportion of their time was spent in watching the play of others. The attending behaviors in boys from divorced families were often accompanied by negative nonverbal behaviors such as pouting and self-manipulation. These behaviors seem very similar to the hovering behavior in unpopular children recently described by Gottman (1978). If we break down the type of peers involved in these initiations, we find that boys from divorced families were more successful in gaining entry when making initiations toward younger children and toward girls. We argue later that this may in part explain why in this study and some previous studies more feminine play patterns and sex-typed preferences in boys from mother-headed one-parent households have been found.

When teachers interacted with boys from divorced families they also showed more negative behaviors than they did with boys from nondivorced families. In the first year following divorce they showed more negative requests or commands, more opposition, more negative terminations of interactions, and fewer positive responses. These differences were gone by 2 years following divorce.

Girls in divorced families seemed to elicit very different responses from their peers than did boys. There were no differences in responses from male peers toward girls from divorced or nondivorced families. Female peers showed more hostile verbal aggression and negative terminations in interacting with girls from divorced families, but they also showed more constructive social behavior such as sympathy, helping, and sharing at 2 months and at 1 year after divorce. There were no differences at 2 years after divorce. In the first year following divorce, teachers similarly seemed to make rather ambivalent responses toward girls from nondivorced families. They not only exhibited more negative commands and more negative verbal and physical responses but also exhibited more positive verbal and physical responses. In the first year following divorce, teachers seemed to be both more supportive and more critical of these girls. There were no teacher differences in treatment of girls from divorced and nondivorced families 2 years following divorce.

Although we have noted the greater ambivalence of the responses of peers and teachers toward girls from divorced than nondivorced families, it should be pointed out that boys from both divorced and nondivorced families receive more ambivalent responses from teachers, peers, and parents than do girls. A larger proportion of responses to boys, particularly to boys from divorced families, were negative or ambivalent responses. Crying and distress in boys received less frequent and shorter periods of comforting and more ambivalent comforting than did distress signals by girls. By ambivalent comforting we refer to instances in which a positive and negative or denying response were combined in dealing with distress in boys—A hug with "There, there! Boys don't cry," or "You're all right now," as a boy gloomily observed a bloody knee. In contrast, in the few cases where physical injury was observed in girls, the response of adults, both in the home and school, was usually either commenting on the quality of the injury ("That hurt, didn't it?") or unconditional nurturance (positive reassurance that was not accompanied by a qualifying statement).

Why should adults and peers be less supportive of boys than of girls in their attempts to cope with stress or changing life situations? It may be that sex-role standards cause people to perceive girls as requiring more support in times of stress and that signs of emotional neediness are less acceptable in boys than in girls. It also should be kept in mind that acting-out behavior, combined with a high rate of dependency demands and immature behavior, as is found in preschool boys in the first year following divorce, is a particularly noxious combination. People may be responding to the more aversive coping style of boys.

Teacher and Peer Ratings

We have examined the actual behavior of the children in the school setting. How do peer and teachers' perceptions of the children concur with our observations? Teachers rated children as becoming more task oriented, more cooperative and more interpersonally constructive and less hostile with age. Boys were rated as more defiant and aggressive than girls. Girls from divorced families were rated by teachers as being more dependent; boys from divorced families were viewed as more aggressive, impulsive, resistant, and lacking in task orientation.

The peer nomination inventory indicated that, both at 2 months and at 1 year after divorce, boys from divorced families were viewed as more aggressive and less socially constructive than were boys from nondivorced families. They were still viewed by their peers as more aggressive at 2 years after divorce although our observations suggest that this was not the case. This may support the notion that the earlier aversive behavior of boys in the first years after divorce was still being reacted to by their peers. There is further support of this position in the finding that boys who were shifted from one school to another between the first and second year assessments were perceived and responded to more positively by both peers and teachers in the last assessment. This was especially true of boys who had been perceived extremely negatively in that first year after divorce. This finding runs counter to the notion that stability in a child's environment following divorce facilitates adjustment. When a child has been labeled by peers or teachers in a negative fashion, the value of a move and a fresh start in a new environment may far outweigh the deleterious aspects of coping with a new school situation. The only differences in ratings between girls in divorced and nondivorced families were that girls in divorced families were rated as more aggressive at 2 months and more withdrawn, anxious, and dependent at all ages. Boys from divorced families were less popular than boys from nondivorced families both at 1 year and at 2 years following divorce. When boys from divorced families were selected as best friends, it was most likely to be by a younger child or a girl. There were no differences in popularity between girls from divorced and non-divorced families.

Relation Between Home and School Behavior

How consistent is the behavior of children in the home, laboratory, and school situations? In the first year following divorce, there is considerable stability across situations in the behavior of children from divorced families. Observed noncompliance, negative demands, dependency, ignoring, aggression, and sustained activity were all significantly correlated for the home and laboratory situation. All these variables except ignoring were significantly correlated for home and school, and all except aggression were significantly correlated for the laboratory and school observations. In addition, there was considerable congruence between parent and teacher ratings in the first year following divorce. This was true for children in divorced families but not in nondivorced families, for whom there was much less stability across situations. The behavior of the children in divorced families also showed less stability across situations at 2 years after divorce. We could speculate that in the first year following divorce, the distress, anxiety, and problems in coping with their new family situation is most intense for the children. Under such disturbed emotional conditions, the internal state of the child rather than external situational variations may control the behavior of the child. Under high stress, the child may discriminate less well between situations and may respond less appropriately to the behavior of others. An analysis was done of the appropriateness of children's responses in the home, laboratory, and school situation. The behaviors of the child and of the people with whom the child was interacting were classified as positive, negative, or neutral. Conditional probabilities were calculated for the child's contingent positive, negative, or neutral responses to the positive, negative, or neutral responses of others. In the first year following divorce, children from divorced families were more likely than children from nondivorced families to make inappropriate responses to others. For example, they were more likely to make negative responses to a positive act of another and positive responses to a negative act of another. There were no significant differences between the groups in the appropriateness of responding at 2 years after divorce.

THE RELATIONSHIP OF PARENT–CHILD INTERACTIONS
AND COGNITIVE AND SOCIAL DEVELOPMENT
IN CHILDREN

Intellectual Development

Studies of the intellectual development of children from single-parent families have investigated both the overall level of intellectual performance and achievement, and the patterning of intellectual abilities. Two reviews of this research have concluded that children growing up in mother-headed families show deficits in cognitive performance as assessed by standardized intelligence and achievement tests and school performance (Biller, 1974; Shinn, 1978), although these conclusions may not be as consistent and well substantiated as the authors assume (Hetherington, Featherman, & Camara, 1981).

Differences in the intellectual performance of children from single-parent and two-parent households are rarely found in the preschool years; they emerge and increase over the course of development in the school years (Deutsch & Brown, 1964). Several longitudinal studies, where repeated measures over time on the same children were available, found no deficits when the children were young but the emergence of deficits with increasing age (Hess, Shipman, Brophy, & Bear, 1968; Hess, Shipman, Brophy, Bear, & Adelberger, 1969; Rees & Palmer, 1970). It may be that the types of items on preschool tests that involve rote memory, simple vocabulary, and sensorimotor skills are less sensitive than the problem-solving and abstract-reasoning items found on tests for older children, to factors associated with being raised in a single-parent family.

In addition to studies of the overall level of cognitive performance, many investigators have studied the patterning of cognitive abilities. Aptitude and achievement tests in the general population have shown that females are usually superior to males in verbal areas, whereas males are superior to females on quantitative tasks. It has been reported that in single-parent families both male and female children are more likely to show the female pattern of higher verbal than quantitative scores. In most cases, this is associated with a decrement in quantitative scores; however, in middle-class, relatively elite samples such as college students from Harvard, Stanford, or Carleton, or in children from upper middle-class families, being raised in a single-parent family actually may enhance verbal scores (Carlsmith, 1964; Funkenstein, 1963; Lessing, Zagorin & Nelson, 1970; Oshman, 1975). This enhancement has never been found in children from lower socioeconomic levels. The difference on quantitative and verbal scores has been attributed to the effects of lack of a male model and hence a more feminine pattern of cognitive skills (Carlsmith, 1964), and to the fact that tension interferes more with problem solving than with verbal skills (Nelson & Maccoby). In addition, decrements in overall levels of achievement have been related to the presence of fewer adults in the home and to less interaction with adults by children in one-parent households (Shinn, 1977; Zajonc, 1976).

In our study each child had taken the Wechsler Preschool and Primary Scale of Intelligence (WPPSI), the Matching Familiar Figures Test (MFF) and the Embedded Figures Test at 2 months, at 1 year, and at 2 years after divorce. Because intellectual differences between children in two-parent and single-parent households usually do not appear until the elementary school years, and because our children were only an average of 5.81 years of age at termination of the study, we did not anticipate significant differences in test performance between our groups. However we did expect that there would be differences in which parental factors were associated with the children's cognitive measures. Much to our surprise, although there were no differences between groups on the WPPSI at 2 months and at 1 year after divorce, at 2 years children in nondivorced families scored significantly higher than children in the divorced families on performance IQ ($\bar{X}$ = 104.4 and 97.5 respectively) and marginally higher ($p < .07$) on the full scale IQ ($\bar{X}$ = 106.5 and $\bar{X}$ = 100.2 respectively). The only subscales on which significant differences between children in divorced and nondivorced families were found were block designs, mazes, and arithmetic. There were no significant differences on the verbal IQ.

What parental behaviors might be mediating cognitive development in the children from nondivorced and divorced families? The parent variables examined were those that have in past studies been found to be related to cognitive development in children and those that seemed most relevant to the explanations that have been offered for differences in the cognitive development of children in single-parent and nuclear families. What was apparent and is a recurring theme in the rest of the chapter is that over time the divorced fathers had a decreasing impact on their children's development and that different parental factors were important in the development of children in divorced and nondivorced families. It should be kept in mind that this declining importance of the father was occurring in a sample of divorced families in which the fathers were probably more actively involved than those in most divorced families. The fathers were continuing to participate in a time-consuming study.

For boys in the divorced families, at 2 months after divorce, the following parental variables in order of descending significance were related to current measures of total IQ and performance IQ: paternal availability, paternal warmth, maternal control (this is control in the Baumrind sense of authoritative control and there is no implication of excessive restrictiveness), paternal control, family disorganization, conflict, total time spent with adults, and paternal warmth. For verbal IQ, maternal warmth and total time spent with adults moved ahead of family disorganization and conflict. By 2 years after divorce, maternal control, family disorganization, maternal maturity demands, conflict, maternal warmth, total time with adults, and paternal availability were important in total and performance IQ. Again, time with adults and maternal warmth moved up in importance for verbal IQ.

A similar declining pattern of paternal influence occurred with daughters; in fact at 2 years after divorce fathers were having no detectable impact on their daughters' intellectual development. For girls at 2 months after divorce, maternal maturity demands, paternal maturity demands, maternal control, paternal warmth, paternal control, family disorganization, conflict, and total time spent with adults were important in total and performance IQ. In verbal IQ, maternal communication appeared midway in the series. At 2 years after divorce family disorganization, maternal control, maternal maturity demands, total time spent with adults, and maternal communication were associated with all three IQ measures. It can be seen that the tension interference hypothesis received support mainly for boys, as conflict remained an important correlate of boys' IQ at all ages. Similarly, paternal availability and hence perhaps identification with the father continues to be important for boys but not for girls. The importance of the amount of total adult interaction proposed by Zajonc and by Shinn also gains some support. In addition structural equations showed an interesting progression of parent and child behaviors leading to children's final intellectual performance 2 years following divorce. Mothers who at 2 months were erratic and inconsistent and had little control over their children, and who had disorganized, chaotic households, had children who were impulsive, inattentive, and highly distractible in nursery school at the end of the first year. These children who showed deficits in attentional focusing 1 year after divorce, at 2 years after divorce showed decrements on performance IQ, particularly on subscales such as block design, mazes, and arithmetic, which require sustained attention in information processing. This chain of responses is not found for verbal IQ scores or for verbal subscales such as vocabulary, which do not require sustained information processing or reasoning. Arithmetic was the only verbal subscale associated with this progression of parent and child behaviors. These effects were more marked for boys than girls and were more likely to occur in families with high continuing marital conflict. This suggests that it is the poor maternal control and family disorganization, often reported to be present in divorced families, that is leading to the inattention and distractibility that ultimately results in poor performance on tasks requiring sustained attention. Under the conditions of stress and a rapidly changing life situation associated with divorce, the child may have difficulty exerting internal controls and may require the external controls provided by an authoritative mother and a more structured and orderly environment. This sequence of relations did not occur for children in nondivorced families, who it might be assumed are less in need of someone else to order and control their world.

The parent variables that correlated with the intellectual performance of children in nondivorced families were more stable over time than those in single-parent families. They resembled those of the children from divorced families at 2 months after divorce. However with increasing age for boys in nondivorced families, paternal availability and paternal warmth became even more highly correlated with IQ scores.

No differences in scores on the Embedded Figures Test were found for children from divorced or nondivorced families for boys and girls. However on the Matching Familiar Figures Test at 2 years following divorce, children in divorced families made more errors and had shorter latencies, that is, were more impulsive than children in nondivorced families, who were more reflective.

The paternal variables related to children's scores on the MFF were similar to those on the performance scale of the WPPSI and particularly on the block design, mazes, and arithmetic subscales. Low maternal control and inconsistency and family disorganization seemed to be particularly important long-term predictors of impulsivity in children in divorced families.

Sex-Role Typing

Previous studies have shown that some disruptions in the sex-role typing of young boys occurs if they have been separated from their fathers in the first 5 years of life. If they lose their fathers after that age, there are no differences in their sex-role typing from that of boys in nondivorced families. In contrast, sex-role disruption usually is not found in young girls from single-parent mother-headed homes regardless of time of separation from their fathers. Preschool boys and boys in their early school years from mother headed-families have been described as more dependent, less masculine (Santrock, 1970), more feminine in self-concepts and sex-role preferences, and less aggressive than boys from intact families. They have been shown to have play patterns and game preferences more characteristic of girls than of boys (Hetherington, 1966). They also have been reported to show greater verbal than physical aggression, which is a pattern more commonly found in girls (Bach, 1946; Sears, 1961).

There were no long-term significant differences between the sex-role preferences or sex-role orientation of girls in single-parent and nuclear families. Daughters of divorced parents were more dependent at home and in school throughout the course of the study and more aggressive and oppositional in the first year following divorce but not by the end of the second year. There was no difference in the amount of time involved with masculine or feminine toys or activities, or playing with members of the same or opposite sex, by these girls and those from nondivorced parents. Clearly divorce cannot be assumed to have led to disruptions in traditional sex-role typing in these girls, nor, it might be added, was it associated with a more or less androgynous pattern of sex-role typing or behavior.

In contrast although at 2 months and at 1 year after divorce, boys from divorced families showed no difference in sex-role preferences or sex-role orientation from those in nuclear families, differences were emerging in the last test session. At 2 years after divorce boys in the divorced families were scoring lower on male preferences and higher on female preferences on the sex-role preference test. They also were drawing the female figure first more often than were boys in nuclear families. In addition, their male and female drawings showed less sex differentiation than those of the boys in intact families and both groups of girls. By 2 years after divorce boys in single-parent families were also spending more time playing with female and younger peers and were more involved in female activities. We earlier remarked that this was not altogether a matter of choice for these boys from single-parent families because they had more difficulty gaining entry to same-aged male peer groups than to female or younger groups. This may explain why their play patterns and social behavior was less mature and more feminine than those of boys in nuclear families. They may have been modeling and adapting to the behaviors of the children with whom they were playing.

Although in the first year after divorce boys from divorced parents were showing more physical aggression and dependency both in the home and school, by the last testing session, although they were still frequently seeking help and attention, their physical aggression in the school was low and had been replaced by high verbal aggression, a pattern more frequently found in girls.

What parental behaviors were associated with the development of masculine and feminine characteristics in children? Our results for children in nondivorced families substantiated the frequently reported finding that fathers are more important than mothers in sex-role typing. This has been attributed to the fact that fathers usually are much more concerned than mothers about the maintainance of stereotyped sex-role behavior in their children and more likely to vary their role as they relate to male and female offspring. Paternal availability also was related to sex-role adoption. For the boys in nondivorced families, paternal warmth, maturity demands, paternal dominance, and participation in decision making were related to masculine sex-role preferences, orientation, and adoption. Girls who scored as extremely feminine had fathers who showed masculine sex-role preferences on the California Personality Inventory, who liked women and reinforced their daughters for feminine attitudes and behavior, and who were restrictive but warm and involved with their daughters. In contrast, only warmth in mothers was related to femininity in daughters in nondivorced families. Femininity in mothers, maternal attitudes toward sex-roles, and maternal reinforcement for sex-stereotyped behavior surprisingly had no impact on the femininity of girls. Depending on your attitude toward conventional sex-role stereotypes you may view the father as an effective parent or as the villain in the piece. What contributes to the development of androgyny in children? The most androgynous girls, in contrast to traditionally sex-stereotyped girls, had fathers who were warm, had a positive attitude toward their wives and daughters, but encouraged early independence and achievement in their daughters. Maternal employment and maternal encouragement of independence was also related to androgyny in daughters. The most androgynous boys had fathers who themselves felt comfortable with an emotional expressive role, who admired their wives and encouraged a warm relationship between the boy and his mother, who were warm but tended to be dominant and play an active role in decision making and in child care. The main difference in fathers of boys who were traditionally masculine or androgynous is that fathers in the latter group were more supportive of the boy's relationship with his mother and were more emotionally expressive than the former group of fathers. Both groups of fathers tended to be rather dominant, decisive types of men. Maternal warmth was the only maternal factor related to androgyny in boys.

How are these parental factors related to sex typing in children of divorced parents? Will the same pattern of the predominant contribution of fathers to sex-role typing still be found? At 2 months after divorce the pattern resembled that in nuclear families, by 1 year the father was beginning to have less impact, and by 2 years following divorce the only paternal variable related to sex typing in sons and daughters was paternal availability. If fathers maintained frequent contact with their children the children were more stereotypically sex typed. An interesting reversal began to occur in the roles of mothers in sex-role typing in the second year following divorce in contrast to that in nondivorced families. Maternal reinforcement for sex-typed behavior, encouragement of independence and of exploratory behavior, low anxiety, and a positive attitude toward the father were all highly related to masculinity in sons. Many mothers in divorced families were overprotective, infantilizing, and erratically restrictive with their sons. They were apprehensive when their children indulged in adventurous or boisterous activities. This maternal fearfulness and inhibition and discouraging of independent activities in combination with viewing the father as an undesirable role model mediated the timorous, dependent behaviors and feminine sex-role typing sometimes found in some of the boys in the divorced families. Maternal warmth and encouragement of sex-typed activities were also important in the development of daughters in single-parent families.

Self-Control

Finally let us turn to the paternal correlates of self-control in children. In nondivorced families aversive oppositional behavior, destructiveness, tantrums, noncompliance, and aggression in boys was associated with parental hostility, rejection, extremes of permissiveness or restrictiveness, conflict and inconsistency, and low use of explanation and reasoning. For girls it was more likely to be related to parental permissiveness, low maturity demands, and rejection. When parental hostility was accompanied by restrictiveness, it was often associated with inhibition, anxiety, and constriction in girls.

In the divorced families similar patterns were associated with lack of self-control in children at 2 months. However 2 years after the divorce we again found that the father was becoming relatively impotent in shaping his children's behavior as the mother was becoming more powerful. At that time mother's authoritative control, consistency, use of reasoning and explanation, family organization, maternal warmth, and marital conflict were related to self-control in boys. Only paternal availability and control continued to be a significant factor for fathers. For girls a similar pattern occurred except that maternal warmth assumed a more important role, marital conflict and maternal reasoning and explanation were not significant factors, and no paternal factors were related to self-control in girls.

Home and School Environments that Moderate the Effects of Divorce

We have been describing the emotional distress and disturbances in social and cognitive development in children following divorce. It might be asked if there are certain types of home or school environments that can moderate the adverse outcomes of divorce. We found a remarkable similarity in the attributes of the home and the school that were associated with more rapid and satisfactory adjustment of children from divorced families. In both settings an organized predictable environment with clearly defined and consistently enforced standards, roles, and responsibilities and a responsive nurturant atmosphere were associated with low rates of behavior disorders and more adaptive behavior in children. These home and school characteristics are similar to those of authoritative parenting described by Baumrind (1971). The role of structure, organization, rule enforcement, and assignment of responsibilities or maturity demands was more important for children from divorced than from nondivorced families. These characteristics in the school were also associated with greater self-control in children from nondivorced families with high levels of parent–child or marital conflict. It seems likely that young children who have undergone the stress inconsistency and transitions associated with divorce or high rates of family conflict require a more predictable and structured environment than do children not exposed to such difficult life experiences. Under stress young children may have difficulty structuring their own world and exerting self-control, thus external controls and a stable environment may become more important for these children than for less stressed children. The structure and control factors were more salient for boys and the responsiveness, warmth, and maturity demands for girls. However, all these factors in the school were significantly related to positive outcomes in children of both sexes from divorced families 2 years after divorce.

There were few effects related to the physical setting in the classrooms. Density, class size, and type and amount of equipment had little impact on negative or prosocial behavior in children. Variations in children's behavior seemed to be related to how teachers used the setting and encouraged the children to use it. Classrooms that were decorated with the children's work and in which the teacher commented on the children's productions were associated with more critical evaluations by children of their own and others' work, and more persistence on teacher-initiated tasks. In addition, in classrooms that were relatively orderly, where children were responsible for the care of toys and for cleaning up after activities, boys from divorced families exhibited more self-controlled and mature behavior. One finding, that at first glance might seem to be difficult to understand, was that there was more ignoring and negative attending and less individualized attention and positive interaction with children with multiple teachers in the classroom, than with a single teacher. When more than one teacher was present the teachers spent considerable time chatting with each other and passively monitoring the room rather than becoming actively involved with the children.

We may seem to be naive or belaboring the point that schools can successfully modify the impact of stressful family events on children. However, until very recently there has been a pervasive pessimism about the effects of schooling on child development. Since the time of the original Coleman (1966, 1975) reports and the work of such investigators as Basil Bernstein (1970) and Christopher Jencks and his colleagues (Jencks, Smith, Acland, Bane, Cohen, Gintis, Heyns, & Michelson, 1972) family influences, particularly early family influences, have been thought to dominate the development of children. It is only recently, in the work of such people as Michael Rutter and some of his British co-workers (Rutter, Maughan, Mortimer, & Duston, 1979) that the characteristics of schools have been found to attentuate adverse outcomes such as delinquency that might have been expected for children coming from disorganized households and economically deprived neighborhoods. In our study, as in Rutter's, we found that by 2 years after divorce: "some schools were able to exert a positive and beneficial influence on their pupils' progress, to some extent protecting them from difficulties, other schools were less successful in this [Rutter et al., 1979, p. 28]."

SUPPORT SYSTEMS

It is apparent that both parents and children are undergoing a variety of stresses and could benefit from support networks in the period following divorce. The role of the formation of an intimate relation for divorced parents and of the school for children have been discussed previously.

Effectiveness in the parent's relationship with the child was related to support in child rearing from the spouse and agreement with the spouse in disciplining the child in both divorced and nondivorced families. When support and agreement occurred between divorced couples, the disruption in family functioning was less extreme and the restablizing of family functioning occurred earlier, by the end of the first year.

The question is often asked as to whether frequent visitation by the noncustodial father has salutary outcomes for children and mothers. It seems to depend on the characteristics of the parents and their relationship. When there was agreement in child rearing, a positive attitude toward the spouse, low conflict between the divorced parents, and when the father was emotionally mature as measured by the Socialization Scale of the California Personality Inventory (Gough, 1969) and the Personal Adjustment scale of the Adjective Checklist (Gough & Heilbrun, 1965) frequency of the father's contact with the child was associated with more positive mother–child interactions, with less child-rearing stress reported by the mother, and with more positive adjustment of the child. When there was disagreement and inconsistency in attitudes toward the child, and conflict and ill will between the divorced parents, or when the father was poorly adjusted, frequent visitation was associated with poor mother–child functioning and disruptions in the children's behavior. Emotional maturity in the mother was also found to be related to her adequacy in coping with stresses in her new single life and relations with children.

Other support systems such as those of grandparents, brothers and sisters, close friends, especially other divorced friends or male friends with whom there was an intimate relationship, or a competent housekeeper also were related to the nonremarried mother's effectiveness in interacting with the child. When the children's grandparents lived in the area they played a particularly important supportive role for parents and children in terms of helping with finances, child care, and emotional support. Grandfathers in particular became actively involved in skills training and activities with sons in divorced families. However, none of these support systems was as salient as a continued, positive, mutually supportive relationship of the divorced couple and continued involvement of the father with the child. For the father, relatives, women with whom he was intimately involved, and married friends offered the next greatest support in his relationship with his child.

In our sample of divorced couples we were able to identify 11 mothers and 6 fathers who entered therapy and on whom we had records for one year following entry into therapy. In the first two years following divorce, the parents who chose to go into therapy could not be identified on the basis of being more emotionally disturbed or more stressed. The main factor which seemed to motivate parents to enter therapy was in having other friends who had been in therapy and encouraged the divorced parent to try it. Unfortunately, in addition, after therapy most of the treated parents could not be distinguished from the nontreated in terms of adjustment and coping. The only subgroup in which both the divorced mother and the child demonstrated improved adjustment was in a group of 5 mothers who were involved in behavioral programs focused on the improvement of parenting skills and in which 24 hour telephone contact with the parent trainer was available. This is obviously not a large enough group from which to draw firm conclusions about the efficacy of therapy as a support system but it does suggest that focusing on effective parenting may alleviate some of the problems encountered by the divorced mother and child.

REMARRIAGE AND STEPPARENTS

Divorce represents only one transition in the lives of children and parents. By the time of the six year follow-up study approximately 70% of the divorced women and 80% of the divorced men had remarried.

Remarriage lessened many of the stresses experienced by the members of the divorced family. The remarried parents reported higher ratings of happiness and less loneliness and state anxiety than the divorced not remarried sample. However, both of these groups were lower in self-esteem and feelings of competence than the never divorced parents. Economic concerns of women and household disorganization, which had been pervasive problems of divorced women, diminished when women remarried. If divorced men remarried before their ex-spouses their concerns about finances increased. They felt burdened by supporting or partially supporting two households. Women in all groups were less satisfied than men with their life situations, and married and remarried women were less satisfied with their marriages than their husbands were. It has frequently been reported that being a mother of preschool children is a stressful situation. In our study this was particularly true of nonworking mothers, divorced mothers of sons, and blended families in which children from two families had been merged in the same household. Maternal employment was related to life satisfaction, self-esteem, and feelings of internal control for all groups of women; however, it also was related to a sense of task overload, particularly in divorced women. In the 6-year follow up, feelings of task overload in the divorced mothers were substantially relieved by the assumption of household chores by children. When the children were preschoolers, few parents assigned them regular tasks; however, by the time the children were 10, many parents were expecting them to do such things as clean up their rooms, help with meals or dishes, do yard work, and so forth. Colletta (1979) in a comparative study of divorced middle- and lower-class mothers, remarks that one of the reasons that in spite of their greater affluence, middle-class mothers experience greater child-rearing stress is because of their reluctance or inability to involve their children in household responsibilities. If fathers participated actively in child rearing or in household tasks, less task overload and a greater sense of competence and satisfaction in child rearing were reported by all groups of women. It should be noted that in the divorced families, even after 6 years, continued involvement with the child by the divorced father led to positive outcomes for mothers and children, especially for boys. Even after remarriage, continued involvement of the divorced father was associated with more positive attitudes toward child rearing in the custodial father. However, remarried mothers, particularly mothers of sons, benefited from the support of a warm, authoritative stepfather.

The interplay between the gradual alterations in the relationship between divorced partners, the formation of new intimate relations, and the transition to remarriage is a complicated one.

At the time of divorce, in 70% of the families at least one of the spouses had been involved with another person. This relationship had contributed to the divorce, and the involved partner said it was unlikely that they would have carried through with the divorce without the extramarital relationship. However, in less than 15% of the cases did they marry this person following divorce. These seemed to be transitional relationships, which gave support at a time when it was greatly needed during separation and divorce. The divorcing spouse did not have to face the breakup of the marriage alone. Once the initial stress of divorce had passed, the transition person was viewed less favorably and fulfilled fewer immediate needs and the relationship disintegrated.

Remarriage of the spouse was accompanied by a reactivation of feelings of depression, helplessness, anger, and anxiety, particularly in mothers. Many reported that their feelings of panic and loss were similar to those experienced at the time of the original separation and divorce. Even after remarriage about 40% of the women and 25% of the men said that at times they were aware of continued emotional involvement with their former mates. Anger by the mother was almost an invariable concommitant of remarriage by the ex-husband even if the mother was the first to remarry. Sometimes this took the form of reopening conflicts about finances or visitation, sometimes it was directed at the children and their split loyalties, and often it focused on resentment and feelings of competition with the new wife. About half of the men whose ex-wives remarried reported approval of the new husband, in contrast to less than a quarter of the women whose husbands remarried. For men, of course, substantial financial gains may result from remarriage of their divorced wives. Ex-wives sought to minimize contact with new wives, whereas divorced husbands were less likely to be discomforted by encounters with a new husband.

The new wives seemed to exacerbate these feeling by entering into a particularly hostile, competitive relationship with the ex-wife in which criticism of the children and the wife's child rearing and the economic burden of the previous family often were used as the combative focus. A stepmother frequently used one of two strategies in trying to isolate her new husband from his former wife. The first was to urge the father to attempt to gain custody of his children, thus reducing the need for contact with the first wife. Only six changes in custody or living arrangements occurred in the course of the study. Five of the six involved sons, and five of the six occurred when the father but not the mother had remarried. The second strategy used by stepmothers, particularly when they became pregnant or had a child, was to try to shut out the entire former family by making visits difficult or by emphasizing that the fathers' responsibilities and future lay with his new family. Whatever the causes, involvement and visits by the father with his children diminished markedly following remarriage. This decrease was most notable with daughters. Divorced fathers not only visited sons more often and for longer periods of time following divorce, but also were more likely to sustain the contact with sons than with daughters following remarriage.

The two most important factors influencing marital adjustment and responses of children in the mother-custody homes following remarriage were the composition of step relationships and the sex of the child. Significantly more problems and less marital satisfaction were reported by spouses in which the stepfather had brought children from a previous marriage into the new household than those in which the stepfather's children resided with his previous wife. However, this last group had more difficulties than reconstituted families in which the stepfather had no natural children at the time of the remarriage. We shall call these blended families with children from both parents *complex stepfamilies,* and those with children only from the mother *simple stepfamilies.* At the time of the 6-year follow-up, five of the families involved residential complex stepfamilies and 20 involved nonresidental complex stepfamilies. The birth of new children in the second marriage was related to increased reported marital satisfaction. In blended families in which the stepfather had children, particularly children in the new household, both parents were more likely to report high rates of marital conflict, disagreement about child rearing, disatisfaction with the spouse's parental role, differential treatment of natural children and stepchildren. These parents complained that so much time was being spent working out the stepparent roles that there was little time or energy left to resolving marital difficulties. These parental reports were substantiated by direct observation that found higher rates of negative exchanges and lower rates of positive exchanges in complex versus simple stepfamilies.

Interviews and observations confirmed that the relations between stepfathers and stepchildren differed from that of natural fathers and children. In addition these relationships differed for boys and girls. There was greater variability in the responses of stepparents to stepchildren. The amount of involvement of stepfathers was not normally distributed. Stepfathers tended to be either disengaged and inattentive and to give the mother little support in child rearing, or they were extremely actively involved and often restrictive in dealing with their stepchildren, especially stepsons. Stepfathers often expressed dissatisfaction with the mother's control over her sons and a wish to help the mother "get a handle on that kid." The stepfathers' concern about control over sons was a realistic one. We have reported that divorced mothers and sons frequently became involved in a coercive cycle. Although this pattern improved over the first 2 years following divorce, in the 6-year follow-up, problems in control of boys were still found more often in the divorced nonremarried mothers than in the remarried or nondivorced mothers. If the natural parent welcomed the involvement of the stepparent, and the stepparent was an authoritative parent in the sense of being warm, willing to set consistent limits, and communicating well with the stepchild, children in stepparent families, particularly boys, functioned better than those in divorced, unremarried families or conflict-ridden, nondivorced families. In such cases the stepfather proved to be an effective support to both the natural mother and stepson and was associated with a reduced frequency of coercive interactions between mother and son. Statements such as "I feel like I'm emerging from a bad dream," or "I was caught in the vortex of a whirlpool and _____(stepfather) rescued me," or "I finally can enjoy my children again, there were times when I hated _____(son) so much that I thought I might lose control and seriously injure him. I know it sounds awful but sometimes I wanted to kill him," were heard from mothers who had had particularly difficult relationships with their sons. Home observations showed that mothers married to supportive stepfathers were more firm, consistent, warm, communicative, and demanding of mature behavior from their sons than were mothers with noninvolved stepfathers or divorced women who had not remarried.

A positive relationship with a stepfather was also reflected in more mature, independent, controlled behavior in sons both at home and in the school. Young boys often formed intense attachments and warm companionate relationships with their stepfathers. When remarriage had not occurred until the boy was 9 or 10, acceptance and a positive relationship were less likely to occur than in younger children. This is substantiated in an unpublished cross-sectional study of remarriage by Hetherington (1981) where it was found that children in the preadolescent and early adolescent period (9–15) were less likely to accept even a good stepparent than were younger or older children. Children at this age were aware of their own awakening sexuality and did not want to view their parents as sex objects. It is difficult not to be aware that your parent is a sex object to someone when he or she remarries. Normal affection and playfulness between the married couple were distressing to these young adolescents.

It should be noted that for sons a continued positive relationship with the natural father played an important role in the development of social and cognitive competence even if a supportive stepfather was available.

There were few significant differences reported or observed in mother-daughter relationships or in the behavior of girls in the remarried, divorced, or nondivorced families at either 2 years or 6 years after divorce. This finding disagrees with those of Santrock, Warshak, Lindbergh, and Meadows (1981) who report that the presence of a stepfather may be associated with adverse outcomes for girls.

The influence of stepmothers on the behavior of children was less marked than that of stepfathers. However it should be remembered that our target families involved custodial mothers, and the day-to-day living with a stepparent seems likely to make them more salient than a nonresidential stepparent.

COMMENTS AND CAUTIONS

The best statistical predictions indicate that an increasing number of parents and children are going to go through a series of transitions and reorganizations in family ties and household structure. There has been a tendency to take extreme and equally invalid views of these changes. Some writers take a gloom and doom perspective that the effects of divorce are destructive and enduring and that households headed by one parent are a pathogenic deviation from the "normal" nuclear family. Others assume the political stance of denying that one-parent households headed by women have problems in addition to financial exigencies.

In this study, we found that families in which the parents had divorced encountered many more stresses and difficulties in coping, which were reflected in disturbances in personal and social adjustments and family relations, than did nondivorced families. In the families we studied we did not encounter a victimless divorce, that is, a divorce in which at least one family member did not report distress or exhibit disrupted behavior. However, if these effects were not compounded by continued severe stress and adversity, most parents and children adapted to their new family situation within 2 years and certainly within 6 years. It also should be remembered that many households headed by mothers are exposed to excessive stresses and that without adequate support systems such families may show more sustained deleterious sequelae of divorce. It is imperative to identify and develop effective support systems that assist the family members in adjusting to the stresses and changes associated with divorce.

A final precautionary comment needs to be made. This study was done with white middle-class families in which the mother had custody of a preschool child. Surprisingly, the findings are similar to those of preschool children in the Wallerstein and Kelly (1980) study, which took place in Marin County, California, an area with very different rates of divorce and life-styles than the relatively conservative state of Virginia in which our families were studied. It may be that many of the experiences, responses, and changes in family process we described are present in a wide range of divorced parents and their children. However, great care should be used in generalizing to very different populations. There is already considerable evidence that such factors as age of the child, sex of the custodial parent, socioeconomic status, culture, and ethnicity shape the responses to and outcomes of divorce (Hetherington, 1981). An understanding of the roles, complexity, and interaction of such factors in modifying the experience and effects of marital dissolution awaits further study.

REFERENCES

Bach, G. R. Father-fantasies and father-typing in father-separated families. *Child Development,* 1946, *17,* 63–80.

Bane, M. J. Discussion paper: Health Education and Welfare. *Policy toward children youth and family,* 1977.

Baumrind, D. Child care practices anteceding three patterns of preschool behavior. *Genetic Psychology Monographs,* 1967, *75,* 43–88.

Baumrind, D. Current patterns of parental authority. *Developmental Psychology Monographs,* 1971, *4* (1, Pt 2).

Bernstein, B. Education cannot compensate for society. *New Society,* 1970, *387,* 344–347.

Biller, H. B. *Paternal deprivation: Family, school, sexuality, and society.* Lexington, Mass.: Heath, 1974.

Carlsmith, L. Effect of early father absence on scholastic aptitude. *Harvard Educational Review,* 1964, *34,* 3–21.

Coleman, J. S. *Equality of educational opportunity.* Washington: U.S. Government Printing Office, 1966.

Coleman, J. S. Methods and results in the I.E.A. studies of the effects of school on learning. *Review of Educational Research,* 1975, *45,* 335–386.

Colletta, N. D. *Divorced mothers at two income levels: Stress, support and childrearing practices.* Unpublished thesis, Cornell University, Ithaca, New York, 1978.

Deutsch, M., & Brown, B. Social influences in Negro-White intelligence differences. *Journal of Social Issues,* 1964, *20,* 24–35.

Ferri, E. Characteristics of motherless families. *British Journal of Social Work,* 1973, *3,* 91–100.

Funkenstein, D. H. Mathematics, quantitative aptitudes, and the masculine role. *Diseases of the Nervous System,* 1963, *24,* 140–146.

George, V., & Wilding, P. *Motherless families.* London: Routledge-Kegan Paul, 1972.

Glick, P. G., & Norton, A. J. Marrying, divorcing and living together in the U.S. today. *Population Bulletin,* 1978, *32,* 3–38.

Gottman, J. M. *Children's behavior when trying to enter a peer group.* Unpublished manuscript, University of Illinois, Urbana, Illinois, 1978.

Gough, H. G. *Manual for California Personality Inventory.* Palo Alto, Calif.: Consulting Psychologists Press, Inc. 1969.

Gough, H. G., & Heilbrun, A. B. Jr. *The adjective checklist.* Palo Alto, Calif.: Consulting Psychologists Press, Inc. 1965.

Gould, R. *Child studies through fantasy.* New York: Quadrangle Books, 1972.

Hartup, W. W. Peer interaction and the behavioral development of the individual child. In E. Schopler, & R. L. Reichler (Eds.), *Psychopathology and child development.* New York: Plenum, 1976.

Hartup, W. W. Peer relations and the processes of socialization. In M. J. Guralnick (Ed.), *Early intervention and the integration of handicapped and nonhandicapped children.* Baltimore: University Park Press, 1977 (a)

Hartup, W. W. Issues in child development, peers, play and pathology: A new look at the social behavior of children. *Society for Research in Child Development Newsletter,* Fall, 1977, p. 1–3. (b)

Herzog, E., & Sudia, C. E. Children in fatherless families. In B. M. Caldwell, & H. Ricciuti (Eds.), *Review of Child Development Research.* Chicago: University of Chicago Press, 1973.

Hess, R. D., Shipman, V. C., Brophy, J. E., & Bear, R. M. *The cognitive environments of urban preschool children.* Chicago: Graduate School of Education, University of Chicago, 1968. (ERIC Document Reproduction Service No ED 039 264.)

Hess, R. D., Shipman, V. C., Brophy, J. E., Bear, R. M., & Adelberger, A. B. *The cognitive environments of urban preschool children: Follow-up phase.* Chicago: Graduate School of Education, University of Chicago, 1969. (ERIC Document Reproduction Service No. ED 039 270.)

Hetherington, E. M. Effects of paternal absence on sex-typed behaviors in negro and white preadolescent males. *Journal of Personality and Social Psychology*, 1966, *4*, 87–91.

Hetherington, E. M. Children and divorce. In R. Henderson (Ed.), *Parent-child interaction:
Theory, research and prospect*. New York, Academic Press, 1981. (a)

Hetherington, E. M. *A study of family relations in stepparent families with children of three ages.*
Unpublished manuscript, University of Virginia, Charlottesville, Virginia, 1981. (b)

Hetherington, E. M., Cox, M., & Cox, R. The aftermath of divorce. In J. H. Stevens, Jr. & M.
Matthews (Eds.), *Mother-child, father-child relations*. Washington, D.C.: National Association
for the Education of Young Children, 1978.

Hetherington, E. M., Cox, M., & Cox, R. Family interaction and the social emotional and cognitive
development of children following divorce. In V. Vaughn, & T. B. Brazelton (Eds.) *The family:
Setting priorities*. New York: Science and Medicine Publishing Company, 1979. (a)

Hetherington, E. M., Cox, M., & Cox, R. Play and social interaction in children following divorce.
Journal of Social Issues, 1979, *35*, 26–49. (b)

Hetherington, E. M., Featherman, D. L., & Camara, K. *Cognitive and academic functioning of
children from one parent households*. Unpublished manuscript written for the National Institute of
Education, Bethesda, Maryland, 1981.

Jencks, C., Smith, M., Acland, H., Bane, M. J., Cohen, D., Gintis, H., Heyns, B., & Michelson,
S. *Inequality: A reassessment of the effect of family and schooling in America*. New York: Basic
Books, 1972.

Kohn, M., & Rosman, A. A social competence scale and symptom checklist for the preschool child.
Developmental Psychology, 1972, *6*, 430–444.

Lessing, E. E., Zagorin, S. W., & Nelson, D. WISC subtest and I.Q. score correlates of father
absence. *Journal of Genetic Psychology*, 1970, *117*, 181–195.

Martin, B. Parent-child relations. In F. D. Horowitz (Ed.) *Review of child development research*.
(Vol. 4.) Chicago, Ill.: University of Chicago Press, 1975.

Martin, B., & Hetherington, E. M. *Family interaction in withdrawn, aggressive and normal children*. Unpublished manuscript, University of Wisconsin, Madison, 1971.

Oshman, H. P. *Some effects of father absence upon the psychological development of male and
female late adolescents: Theoretical and empirical considerations* (Doctoral dissertation, University of Texas at Austin, 1975). *Dissertation Abstracts International*, 1975, 36, 919B–920B.
(University Microfilms No. 75-16, 719).

Parten, M. B. Social participation among pre-school children. *Journal of Abnormal and Social
Psychology*, 1932, *27*, 243–269.

Patterson, G. Mothers: The unacknowledged victims. *Monographs of the Society for Research in
Child Development*. 1980, *45*, serial number 186.

Patterson, G. R., Ray, R. S., Shaw, D. A., & Cobb, J. A. *A manual for coding of family interaction*, 1969 revision. NAPS Document #01234.

Piaget, J. *Play, dreams and imitation in childhood*. New York: Norton, 1962.

Rees, A. H., & Palmer, F. H. Factors related to change in mental test performance. *Developmental
Psychology Monographs*, 1970, *3*, 1–57.

Reid, J. B. Reliability assessment of observation data: A possible methodological problem. *Child
Development*, 1970, *41*, 1143–1150.

Roff, M., Sells, S. B., & Golden, M. M. *Social adjustment and personality development in children*. Minneapolis: University of Minnesota Press, 1972.

Rotter, J. B. Generalized expectancies for internal versus external control of reinforcement.
Psychological Monographs, 1966, *80*, (1, Whole No. 609).

Rubin, K. H., Maioni, T. L., & Hornung, M. Free play behaviors in middle and lower-class
preschoolers: Parten and Piaget revisited. *Child Development*, 1976, *47*, 414–419.

Rutter, M. *Maternal deprivation, 1972-1977: New findings, new concepts, new approaches.* Invited address to the Society for Research in Child Development, New Orleans, LA, March 1977.

Rutter, M., Maughan, B., Mortemore, P., Ouston, J., & Smith, A. *Fifteen thousand hours.* Cambridge, Mass.: Harvard University Press, 1979.

Santrock, J. W. Paternal absence, self-typing and identification. *Developmental Psychology,* 1970, *2,* 264–272.

Santrock, J. W., Warshak, P., Lindbergh, C., & Meadows, L. Children's and parents' observed social behavior in stepfather families. *Child Development,* 1981, in press.

Schaefer, E. S., & Aaronson, M. R. *Classroom behavior inventory: Preschool to primary.* Bethesda, MD: National Institute of Mental Health, 1966 (mimeo copy).

Sears, P. S. Doll-play aggression in normal young children. *Psychological Monographs,* 1961, *65* (Whole No. 6).

Sears, R. R., Rau, L., & Alpert, R. *Identification and child rearing.* Stanford, Calif.: Stanford Press, 1965.

Shinn, M. Father absence and children's cognitive development. *Psychological Bulletin,* 1978, *85,* 295–324.

Singer, J. L. *Television, imaginative play and cognitive development some problems and possibilities.* Paper presented to the American Psychological Association, San Francisco, September 1977.

Singer, J. L., & Singer, D. G. Imaginative play and pretending in early childhood: Some experimental approaches. In A. David (Ed.), *Child personality and psychopathology: Current topics.* (Vol. 3). New York: Wiley, 1976.

Spanier, G. B., & Castro, R. F. Adjustment to separation and divorce: An analyses of 50 case studies. *Journal of Divorce,* 1979, *2,* 241–253.

Speilberger, C. D., Gorsuch, R. L., & Lushene, R. *State-Trait Anxiety Inventory.* Palo Alto, Calif.: Consulting Psychologist Press, 1970.

Sutton-Smith, B. A syntax for play and games. In R. E. Herron, & B. Sutton-Smith (Eds.), *Child's play.* New York: Wiley, 1971.

Wallerstein, J. S., & Kelly, J. B. *Surviving the breakup: How children and parents cope with divorce.* New York: Basic Books, 1980.

Weiss, R. *Marital separation.* New York: Basic Books, 1975.

Weiss, R. The emotional impact of marital separation. *Journal of Social Issues,* 1976, *32,* 135–146.

Zajonc, R. B. Family configuration and intelligence. *Science,* 1976, *192,* 227–236.

10
Social Development and Parent–Child Interaction in Father-Custody and Stepmother Families

John W. Santrock
The University of Texas at Dallas

Richard A. Warshak
The University of Texas Health Science Center at Dallas

Gary L. Elliott
The University of Texas at Dallas

Although there has been a long history of interest in the effects of family structure on children's social development (Freud, 1949; Sears, Pintler, & Sears, 1946), it has been only in the last several years that extensive, systematic research has been conducted in this area (Hetherington, Cox, & Cox, 1976, 1978; Lamb, 1976). Early research (Sears, 1951) focused on a comparison of father-absent and father-present families, emphasizing the importance of the son's identification with the father as a precursor for competent social development. Recently a more fine-grained approach to studying single-parent families has been adopted. For example, rather than comparing children in father-absent and father-present homes, specific types of father-absent families have been studied (Hetherington, 1972).

For nearly a century, child custody decisions in America have been guided by the stereotype that mothers are, by nature, uniquely suited to care for children. The child will suffer irreparable damage, so the argument goes, if separated from mother during the formative "tender years." This idea is so entrenched in our culture that, until recently, fathers were awarded custody only if the mothers were proved grossly unfit. Psychological research on the effects of different custodial arrangements could help to decrease our reliance on cultural stereotypes in formulating custody decisions.

By far the greatest quantity and quality of research has been directed toward children growing up in mother-custody divorced families. As part of the investigation of mother-custody divorced families, attempts have been made not only to document how children function in divorced mother-custody compared to intact father-present homes, but also to detail the various processes in the family system that mediate the effects of family structure. Such factors as the mother's social interaction with the child, her attitudes toward the ex-spouse, and the availability of support systems, such as day care, baby-sitting, and help from relatives have been investigated (Hetherington, 1972; Hetherington et al., 1976; Santrock & Warshak, 1979; Wallerstein & Kelly, 1980).

Although our knowledge of the effects of divorce on children living with their mothers has increased substantially, we have very little information about children growing up in father-custody families. One of the main goals of our recent research is to study comprehensively the social development of children in father-custody families by comparing them with children in mother-custody and intact families. Some of the results of our research on the effects of father-custody on children have been reported earlier (Santrock & Warshak, 1979; Warshak & Santrock, in press). These results are summarized here, along with additional information on the effects of father-custody on children. The majority of the results reported earlier were derived from videotaped observations of the child with the custodial parent. In addition, the child's behavior during his or her interview with an adult also was videotaped, providing a set of observations that are independent of data reported earlier. Our discussion focuses on whether these independent observations reveal more competent social behavior by children in same-sex–child–custodial-parent families then opposite-sex–child–custodial-parent families. Other new information to be reported includes comparison of observed parental behaviors in different family structures and the relation of parental behavior to child behavior analyzed separately for the sex of the child within each of the custodial arrangements.

Not only has there been almost a complete lack of information about the effects of father custody on children, but there also have been few empirical studies of children from stepparent families. We currently are studying children in stepmother and stepfather families. Data on stepmother families are reported here in an effort to compare children's social behavior in father-custody, stepmother, and intact families.

SOCIAL DEVELOPMENT AND PARENT–CHILD INTERACTION IN FATHER-CUSTODY AND MOTHER-CUSTODY FAMILIES

The few studies of the effects of father custody have involved either an interview or a questionnaire (Gasser & Taylor, 1976; George & Wilding, 1972; Gersick, 1975; Gregory, 1965; Mendes, 1976; Orthner, Brown, & Ferguson, 1976; Schlesinger & Todres, 1976). Characteristically, a small set of fathers with custody are interviewed about their general life-styles, psychological characteristics, social adjustment, parental attitudes, and the use of support systems, such as day care. For example, Orthner et al. (1976) interviewed 15 custodial fathers, Gersick (1975) interviewed 20 custodial fathers, and Gasser and Taylor (1976) interviewed 25 custodial fathers. In all three studies, the custodial fathers expressed confidence in their ability to raise their children and reported that household functioning was proceeding smoothly. However, such studies provide an incomplete description of father-custody families. In particular, they reveal no comparison with mother-custody or intact families, and they include no direct study of children.

Methodology

We are studying 64 white, predominantly middle-class families in which the children range in age from 6 to 11 years. Half of the children are boys and half are girls. Approximately one-third of the children come from families in which the father was awarded custody following divorce, one-third come from families in which the mother was awarded custody, and one-third live in intact families. The three different types of families were matched for age of the children, family size, and socioeconomic status (SES) (Hollingshead Index). The two groups of children from divorced homes also were matched for sibling status and when the parents separated. Parents had been separated an average of 3.3 years and were in their early to middle thirties. Age of child at onset of parental separation was used as a control rather than age at onset of divorce because parental separation reflects the earliest splitting of the parents. Divorce followed parental separation by an average of 10 months in the present sample.

The procedure for obtaining the sample of families involved visiting various community agencies and Parents without Partners, and following leads given by students and professors at various colleges and universities in the Dallas–Fort Worth metropolitan area. The father-custody group was selected first because it was expected that it would be the most difficult set of families to find. Then a mother-custody family was matched on a one-to-one basis to a father-custody family, followed by the matching of the intact family group to each of the first two groups. Analyses of variance revealed no significant group differences on any of the matching variables. Although there were no social class differences, postdivorce annual income was significantly lower in mother-custody families.

Because when there is a custody dispute, it has been the practice of courts in America to award custody to fathers only when the mother is proven grossly unfit, we think it important to note that, in our sample, this did not appear to be the case. In only one case was a mother found to be "unfit." Furthermore, there were no differences between the father- and mother-custody groups in the number of custody decisions that had been reached by a court in a contested case. Nor was there any difference in the general reasons for custody assignment. With few exceptions, in both groups custody was agreed upon before a court hearing, and most ex-spouses relinquished custody because they either did not care, whether they had custody, were actively opposed to it, or were convinced that the children would be better off with the other parent.

A multimethod approach to studying family interaction was followed. Parents and children were observed interacting in a laboratory situation and the child was observed while being interviewed; structured interviews and self-report scales were given to parents and children; a projective task was administered to parents and children; and teachers were asked to report their perceptions of the children.

When the family came to the laboratory, the parent with custody and the child were videotaped in a structured interaction situation. In the intact family group the mother and the father participated in the laboratory sessions on different days. During two videotaped 10-minute laboratory sessions the parent and the child were asked to: (1) plan an activity together; and (2) discuss the main problems of the family. The parent–child interactions were rated on 9-point scales for a broad range of observational categories. This Chapter presents results from analyses on 7 of the scales on which parents were rated: control (amount of firm control the parent exerted over the child); engages child in intellectually meaningful interaction; encourages independence; attentiveness; authoritative parenting; authoritarian parenting; and permissive parenting. Children were rated on 9 categories: warmth; self-esteem; anxiety; anger; demandingness; maturity; sociability; social conformity; and independence. Many of the parent categories were derived from and modified from those developed by Baumrind (1971).

The videotaped interactions of the parent and child behavior were rated by an advanced graduate student in psychology with a clinical background. In addition, another graduate student independently rated one-fourth of the interactions. Both raters were kept naive about the group membership of the participants, although occasional comments during the interaction provided clues about family structure. The interrater reliabilities, based on Pearson r correlations for the parent scales, ranged from $+.67$ for encourages independence to $+.92$ for authoritative parenting, and for the child scales from $+.54$ for anxiety to $+.92$ for social conformity. In the intact families, the children and their fathers served as the control group for the father-custody families whereas these same children and their mothers were the control group for the mother-custody families.

The videotaping of the structured family interaction was followed by a short break, after which the child was taken back to the laboratory to be interviewed. The entire interview was audiotaped and, in addition, the first 10 minutes of the interview were videotaped. The portion of the interview that was videotaped consisted of 23 highly structured questions that were specifically worded so as not to elicit any cues about family structure. Examples were: "What school do you go to?"; What is your favorite T.V. show?"; and "If you could have three wishes, what would they be?" The child's behavior during the structured interview was rated from videotapes on the following 5-point categories: self-esteem; anxiety; dress and appearance (very neat to very sloppy); traditional femininity;

traditional masculinity; social competence; affect (very happy to very sad); and clarity of expression. One person (not the same person who coded the parent–child interaction) coded all the videotapes of the interview while another person coded one-fourth of the videotapes. These raters were completely naive about the family structure of the children being rated. Reliability between raters was calculated by the formula $a/(a + d)$, where a = number of agreements and d = number of disagreements. Agreement ranged from 67% for anxiety to 100% for appearance, with an average of 83%. In addition, the interviewer rated the child on a series of personality categories after he or she had completed the entire child interview. These 5-point scales were: self-esteem; anxiety; honesty; mood (happy–sad); overall appeal; and cooperativeness. One-fourth of the audiotapes of the child interview were independently rated. The interrater reliabilities ranged from $+.06$ to $+.67$. It is difficult to interpret this relatively weak agreement because the data are not equivalent. An audiorecording does not provide the important visual cues that can be expected to influence inferential judgements of the type invoked in these ratings. However, less confidence should be placed in the ratings of self-esteem, anxiety, and honesty (reliability below $+.50$), and more confidence in the ratings of overall appeal, cooperativeness, and mood (reliability above $+.50$).

Summary of Previously Reported Results

Based on the observations of parent–child interaction in the laboratory, we found that boys showed more problems in social development than girls in mother-custody families (Santrock & Warshak, 1979), a result that supports the multimethod data on boys and girls collected by Hetherington (Hetherington et al., 1976, 1978). (See Table 10.1 for a summary of the results.) However, in father-custody families, boys showed more competent social behavior than girls. On each of the observational measures, the mean score for boys in father-custody homes was higher than for girls, whereas the children's behavior was reversed in mother-custody homes. Significant differences were found on four of the child dimensions—boys whose fathers have custody were less demanding than girls in this type of family structure, whereas girls were less demanding than boys in mother-custody families. A similar, significantly positive same-sex-child and-parent effect was shown in the children's maturity, sociability, and independence.

We also found that the quality of the ongoing relationship between the custodial parent and the child was related to the child's behavior. Three observed parenting styles—authoritarian, authoritative, and laissez-faire—were correlated with the child's observed behavior. These three categories were chosen because they represent Baumrind's widely adopted set of parenting strategies. Regardless of the custodial arrangement, authoritative parenting (warmth, clear setting of rules and regulations, and extensive verbal give-and-take) was significantly correlated with six of the nine child observation scales: self-esteem, maturity, socia-

TABLE 10.1
Children's Behavior with Their Parent in Laboratory Situations:
Comparisons of Father-Custody with Mother-Custody Families

Child's Behavior[a]	Family Structure								F^b	p
	Father Custody				Mother Custody					
	Boys		Girls		Boys		Girls			
	$\bar{X}$	σ	$\bar{X}$	σ	$\bar{X}$	σ	$\bar{X}$	σ		
Warmth	6.8	1.6	6.0	1.5	5.4	1.6	6.1	1.2	—	—
Self-esteem	6.2	1.6	5.3	1.9	4.9	0.8	5.8	1.6	3.61	.06
Anxiety	6.0	1.6	5.3	2.3	5.4	1.6	6.1	1.0	—	—
Anger	7.7	1.3	6.6	2.6	6.8	2.0	7.1	2.1	—	—
Demandingness	6.4	1.4	4.4	2.5	4.9	2.1	6.3	1.7	7.57	.01
Maturity	6.3	1.8	4.7	2.2	4.6	1.5	6.2	1.4	8.75	.01
Sociability	6.7	1.5	5.7	1.8	5.2	1.5	6.4	1.2	5.53	.01
Social conformity	6.0	1.6	5.2	2.4	4.5	2.4	6.1	1.9	—	—
Independence	6.3	1.6	4.7	2.2	5.7	1.6	6.3	0.8	4.63	.04
	$N = 10$		$N = 11$		$N = 10$		$N = 9$			

[a]Higher scores indicate the favorable pole of the variable.
[b]All significant F's are interaction terms.

bility, social conformity, anger, and demandingness. The correlations of authoritarian and laissez-faire parenting styles and child behavior in the laboratory were not as consistent as they were for authoritative parenting. However, overall authoritarian and laissez-faire parenting were more likely to be associated with social incompetence than competence on the part of children.

To cope with the demands of single parenting, divorced parents were enlisting the aid of additional caretakers, such as the noncustodial parent, baby-sitters, relatives, day-care centers, and friends. Overall, support systems were being used more by fathers with custody than mothers with custody (24 hours per week versus 11 hours per week). Father-custody children also had more contact with the noncustodial parent than their counterparts in mother-custody homes. In both types of custody dispositions, total contact with adult caretakers was positively related to the child's warmth, sociability, and social conformity as observed in the laboratory.

An analysis of the interviewer's perceptions of the child during the child interview led to virtually the same pattern of results found in the observations of parent-child interaction (Warshak & Santrock, in press). On each of the interviewer's ratings the mean score for boys in father-custody homes was higher than the mean score for girls in father-custody homes, whereas the children's scores were reversed in mother-custody homes. Significant differences were found in cooperativeness, honesty, and overall appeal. For example, father-custody boys and mother-custody girls were perceived to be more honest than father-custody girls and more appealing than mother-custody boys.

In the Warshak and Santrock (in press) paper, information about children's reactions to divorce and the custodial parent's perception of the effects of the divorce on the child was presented. Type of custody was not linked with any of the children's acute reactions to the divorce, except when changes in their relationship with the noncustodial parent were evaluated. Mothers with custody indicated that the father–child relationship began to deteriorate in the weeks and months following the divorce, but in contrast, half the custodial fathers who detected changes in their child's relationship with their mother saw the changes as positive. This pattern of results also appeared when parents were asked about how things were now compared to how they had been before the divorce. Mothers with custody reported a deterioration in the father–child relationship , whereas fathers with custody reported improvement in the mother–child relationship.

There were some interesting differences in what parents told us about their children's perception of the divorce and what the children reported themselves. A large majority (80%) of the parents stated that their child initially wanted the parents to get back together, but only 40% indicated that their children still had this wish. However, 85% of the children interviewed said that they still would like their parents to get back together again. More than two-thirds of the children said that overall, things were better before the divorce. The children from divorced homes enjoyed visiting with the noncustodial parent, a majority reporting that they would like to have more visits. And a majority of these children said they they would like their custodial parent to get married again. In sum, such information suggests that children want to live in two-parent families rather than one-parent families.

Not Previously Reported Results

The following sections present additional data on father- and mother-custody families that have not been previously reported. The data include observations of the parent's behavior during parent–child interaction in the laboratory, observations of the child's behavior during the child interview, the relation of parent behavior to child behavior during parent–child interaction, and the relation of parent behavior in parent–child interaction to child behavior during the child interview. Analysis of the parent's behavior and assessment of its relation to the child's behavior emphasizes the importance of searching for how the parent's behavior may mediate the effects of family structure on the child's behavior. By assessing these effects in more than one setting (e.g., child's behavior with parent, interviewer's perception of child, and child's observed behavior with interviewer), more confidence in the generalization of the findings can be obtained.

Observation of Parent Behavior during Parent–child Interaction in the Laboratory. A 4 by 2 analysis-of-variance (ANOVA) test was conducted on the seven parent scales coded from videotaped observations of parent–child interaction. The factors were: family structure (mother with custody, father with custody; mother in intact family; father in intact family); and sex of child. Duncan Multiple Range Tests were used to specify the effects revealed by the ANOVAS. Significant main effects occurred for controlling [$(F(3,66) = 5.22, p. < .003)$] and permissive [$F(3,66) = 5.71, p. < .002$] parenting orientations. The control variable reflects firm versus lax enforcement of control and ranges from 1 (the child controls the parent, parent has no control over child) to 9 (very firm, consistent control of the parent over the child). Mothers with custody were more likely to allow the child to control them ($\overline{X} = 4.05$) than were fathers with custody ($\overline{X} = 6.00$), and intact-family mothers ($\overline{X} = 6.06$) and fathers ($\overline{X} = 6.12$). In similar fashion, mothers with custody ($\overline{X} = 6.71$) were more permissive than intact-family fathers ($\overline{X} = 3.75$) and mothers ($\overline{X} = 4.18$) more permissive than fathers with custody ($\overline{X} = 4.90$).

The difficulties mothers with custody have in controlling their children were also found by Hetherington et al. (1976). However, as just noted, we found that fathers with custody were in more firm control of their children than mothers with custody. Although we have found a relationship between authoritative parenting and competent social behavior in children from mother- and father-custody homes, we did not find that authoritative parenting is used by one set of custodial parents more than the other.

Observations of The Child's Behavior During the Child Interview. A 3 × 2 analysis-of-variance (Family Structure and Sex of Child) was applied to the videotaped observations of the child's behavior during the highly structured first 10 minutes of the child interview. When appropriate, the Duncan Multiple Range test was also used.

As indicated in Table 10.2, significant interaction effects occurred for the children's self-esteem, anxiety, and social competence. Mother-custody boys were observed to have lower self-esteem than intact-family girls, and intact-family girls were rated as higher on self-esteem than father-custody girls. Father-custody girls were rated as showing more anxiety than intact-family girls. In addition, mother-custody girls and intact-family girls were observed to be more socially competent than mother-custody boys, whereas intact-family girls were viewed as more socially competent than father-custody girls.

Taken together, these results support our earlier data on observations of children's behavior with their parents (Santrock & Warshak, 1979), namely that competent social behavior is more characteristic of children whose custodial parent is the same sex as they are. Recall that this same patterning of findings was found also when the child interviewers rated the child's behavior at the end of the child interview (Warshak & Santrock, in press). As further indication of

TABLE 10.2
Observations of the Child's Behavior During the Child Interview: Effects of Family Structure and Sex of Child

	Family Structure												
	Father Custody				Mother Custody				Intact Family				
	Boys		Girls		Boys		Girls		Boys		Girls		
Child's Behavior	$\bar{X}$	σ	$\bar{X}$	σ	$\bar{X}$	σ	$\bar{X}$	σ	$\bar{X}$	σ	$\bar{X}$	σ	F^a	p
Self-esteem	3.38	1.30	2.91	1.22	2.13	.99	3.75	1.17	3.29	1.11	4.11	1.05	3.66	.03
Anxiety	2.13	1.36	3.73	1.35	3.50	1.60	2.38	1.19	2.86	1.57	1.89	1.05	5.60	.01
Dress and appearance	3.75	1.04	3.73	1.10	3.13	1.13	4.00	1.31	3.57	.54	4.33	.71		
Social competence	3.50	1.31	3.00	1.34	2.13	.99	4.00	1.20	3.43	1.13	4.33	1.32	4.05	.02
Affect	3.00	1.20	2.82	.98	2.25	1.04	3.38	.92	2.86	1.07	3.56	1.33		
Clarity of expression	2.75	1.04	2.91	1.04	1.75	1.04	3.50	.93	3.14	1.46	4.00	.71		
Femininity	2.25	.89	3.73	1.10	1.75	1.04	3.63	1.30	2.00	1.16	3.78	1.30		
Masculinity	2.25	1.39	2.18	1.54	3.63	1.41	2.25	1.49	2.86	1.46	2.00	1.12		
	$N = 8$		$N = 11$		$N = 8$		$N = 8$		$N = 7$		$N = 9$			

[a]All significant F's are interaction effects.

the robustness of this effect, the analyses of all three sets of measures (observations of the child's behavior with the parent, interviewer's ratings of the child, and observations of the child's behavior during the interview) yielded no main effects, only interaction effects. Sometimes the significant interaction effects represent less socially competent behavior on the part of mother-custody boys when they are compared with father-custody boys, sometimes the interaction indicates more socially competent behavior by mother-custody girls when compared to father-custody girls, sometimes it suggests more socially competent behavior by mother-custody girls compared to mother-custody boys, and finally it sometimes reveals that father-custody boys are more socially competent than father-custody girls. However, in none of the analyses of the three sets of information discussed here have we found significant effects in favor of opposite-sex-child–custodial-parent family structures.

The Relation of Observed Parental Behavior to Observed Child Behavior During Parent–Child Interaction. Previously we reported that an authoritative parenting style is positively correlated with competent social behavior in children in both father-custody and mother-custody families (Santrock & Warshak, 1979). We also reported that an authoritarian parenting style was more likely to be associated with more socially incompetent behavior by children in father-custody families and that a laissez-faire parenting style was more likely to be linked with socially incompetent behavior in mother-custody families, although these associations were not nearly as strong as the relationship between authoritative parenting and competent social behavior. Those analyses were not conducted separately for sex of child within each custody disposition. For our purpose here, we correlated observed parent behavior with observed child behavior separately for sex of child within each custodial arrangement.

In Table 10.3, the Pearson r correlations suggest that regardless of the sex of child–custodial parent structure, authoritative parenting was correlated in highly positive ways with socially competent behavior on the part of children. For example, in father-custody boy families, authoritative parenting was correlated +.84 with the son's self-esteem, −.54 with anxiety, and +.72 with social maturity. And in mother-custody girl families, the correlation with the girl's warmth was +.61 and with social maturity it was +.57.

Although there were fewer significant correlations of authoritarian and permissive parenting with the children's behavior, the pattern of those correlations is interesting. Permissive parenting was correlated with socially incompetent behavior for mother-custody girls but was not significantly correlated with children's social behavior in the other sex of child–custodial parent arrangements. For example, permissive parenting by the mothers with custody showed the following correlations with their daughters' behavior: warmth (+.57), anger (+.76), demandingness (+.68), and sociability (−.70). However, the most significant relationship between authoritarian parenting and children's social behavior occurred for father-custody boys. The following relationships between the

TABLE 10.3

Correlations Between Observed Parental Behavior and Child Behavior During the Parent–Child Interaction

| Child's Behavior | Authoritarian | | | | Permissive | | | | Authoritative | | | |
| | Father Custody | | Mother Custody | | Father Custody | | Mother Custody | | Father Custody | | Mother Custody | |
	Boys N=10	Girls N=10	Boys N=11	Girls N=10	Boys N=70	Girls N=10	Boys N=11	Girls N=10	Boys N=10	Girls N=10	Boys N=11	Girls N=10
Warmth	-.17	.09	.15	-.05	-.11	-.07	-.47	-.57*	.61*	.46	.55*	.61*
Self-esteem	-.44	.27	-.19	.03	-.01	-.31	-.13	-.45	.84*	.50	.31	.52
Anxiety	+.57*	-.26	.29	-.16	-.33	.35	.10	.12	-.58*	-.53*	-.61*	-.15
Anger	+.32	.57	-.23	-.24	.02	-.20	.23	.77*	-.27	-.59*	-.42	-.50
Demandingness	-.06	.07	-.15	-.19	.36	.15	.39	.68*	-.63*	-.63*	-.45	-.54*
Maturity	-.46	.03	-.37	.12	-.02	-.19	.20	-.46	.71*	.71*	.56*	.57*
Sociability	-.18	-.22	-.16	.17	-.17	.08	-.06	-.70*	.67*	.52	.43	.52
Social conformity	.27	-.32	.23	.27	-.61*	-.09	-.52*	-.71*	.41	.93*	.57*	.64*
Independence	-.54*	-.29	-.51*	-.21	.59*	.15	.37	-.31	.31	.58*	.15	.65*

*p < .05.

use of authoritarian behavior by the fathers with custody and their son's social behavior occurred: anxiety (+.57), social maturity (−.46), and independence (−.54). These correlations suggest that when fathers with custody use authoritarian behavior with their sons it is associated with socially incompetent behavior.

Recall that mothers with custody were the most permissive of the family structure groups, and also that mother-custody girls generally showed a pattern of socially competent behavior. However, although mother-custody girls show a pattern of socially competent behavior, these data-suggest that when mothers with custody adopt a permissive child-rearing strategy with their daughters it is an ineffective way of socializing the daughters. And although father-custody boys also showed a pattern of social competence, the data suggest that when fathers with custody act in an authoritarian manner toward their sons it is an ineffective strategy. Authoritarian parenting is more sterotypically linked to the child-rearing practices of fathers than of mothers, and permissive parenting more with mothers. It may be that for a father to be rated high on authoritarian parenting it reflected this style in a relatively strong manner, and likewise for permissive parenting on the part of mothers. In sum, an authoritative parenting strategy seems to be associated with more competent child behavior regardless of the custodial arrangement, but permissive parenting in mother-custody homes is associated with poorer adjustment in girls, whereas authoritarian parenting in father-custody homes is correlated with poorer adjustment. However, caution should be exercised when positing causal mechanisms to explain correlations between observed parenting style and child behaviors. Although parental behavior is often seen as the cause of child behavior the process may also work in reverse.

Because on the whole, children living with the same-sex parent seem to cope better with divorce, those children living with the same-sex parent who do not cope well may be exhibiting serious interpersonal difficulties. It may be that these less well-adjusted children provoke their parents into adopting less effective parenting strategies. Under such pressure it may be more likely for fathers to move in a direction of greater control and for mothers to move towards greater permissiveness.

The Relation of Observed Parent Behavior During Parent–Child Interaction to Observed Child Behavior During the Child Interview.   As expected there were fewer significant correlations between parenting behavior and observations of the child's behavior during the child interview, because of the independence of the data sources. However, there were some interesting significant correlations. For example, authoritarian behavior by mothers with custody was significantly correlated with the son's social incompetence during the child interview ($r = +.62$).

However, the most consistent and remarkably strong relationships between observed parental behavior and observed child behavior during the child interview occurred on the variables of masculinity and femininity. Females and males were rated high on feminity when they displayed passivity, a low quiet volume of speech, excessive politeness, and shy, submissive behavior. If girls responded that they liked to go to dance class, play with dolls, and dress up, a higher rating of femininity was indicated. Their dress also contributed to this rating—girls wearing frilly clothes and ribbons in their hair were rated more feminine, particularly if they were older. Males and females were rated high on masculinity if they displayed aggressive, assertive behavior. Those who wore athletic clothes, like jogging shoes, T-shirts, and blue jeans were rated more masculine. When children said they liked sports, such as football, soccer, and basketball, they were rated more masculine. Girls who were rude and spoke loudly were rated more masculine. Short, boyish haircuts contributed to a masculine rating for girls, as did body language—girls who sat sprawled out in their chairs and were very active were rated more masculine.

Intriguing findings emerged when the correlations for father-custody girls and mother-custody sons were compared. When the father with custody was attentive to his daughter she was observed to be traditionally more masculine than feminine (correlations of $-.76$ with femininity and $+.68$ with masculinity). When the father with custody acted in an authoritarian manner with his daughter, she was observed to act in traditionally more feminine ways during the child interview (correlations of $+.53$ with femininity and $-.66$ with masculinity.) However, mothers with custody who acted in an authoritarian manner had daughters who showed more traditional masculinity ($r = +.53$).

Most reviews of the father-absence literature (Lynn, 1974) conclude that boys show a more feminine patterning of behavior in father-absent than in father-present homes—however, close inspection of the father-absence literature suggests that this conclusion seems more appropriate for young children, and that the findings for the elementary school and adolescent ages are more mixed. Hetherington's (Hetherington et al., 1978) recent research on mother-custody divorced families suggests that the effects of divorce on children's sex-typed behavior reflect more than just the unavailability of a consistent adult male model. She found that whereas many single-parent mothers are overprotective and apprehensive about independent behavior on the part of their sons, when the single-parent mothers do encourage masculine and exploratory behavior and do not have a negative attitude toward the absent father, disruptions in sex typing are less likely to result.

The findings reported here clearly support the conclusion that the sex-typed behavior of children is influenced by much more than the absence of the mother in father-custody divorced homes. Recall that there were no significant family structure or family structure × sex of child differences for the observations of traditional masculinity and feminity.

It is only when we look at the custodial parent's social interaction with the child that significant differences emerged in masculine and feminine behavior in children.

We have collected data on children's androgyny, but they have not yet been analyzed. It will be interesting to see how the parenting behaviors link up with the measures of androgyny in comparison with the observations of traditional femininity and masculinity reported here.

Discussion

The data presented here provide further support for our conclusions reported in earlier papers (Santrock & Warshak, 1979; Warshak & Santrock, in press). The first conclusion is that there may be systematic effects of divorce on children that favor a same-sex child–custodial-parent family structure. There are a number of reasons to explain these effects. Freudian psychoanalytic theory stresses the importance of the child's identification with the same-sex parent. Social learning theory has continued this emphasis, but with more importance attached to the behavioral aspects of the modeling process. Also, parents may know how to interact more effectively with a child of the same sex because of their own childhood experiences as a boy or girl. Fathers likely do a more competent job of discussing sexually sensitive issues with sons than with daughters, and mothers probably are better at this with daughters than with sons. There is also a greater likelihood that fathers will share more rough-and-tumble play and athletic experiences with their sons than mothers, and that mothers will be more likely to interact with their daughters in traditionally feminine activities, such as sewing, cooking, and so forth.

There are several other reasons that explain the negative cross-sex effects we found. In discussing our findings with various parent groups, some intact-family mothers reported that if they had one or two boys and the father had left the family, they would harbor a considerable amount of resentment toward him, which might influence their effectiveness in raising their sons. The mothers believe that fathers are important in helping them control the behavior of their sons and in making themselves available to play with their sons in traditional male activities, particularly athletics.

There is also another possibility. A child of the opposite sex may in some ways represent a substitute for the now absent spouse. If so, expectations and interactions of the custodial parent with the opposite-sex child might lead to a relationship that is overly coercive and demanding in some cases, smothering and too nurturant in others.

The second conclusion these data support is that the effects of father and mother custody on children are mediated by many factors. Although we have found strong evidence for the importance of same-sex-custodial-parent–child family structures, we clearly do not recommend that in custody decisions the girl should always be given to the mother and the boy to the father. In the past, custody decisions have been based on cultural stereotypes and historical biases that give mothers preferential claim to children. Clearly, we have found that some children, particularly boys, function in socially competent ways in father-custody families, suggesting that an a priori decision to award the child to the mother is not a wise decision. The impact of a custody disposition is mediated by a host of factors in addition to sex of child. We have found that the child-rearing practices of the custodial parent show important linkages with the child's social competence and that the availability of support systems to the custodial parent are important to consider as well.

There are obvious limitations to the application of findings such as those reported here to the decisions involved in an individual custody case. Each custody case should be considered on its own merits, although it is hoped that the data presented will contribute to the demise of a judicial system that dictates an a priori award to one parent or the other. Scientific research such as that reported here produces probabilities rather than exact generalizations, and there may be unique circumstances in an individual family that warrant attention and consideration in custody decisions. It also should be noted that this sample was comprised of elementary school-aged children from middle-class families with an average of two children. Generalizations to other social classes, other-aged children, and other-sized families obviously are more limited. The results of the present study should not be used to infer the splitting of siblings along sex-related lines in custody disputes either. Neither in this study, nor in other investigations of custody, have sibling relationships been explored. The results reported here also do not apply in cases where a reversal of a prior custody decision is being considered. The continuity of caretaking by one parent may override other concerns. Finally, we know nothing about the long-term effects of children growing up in mother-custody compared to father-custody families.

Future changes, such as the remarriage of one or both parents, are likely to have significant effects on the child. Children whose single-parent custodial fathers remarry are introduced to life with a stepmother. In the second half of this chapter, we explore what effects living in a stepmother family have on children and compare this information with our data on father-custody and intact families.

SOCIAL DEVELOPMENT AND PARENT–CHILD INTERACTION IN STEPMOTHER FAMILIES

There are an increasing number of "blended families" in which one or both of the spouses has been married in the past and brings children from the first marriage to live in the newly arranged stepparent family. Over 6 million children in the United States live in stepparent families (Current Population Reports, 1977). These "blended families" equaled 11% of all American households in 1977 (Eiduson & Zimmerman, 1978).

Unfortunately, much of our stepparenting knowledge is not empirically based. Folklore has painted the stepmother as a "wicked witch." Childhood stories of Cinderella and Hansel and Gretel both portray the stepmother in the role of a wicked woman.

The study of stepmother families requires that the child's relationship with his or her natural father be explored to comprehend fully the changing family dynamics he or she has been exposed to. The usual sequencing of events the child has experienced in such situations is: living with his or her natural mother and father; living with his or her natural father alone; and then living with a stepmother and his or her natural father. The family structure actually is more complex than this, as it is also necessary to focus on the reason for the dissolution of the ''natural,'' intact family—was it death or divorce, for example? For our purpose here, only those stepmother families in which the ''natural'' intact family was broken due to divorce are considered, in order to control for the reason for the dissolution of the intact family.

Stepparent Research

Representative studies of stepparent families include those by Bowerman and Irish (1962), Broderick (1976), Chapman (1977), Duberman (1973), Fast and Cain (1966), Heilpern (1943), Jenkins (1968), Messer (1969), Nadler (1976), Oshman and Manosevitz (1976), Santrock (1972), Stern (1977), Visher and Visher (1978), and Wilson, Zurcher, McAdams, and Curtis (1975). In none of those clinical reports were efforts made to assess the reliability of the ratings of the clinical judges.

Other studies of stepparent families often rely solely on data from questionnaires or surveys given to only one family member, usually the stepparent or the stepchild (Bowerman & Irish, 1962; Wilson, et al., 1975). An accurate picture of stepfamilies is not possible when information is obtained through the perceptions of only one family member. For too long, most of our information about parent-child relations came from the eyes of the mother via maternal interview data (Sears, Maccoby, & Levin, 1957).

In one widely cited investigation that included data collected from stepchildren, Bowerman and Irish (1962) had teachers administer questionnaires to junior and senior high school students. The 2145 stepchildren were among almost 29,000 students involved in the study. The investigators concluded that the students perceived their stepfamilies to have more internal stress, participant ambivalence, and low cohesiveness than students from intact families. Students in stepfamilies indicated that their stepparents were less affectionate than students' ratings of their parents in intact families. More specifically, in stepmother homes students rated this affection to be less than in stepfather and intact homes. Some additional findings in the Bowerman and Irish (1962) investigation suggested that stepchildren preferred one parent more than was the case in intact families and perceived that their stepparents discriminated against them more than their natural parents did. Stepchildren reported that their stepmothers were more likely to discriminate against them than were their stepfathers. And girls said they experienced parental rejection in stepfamilies more than boys. No statistical analyses were used in this widely quoted study.

In another investigation, Fast and Cain (1966) examined the child treatment center records of 50 children from stepparent families. They concluded that the stepparent family is particularly vulnerable to adjustment problems because of role difficulties. Their point about the identity problem of the stepparent as "parent," "stepparent," and "nonparent" was mentioned earlier.

However, several investigators have concluded that the stepparent family does not necessarily show more maladjustment than the intact family. Duberman (1973) obtained a random sample of families from the marriage license bureau. She then contacted the families and asked the parents to give their perceptions of the stepfamily. The results indicated a more positive picture of the stepfamily than was found by Bowerman and Irish (1962).

Another widely reported study of stepparent families (Wilson et al., 1975) also concluded that stepfather families do not show more problems than intact families. They examined data from two national surveys and found no substantial differences between individuals who had a stepfather and those who did not. However, on one important factor, marital relationship, the stepfamily respondants said they currently were less happy with their marriage than intact-family respondents. Overall, though, on a large number of variables there were no differences between stepfather and intact families.

An important issue in the development of the stepfamily was investigated by both Duberman (1973) and Bowerman and Irish (1962), namely, the initial reason for the separation of the child's biological parents. Duberman (1973) found that divorce was linked with more problems in the stepfamily, whereas the death of the child's biological parent was found to lead to more stepfamily difficulties by Bowerman and Irish (1962). Although such opposite findings are not easily reconciled, one clearly important point of difficulty in their interpretation is the data source from which they were obtained—the Duberman (1973) data were based on parental perceptions whereas the Bowerman and Irish (1962) data were based on children's perceptions. It should be noted also that no statistical analyses were used in the Duberman (1973) study.

Research on stepparent families that control for or investigate the age of onset of the natural parent's absence also is limited. Three studies have controlled for the age of onset of father absence in their evaluation of stepfather families (Chapman, 1977; Oshman & Manosevitz, 1976; Santrock, 1972); but only in the investigation by Santrock (1972) was type of absence controlled. No investigations of stepmother families have controlled for these relevant factors.

In surveying the stepparent literature, we find that to date direct observations of children growing up in stepfather and stepmother families have not been made.

It is not only important to study the perceptions of stepfamily members; it is equally important to observe their behavioral interaction. Administering personality tests to the parents and the child provides another means of obtaining important information about the psychological makeup of the stepparent family members. Further, by obtaining information about the child's behavior in other settings, such as with peers and at school, a more complete picture of the child in the stepfamily can be obtained. Virtually no studies of stepparent families have assumed this multimethod approach.

One recent investigation of stepmother families (Nadler, 1976) did include several different measures in a comparison of stepmother and intact-family mothers. The Multiple Affect Adjective Check List was used to measure anger, anxiety, and depression. The Marriage Adjustment Form was included to assess marital relations, several TAT cards were selected to provide a projective indication of anger, anxiety, and depression, and, a Conflict Questionnaire was developed to assess conflict in family life, with relatives, and in the community. Nadler (1976) found that stepmothers experienced more intrapersonal conflict and had more feelings of anxiety, depression, and anger regarding family relations than did mothers from intact families. In a recent review of marital conflict, Barry (1979) also concluded that stepmothers experience an inordinate amount of such stress when compared with mothers in other family structures.

There do seem to be some vulnerabilities that children growing up in stepparent families face that children from intact families, and in some cases single-parent families, do not. When a remarriage occurs, adjustment to the new family may be overwhelming. The father who remarries not only has to adjust to having another mother for his children, but also has to adjust to being a husband again. As Visher and Visher (1978) point out, there is virtually no time for the husband–wife relationship to develop in stepfamilies.

Stepmother and Father-Custody Families

There have been no investigations of stepmother families that have included a comparison of these families with father-custody families, the type of family most children in stepmother families have been exposed to earlier in their development. Recall that our father-custody data suggest that father-custody boys show more competent social development than girls. Is it likely that the same kind of findings might continue when the child enters the stepmother family? There are many new adjustments that have to be made after the stepmother arrives. Her arrival may be particularly disruptive for boys who seem to be functioning in socially competent ways in father-custody families. The difficulties may be evidenced as much or more in the interaction of the son with his father as with the stepmother. It is expected, then, that boys will show less competent social behavior in stepmother families than in father-custody families.

Also, there may be advantages to gaining a same-sex parental model for girls coming from a father-custody family and entering a stepmother family, particularly as girls show less competent social behavior than boys in father-custody families. Wallerstein and Kelly (1980) found that, for young boys, the entry of a stepfather triggered excitement and growth and a rapid attachment. A similar process may occur for girls in stepmother families.

Methodology.   Forty of the 64 children and their families on which data were reported earlier in this chapter were included in the analysis reported here. The 40 families were 20 father-custody families and the 20 matched intact families. In addition, 12 children, half boys and half girls, who were living with their natural father and stepmother, were studied. In all instances the severing of the intact family had been due to divorce. The mean age of separation of parents in the stepmother families was 4.4 years and for the father-custody families it was 5.7 years. SES status as measured by the Hollingshead Index was $\overline{X} = 2.25$ for stepmother families and $\overline{X} = 2.15$ for father-custody families. The mean income for father-custody families was $23,000 and for stepmother families it was $29,000, suggesting that both the father-custody and stepmother families can be characterized as middle class. Intact family SES and income were similar to these figures as well. The children ranged in age from 6 to 11 years, with the mean of the stepparent children being 9.0 years, the father-custody children being 8.2 years, and the intact-family children being 8.2 as well. There were an average of 2.25 children in the stepmother families, 1.9 children in the father-custody families, and 2.1 children in the intact families, indicating similarity of family size across the three family structures.

The same measures and procedures used in the investigation of father-custody families were adopted for the study of stepmother families. In addition, each child was observed while interacting individually with his or her stepmother and biological father—the order of these observations was balanced so that an equal number of biological fathers were observed first with their child, as were an equal number of stepmothers.

The data reported here come from the videotaped observations of parent–child interaction. The same categories used to code the child's behavior in the report of father-custody data earlier were employed—these include the child's warmth, anger, self-esteem, demandingness, maturity, and so on. Checks on the reliabilities of these ratings with stepmother families was continued and remained high. For example, reliability for demandingness was $+.74$, for maturity $+.83$, and for sociability $+.74$. The parent data have not yet been coded and analyzed.

Observations of Children's Behavior with Fathers in Father-Custody, Stepmother, and Intact Families.   A 3×2 analysis of variance was performed on the observations of the child's behavior during interaction with his or her father, with family structure (father-custody, stepmother, and intact) and sex of child as the main factors. Duncan Multiple Range Tests were conducted where appropriate.[1] The means, standard deviations, and significant F's are presented in

---

[1]Note that although data have been collected on 42 father-custody and intact families, not all of these were used in the present analyses, in order to control for factors such as SES, family size, etc. Consequently, data for the child's behavior with the father are based on 12 stepmother families, 16 father-custody families, and 17 intact families.

TABLE 10.4

Children's Social Behavior During Interaction with
Their Fathers in Father-Custody, Stepmother, and Intact Families

Children's Observed Behavior	Family Structure											
	Father Custody				Stepmother Families				Intact Families			
	Boy		Girl		Boy		Girl		Boy		Girl	
	$\bar{X}$	σ	$\bar{X}$	σ	$\bar{X}$	σ	$\bar{X}$	σ	$\bar{X}$	σ	$\bar{X}$	σ
Warmth	6.80	1.47	6.00	1.41	4.00	1.10	6.50	1.18	6.00	.87	7.25	1.09
SE lab	6.20	1.54	5.30	1.79	4.80	.75	6.25	1.50	4.88	1.27	7.25	1.48
Anxiety lab	6.00	1.48	5.30	2.15	5.20	1.17	6.75	1.64	5.63	1.49	7.00	1.22
Anger lab	7.70	1.19	6.60	2.42	6.40	1.36	7.50	.50	8.00	1.00	8.38	.86
Demand	6.40	1.36	4.40	2.61	5.60	1.96	7.00	.50	5.63	2.50	8.00	.50
Maturity lab	6.30	1.73	4.70	2.10	4.60	.80	5.00	1.80	4.88	2.42	7.25	1.48
Sociability	6.70	1.42	5.70	1.76	5.00	.63	6.25	1.09	5.88	.78	7.13	1.05
Social conformity	6.00	1.55	5.20	2.23	6.00	1.41	7.00	.71	5.88	2.03	7.63	1.22
Independence lab	6.30	1.49	4.70	2.10	5.80	1.20	5.25	.83	5.38	.81	6.50	1.41
	$N = 10$		$N = 10$		$N = 5$		$N = 4$		$N = 8$		$N = 8$	

Behavior	F	p
Warmth	$F^* = 3.92$	.03
	$F^{**} = 5.59$	.007
Self-esteem	$F^{**} = 5.05$	.01
Maturity	$F^{**} = 4.78$	.01
Sociability	$F^{**} = 3.87$	.03

*Significant main effect for family structure.
**Significant interaction effect.
Note: Higher scores represent more favorable pole of variable.

Table 10.4. The only signficant main effect of family structure was revealed in the warmth of the children. Less affectionate behavior was shown with the father in stepmother than in father-custody and intact families ($p < .01$). However, a significant interaction effect for warmth suggested that less affection was displayed by boys with their father in stepmother families than boys in father-custody and girls in intact families ($p < .01$). Intact-family girls also showed more self-esteem and social maturity than the other five groupings of family structure and sex of child ($p < 4.05$). Finally, boys in stepmother families were observed to be less sociable during interaction with their fathers than boys in father-custody and girls in intact families ($p < .05$).

TABLE 10.5
Children's Social Behavior During Interaction with
their Stepmother and Intact-Family Mother

Children's Observed Behavior	Family Structure									
	Stepmother				Intact Family					
	Boy		Girl		Boy		Girl		F	p
	$\bar{X}$	σ	$\bar{X}$	σ	$\bar{X}$	σ	$\bar{X}$	σ		
Warmth	5.33	1.11	6.83	1.07	4.63	1.53	7.44	.83	$F^a = 19.02$	$p < .0001$
Self-esteem	6.00	1.35	6.17	.69	3.38	1.89	7.11	.74	$F^a = 8.74$	$p < .007$
									$F^b = 9.00$	$p < .0003$
Anxiety	5.33	1.80	6.67	.47	4.25	1.85	7.33	.47	$F^a = 17.40$	$p < .0001$
Anger	7.33	1.11	7.50	.50	7.13	1.54	8.33	.47		
Demandingness	6.77	.75	7.17	.69	6.25	1.98	8.22	.79	$F^a = 5.78$	$p < .02$
									$F^b = 4.09$	$p < .05$
Maturity	5.67	.94	7.17	.90	5.25	2.05	7.00	1.70		
Sociability	5.50	1.26	7.00	.91	5.50	1.58	7.11	.99		
Conformity	6.17	1.46	7.33	.47	5.00	2.24	7.78	.92		
Independence	5.50	.96	6.50	.96	5.88	1.27	6.11	1.52		
	$N = 6$		$N = 6$		$N = 8$		$N = 9$			

[a]Sex-of-child main effect.
[b]Interaction effect.
Note: Higher score reflects more favorable pole of variable.

Observations of Children's Behavior with Mothers in Stepmother and Intact Families.   Recall that the mother's behavior in father-custody families was not observed, because a majority of the fathers with custody did not want her to be contacted. Consequently, only comparisons of the child's behavior during interaction with the stepmother and the intact-family mother were made. The means, standard deviations, and significant F's for the 2 × 2 analyses of variance are shown in Table 10.5.

A number of sex-of-child effects indicated that boys showed less competent social behavior than girls. And two significant interaction effects revealed that intact-family boys were lower in self-esteem than the other three groupings of children ($p < .01$) and that intact-family girls were less demanding than the other three groups ($p < .05$).

Observations of Children's Behavior during Interaction with their Stepmother and Biological Father in Stepmother Families.   A 2 × 2 analysis of variance was performed on the observations of the child's behavior during social interac-

TABLE 10.6

Children's Social Behavior During Interaction with their Stepmother
and Biological Father in Stepmother Families

Children's Observed Behavior	Parent								F	p
	Stepmother				Biological Father					
	Boy		Girl		Boy		Girl			
	$\bar{X}$	σ	$\bar{X}$	σ	$\bar{X}$	σ	$\bar{X}$	σ		
Warmth	5.33	1.11	6.83	1.07	4.00	1.10	6.50	1.18	$F* = 13.08$	$p < .002$
Self-esteem	6.00	1.35	6.17	.69	4.80	.75	6.25	1.50	—	—
Anxiety	5.33	1.80	6.67	.47	5.20	1.17	6.75	1.64	$F* = 4.72$	$p < .04$
Anger	7.33	1.11	7.50	.50	6.40	1.36	7.50	.50	—	—
Demandingness	6.67	.75	7.17	.69	5.60	1.96	7.00	.50	—	—
Maturity	5.67	.94	7.17	.90	4.60	.80	5.00	1.80	$F* = 6.15$	$p < .02$
									$F** = 14.18$	$p < .002$
Sociability	5.50	1.26	7.00	.91	5.00	.63	6.25	1.09	$F* = 9.45$	$p < .007$
Conformity	6.17	1.46	7.33	.47	6.00	1.41	7.00	.71	—	—
Independence	5.50	.96	6.50	.96	5.80	1.20	5.25	.83	—	—
	$N = 6$		$N = 6$		$N = 5$		$N = 4$			

*Main effect for sex of child.
**Main effect for parent.

tion with the stepmother and biological father in separate situations. The means, standard deviations, and significant F's are displayed in Table 10.6. Again, consistent sex differences portrayed boys as less socially competent than girls, regardless of whether they were with their stepmother or biological father. Only one main effect for parent occurred, and no interaction effects occurred. Children behaved in a more socially mature fashion when they were with their stepmother than when they were in the company of their biological father.

Discussion. When a single parent remarries and children become members of a new family, "the stepfamily," a disequilibrium results. During the early years of the stepfamily, children are confronted with many changes, adjustments, and possible new attachments. The disequilibrium created by the father's remarriage seems to produce a positive effect for his daughter but a negative effect for his son. His children have already undergone at least one major traumatic change in their lives, the severing of their parents' marriage. Several years after the divorce, boys whose fathers have obtained custody seem to have adjusted well to the change of living in a single-parent family whereas girls have not. When a second major family structure change occurs in the child's life, namely, the custodial parent's remarriage, it undoubtedly, like divorce, triggers a period of disequilibrium. For the boy who seems to be getting along well in a single-parent father-custody family, the entrance of the stepmother may produce conflict. It may mean that he now has to spend less time with his father and to share his father with the stepmother and her children. Although the young girl also must share her father with the stepmother and her children, her circumstances when coming into the stepmother family were not as positive as the boy's. Based on our father-custody data, she likely was not very happy in the father-custody family, so the disequilibrium generated by the arrival of the stepmother may lead to a more positive set of relationships for her. She now has a same-sex "parent" who may understand her needs and with whom she can identify.

The data on children's behavior in stepmother families represent a small number of families. We currently are collecting data on more stepmother families, as well as an equal number of stepfather families. Even though the analyses involve data from only 12 stepmother families, the patterning of findings lends support to our hypothesis that boys are likely to show less competent social behavior in stepmother families than girls in stepmother families and boys in father-custody families. In no instance did data favor more competent social behavior for boys in stepmother families.

Prior studies of stepparent families have failed to reveal the rather strong sex differences in children found in our current investigation. There are several reasons for this discrepancy. First, a majority of the investigations of stepparent families focus on stepfather rather than stepmother families, or lump all the stepparent families together. Second, prior investigations of stepparent families have not involved the use of behavioral observations, but rather have relied on the parent's or the child's perception of their family life and/or the child's personality. And, third, in prior investigations of stepparent families comparisons with single-parent divorced families generally have not been made.

Our plans are to collect information about 24 stepmother and 24 stepfather families. These data will be compared with the information collected from father-custody, mother-custody, and intact families. Measures of family and marital conflict are being included in the assessment of stepparent and intact families. In addition, we hope to bring the stepfamily members together at the end of our data collection procedure and observe how they interact with each other as a family system. Attention will be given to sibling relations as well, as virtually no empirical data have been collected about stepsibling and sibling relationships in stepfamilies.

Our current research plan has involved controlling for rather than investigating the child's age. To our knowledge, no research on stepparent families has investigated the child's developmental status. Similarly, we do not have good information about the role of the child's developmental status in studies of the effects of father and mother custody. Only the work of Wallerstein and Kelly (1980) has taken a strong developmental stance in looking at how divorce affects children of different ages, and even those data are somewhat flawed in that they do not include a control group of intact families and are based solely on clinical judgments of unknown reliability.

SUMMARY

In conclusion, although we clearly are beginning to develop a better understanding of the effects of divorce on children, the majority of this information has been derived from mother-custody families. It is hoped that more studies of divorced single-parent and stepparent families will include more than one family structure, so that comparisons across different types of family structures can be made. In addition, future studies of children in divorced single-parent and stepparent families should include information from a variety of persons in the family rather than relying on a single data source, such as the stepmother's perception of herself and the rest of the family. And far too many of our studies of single-parent and stepparent families fail to make even rudimentary efforts to assess the reliability of questionnaires, interviews, observations, and clinical judgments.

So far, in our investigations of children growing up in alternative family structures, we are finding that the sex of the child in combination with the sex of the custodial parent and the stepparent have rather strong influences on the child's social behavior. It will be interesting to see if the same-sex child–custodial parent–stepparent relationships hold when we compare mother-custody families with stepfather families, and stepmother families with stepfather families. If our predictions about the importance of a match between sex of child and sex of custodial parent or stepparent are accurate, then, boys will show more competent social behavior in stepfather families when they are compared with girls in stepfather families and boys in mother-custody families. And, similarly we predict that girls in mother-custody families will show more competent social behavior than girls in stepfather families.

ACKNOWLEDGMENTS

We give special thanks to Ann Minnett, who diligently conducted a number of statistical analyses for this chapter. Thanks also go to Janet Burrage and Jeffrey Burke, who coded the videotapes of the child's behavior during the interview. Cheryl Lindbergh also spent numerous hours on the collection of mother-custody and father-custody data. Special thanks also go to Laurie Bura for typing this manuscript. The portion of the chapter pertaining to father custody was funded by a grant from the Hogg Foundation to the first author. However, the comments made and conclusions arrived at do not necessarily reflect the opinion of the Hogg Foundation.

REFERENCES

Barry, W. A. Marriage research and conflict: An integrative review. *Psychological Bulletin*, 1979, *73*, 41–45.

Baumrind, D. Current patterns of parental authority. *Developmental Psychology Monographs*, 1971, *4*(Pt. 2)

Bowerman, C. E., & Irish, D. P. Some relationships of stepchildren to their parents. *Marriage and Family Living*, 1962, 24, 113–121.

Broderick, C. *Fathers*. Presidential address to the National Council of Family Relations. New York City, October 1976.

Chapman, M. Father absence, stepfathers, and the cognitive performance of college students. *Child Development*, 1977, *48*, 1155–1158.

Current Population Reports. Household and Family Characteristics: August 1977. Populations Characteristics, Series P-20, No. 311, U.S. Bureau of the Census, Washington, D.C.

Duberman, L. Step-kin relationships. *Journal of Marriage and the Family*, 1973, *35*, 283–292.

Eiduson B., & Zimmerman, I. *Implications of research on the family for policy*. Paper presented to the American Psychological Association, Toronto, Canada, August 1978.

Fast, I., & Cain, A. The stepparent role: Potential for disturbance in family functioning. *American Journal of Orthopsychiatry*, 1966, *36*, 485–491.

Freud, S. *An outline of psychoanalysis*. New York: Norton, 1949.

Gasser, R. D., & Taylor, C. M. Role adjustment of single parent fathers with dependent children. *The Family Coordinator*, 1976, *25*, 397–401.

George, V., & Wilding P. *Motherless families*. London: Routledge & Kegan Paul, 1972.

Gersick, K. *Fathers by choice: Characteristics of men who do and do not seek custody of their children following divorce*. Unpublished doctoral dissertation, Harvard University, 1975.

Gregory, I. Anterospective data following childhood loss of a parent: Delinquency and high school dropout. *Archives of General Psychiatry*, 1965, *13*, 99–109.

Heilpern, E. Psychological problems of stepchildren. *Psychoanalytic Review*, 1943, *30*, 163–176.

Hetherington, E. M. Effects of father absence on personality development in adolescent daughters. *Developmental Psychology*, 1972, *7*, 313–326.

Hetherington, E. M., Cox, M., & Cox, R. Divorced fathers. *The Family Coordinator*, 1976, 25, 417–428.

Hetherington, E. M., Cox, M., & Cox, R. The aftermath of divorce. In J. H. Stevens & M. M. Matthews (Eds.), *Mother–child, father–child relations*, Washington, D.C.: NAEYC, 1978.

Jenkins, R. The varieties of children's behavioral problems and family dynamics. *American Journal of Psychiatry*, 1968, *124*, 1440–1445.

Lamb, M. E. The role of the father: An overview. In M. E. Lamb (Ed.), *The role of the father in child development*. New York: Wiley, 1976.

Mendes, H. A. Single fathers. *The Family Coordinator*, 1976, *25*, 439–444.

Messer, A. The phaedra complex. *Archives of General Psychiatry*, 1969, *21*, 213–218.

Nadler, J. H. *The psychological stress of the stepmother*. Unpublished doctoral dissertation, California School of Professional Psychology, Los Angeles, 1976.

Orthner, D., Brown, T., & Ferguson, D. Single-parent fatherhood: An emerging lifestyle. *The Family Coordinator*, 1976, *25*, 429–437.

Oshman, H., & Manosevitz, M. Father-absence: Effects of stepfathers upon psychosocial development in males. *Developmental Psychology*. 1976, *12*, 479–480.

Santrock, J. W. The relations of onset and type of father absence to cognitive development. *Child Development*, 1972, *127*, 201–213.

Santrock, J. W., & Warshak, R. A. Father custody and social development in boys and girls. *Journal of Social Issues*, 1979, *35*, 112–125.

Schlesinger, B., & Todres, R. Motherless families: An increasing societal pattern. *Child Welfare,* 1976, *55,* 443-458.

Sears, P. S. Doll-play aggression in normal young children: Influences of sex, age, sibling status, father's absence. *Psychological Monographs,* 1951, *65*(Whole No. 323).

Sears, R. R., Maccoby, E. E., & Levin, H. *Patterns of childrearing.* Evanston, Ill.: Row Peterson, 1957.

Stern, P. N. Integrative discipline in stepfather families. *Dissertation Abstracts International,* April 1977.

Visher, E., & Visher, J. Common problems of stepparents and their spouses. *American Journal of Orthopsychiatry,* 1978, *48,* 252-262.

Wallerstein, J. S., & Kelly, J. B. *Surviving the break-up: How children and parents cope with divorce.* New York: Basic Books, 1980.

Warshak, R. A., & Santrock, J. W. Children of divorce: Impact of custody disposition on social development. In E. J. Callahan & K. A. McCluskey (Eds.), *Life-span developmental psychology: Non-normative life events.* New York: Academic Press, in press.

Wilson, K., Zurcher, L., McAdams, D., & Curtis, R. Stepfathers and stepchildren: An exploratory analysis from two national surveys. *Journal of Marriage and Family,* 1975, *37,* 526-536.

11 Comparative Socialization Practices in Traditional and Alternative Families

Bernice T. Eiduson, Madeleine Kornfein, Irla Lee Zimmerman, and Thomas S. Weisner
University of California, Los Angeles

In the 1960s, middle America was shaken by an important sociocultural movement, the counter culture or youth rebellion (Eiduson, 1978). It was regarded as a momentous social phenomenon with far-ranging consequences, in part because middle- and upper-class Caucasian young adults began to question, reject, and seek alternatives to the traditional nuclear family in which they had been reared. They thought the conventional family unit was not the necessary nor even the optimal way to rear children. The traditional nuclear family became the symbol of the status quo, the life-style that fostered the success-oriented, materialistic attitudes of our dehumanized, technological society. They sought alternative family forms that would allow them to live in ways consonant with their values; they sought life-styles that were fulfilling and gratifying in the present, in which nature provided patterns and pleasures to be followed and enjoyed rather than conquered and obliterated; they sought ways of living that respected individual differences and fostered greater interpersonal involvement and cooperation.

The family models they chose differed in terms of composition, legality, and way of functioning from the conventional family. Some purposely and unashamedly became single mothers; others became "social contract" families, remaining unmarried because a legal contract seemed unnecessary or even damaging to their emotional ties; and others chose communal living groups in order to share important parts of their everyday lives with like-minded people.

Because the young adults were of childbearing age, they offered an opportunity for naturalistic study of how their values and attitudes would shape families and how these families would rear children. Therefore at the end of 1973, a UCLA interdisciplinary group embarked on a child development study of these different life-styles. Two hundred children were in the Family Styles Project: 50

from single-mother families, 50 from social-contract couples, and 50 from families in communal living groups, as well as a control group of 50 children from traditional two-parent nuclear families. Parent participants were Caucasian, came from middle-class or upper middle-class backgrounds, were aged 18–35, and thus were comparable to the young adults in the counterculture who were instrumental in electing these new family forms (Cohen & Eiduson, 1975). To be recruited, mothers had to be in the third trimester of pregnancy with their first child, or, in some one-quarter of the cases, their second child.

In deciding which of the many extant American variations in family structure to study, we limited selection to those that had been shown to be most viable and that provided some range of conceptual interest, such as number of parents available to the child or extent to which life-styles varied from two-parent nuclear families. Within the three family variants chosen, we tried to include a range of family types so that child development issues of interest—such as multiple caregiving, fathering behaviors, role modeling along sex egalitarian lines—could be addressed with as much generality as possible. This methodological position was supported by findings in our pilot work that showed no "typical" or representative commune, social-contract marriage, single-mother household, or even traditionally married couple in a nuclear unit (Eiduson, Cohen, & Alexander, 1973). In fact, our data thus far show considerable internal variability in terms of family structure, motivation, and resources within each of three alternative life-style groups (Eiduson & Weisner, 1978).

The alternative groups were identified through a combination of referrals from professional agencies and resources, and the indigenous networks in which these populations moved. Referral resources included Lamaze teachers, birth centers, and women's organizations. In addition, notices addressed to prospective parents were posted at universities, natural food stores, co-op centers, and other appropriate places. The traditional married group was obtained by randomly sampling the obstetricians in the California American Medical Association Directory and asking each doctor to nominate one pregnant woman who met our criteria. The woman was then encouraged to contact the project (Eiduson, 1974).

Incentives for participating were of two kinds: (1) parents were paid $5.00 per procedure to cover expenses involved; (2) $80.00 per year for each child was given to any provider of pediatric services selected by the parent. The service provider shared with the project codifiable information concerning the nature of illness, reason for contact, diagnosis, and recommended treatment.

At the time they entered the study, 50% of the families lived in Los Angeles and its environs, with the remainder fairly evenly divided among San Diego, San Francisco, and the northern California area. Eighty-three percent of the families resided in urban settings, with the remainder in rural settings.

We have been studying this sample of over 200 families and children for 6 years. Our formal contacts began during the last trimester of the pregnancy and continued throughout the child's first 6 years of life. We used a variety of data collection techniques: parents' reports including interviews and questionnaires; field studies including naturalistic home observations, dwelling maps, and census forms; standardized tests including structured and semistructured psychological tests, experimental situations, and play observations. A small portion of the data, derived mainly from parental interviews and questionnaires and home observations, are reported in this chapter.

The main intent of the Family Styles Project has been to study the relationship between family life-style and child development, focusing particularly on the pertinent variables affecting child socialization. The project strategy conceives of family socialization in terms of four categories of variables; these variables are obviously interrelated but can also be considered independent variables in terms of their ultimate impact on child development:

1. Family history: Demographic and background history of the parents in their families of origin.
2. Parental values.
3. Current family milieu.
4. Child-rearing attitudes and practices.

The family history variables, the history of the parents in their families of origin, serve as background or frame-of-reference variables. Included here are demographic characteristics as well as variables in family history considered pertinent for parenting role and attitudes. Currently being collected and ultimately to be analyzed among these background variables are measures of the parents' personalities and IQs, as such parental resources are considered critical for parenting attitudes and parenting skills as well as contributing to the understanding of child outcome variables.

Because the search for new family forms was given impetus by the desire of young people to live their daily lives in ways consonant with their values, we include, as an important set of independent variables, the values that alternative families strongly espouse. Our pilot studies of the value systems of alternative life-style adults (Eiduson, 1981; Rocheford, 1978) had elaborated eight dimensions that defined the alternative ideology: (1) the desire for humanism or strong interpersonal relationships, with the aim of building a sense of generalized trust in others; (2) a striving to break away from conventional achievement goals, in favor of achievement that is more creative and personally fulfilling; (3) sex egalitarianism, a recasting of traditional stereotyped roles and responsibilities; (4) a preference for natural–organic ways, making daily life more harmonious with the natural environment; (5) a desire for gratification in the "here and now" as compared to planfulness and an orientation toward the future; (6) antimaterialism; (7) an antiauthority perspective that goes along with the desire for less dependence on medical, social, and educational institutions in society, and an interest in self-help and taking control of one's own fate; (8) an antiscience, antiintellectual bent, in which sensory and intuitive data and mystical sources of knowledge are regarded as worthy supplements to objective, rational ways of problem solving, and knowing.

We hypothesized that the traditional families and alternatives would differ significantly in adherence to such values and, in fact, this was borne out, as discussed later. Because these value dimensions are likely to impact on a number of developmental domains, we are currently studying whether the family's affiliation with each dimension or sets of dimensions will predict certain child-rearing attitudes and practices and whether, in turn, certain aspects of the child's intellectual, social, and emotional behavior will be affected.

Of course the literature on nonnuclear families has also suggested that certain child development outcomes are associated with families that are nonnuclear and non-two parent (Blanchard & Biller, 1974; Hoffman, 1973; Marsella, 1974; McCord, McCord, & Thurber, 1962; Mischel, 1961; Santrock, 1972). Consequently, we are studying relevant family milieu variables likely to be influential in child socialization and development: family organization and functioning; familial changes and mobility; relationship and interaction patterns; parent and parent–surrogate roles and responsibilities; parental occupation and income; adult support system; conflicts, satisfactions, and attitudes towards the family's life-style. We feel that these variables will be particularly important as we study the current consequences of growing up in alternative family life-styles. The family life choices are often seen as voluntary alternatives, rather than as inescapably deviant or pathological aberrations. This may change the outcomes usually expected.

The major thrust of our data collection efforts has been to gain detailed information about specific child-rearing attitudes and practices. The domains of particular interest are those derived from the values of the parents in alternative lifestyles: their natural–organic perspective, attitude to authority, anticonventional achievement orientation, "here-and-now" perspective, and so on. Therefore we studied use of natural foods, attitude toward and types of discipline, motivations, encouragement for learning, etc.

The remainder of this chapter is devoted to summarizing our early findings about these four categories of variables: Family History, Parental Values, Current Family Milieu, and Child-rearing Attitudes and Practices. Although there are numerous ways to analyze and present these data, for now we are looking at important life-style differences and similarities. We highlight first the differences between alternative and traditional families, pointing out as well the important areas in which no significant differences were observed or reported. We then look separately at each of the alternative life-styles, pointing out significant within-group differences and comparing this life-style to the other alternatives.

COMPARISONS OF TRADITIONAL MARRIED AND ALTERNATIVE LIFE-STYLE FAMILIES[1]

Family History

We found relatively few background variables and attitudes that seemed to differentiate the traditional and nontraditional life-style groups; however, the ones that were significant added to our understanding of the motivations and resources of those seeking an alternative family (Cohen & Eiduson, 1975; Kornfein, Weisner, & Martin, 1977). We found that there was a significant difference in parent age by life-style, with traditional mothers 26.7 ± 2.9 years (mean ± standard deviation), and the single mothers 2 years younger (24.6 ± 4.4); variances also differed significantly. The mean age of fathers was older than the mothers (28.4), but not significantly different by family style.

As would be expected from the literature on young adults attracted to the counterculture movement in the late 1960s, the alternative group interrupted their education more frequently than the traditional group (Keniston, 1965). Paralleling the difference in age, the single mothers had significantly less schooling (13.3 years) than the traditional married mothers (14.7 years). However, the social-contract mothers, who were similar in age to the traditional mothers, also had significantly fewer years of education (13.3), reflecting perhaps their different attitudes toward conventional achievement and success or, possibly, different levels of ability. Although the fathers did not differ significantly in terms of age, the social-contract fathers also had significantly less education (14.0 years) than traditional married fathers (15.5 years). Forty-eight percent of the traditional mothers had at least a BA degree, a significantly higher proportion than other mothers (living group, 36%; single mothers, 23%; social contract, 12%). Fifty-two percent of traditional fathers had college degrees, compared to 38% of communal living-group fathers and 30% of social-contract fathers.

No significant difference between alternative and traditionally married families was found in the level of education of their families of origin (maternal or paternal grandparents of the children in the study), nor in the families of origin's overall SES level. This similarity in family backgrounds is very interesting particularly because the alternative parents' own education, income, and occupational levels were significantly lower than those of their traditional married peers (see Current Family Milieu).

Significant differences on a few other family historical variables were of interest, for they suggested that more family instability was experienced by

---

[1]Data in the form of charts and tables have been filed with the National Technical Information Service, Springfield, Virginia and may be accessed in microfilm form upon request.

alternative than by traditional life-style parents. Alternative parents moved more often than traditionals during their childhood (58% of the alternatives moved three or more times, compared to 28% of the traditional families). Alternative maternal grandparents also showed a significantly greater number of divorces and remarriages (90% of the traditional married maternal grandparents were still married to each other, compared to 66% of the families of origin of the communal living groups, 63% of the single mothers, and 52% of the social contracts). Paternal grandparents of our alternative families were also divorced more often than were the paternal grandparents of the traditional married families. These data may be more influential than they might at first appear, as they relate to separations, divorces, and remarriages that occurred a generation ago, when family dissolution was less common and even more stressful to family members.

There was a significantly greater tendency for the alternative group to view their early childhoods as unhappy; traditional mothers tended to maintain a better relationship with their parents throughout childhood and adolescence than mothers who chose alternative life-styles. Interview data from fathers showed the same trend in relationship with their parents.

Other demographic and family-related variables, such as number of siblings in the family or ordinal place in family, did not differentiate traditional from alternative groups.

Parental Values

When we first met these families there were strong differences in values between the alternatives and the traditionally married families. On seven of eight domains measured, there were significant alternative/traditional married life-style differences. The alternatives were more apt to reject conventional definitions of achievement, be more sex egalitarian, prefer natural ways of doing things, be more oriented towards immediate gratification and less oriented towards the future, be less materialistic, rely more on intuitive and mystical sources of knowledge, and be antiauthoritarian. It is important to note that considerable variability exists within each of the three alternative life-style groups in terms of their values; this variability is particularly evident in the communal living-group sample and is discussed in that section.

Traditional and alternative families did not differ significantly in terms of humanistic values, in their desire for strong interpersonal relationships and concern for the problems of others: instead, the total sample reflected the self-examinational interest and the desire to intensify relationships and meaningfulness that corresponded to the surge of the personal awareness movement in the '70s among the general population (Delora & Delora, 1972; Ehrenberg, 1975; Eshleman & Clarke, 1978). Traditional married mothers and fathers were identified particularly by the high values they placed on materialism, scientific ways of knowing, and conventional authority attitudes, which we hypothesized would be particularly distinctive in shaping their goals and child-rearing practices.

Current Family Milieu

The traditional child was more likely to be born into a more affluent family than was an alternative child. When we first met the parents, the traditional families' incomes averaged more than $1200 a month, more than three times greater than the single mothers' ($390), twice that of the social contracts' ($588) and a third higher than the "equivalent" income level of communal living-group families ($866).[2] This difference in financial status continued for every period throughout the children's first 5 years of life. Furthermore, the income of the traditional family increased slowly over time, and with a regularity that was absent in alternative families, even though in these, too, income increased with child age. Significantly fewer members of the traditional married groups were welfare recipients, or dependent on grandparents for economic assistance.

The fathers' occupational level, as expected, related to the higher average income. A disproportionate number of fathers in traditionally married families were found in the three highest level Hollingshead–Redlich categories, and significantly fewer in the two lowest categories. This differential, identified at the time families entered the study, continued throughout the children's first 5 years. The picture for mothers' occupational level was similar, once mothers returned to the work force. Traditional mothers also earned more per hour than alternatives. The timing of mothers' reentry into the work force and the extent of their participation was not an alternative/traditional difference, as is discussed later.

Hours of employment also covaried with the traditional/alternative distinction for the fathers. Over 90% of traditionally married fathers worked on a full-time basis at the point of entry, significantly more than the alternative fathers, a pattern that continued throughout the first 5 years of the children's lives. For example, at 3 ½ years, 92% of the traditional married fathers worked full time, as compared with 53% of the communal living group and 65% of social-contract fathers.

Thus, children from traditionally married homes started life in a comparatively financially advantaged situation. The work model presented by fathers was of an achiever and the main wage earner in the family during the child's first few years—that he worked consistently and regularly in occupations that were at the

---

[2]It is difficult to evaluate the exact income level of communal living-group families as work for the group may be exchanged for services, room and board, etc., rather than a paycheck. In these cases, project staff members estimated an equivalent income level for the particular standard of living.

high ends of vocational competency scales. These findings correspond to the traditional married sample's higher value of conventional achievement and material success and their identification with conventional sources of authority.

In line with status ambitions and financial resources, traditionally married families lived in abodes with significantly more floor space than alternatives. They had more areas divided by function and more private areas not shared by all family members. Their homes were more frequently detached dwellings rather than apartments, duplexes, small cabins, etc. A significantly larger percentage of children in traditionally married homes had their own rooms and slept in their own beds, beginning at birth and continuing through the early years.

Traditionally married families were also more likely to own certain possessions—cars, personal laundry facilities, savings accounts, insurance, and television. Everyone was likely to own a stereo, however! Also, in line with the more materialistic orientation of parents, the traditional child owned more types of toys. However, this significant difference did not mean a paucity of toys for alternatives, as all children had a sizable number and variety; although some alternative children had to share toys, they were accessible if not owned. As with the amount and use of dwelling space, these are stylistic features, but also features influenced by availability of income.

Although there were differences in quantity of possessions, there were no differences by life-style in terms of the decorative complexity or warmth/child orientation of the household. However, traditional married households ranked lowest in disorderliness and in potential dangers observed.

A major difference between alternative and traditional family life-styles is revealed in studies of mobility rates. Traditionally married families are more stable than alternatives. During the children's first 18 months, 19% of the traditional married moved two or more times compared to 46% of the alternatives. From 18 months to 3 years, 12% of the traditional married and 31% of the alternatives moved two or more times; likewise, during the first 18 months almost one-half of the alternatives but only 15% of the traditional married changed household residents (other than mates) by moving in or out of a relative's home, communal living group, or roommate situation. During the subsequent 18 months, 30% of the alternatives and 6% of the traditional married changed household residents. Similarly, by the time the children were 4 years old, 84% of the original group of traditional married were still together, compared to 52% of the social contracts; 4% (2) of the single mothers were with the child's father, 32% had married and 8% (4) were living with a man other than the child's father. Some of the alternative families were repeating the pattern of mobility and life-style changes of their families of origin.

The nature of relationships with the extended family (the child's grandparents) was an area in which there were significant differences between alternatives and traditionals (and among the alternatives as well). Grandparents of traditionals visited more often, and relationships of parents with their own parents were perceived more positively. When the children were 6 months, 1 year, 18 months, and 2 years old, the mean number of contacts per year was greater for the traditionals; in the alternative groups, the single-mother family showed the next closest number, and the communal living groups the lowest. In our preliminary studies of support systems characteristic of each family life-style, the grandparent family is seen as a model and source of psychological but not financial support for traditionals; for some alternatives, it is the reverse.

In summary then, in comparison to the alternatives, the traditional married family environment is characterized by less geographic and life-style change, by economic advantage, and by some of the possessions and variability in material appurtenances that accompany an initially higher and consistently improving financial status. They also have more contact with the child's grandparents and view them as models to follow.

Childrearing Attitudes and Practices

Beginning with anticipatory socialization, it appears that there were significant differences in the parental desire for a child between the traditional married mothers and those in the single-mother and even social-contract life-styles; the traditional marrieds were significantly more likely to have planned the birth of the child. Traditional married mothers had a history of fewer abortions than single-mother and social-contract participants. There were no differences in the use of pregnancy preparatory courses, in the obtaining of prenatal care, and general health care of mothers as birth approached.

During the course of the pregnancy, alternative parents tended to modify some of their previous unconventional practices in the areas of diet, drugs, and health care. Although the alternatives had had a significantly higher history of drug use prior to pregnancy, including social use of marijuana and experimental and social use of the psychedelic drugs, drug use by all participants declined by the last trimester of the pregnancy, with alternatives showing a particularly dramatic drop. Fathers' patterns followed mothers' in terms of reduced drug use.

Despite the tendency of alternatives to follow traditional health-care practices during the prenatal period, there were strong traditional married/alternative differences in birth practices. The alternatives were significantly more likely to have natural childbirth and home births; the traditionals were more likely to have instrument-assisted deliveries and Caesarian sections.

For the total sample, 80% of the children were breast-fed initially, but by 1 year, significantly more traditional married children were being bottle-fed than were alternative children. In general, breast-feeding extended longer in alternative populations, in some few cases until 3 years (Weisner & Martin, 1979).

The life-style groups did not differ significantly in use of traditional health-care services, number of well-child visits to physicians, or in relative number of physician visits by type of illness. Likewise, they did not differ in frequency of immunizations. However, children in the traditionally married population were taken to physicians more frequently for minor respiratory illnesses such as colds than children in the alternative life-styles, reflecting the alternatives' greater tendency to deal with minor illnesses through home remedies, etc.

Surprisingly, there were no significant traditional/alternative differences in terms of the child's primary caretaker during infancy. In all families, mothers were the main caretakers throughout the child's first 18 months. Even in communal living groups where more "substitute" parents were involved, mother was most often the main caretaker until the children became older.

Few differences were noted in psychological aspects of caretaking. Home observations when the children were 6 months and 18 months old permitted detailed studies of affective interchanges between caretaker and child, frequency of child-initiated behaviors, and of parent-initiated behaviors to child, and kind or extent of responsiveness to initiated behaviors. It was striking to note that few significant differences between alternatives and traditionals were observed. Mutuality of affect, observable visual, vocal, and sensory interchanges, tactile and physical stimulations, display of warmth, attentiveness and concern for the child, and appropriate supervision characterized each life-style.

Parental reports through baby books and interviews obtained at 6-month intervals also showed that as the infant matured there were few significant differences in caretaking behaviors. Ways of playing with the child, toilet training, adult responses to a child waking at night, were similar across the four groups. However, a number of differences were found between traditional marrieds and alternatives in caretaking styles, where the alternatives' "natural" perspective seemed to influence their child-rearing practices. Alternatives were more likely to feed their children natural, homemade foods, rather than products purchased in stores. Alternatives, even from birth, tended to take their infants along wherever they went and carried them physically close, using slings. The traditional marrieds were more likely to use "infant seats" and strollers. Traditional marrieds gave vitamin supplements more often and were significantly more likely to use fluorides (Weisner, Bausano, & Kornfein, in press).

We hypothesized that discipline would be one area in which differences between alternatives and traditionals would emerge in line with the differences noted between them in their affiliation with conventional authority. Although there were no significant differences in the kinds of child behaviors for which they disciplined at the 18-, 24-, or 36-month periods, there was a significant difference in the number of different things for which the child was disciplined, with the traditional married (and the creedal living group)[3] parents disciplining

---

[3]The living-group sample is comprised of two subsets—creedal, or religiously oriented communal groups, which are usually leader directed, and the domestic living group, comprised of families who live together because they share common interests, social goals, and friendships.

for more types of behaviors than the domestic living-group members. All participants reported common modes of disciplinary behavior. The traditional marrieds
(again in common with the creedal living group) placed a much higher value on
teaching their children obedience and respect for authority.

Compliance styles also were studied in the home observations as a way of
assessing disciplinary practices. Although differences in compliance styles and in
number of successful compliance requests were not significant, a significant
difference was found in the number of unsuccessful compliance attempts: traditional marrieds, like the social contracts and single mothers, made a greater
number of unsuccessful attempts than did creedal living-group parents. Traditional married parents were rated as being more directive in their caretaking
than social contract and domestic living-group parents, and they were significantly more likely to hover around the child than were caretakers in domestic
living groups. No difference was found by life-style in the amount of father
control over the child. Observers noted that single mothers were significantly
more child focused in their activities than were traditional married parents.

The traditional marrieds (and creedal living groups) were more involved than
most of the alternatives with formal religious activities. In this, the traditional
family's stance and the creedal group's stance were in line with their strong
authority orientation.

The traditionally marrieds described their own households, and were similarly
rated by our observers, as organized and scheduled significantly more often than
the alternatives, particularly the social contracts.

There were no differences between traditionals and alternatives in their
positive/negative perception of their child, as taped in parental interviews 2
weeks after the child was born, and at 6 and at 12 months. Furthermore, at the
18-month period, over 90 adjectives were checked off by the parent as descriptive of the child. Subsequently data were summarized, using a factor analysis,
and produced four factors: different, shy, independent, and confident. No significant differences by family group emerged on any of the factors at any age
period. However, there was a high level of consistency (from .50 to .65) across
time periods in parental ratings. The traditionals tended to perceive children at
the high end of the independent and confident dimensions, and at the low end of
the shy and difficult dimensions. Single mothers' children scored in the opposite
direction, but the overlap among groups was considerable.

DIFFERENCES AMONG ALTERNATIVE LIFE-STYLES: COMMUNAL LIVING GROUPS

The living-group sample was purposely selected in order to be representative of
the heterogeneity in this family unit found in our pilot studies (Eiduson, 1979).

The sample consists of 29 families in creedal living groups who are identified with established religious or spiritual philosophies or who have a charismatic leader; and 25 families who were in domestic living groups (i.e., people who banded together because they liked each other, wanted to reside closely so they could share meals and experiences, and so solidify their friendships). Included in the latter are a few triads (i.e., two men and one woman, or two women and a man living ostensibly as a "three-parent" family).

Family History

Thus far, we have not uncovered any strong and consistent differences in Family History variables between members of creedal and domestic living groups. This absence of differences in backgrounds is particularly interesting because there is considerable divergence between these groups in terms of their basic values and related child-rearing practices and attitudes.

The only statistically significant difference was the mothers' occupational levels at the time they entered the project. The domestic living group mothers had a higher occupational level than the creedal mothers ($p = .045$); the domestic fathers also tended to have higher occupational levels, but the difference only approached significance ($p = .09$); similarly, the mothers and fathers in domestic living groups tended to have more years of education, but again, the difference only approached significance ($p = .10$). Although the communal living-group families contributed to the alternative/traditional married differences reported earlier, there was no strong differences in Family History separating the communal living group from the social contract or single-mother family backgrounds.

Parental Values

Most members of communal living group households did not value the pursuit of conventional achievement or material success; they did not rely on the use of scientific sources of information, for they listened as well to intuitive feelings to guide their actions. They placed a high importance on doing things the "natural" way and were oriented to gratification in the "here and now". In these values the communal living group families were most like the social contract and different from the traditional married families.

The two types of communal living groups strongly differed in their attitudes towards authority and sex egalitarianism. As expected, most members of creedal groups placed a high value on obeying authority; likewise, they did not identify with the goals of the Woman's Movement and did not value sex egalitarianism. In contrast, members of domestic living groups were antiauthoritarian and strongly sex egalitarian in their values.

Current Family Milieu

Living arrangements for communal living groups showed an enormous variability, including adapted motels, rural acreage with permanent and/or temporary dwellings, buses, handhewn houses, large Hollywood mansions. All had combinations of public and private spaces and were not necessarily under one roof. Private spaces were smaller in square footage than in abodes of other family groups.

In our sample some of the creedal living groups had separate quarters for children, and a few had nonbiological parent caretakers on a 24-hour basis, or caretakers who alternated with each other and with parents. In most groups, children resided with their parents, sharing a room or a small apartment. Children generally shared meals with community members, although in a few cases, they ate separately from the adults, or together with their nuclear family. The variability in milieu and eating arrangements was striking.

Twenty-five percent of the communal living groups, like our social contract families, were found in rural areas; these two life-styles comprised over 90% of the rural participant families.

Religious and philosophical tracts had positions of prominence in the communal home, so that when home observers rated households on more than 25 adjectives, which then were summarized by four orthogonal factors, communal living groups were rated as highest on the presence of books being easily visible.

Income of communal living groups was difficult to establish, because in many of the groups personal income was pooled and work for the group was regarded as part of the contribution. However, exploration of the standard of living and finances of the participants revealed that the income equivalent of communal living group families was significantly lower than the level found in traditional married homes, but higher than that of the other alternative life-styles. Many possessions tended to be shared—again, for some, a motivation for moving into and remaining in the life-style.

It was necessary to study both the nuclear unit and the larger unit or extended household to obtain a picture of what participants called "family." Some single mothers, married couples, and unwed couples resided within the communal living groups. As expected, there were more people residing in each household (mean of 5.0 as compared with 2+ for the other life-style groups), including more children as well as more adults. Group size tended to covary with the need for a hierarchical structure, and the presence of formal rules and regulations to divide work, ascribe roles and tasks, etc. Such hierarchical structuring was typical of the creedal groups but not of the domestic living groups.

As expected, from the work of others pointing to criteria for the stability of a "new" family, the domestic groups were less viable. Mobility out of the domestic group proved to be the highest of any life-style, so that by the time children were 3 years old, only eight families remained in domestic groups: four became social contracts, four became single mothers, and nine became traditional married nuclear families. The picture for the creedal group suggests much more stability; by the time the children were 4½, 21 of the 29 original creedal group members were still in the same groups. The commitment to their stable, highly regularized, often hardworking lives came, at least in part, out of their adherence to group goals, which were regarded as more important than personal goals. In contrast, the domestic groups were more tenuously tied together; for some participants they were advantageous for a particular period in their lives, but then proved frustrating because of conflicts and incompatibility, often centering around child rearing; in some cases there were too many adults giving input to the parents and child; in other cases, there was a disappointing lack of shared responsibility and caretaking.

Consideration of the personal motivations and conditions that lead to movement out of a communal life-style must include not only the degree of personal satisfaction and identification with group goals, and ease of moving out of the unit, but also the family's feeling of competency about making it on the outside. For the most part, the communal living-group members, particularly the creedal mothers and fathers, had lower occupational skills than their traditional married peers "on the outside"; this may have been a factor in their remaining in the groups.

Creedal group populations are also maintained by proselytizing. Proselytizing (and keeping women busy) are served by having more births subsequent to the target child than in any other family group (traditionals are second in this characteristic, for reasons that seem to have more to do with the reluctance to have an "only child" family).

Child-Rearing Attitudes and Practices

The literature (Berger, 1967, 1971; Blois, 1971; Cavan, 1972; Kanter & Furcher, 1973) and our own work (Eiduson & Alexander, 1978) had suggested that philosophy (viz. a stated preference for children to learn generalized sense of trust and to be attached to others, as well as availability of other potential caretakers) would result in significant differences in terms of who served as the caretaker of the child throughout the early years. During infancy there was more multiple caretaking in communal living groups than in traditional married families; more adults were present and did some caretaking; this life-style had the highest amount of social stimulation and variety of people present during our home observations. However, even in these groups, in almost every case, the mother was still the infant's *primary* caretaker. By the time the children were 2 years old, the mothers in communal groups were significantly less likely to be the child's primary caretaker; in many of the groups, group care situations existed in which the children spent a good part of their day. Likewise, at 3, 3 ½, and 4 years there was a significant difference between traditional married families and those remaining in communal living situations; the communal child was less likely to have mother as primary caretaker and more likely to be exposed to other caretakers.

Although in most groups children resided with their parents, in some group settings, child and mother were geographically separated by choice of leader or other roles the mother might play (one group that has a number of residences in this country separates mothers and children who become too "tied" to each other; however, even in this extreme example, the children know who their parents are and differentiate them from the other adults.)

Relevant to caretaker roles are the data that from the beginning, communal living-group mothers were also less likely than mothers in other life-styles to do household tasks alone, for they had other household members with whom they shared these responsibilities.

One of the most dramatic characteristics of creedal living group members was their strong identification with spiritual and religious goals. They attended church more regularly. They valued spiritual training for their children significantly more than did domestic living group or social-contract families. Most children received informal, if not formal spiritual training. (In some Eastern religious groups, this means special schools, apart from parents by age 18 months.) This emphasis on spirituality was reinforced by a reduction in other "worldly" stimulation: fewer toys for children, less exposure to TV and other mass media. Again there are examples of significant within-group variance: one communal group had a television on in the children's quarters 24 hours a day. This latter idiosyncratic family notwithstanding, 53% of children in communal living groups watched no TV, a higher percentage than in any other life-style.

The communal living group child had the most nonbiologically related peers in the household, but the fewest social contacts outside the home. Children were significantly less often left at someone's house outside the group. Also, visits by grandparents occured most infrequently (about two times a year) for this family group; this difference is significant as compared to the traditional and single-mother samples. Their insularity from outsiders was also reinforced by school attendance; only one-third to one-half attended an outside school.

The creedal living group child was likely to be disciplined in line with the group's needs for conformity to operate, and in line with their focus on the child's need to respect authority. Unlike the domestic living group members who did not emphasize obedience and who "reasoned" with their children, creedal group members felt it was paramount to teach obedience and respect for authority. Creedal group parents disciplined for more types of behaviors than domestic group parents, although they did not differ overall in modes of discipline. Creedal group parents saw their own disciplinary practices as harsher than those of their own parents. The domestic group's disciplinary outlooks and practices were more like those of the social-contract families.

DIFFERENCES AMONG ALTERNATIVE LIFE-STYLES:
SOCIAL-CONTRACT FAMILIES

Family History

The social-contract fathers had the lowest level of educational and vocational competencies of all groups when entering into the project. Fathers averaged more than 1 year less training than other male parents—this in part reflecting their early "drop-out" status from school. Although the social-contract mothers had fewer years of education than their traditional married peers, and later worked at lower occupational levels, there was not a significant difference in occupational status between mothers in social-contract and other life-styles at the point of entry into the project.

Parental Values

The social-contract parents were the most deviant in terms of nonconventional beliefs and values (Rocheford, 1978). At the point of entry, on six of the eight dimensions they were at the polar end of each scale, signifying high affiliation with unconventionality. They were the least oriented toward conventional achievement; the family group most pulled toward here-and-now gratifications; they identified with using intuitive and sensory modes of input in problemsolving; they showed the most preference for the natural–organic orientation in environmental concerns, foods, and so forth. On all these dimensions they were significantly different from the traditional marrieds and from single mothers. On the sex-egalitarianism dimension they appeared as the most egalitarian-oriented family group, being significantly different from traditionals and creedal living groups. In regard to materialism, they were significantly different from traditional marrieds, but not from the other two alternative family groups, all of whom expressed an antimaterialistic stance. They rejected conventional sources of authority and, further, their antiauthority position remained significantly stronger at 3 years than that of single parents, traditional marrieds, and creedal living group samples—comparable only to the position taken by the domestic living-group families, whose perspectives generally resembled theirs.

Current Family Milieu

Social-contract families had the lowest number of fathers working full time at each period from the birth of the child through 4 years. For example, slightly more than 60% of the social-contract fathers worked full time at the 1- and 3-year periods, a lower proportion than in other life-styles. Vocational level of competency may have played a role in their employment status: 50% of fathers worked in middle-level occupations when children were of preschool age, and a significantly larger number of social-contract fathers compared to other groups were also in the lowest occupational levels. Further, there were fewer social contracts returning to school, and fewer in college or professional training at the 4-year period, when data showed many indications that some alternatives were returning to mainstream activities.

Social-contract mothers also were the last group to return to the work force—again their later entry, and the numbers entering, were different from other groups. When their children were 3 years old, only 12% were working on a full-time basis, compared to 40% of the single mothers and 27% of the traditional marrieds. Like the fathers, their work activities were dispersed primarily in middle and lower occupational levels; at 3 years these mothers had the lowest occupational level of any life-style group. Their occupational level may be related to their preference for part-time employment and the usual low level of jobs available on this basis.

These significantly lower levels of vocational competency and work involvement are reflected in the low income of this family group. In part, their low income is voluntary, consonant with their antimaterialistic, antimainstream-success positions, for they are among the "voluntary poor," taking seasonal or casual jobs in order not to be constrained by their jobs and to be available for their families and pursue other interests (Eiduson, 1978). However, it is conceivable that their distance from success-oriented work involvements also rationalizes feelings (and possibly actual indices) of incompetence.

Many social-contract households were in rural or small-town areas to which the adults emigrated feeling they could live closer to nature and have greater control over their lives. A number of their houses were handmade and, although small and primitive in terms of middle-class amenities, quite colorful and creative with the use of recycled wood, stained glass, plants, and wall hangings. Social-contract households were rated as the most "funky" and disorderly. At the same time these homes were also rated as having the most indices of potential danger spots for an infant or young child. In these characteristics, their homes were significantly different from the other life-style groups.

The initial group of social-contract mothers reported greater overall satisfaction than did traditional marrieds in their personal growth and work/homemaker roles as measured over a 3-year period. However, there were no differences in reported satisfaction with their life-style choices, though by the time their children were 4½ years old, 62% of the social contracts had changed life-styles, compared to 16% of the traditional marrieds: 13 married (the largest proportion to their original mates); 16 became single; and 4 moved into communal groups.

Child-Rearing Attitudes and Practices

In line with their value perspectives, this group was more alternative and clearly delineated from other family groups in terms of some infant child-rearing practices. For example, they had a significantly higher number of home births (32% compared to 8% of the traditional marrieds). Most breast-fed, and for a longer period than traditionals or single mothers; they tended to feed the infant significantly more often and to be particularly oriented toward demand feeding. The breast was regarded as a pacifier for many, not only as the main nutritional source. Natural organic foods were commonly used. Many restricted use of meat, and the use of fluorides.

Children tended to be carried in slings, travel with parents at night, were less often placed in playpens than most other children, and generally were exposed to all family experiences, without much attempt on the parents' part at differentiating the child's experience from the adults'. The parents saw themselves as giving much more time to their child than did their own parents to them.

Social contracts' unconventionality was interesting when discipline was an issue. They did not stress obedience and respect for authority; they considered it important that even a 3-year-old child have a reason to obey. When comparing their discipline practices with those encountered in their families of origin, they described themselves as more lenient.

Their more permissive life-style was also evident in regard to attitudes towards sexuality. Data collected at the 3-year period suggested that social-contract mothers and fathers bathed more frequently with their children, fathers went nude more frequently in front of children, and children were allowed to be nude in front of other children more frequently than in other family groups. For example, 67% of the social-contract parents were casual about or encouraged their child to play nude in front of other children, compared to 46% of the communal parents, 44% of the single mothers and 22% of the traditional marrieds.

The social contracts felt school was important to children. By 3½, 67% of social-contract children were in nursery school; the mean for the total sample was 54%. At 5 years, 79% of the social-contract children were in some type of school, only slightly less than the children of traditional married parents. These data are interesting in terms of their antiauthoritarianism and general distaste for dependence on existing social institutions. However, they were attracted to schools with alternative programs and used these significantly more than the traditional marrieds and single mothers. For their children they wanted nature appreciation, social adjustment, and happiness stressed—and ranked such educational goals significantly higher than did other families; spiritual training was lowest in importance for the child to learn.

DIFFERENCES AMONG ALTERNATIVE LIFE STYLES: SINGLE-MOTHER FAMILIES

Family History

The elective mother was the youngest of the groups. She averaged approximately 13.3 ± 2 years of schooling; 14% lacked a high school diploma, and 23% had

college degrees. On the basis of their educational level and vocational competency, as well as their motivation for pregnancy, it was possible to identify
certain subsets within the population: the "nest builder," "post hoc adaptors,"
and "unwed mothers" (Kornfein et al., 1976; Eiduson, in press). The nest
builders, who comprised one-fourth of the group, had consciously planned to
become pregnant and selected a man who might be a suitable father. These were
the older, more career-oriented and experienced of the single mothers; they
usually lived by themselves, had the highest income, and were the most economically, socially, and psychologically self-sufficient. The post hoc adaptor
group was made up of women who had not intended to become pregnant, but
once aware that they were, felt sufficiently happy about the pregnancy and were
able to adjust to the circumstances. Their work experience had been in lower-
level administrative and clerical jobs, because their education was more limited
than that of the nest builders, and vocational goals less specific. These single
mothers often shared small houses or apartments with friends or relatives such as
siblings or aunts. For the unwed mothers pregnancy was unhappily anticipated.
They were the youngest and least vocationally competent group; they worked
prior to pregnancy in clerical, skilled, or semiskilled areas. They were rarely
financially independent, using welfare or their parents for economic assistance.
They either lived with roommates or with relatives, often returning to the
neighborhood or dwelling of their own parents for practical support.

Parental Values

The most salient finding in regard to the values of single mothers was their
ambivalent alignment with alternative values. As a total group, they were at
times more like the traditional married family sample, and at other times more
like their alternative cohorts. For example, the single mother shared the same
high values placed on conventional achievement as did the traditional marrieds,
but she was much less concerned with materialism, and drawn to sensory and
intuitive modes of thinking, as a useful supplement to scientific and rational
thought.

The notable within-group variability that led us to identify a number of sub-
types of single mothers in the sample was reflected in their values. The career-
oriented nest builders were high on the sex-egalitarian dimension; the post hoc
adaptors scored in the middle range; and the unwed single-mother subgroup
scored very low on the sex-egalitarian dimension. This same kind of within-
group variance was found in regard to planfulness and future orientation. Although we had hypothesized a strong anticonventional, antiauthority thrust in the
single parents as a group because of their antimainstream behavior in regard to
having a baby without benefit of wedlock or a man in the picture, analysis of data
again showed significant variance.

Current Family Milieu

Of the single mothers, 96% were urban, much like the traditional married population. Like the other alternatives, they were less likely than traditional marrieds to live in a single-family home and they had fewer rooms and functionally distinct areas than were present in traditional married households. Their households were significantly more often rated as disorderly/funky than traditional marrieds, however, they were not as disorderly and funky as social contract households.

Income was comprised of a number of sources: part and full-time work, welfare, grandparents, and in some few cases, father support. During the child's early years, total income tended to be the lowest for the samples studied, with a mean of approximately $5000 a year during the first 3 years of the child's life. During infancy only 10% of the single mothers were in high socioeconomic status groups, 36% were in the middle, and over 50% were in the lowest groups.

Few single mothers were employed when their children were infants, and about 51% were not working when the children were 3. This was related to the fact that about 25% had married by then and had life-styles in which fathers were the main wage earners. When the single mothers did work, they were more likely than other mothers to work full time.

When single mothers did work during their child's infancy, they were more likely than social contract and communal mothers to be in the three highest Hollinghead–Redlich categories, second only to the traditional married women. This suggests of course that it may be most satisfying and financially worthwhile for the woman with a higher occupational status to return to work.

Of all the alternative groups, the single mothers made significantly more residential moves. Furthermore, through the child's first 18 months, the single mother had a higher number of total changes (moves, life-style changes, separations from child) than did any other group. From 18 months to 3 years, and again from 3 to 4 ½ years, the single mother made significantly more changes than the traditional married group. Variance here was significant, suggesting that within this sample were a few members who were more stable, and others particularly prone to resolving difficulties or conflict situations through environment change.

Related to these change behavior data was the finding that by 1 year the single mother was, of all the mothers, the least satisfied with her fate. Some 42% expressed ambivalence about the life-style and 20% were openly negative. At 3 years, the single-mother group again appeared to have the most negative feelings concerning life-style status. These attitudes may be related to their low economic status, and to the data showing that the single-mother group, from infancy on, was the family unit in which the mother was responsible for more household and child-care tasks by herself than were women in any other group.

Child-Rearing Attitudes and Practices

Our single mothers had significantly more abortions than traditional marrieds prior to this pregnancy, and most reported not planning to have this baby.

Therefore our calling them "elective" single mothers refers to their decision to have a baby once pregnant, not their attitudes toward planning the pregnancy (with the exception of the nest builders).

Like the traditional marrieds, almost all (94%) single mothers opted for a hospital delivery with a medical doctor present; 74% had an anesthetic, significantly more than did other alternatives. Generally, they had long labors, in fact significantly longer than traditional married mothers. Although these mothers had fewer males present to lend support at birth, they had a higher number of female and other adult friends present to compensate.

Infancy and early childhood patterns of caretaking did not distinguish this group from the other alternative groups. There were few differences that were significant in terms of feeding or sleep arrangements, nor in psychological patterns such as mother/child attentiveness or involvements. In extent or kind of caretaker responsiveness to child-initiated contacts, affective interchanges, verbalizations or contact initiated by the mother, a home observation at 6 months revealed no significant differences between the single-mother sample and any other group. Some differences, however, were noted in summary scores of intensity and variability of social and nonsocial stimulation, with the single mother slightly lower.

As noted earlier, there were no significant differences by life-style in the ways parents perceived children. However, it is noteworthy, although not significant, that single mothers tended to have more children in the "difficult" and "shy" categories than did the other groups. Similarly, on a self-report measure (Ireton) in which mothers reported development of their children in a number of areas, such as self-help, comprehension, perceptual–motor development, and so on, the single mothers' boys emerged in the borderline or problem areas more often than did children from other groups, although overall, very few children were so rated in the total sample.

Although our population did not differ in use of traditional medical care, number of well-child visits to physicians, or in relative number of visits by type of illness, single mothers did tend to take their children to physicians more frequently for psychological or behavioral problems than parents in other alternative life-styles. This tendency may not indicate greater frequency of problems, but rather reflect the single mothers' lack of practical and psychological support within their own households, and perhaps attributing their own psychological difficulties to their children.

A greater percentage of single-parent children attended day care or preschool than did children in any other alternative group: over 75% by age 3½. Such exposure to outside inputs was in line with findings earlier that the single mother's child had more exposure to radio, television, and other forms of mass media than other alternative groups. Again, the single mother was like the traditional mother population, and different from alternatives, to a significant degree.

As a group, the single mothers' child rearing was distinctive in terms of conscious desire on the parent's part not to sex-stereotype children's toys, activities, or personalities. This is particularly interesting in light of the single mothers' voiced preference for girls at birth.

As we try to understand the kinds of stresses to which the single-mother family was subjected, it is noteworthy that the single mother had the highest total stresses for almost every period. The single-mother families had the highest number of potential stresses related to residence and life-style change as well as other stresses potentially affecting the child (Eiduson & Forsythe, in press).

DISCUSSION

Some of the compelling modifications of family in America initiated during the 1970s have been projected as continuing into the 1980s (Masnick & Bane, 1980). It is anticipated that one-third of all children born during the '70s will be spending part of their childhood living with a single parent. Only one-quarter of all American households will be conventional ones, if "conventional" is defined as including mother, father, and children. Thirteen separate types of households will eclipse in numbers the conventional units. Most of our understanding of the ways children in families are socialized is derived from studies of conventional two-parent nuclear units. However, because Bureau of Census data are "eliminating the typical family," as reported in one announcement (Peirce, 1980), normative data on values and practices relevant to child development in family variants are essential in order to assess the implications for the child who grows up in a variant family form. Our data are suggesting that what parents want for their children, the behaviors they value as competencies and try to foster, are different in traditional two-parent families, and some of the pluralistic family forms. These differences are expressed in child-rearing attitudes and practices.

What are the implications for the child who is growing up in one of the alternative family forms? Until now our understanding of the ways in which child functioning is affected by growing up in variant family forms rests mainly on data obtained on families whose nonconventional status arose by default, not choice—widowhood, desertion, unwanted pregnancy. Child outcome data in these studies have suggested wide-ranging negative consequences for cognitive growth and socioemotional development, which fostered an association of deficit family or deviance with the family that was nontraditional and non-two parent. These findings have been put into question because studies on which they were based are fraught with methodological problems (Biller, 1974, Herzog & Sudia, 1970, Hetherington, 1967, Pedersen, 1976). However the association of deficit with nontraditional families remains, and needs the kind of reexamination that this study is providing.

We have had the opportunity to study nontraditional, nonnuclear families who elected their family style and who felt that certain values could better be expressed in one of the pluralistic family forms than in the traditional unit. Further, they regarded these family forms as developing in the child competencies and knowledge that were desirable, and also adaptive for tomorrow's world (Brim, 1975).

What competencies would a nontraditional family put a premium on, and reward in a child? On the basis of our findings about their family functioning, values, and child-rearing preferences and practices in the early years, we hypothesized that a social-contract family child would be rewarded were he or she creative, tended to act on his or her own impulses, rather than being compliant and meek, be able to evade and not be felled by frustrating situations, have high personal sensitivity, and be strongly self-motivated. For the communal living group we felt that successful functioning in a creedal living group might demand a child who was selfless, who would deny impulses, and have a great deal of social poise, have a single-minded pursuit of goals of the group, be compliant, nonassertive, and be able to integrate personal and group needs. In the domestic living group, we thought that the most highly valued would be a flexible child, who was able to express himself or herself, be able to tolerate group conflict, and be able to adapt without being distressed by change. We thought the single-mother population would value a child who was dependent on the mother for affective needs, and who could also be affectionate and nurturing of the mother, be independent and self-reliant in other areas, and able to play alone; be assertive if a girl and resemble the mother, especially if she were interested in women's causes; be able to face the reality of not having a father but nevertheless behave in ways that were so "normal" that the child would not feel differentiated from other children. The traditional married two-parent family, by contrast, would value an achievement-oriented, task-oriented child, one who set goals and subgoals, who was organized, energetic, able to delay immediate satisfactions for future pleasures, and who showed good control.

As yet, these anticipated differences among the children are not evident. However, at 6 years, when assessment measures are stronger, we think that we shall see differences in the expected directions. Further, we think that at that point we shall be able to delineate the variables that when considered together with family structure and composition, account for differences in child competencies.

To what extent are the family forms developed for the '80s able to prepare a child for a world in which rapid change, mobility, population pressure, and stress are considered commonplace? The family forms under study seem to be adopting a variety of ways of coping with the contemporary way of life. Some family forms remain a part of society but resist certain pressures when they see them as antithetical, even destructive of human needs, and in those aspects they find ways to live differently from mainstream families. Other families attempt to modify society through extolling group goals that they think have the potential of meeting social needs in an enriched way. Still others insulate themselves through retreating geographically to a more "simple" life. Some families continue to try to swim upstream in order to demonstrate that determination can make what looks outwardly like a "handicapped" family, a normal, and even forward-looking one.

These are goals set by adults. The children, who are faced with the consequences of having to adjust to mainstream institutions, will tell us, through the adaptiveness of their coping strategies, their conflicts, anxieties, and symptoms, the usefulness and effectiveness of these family styles for child adjustment. Do any of these family styles put a child at intellectual, social, or emotional risk? What family strategies are adjustment producing, and what are limiting or handicapping? Are there ages or conditions when these family situations are more risk producing than others? Our studies of families continue to elucidate many such mental health issues and point to the extent to which each of these families meets the needs of children.

DEVELOPMENT OF CHILDREN

We conclude with some initial findings on child outcome measures. Children were essentially a normal sample at birth. Data on the Obstetrical Complications Scale adjusted (OCS) revealed mean scores that were average or better for each life-style (total mean 111.2 ± 21.4 as compared to the standardization mean of 111 ± 11), suggesting that births were generally uneventful. Results on the Newborn Neurological Examination (NNE) also indicated that mean scores were average or better for each life-style (total mean 101.6 ± 21.5 versus standardization mean of 100 ± 20). There appeared to be no relationship between the two measures (Pearson $r = .01$) nor between children flagged at risk (1 or 2 SD below average) by either measure.

No differences attributable to life-style were significant on these measures; although single mothers' infants were lowest in rank, there was in all only a 7-point difference between the lowest ranking (single-mother) infants and the highest ranking (living-group) infants (100.0 versus 106.9, $p = .28$). When NNE scores were dichotomized to identify those infants scoring below 80, or at risk (one standard deviation below average), 22 or 11% met this criterion, randomly dispersed over all life-styles.

On the Obstetrical Complications Scale, life-style differences approached significance, specifically because scores for single mothers were 8 or more points lower than those of the other groups (104.3 versus $111.6+$, $p = .07$). Other groups were generally similar to each other. From these data we proceeded on the assumption that essentially no children in any group would demand differential caretaking because of neurological difficulties evident at birth, and that any differentials that existed in caretaking practices would reflect family values, preferences, and propensities, rather than responses to identified anomalies or deficits.

Our first studies of the ability of the child to meet developmental milestones came in the home observations at 6 months, and in the administration of the Bayley Scales of Infant Development at 8 months and 12 months. At 6 months, the child's range of affective behaviors, ability to initiate responsiveness to caretaker-initiated behaviors, and smiling and crying behaviors were studied through time and event sampling methods at a feeding period. In general, all babies showed a normal range of behaviors, and no notable difference between groups on such maturational parameters was found. At 8 months, children as a whole were average (MDI 103.6 ± 14.9, PDI 105.6 ± 12.1). Slight life-style differences favoring traditional married over living-group children on mental developmental measures were noted ($p = .06$). In development focusing on motor behavior, single-mother children scored significantly higher ($p = .05$) than living-group children.

These differences disappeared by one year (MDI 109.6 ± 10.6, $p = .75$, PDI 98.3 ± 13.5, $p = .14$) in part revealing a regression to the mean. However, scores on mental development rose significantly for all but children in traditional homes. Motor development scores dropped significantly for all groups. When 8-month and 1-year scores were compared to birth status as revealed in Obstetrical Complications Scale and the Newborn Neurological Examination Scores, no life-style-dependent differences were seen.

In order to assess the child's reaction to separation from mother as an indication of extent and kind of attachment to her, all 1-year-old infants and their mothers were observed at 1 year of age in the Strange Situation and Mother Attachment Procedure developed by Ainsworth for 1-year-olds (Ainsworth, Blehar, Waters, & Well, 1978). Using Ainsworth's classification, attachment is of three kinds: (1) Group A (avoidant), in which there is "little or no tendency to seek proximity to or interaction or contact with the mother, even in the reunion episodes" (p. 59). In general, "either the baby is not distressed during separation, or the distress seems to be due to being left alone rather than to his mother's absence." In this study 15% of the children were rated A. (2) Group B (attached) consisted of children who wanted "either proximity and contact with the mother or interaction with her, and actively seek it, especially in the reunion episodes." In this sample 76% were rated B. (3) Group C (anxious–resistant) identified the child who might display "generally 'maladaptive' behavior in the strange situation. Either he tends to be more angry than infants in other groups, or he may be conspicuously passive." Only 19% of the sample rated C.

We had hypothesized that differences in family composition and structure, as well as differences in experiences during year 1 would result in life-style-dependent differences. However, differences in the Stranger Test attributable to life-style were negligible and undoubtedly due to chance.

We had also hypothesized that parental differences on the sex-egalitarian dimensions might emerge on the children's tests. On the Strange Situation Test, we had some first indications of sex differences, albeit few. Surprisingly, girls moved more often than boys as assessed in the situation as a whole ($p = .04$). When the mother returned after an absence, girls differed by more often showing toys, smiling, and speaking than boys ($p = .009$), and girls also more often stopped crying within 30 seconds of the mother's return ($p = .02$). In addition, few sex differences in toy preference were noted—an issue about which there are controversial findings in the literature. However, when the child was joined by the stranger in the last episode, no sex differences were elicited, as others have noted. In the last episode, when the mother returned, girls more frequently smiled at the mother than did boys ($p = .05$).

In the Strange Situation Test we also had the opportunity to study comparatively aspects of children's visual, locomotive, and manual manipulative behaviors under the familiar situation of mother present, with a stranger present, and while alone in a strange room. Also, the coping styles used when secure with mother, or in distress occasioned by the mother's absence (such as seeking or avoiding proximity and contact) are thought to be possible precursors of later reaction in the child. Our sample showed a range of behaviors comparable to the data presented by Ainsworth. Very minimal differences by our four family groups emerged, thus supporting the position that reactions to separations at this early point may be maturational, rather than family-environment dependent. Although differences did not reach significance, traditional children seemed to have a differentially strong need for "mothering" as revealed by their wanting to be held more often, doing less exploratory or manipulative toy play, and refusing to be soothed following separation.

Because children were not seen for developmental assessment between ages 1 and 3, parent-report measures on child maturation were embedded in other data being collected.

On the Ireton Minnesota Child Development Inventory, a parent-report measure given at 18 months, the general development index for the total population was average (101.8 ± 14.1). Neither sex nor life-style differences reached significance. Ireton recommends using this measure to identify children at risk, rather than to focus on minor deviations from average. Children who were rated by their mothers at 18 months as falling 30% below average on general development or, in terms of a ratio score, to be functioning at the defective level (DQ 70) were identified. In all, only seven children (or 4%) were so rated. Of responding parents who so labeled their child, there were three single mothers, two social contracts, one living group, and one traditional married. Twenty-two parents reported developmental levels which gave their children borderline scores: eight single mothers, six social contracts, five in living groups, and three traditional married.

At 2 years the children were again rated by their parents, with the sample as a whole rated average (104.3 ± 14.7). Here sex differences favored boys, but no life-style differences were found. However the number of children rated as defective in general development rose to 19 (14%): social contract six, single mother six, living group five, traditional married two. Nineteen other children were rated as borderline (14%): social contract four, single mother five, living group seven, and traditional married three. Because these are parent-report measures, the discrepancies between parent report and scores on another measure were studied. Only two of the ten children who were rated as borderline or below by the parent at two successive time points, 18 months and 2 years, had significantly low Binet scores, whereas one seen by the mother as average at the second test had a low Binet at age 3. These data suggest differences in parent perception of child ability, even though no significant differences were supported by our direct assessment data.

When children reached 3 years of age, we hypothesized that measures of competence could be more diverse and would be more reliable and valid. On the Stanford–Binet, a test admittedly heavily loaded in verbal areas, the sample again scored as normal, verifying earlier data indicating that the children constituted a normal sample so far as general functioning level was concerned. The mean IQ was 102.9, standard deviation 15.0, very close to the national average. Comparison of children by life-style did not reveal more than minimal differences by group. Both social contracts and traditional marrieds revealed identical means (103.0) slightly surpassed by living-group children (104.2) who were, incidentally, the most diverse (SD 17.7, $p = .09$). Single mother children showed the lowest mean score (101.1).

Scores on Binet correlated significantly with both 8-month and 1-year developmental measures (MDI r = .20 and .25, p's = .01; PDI r = .17 and .13, p = .05). The higher correlation of the MDI at 1 year with the Binet probably reflected the increasing amount of language being measured by age 1.

We had hypothesized that some gross differences noted in environments might affect object recognition, and the subsequent ability to label objects. However, on the Peabody Picture Vocabulary Test, scores for the total sample were average (102.4, SD 16.6) and again life-style differences were not significant. Again single-mother children had the lowest mean score (98.2), whereas traditional married children scored highest (104.5), and social contract and living group were close to traditional marrieds. Rural/urban differences, differences in parent education level and/or SES did not appear to discriminate family groups. Hypotheses relating verbal competency to large family size (and therefore more verbal interaction) were not confirmed, although the one-parent family showed slightly lower scores. When an "intellectual risk" score summarizing performance on both the Peabody and Binet was calculated, a total of 18 children were identified as at risk. The four groups contributed almost evenly to this group. The three children from the traditional married group seemed to be those with possible minimal brain damage, although only one had evidence of difficulty at birth.

A number of other cognitive-related abilities were also tested at 3 years;

because language development is a critical milestone by age 3, our tests of verbal development and language receptivity were supplemented by a test of articulation ability. Findings showed that these children had typical articular skills for their age, although living-group children tended to surpass single-mother children.

A global assessment of creativity was based on amount and kind of originality shown in fantasy play on the semistructured World Test as well as nonconventional responses on the Rorschach. Results did not reach significance, but traditional married and social-contract children appeared more free to express their fantasy as compared to the communal living-group children.

Persistence, a characteristic related to task orientation, was based on a number of verbal tasks well completed, continuous pulls on an insoluble drawer task, and number of attempts to overcome a barrier without showing distress. There was considerable variance within groups, and no significant difference by lifestyle. Traditional and single-mother children were most persistent however, and social-contract children least. This appeared to be related to ability level, with social-contract children who scored lower on receptive vocabularly more apt to refuse the verbal tasks.

The Strange Situation Test was repeated at 3 years, assessing a number of socioemotional behaviors. We hypothesized that there would be no spread in these data because at this age, the separation anxiety elicited when mother leaves is a developmental phase already passed. We found only eight children (4%) rated as avoidant–anxious or "C." None of these had been so rated at year 1. Four were from the traditional married sample, three from single mothers, and one was a social-contract child. Examination of environmental data for these children showed that all but one had recently been subjected to marked stresses such as parental divorce, separation, and hospitalization. Yet other children experiencing such stresses rated in accordance with the total sample in the A (56%) or B (39%) categories, both of which suggest ability to experience separation without visible distress.

The stability of the Stranger Test from age 1 to 3 was assessed for the 172 children who took both tests. Of the total sample 37% did not change classifications, with the most (70%) remaining securely attached (B rating), and the rest remaining avoidant of mother (A). No child in any life-style was rated insecurely–anxiously attached (C) at both time periods. By life-styles, stability (i.e., those rated either A or B at both time periods) ranged from 31% for children of single mothers to 42% for living-group children, who changed least. Both two-parent family samples were identical in stability (38% social contract and 37% traditional married).

A conceptually related variable, fearfulness and/or anxiety, was developed as a summary variable based on frightening themes produced in the World Test, a global rating of behavior as fearful, and the frequency of frightening or anxious content on the Rorschach. Results showed a tendency for traditional married children to be least fearful and living-group most.

Because of the antiauthority stance of some alternative families, such child behaviors as aggression, hostility, and failure to cooperate also were assessed. Aggression, rated on the basis of extent of aggression expressed motorically or verbally during the play on the World Test; and hostility, assessed in terms of hostile ideation (for example, mistreatment of dolls), expressed on the World Test were nonsignificant by family group. However, social contracts were slightly high and living-group children a bit low.

Although differences were minimal, measures of cooperativeness (identifying children who were able or willing to follow instructions on a Simon Says task, and in a global rating by the psychologist) showed that living-group and single-mothers' children tended to be more cooperative, whereas social-contract children were least. Thus although differences between children were not significant, we have a first indication of compliance in the living-group sample's children, a characteristic hypothesized as desirable for adaptation in this large family unit, and some anticompliance tendencies in our most permissive and alternative family group, the social contracts.

Also of interest because of the alternative families' orientation toward the "here and now," was the child's tolerance for frustration. Tolerance for frustration under stress was rated on the basis of response to the Drawer Barrier and a frustrating (Room Barrier) situation. Single-mother children tended to be most tolerant, social-contract least. Activity level was measured in terms of mobility under stress in the Strange Situation Test and on an overall rating from the Bayley Behavioral Record; no life-style differences were significant, but social-contract children were more apt to approach a rating of "hyperactive" and living-group children least.

Extent of attentiveness, based on a rating of distractable behavior as observed on four difficult tasks (including Drawer Pull and Competing Sets) again revealed no significant life-style differences, but single-mother children were rated highest and social-contract children were lowest.

Some global measures of social maturity were obtained. Mothers provided data for the Vineland Scale, a well-standardized social maturity measure. Scores were slightly above average for the sample as a whole (107.6 ± 14.5) and revealed no life-style differences. Single-mother children had the highest mean (surprising in light of their reports on the written Minnesota Child Development Inventory) and the most dispersion (108.8 ± 16.0), and living-group children had the lowest mean and least dispersion (106.5 ± 13.5).

Also, a summary adjustment variable was developed in terms of use of play during separation in the Stranger Test; the ability to perform a task when confronted with a frustration barrier (Room Barrier); and attempts at finding a solution during an insoluble task (Drawer Barrier), as well as the number of responses showing personal resources on the Rorschach (M & FM). On this variable, single-mother children tended to be rated highest, social-contract lowest.

Further, general maturity was assessed from a composite of the Vineland, level of articulation, cooperativeness in test taking, and the number of mature perceptions (P, M) on the Rorschach. Again single-mother children tended to be rated more mature; social-contract, less mature.

Finally, social, intellectual, and emotional competence scores summarizing the child's performance on all 3 year tests revealed no differences by life-style. All three scores were highly interrelated for all groups ($r = .45-.55$).

In sum, the psychological development of the children was assessed thoroughly and repeatedly during the first three years of their lives. Although a number of developmental constructs were assessed, the life-style of the family in which the children were being raised had no systematic effect on the children's development. Stated differently, the children in all groups appeared to be developing normally.

ACKNOWLEDGMENTS

This work is supported in part by the National Institute of Mental Health Research Scientist Career Aware No. 5 K05 MH 70541-09 to Bernice T. Eiduson, and by the United States Public Health Service Grant No. 1 R01-MH 24947-08 and Carnegie Corporation Grant B3970-08.

REFERENCES

Ainworth, M. D. S., Blehar, M. Waters, E. & Wall, S. *Pattern of attachment*. Hillsdale, N.J.: Lawrence Erlbaum Associates, 1978.

Berger, B. Hippie morality, more old than new. *Trans-Action,* 1967, *5,* 19-23.

Berger, B. *Child rearing practices of the communal family*. Progress report to the National Institute of Mental Health, Bethesda, Maryland, 1971 (Mimeo).

Biller, H. B. *Paternal deprivation: Family, school, sexuality, and society*. Lexington, Mass.: D.C. Heath, 1974.

Blanchard, R. W., & Biller, H. B. Father availability and academic performance among third-grade boys. *Developmental Psychology,* 1974, *4,* 301-305.

Blois, M. S. Child rearing attitudes of hippie adults. *Dissertation Abstracts,* 1971, *31,* 3329-3330.

Brim, O. G. Socialization through the life cycle. In O. G. Brim & E. Wheeler (Eds.), *Socialization after childhood*. New York: Wiley, 1975.

Cavan, S. *Hippies of the Haight*. St. Louis, MO.: New Critics Press, 1972.

Cohen, J., & Eiduson, B. T. Changing patterns of child rearing in alternative life styles: Implications for development. In A. Davids (Ed.), *Child personality and psychopathology: Current topics*. New York: Wiley, 1975.

Cole, M., Gay, J., Glick, J. A., & Sharp, D. W. *The cultural context of learning and thinking*. New York: Basic Books, 1971.

Delora, J. S., & Delora, J. R. *Intimate life styles: Marriage and its alternatives*. Pacific Palisades, Calif: Goodyear, 1972.

Eiduson, B. T. Looking at children in emergent family styles. *Children Today,* 1974, *4,* 2-6.

Eiduson, B. T. Child development in emergent family styles: A research update. *Children Today,* 1978, *7,* 24–31.

Eiduson, B. T. Emergent families of the 1970's: Values, practices and impact on children. In D. Reiss & H. Hoffman (Eds.), *The family: Dying or developing.* New York: Plenum Press, 1978. (b)

Eiduson, B. T. The commune-reared child. In J. Noshpitz (Ed.), *Basic handbook of child psychiatry*(Vol. 1). New York: Basic Books, 1979.

Eiduson, B. T. Changing sex roles in alternative family styles: Implications for young children. In E. J. Anthony & C. Chiland (Eds.), *The child in his family: Changing roles of children and parents*(Vol. 6). New York: Wiley Interscience, 1980.

Eiduson, B. T. The child in the non-conventional family. In M. Lewis & L. Rosenblum (Eds.), *The genesis of behavior: The uncommon child.* New York: Plenum Press, 1981.

Eiduson, B. T. *Child mental health in alternative family styles.* Progress report submitted to the National Institute of Mental Health, Bethesda, Md. Grant No. MH 24947–08, February 1981. (a)

Eiduson, B. T. Parent–child relations and the socio-emotional development of the child. In B. T. Eiduson (Chair), *The development of the child in alternative life styles: Years 1–3.* Symposium presented at the meeting of the Society for Research in Child Development, Boston, April 1981.

Eiduson, B. T. Contemporary single mothers. In L. G. Katz (Ed.), *Current topics in early childhood education* (Vol. 3). *Children of the 80's: Perspective for action.* Norwood, N.J.: Ablex, in press.

Eiduson, B. T., & Alexander, J. The role of chidlren in alternative family styles. *Journal of Social Issues,* 1978, *34,* 149–167.

Eiduson, B. T., Cohen, J., & Alexander, J. Alternatives in child rearing in the 1970's. *American Journal of Orthopsychiatry,* 1973, *43,* 721–731.

Eiduson, B. T., & Forsythe, A. Life change events in alternative family styles. In E. J. Callahan & K. A. McClusky (Eds.), *Life-span developmental psychology: Non-normative life events.* New York: Academic Press, in press.

Eiduson, B. T., & Weisner, T. S. Alternative family styles: Effects on young children. In J. Stevens & M. Mathews (Eds.), *Mother/child, father/child relationships.* Washington, D.C.: National Association for the Education of Young Children, 1978.

Ehrenberg, D. The quest for intimate relatedness. *Contemporary Psychoanalysis,* 1975, *2,* 320–331.

Eshleman, J. R., & Clarke, J. N. *Intimacy, commitments, and marriage: Development of relationships.* Boston: Allyn & Bacon, 1978.

Herzog, E., & Sudia, C. E. *Boys in fatherless families.* Washington, D.C.; Office of Child Development, 1970.

Hetherington, E. M. The effects of familial variables on sex typing, on parent–child similarity, and on imitation in children. In J. P. Hill (Ed.), *Minnesota Symposium on Child Psychology.* Minneapolis: University of Minnesota Press, 1967.

Hoffman, M. L. Father absence and conscience development. In F. Rebelsky & L. Dormon (Eds.), *Child development and behavior*(2nd ed.). New York: Knopf, 1973.

Kanter, R., & Furcher, L. A. (Eds.). Issue on alternative institutions. *Journal of Applied Behavioral Science,* 1973, *9,* 144–163.

Keniston, K. *The uncommitted: Alienated youth in American society.* New York: Dell Publishing, 1965.

Kornfein, M., Weisner, T. S., & Martin, J. C. Women into mothers: Experimental family lifestyles. In J. R. Chapman & M. J. Gates (Eds.), *Women into wives: The Legal and Economic Impact of Marriage.* Beverly Hills, Calif.: Sage Publications Inc., 1977.

Marsella, A. J. The effects of father presence and absence upon maternal attitudes. *Journal of Genetic Psychology,* 1974, *125,* 257–263.

Masnick, G., & Bane, M. J. *The nation's families: 1960–1990.* Cambridge, Mass.: Joint Center for Urban Studies of MIT and Harvard University, 1980.

McCord, J., McCord, W., & Thurber, E. Some effects of paternal absence on male children. *Journal of Abnormal and Social Psychology,* 1962, *64,* 361–369.

Mischel, W. Father absence and delay of gratification. *Journal of Abnormal and Social Psychology,* 1961, *63,* 116–124.

Pedersen, F. A. Does research on children in father-absent families yield information on father influences? *Family Coordinator,* 1976, *25,* 459–464.

Peirce, N. T. Census eliminates the 'typical' family. Editorial, *Los Angeles Times,* September 7, 1980

Rocheford, E. B. Values of alternative and traditional contemporary families. In J. Alexander (Chair), *Alternative families of the 1970's.* Symposium presented at the meetings of the American Orthopsychiatric Association, San Francisco, April 1978.

Santrock, J. W. Relation of type and onset of father absence to cognitive development. *Child Development,* 1972, *43,* 455–470.

Weisner, T. S. *As we choose: Family life styles, social class, and compliance behavior.* Unpublished manuscript. University of California, Los Angeles, 1981. (a)

Weisner, T. S. Authority, discipline and compliance styles in alternative families. In B. T. Eiduson (Chair), *The development of the child in alternative life styles: Years 1–3.* Symposium presented at the meeting of the Society for Research in Child Development, Boston, April 1981. (b)

Weisner, T. S., Bausano, M., & Kornfein, M. Pro-Natural California Families: Putting Family Ideals Into Practice. *Ethos,* in press.

Weisner, T. S., & Martin, J. C. Learning environments for infants: Communes and conventionally married families in California. *Alternative Lifestyles,* 1979, *2,* 201–241.

Zimmerman, I. L. Intellectual and cognitive development of children in alternative life styles. In B. T. Eiduson (Chair), *The development of the child in alternative life styles: Years 1–3.* Symposium presented at the meeting of the Society for Research in Child Development, Boston, April 1981.

Author Index

Numbers in *italics* denote pages with complete bibliographic information.

A

Aaronson, M. R., 242, *288*
Abbott, M. S., 82, *116*
Aberle, D. F., 200, *202*
Abrahams, B., 151, 154, *170* 175, 177, 181, *202*
Acland, H., 279, *287*
Adamson, J., 56, *68*
Adelberger, A. B., 272, *286*
Ainsworth, M. D. S., 55, *63*, 88, 89, 97, *111*, 339, *344*
Aldous, J., 20, 33, *38*, 104, *112*, 175, *202*, 217, *230*
Alexander, J., 316, 328, *345*
Alexander, J. W., 205, 212, *230*
Almquist, E. M., 32, *38*, 59, 60, *63*
Alpert, R., 236, *288*
Als, H., 130, *137*
Ambron, S., 93, *112*
Anderson, P., 97, *112*
Andres, D., 56, 57, 58, 59, *66*
Andrisani, P. J., *38*
Angrist, S. S., 32, *38*, 59, 60, *63*
Antill, J., 141, 142, 151, *171*
Arend, R., 89, 92, *112*, *114*
Aries, P., 3, *11*

Arkin, W., 36, *38*
Armstrong, R. F., 59, *64*
Arnold, F., 131, *135*
Astin, H. S., 60, *64*
Avgar, A., 227, 228, *230*
Avis, C., 81, *112*
Axelson, L. J., 58, 60, *67*

B

Bach, G. R., 275, *285*
Bahr, S. J., 27, *38*
Bailyn, L., 17, 24, 28, 29, *38*, 142, *170*
Baker-Ward, L., 93, 103, *115*
Bales, R. F., 4, *12*, 29, *41*, 206, *232*
Banducci, R., 59, 60, *64*
Bandura, A., 177, *202*
Bane, M. J., 13, 34, 38, *41*, 233, 279, *286*, *287*, 336, *346*
Barnes, R. D., 4, *11*
Barnett, M. A., 177, *202*, 219, *230*
Barrett, C., 32, *39*
Barry, W. A., 306, *313*
Baruch, G. K., 58, 59, 60, *64*
Baumrind, D., 93, *112*, 236, 242, 278, *286*, 292, *313*

Bear, R. M., 272, *286*
Beit-Hallahmi, B., 225, *230*
Bell, C. S., *39*
Beller, E., 82, *112*
Below, H. I., 60, *64*
Belsky, J., 62, *64,* 77, 80, 85, 86, 87, 88, 89, 92, 97, 100, 104, *112,* 130, *135*
Bem, S. L., 61, *64,* 121, 123, *135,* 140, 142, 145, 148, 150, 169, *170,* 177, 178, 179, *202,* 215, *230*
Berger, B., 328, *344*
Berger, M., 15, *39*
Berk, R. A., 27, *39*
Berk, S. F., 27, *39*
Berman, P. W., 5, *11*
Bernstein, B., 279, *286*
Best, F., 31, *39*
Bettelheim, B., 5, *11*
Biemiller, A., 81, *112*
Biller, H. B., 174, 175, 178, 179, *202, 204,* 272, *286,* 318, 337, *345*
Birnbaum, J. A., 24, *39,* 48, 56, 58, 59, 60, *64*
Blanchard, M., 53, *64,* 90, *112*
Blanchard, R. W., 318, *345*
Blau, P. M., 23, *39*
Blauner, R., 25, *39*
Blehar, M. C., 53, 55, *63, 64,* 89, 90, *112,* 339, *344*
Block, J., 220, *230*
Blois, M. S., 328, *345*
Blood, R. O., Jr., 51, *64,* 179, *202*
Borke, H., 178, *202,* 219, *230*
Borstelmann, L. J., 174, 175, *202*
Bott, E., *39*
Bowerman, C. E., 304, 305, *313*
Bowlby, J., 53, *64,* 88, *112*
Boyle, P., 84, 90, 96, *115*
Bradley-Johnson, S., 216, *232*
Brassard, J. A., 168, *170*
Brazelton, T. B., 5, *11,* 130, *137*
Bridge, R. G., 200, *202*
Brim, O. G., 337, *345*
Broderick, C., 304, *313*
Bronfenbrenner, U., 30, *39,* 76, 78, 98, 99, 104, 109, *112,* 175, 200, *202,* 217, 227, 228, *230*
Bronson, S. K., 9, *11,* 173, 197, *203,* 221, *231*
Brookhart, J., 53, *64*
Brophy, J. E., 272, *286*
Broverman, D. M., 60, *69*
Broverman, I. K., 60, *69*

Brown, D. G., 178, *202*
Brown, P., 176, *203*
Brown, S. E., 57, *64*
Brown, S. W., 58, 59, *64*
Brown, T., 205, 218, *232,* 290, 291, *313*
Brownlee, M., 87, 95, *113*
Bryson, J., 32, *39*
Bryson, R., 32, *39*
Bulatao, R. A., 131, *135*
Burchinal, L. B., 57, 58, 59, *64*
Buripakdi, C., 131, *135*
Burke, R., 55, *64*
Burton, R. V., 123, *137*

C

Cain, A., 304, *313*
Camara, K., 272, *287*
Cambier, A., 57, 59, *65*
Campbell, F., 93, *115*
Campbell, E. A., 200, *203*
Campbell, F. A., 87, 102, *115*
Campbell, J. D., 123, *137*
Carew, J., 83, 94, 95, *112, 113*
Carlsmith, L., 272, 273, *286*
Carlson, B. E., 178, 180, *203*
Castro, R. F., 244, *288*
Cavan, S., 328, *345*
Chandler, M. J., 177, *203*
Chapman, M., 304, 305, *313*
Chase-Lansdale, P. L., 52, 54, 55, 61, *67, 68,* 120, 121, 122, 123, 125, 126, *136,* 220, *231*
Chernovetz, M., 181, *203*
Cherry, D., 57, 58, *68*
Christman, K., 54, 55, *66*
Chu, C., 56, *64*
Chung, B. J., 131, *135*
Clark, R. A., 20, 32, *39*
Clarke, J. N., 320, *345*
Clarke-Stewart, K. A., 73, 82, 85, 90, 94, 95, 97, 98, 102, *112, 113,* 130, *135,* 168, *170*
Clarkson, F. E., 60, *69*
Cobb, J. A., 238, *287*
Cochran, M. M., 53, *64,* 80, 84, 87, 93, *112,* 168, *170*
Cohen, D., 279, *287*
Cohen, J., 316, 319, *345*
Cohen, S. E., 54, *65*
Cole, M., 337, *345*
Coleman, J. S., 200, *203,* 279, *286*
Colletta, N. D., 281, *286*

Congalton, A. A., 142, 150, *170*
Connell, D. B., 81, *112*
Corry, T., 117, 127, *135*
Corsini, D., 53, *67*
Cox, M., 6, *11*, 205, *231*, 234, *287*, 289, 290, 293, 296, 301, *313*
Cox, R., 6, *11*, 205, *231*, 234, *287*, 289, 290, 293, 296, 301, *313*
Cummings, E. M., 96, *112*
Cunningham, J., 141, 142, 151, *170*
Current Population Reports, 303, *313*
Curtis, E. A., 60, *68*
Curtis, R., 304, 305, *314*

D

David, T., 79, *115*
Dawson, F., 59, *65*
De Frain, J., 144, 154, 164, *170*, 174, 180, *203*, 212, 221, *230*
Dela-Pargola, S., 223, *230*
deLeeuw, L., 51, 57, 58, *69*
Delora, J. S., 320, *345*
Delora, J. R., 320, *345*
Delys, P., 178, *204*
Dempster-McClain, D., 31, *41*
Dickerscheidt, J. D., 130, *136*
Dino, G. A., 177, *202*, 219, *230*
Dits, A., 57, 59, *65*
Dixon, S., 130, *137*
Dobrofsky, L. R., 36, *38*
Donovan, W. L., 205, *231*
Dorval, B., 93, 103, *115*
Douvan, E., 25, 29, 38, *39*, 57, 58, 60, *65*
Doyle, A-B., 53, *65*, 88, *112*
Duberman, L., 304, 305, *313*
Dubin, R., 24, *39*
Dubnoff, S. J., 48, 61, *65*
Duncan, B., 23, *39*
Duncan, O. D., 23, *39*
Duncan, R. P., *39*
Durham, M., 17, 20, 27, *40*
Duvall, E. B., 58, *65*
Dyer, W. G., 23, *39*

E

Easterbrooks, M. A., 52, 54, *67*, 122, *136*
Egeland, B., 56, *69*, 88, 91, 92, 96, 98, *116*
Ehrenberg, D., 320, *345*

Eiduson, B. T., 174, *203*, 205, 212, *230*, 303, *313*, 315, 316, 317, 319, 325, 328, 331, 333, 336, *345*
Elder, G. H., Jr., 31, *39*
Emlen, A., 74, 83, 85, *113*
Eshleman, J. R., 320, *345*
Estes, D., 56, *69*
Etaugh, C., 52, 57, 61, *65*, 226, 228, *230*

F

Falender, C., 102, *113*
Farel, A. M., 51, *65*
Farley, J., 58, 59, *65*
Farran, D., 102, *113*, *114*
Farran, D. C., 53, *65*, 102, *115*
Fast, I., 304, *313*
Fawcett, J. T., 131, *135*
Featherman, D. L., 23, *39*, 272, *287*
Fein, G., 73, 82, *113*
Feld, S., 24, 25, *39*, *40*
Feldman, S. S., 5, *12*, 53, *65*, *67*, 151, 154, *170*, 175, 177, 181, *202*
Ferguson, D., 205, 218, *232*, 290, 291, *313*
Ferree, M. M., 23, 24, *39*
Ferri, E., 244, *286*
Field, T., 130, 132, *135*, 167, *170*, 173, *203*
Finkelman, J. J., 58, *65*
Fish, K. D., 59, *65*
Form, W. H., 25, *39*
Forsström, 117, 127, *135*
Forsythe, A., 336, *345*
Fosburg, S., 82, *113*
Foster, M., 15, *39*
Fox, N., 53, *65*
Fraiberg, S., 86, *113*
Franke, H. B., 58, *65*
Frankel, E., 57, 59, *65*
Frankie, G., 174, *203*
Freed, D., 205, *231*
Freenan, H., Jr., 87, 95, *113*
French, J. R. P., Jr., 25, *39*, *40*
Freud, S., 289, *313*
Fried, M. A., 25, *39*
Friedman, D., 81, *113*
Frieze, I., 60, *65*
Frodi, A. M., 117, 120, 125, 127, 131, 132, *135*, *136*, 205, 207, 210, 218, *231*
Frodi, M., 117, 120, 125, 127, 131, 132, *135*, *136*, 205, *231*
Frye, D., 53, *65*

Funkenstein, D. H., 272, *286*
Furcher, L. A., 328, *346*

G

Garbarino, J., 62, *65*
Garland, T. N., 16, 17, 26, *39, 42*
Gasser, R. D., 205, 220, *231,* 290, 291, *313*
Gay, J., 337, *345*
Gecas, V., 20, 32, 33, *39,* 179, *203*
George, E. I., 59, *65*
George, V., 244, *286,* 290, *313*
Gersick, K. E., 173, 174, *203,* 290, 291, *313*
Gerwirtz, J. L., 177, *203*
Gillis, G., 83, *113*
Gintis, H., 279, *287*
Glenn, N. D., 50, *65*
Glick, J. A., 337, *345*
Glick, P. C., 6, 9, *11,* 45, 46, 47, 48, 49, 62, *66,* 173, *203,* 233, *286*
Glorieux, J., 56, *66*
Gold, D., 56, 57, 58, 59, *66*
Goldberg, R. J., 56, *66*
Goldberg, W. A., 5, *11,* 205, *231*
Golden, M., 87, 95, *113*
Golden, M. M., 264, *287*
Goldfarb, W., 88, *113*
Goldstein, B., 32, *39*
Goodson, D., 81, *112*
Gorsuch, R. L., 236, *288*
Gottman, J. M., 269, *286*
Gough, H. G., 236, 280, *286*
Gould, R., 264, 266, *286*
Gove, F., 56, *69,* 88, 89, 91, 92, 96, 98, *112, 116*
Gowler, D., 28, *39*
Grant, C. W., 24, 29, *40*
Graham, P., 5, *11*
Green, C., 78, 79, 83, 84, 103, *116*
Greenberger, E., 100, *116*
Greenspan, S., 177, *203*
Gregory, I., 290, *313*
Greif, J. B., 205, *231*
Gronseth, E., 36, *40*
Grossi, M. T., 87, 95, *113*
Grossman, A. S., 30, *40*
Gunnarson, L., 87, 93, *113*
Gurin, G., 25, *40*
Gurin, P., 25, *40*
Gutmann, D., 140, *170*

H

Haas, M. B., 52, *68*
Hacker, H. M., 24, *40*
Hall, A., 83, *113*
Hall, F. T., 51, *66*
Hall, R., 17, 21, 23, *41*
Haller, M., 24, *40*
Hamblin, R. L., 51, *64*
Hand, H. B., 57, *66*
Hansson, R. O., 181, *203*
Harberg, E., 176, *203*
Hartley, R., 32, *40*
Hartley, R. E., 58, *66*
Hartup, W. W., 264, *286*
Haskins, R., 87, 102, *113, 115*
Hawkins, P., 83, *113*
Hayghe, H., 22, *40*
Heath, D. H., 218, *231*
Heber, R., 102, *113*
Heilbrun, A. B. Jr., 236, 280, *286*
Heilpern, E., 304, *313*
Heinicke, C., 81, *113*
Heinig, C., 51, 57, 58, *69*
Henderson, C. R., Jr., 227, 228, *230*
Herbert-Jackson, E., 93, *114*
Herzog, E., 245, *286,* 337, *345*
Hess, R. D., 272, *286*
Hetherington, E. M., 6, *11,* 62, 66, 96, *113,* 174, *203,* 205, *231,* 233, 234, 236, 272, 275, 284, 285, *287,* 289, 290, 293, 296, 301, *313,* 337, *346*
Heyns, B., 279, *287*
Hicks, M., 33, *38*
Hill, R., 17, 21, 23, *41,* 140, *170*
Hill, C. R., 27, *40,* 56, *66,* 76, 78, *113*
Hitchcock, E. A., 56, *68*
Hobson, C. J., 200, *203*
Hock, E., 53, 54, 55, 60, *64, 66,* 86, 87, 89, 97, 99, *113*
Hock, M., 54, 55, *66*
Hofferth, S. L., 50, *67,* 76, 105, *113*
Hoffman, L. W., 5, *11,* 13, 24, 27, 28, 31, 32, *40,* 51, 52, 56, 57, 58, 60, 61, 62, *66, 68,* 145, 165, *170,* 173, 174, 176, 200, *203,* 205, 215, 216, *231*
Hoffman, M. L., 217, 218, 219, *231,* 318, *346*
Hollingshead, A. B., 177, *203*
Holme, A., 52, *69*
Holmstrom, L. L., 17, 23, 30, *40,* 51, *66*
Holter, H., 26, *40*

Hornung, M., 264, *287*
Howard, J. A., 177, *202,* 219, *230*
Howes, C., 79, 80, 82, 84, 87, 90, 96, *113, 115*
Hubbell, U., 98, *114*
Hultsch, D. F., 145, 156, *170*
Hunt, J. G., 28, *40*
Hunt, L. L., 28, *40*
Huser, W. R., 24, 29, *40*
Hwang, C-P., 117, 120, 125, 127, 131, 132, *135, 136,* 205, *231*
Hyde, J. S., 175, 181, *203*

I

Ickes, W., 4, *11*
Institute for Social Research, 30, *40*
Irish, D. P., 304, 305, *313*
Iritani, T., 131, *135*

J

Jacklin, C. N., 175, *204*
Jencks, C., 279, *287*
Jenkins, R., 304, *313*
Joffee, C., 81, *114*
Johnson, C. L., 58, *66*
Johnson, M., 32, *39*
Jones, E., 80, *115*
Jones, J. B., 59, *66*
Jones, W. H., 181, *203*

K

Kagan, J., 53, *67,* 174, 175, 177, 178, *203,* 221, *231*
Kahn, A., 73, 74, 75, 107, *114*
Kahn, A. J., 37, *40*
Kahn, R. L., 24, 25, *40*
Kamerman, S., 37, *40,* 73, 74, 75, 107, *114*
Kanter, R., 15, *40,* 328, *346*
Kappel, B. E., 57, 59, *67*
Kearsley, R., 53, *67*
Keidel, K. C., 59, *67*
Keister, M., 83, *116*
Kelly, J. B., 233, 234, 262, 285, *288,* 290, 306, 311, *314*
Keniston, K., 107, *114,* 319, *346*
Kennell, J., 5, *11*
Kermoian, R., 96, *114*
King, K., 58, 60, *67*
King, L. M., 177, *202,* 219, *230*
Klaus, M. H., 5, *11*

Klein, V., 28, *41*
Kleinman, C., 106, *114*
Kliger, D., 51, 56, *67*
Kohlberg, L., 175, 176, *203,* 217, *231*
Kohn, M. L., 24, *40,* 242, *287*
Komarovsky, M., 50, *67*
Konner, M. J., 223, *232*
Kornfein, M., 319, 333, *346*
Kornhauser, A., 20, 25, *40*
Kreps, J., 36, *40*
Kritchevsky, S., 80, *115*
Krolick, G., 93, *116*
Kulka, R., 25, 29, 38, *39,* 48, 61, *65*

L

Lally, R., 103, *114*
Lamb, M. E., 5, 8, 9, *11,* 51, 52, 53, 54, 55, 56, 61, 62, *67, 68, 69,* 86, *115,* 117, 118, 120, 121, 122, 123, 125, 126, 127, 130, 131, 132, *135, 136,* 144, 168, *170,* 173, 197, *203,* 205, 207, 209, 210, 215, 218, 219, 220, 221, *231,* 289, *313*
Lambert, R. D., 57, 59, *67*
Lang, L., *42*
Layzer, J. I., 81, *112*
Lazar, I., 98, *114*
Leavitt, L. A., 205, *231*
Lee, R. B., 2, *12*
Lee, S-J., 131, *135*
Legge, K., 28, *39*
Lein, L., 17, 20, 27, *40,* 105, *114*
Leite, J., 120, *136*
Lemkin, J., 178, *203,* 221, *231*
Lenney, E., 61, *64,* 140, 145, *170*
Lessing, E. E., 272, *287*
Levin, H., 304, *314*
Levine, J. A., 118, *136,* 140, 165, *170,* 173, *203,* 205, 206, *232*
Lieberman, A. F., 53, *67,* 73, *114*
Lightfoot, S., 101, *114*
Lindbergh, C., 284, *288*
Lindsay, A., 81, *112*
Lippit, R., 101, *114*
Litwok, E., 82, *112*
Loeb, R. C., 176, *203*
Lott, B. E., 111, *114*
Lovell, L., 58, *64*
Lozoff, M. M., 220, *232*
Ludsteen, S. W., 59, *66*
Lushene, R., 236, *288*

M

Maccoby, E. E., 53, 62, *67,* 175, *204,* 304, *314*
MacPhee, D., 93, *115*
Macrae, J. W., 93, *114*
Main, M., 53, *64,* 90, *112*
Maioni, T. L., 264, *287*
Manion, J., 212, *232*
Mann, F. C., 20, 29, *41*
Manosevitz, M., 304, 305, *313*
Marsella, A. J., 318, *346*
Martensson, S., 105, *114*
Martin, B., 236, 255, *287*
Martin, J. C., 319, 323, 333, *346*
Martyna, W., 61, *64,* 145, *170*
Masnick, G., 13, 34, 38, *41,* 336, *346*
Matas, L., 89, *114*
Mattessich, P., 140, *170*
Maughan, B., 279, *288*
McAdams, D., 304, 305, *314*
McCord, J., 57, 58, *67,* 318, *346*
McCord, W., 57, 58, *67,* 318, *346*
McIntyre, J., 58, 60, *67*
McLaughlin, Q., 20, 29, *41*
McPartland, J., 200, *203*
Meadows, L., 284, *288*
Meier, H. C., 58, 60, *67*
Mendes, H. A., 173, *204,* 205, 212, *232,* 290, *313*
Messer, A., 304, *313*
Meyer, B., 176, *204*
Michael, W. B., 59, *66*
Michelson, S., 279, *287*
Michelson, W., 105, *114*
Miller, J., 24, *40*
Miller, K. A., 24, *40*
Miller, S. M., 58, *67*
Mills, J., 102, *115*
Mischel, W., 177, 178, *204,* 217, 220, *232,* 318, *346*
Moen, P., 22, 31, *41*
Molm, L. D., *41*
Money, J., 175, *204*
Moock, P. R., 200, *202*
Mood, A. M., 200, *203*
Moore, K. A., 50, *67*
Moore, T. W., 53, *67,* 86, *114*
Mortimer, J. T., 17, 20, 21, 23, 24, *41*
Moskowitz, D., 53, *62*
Mott, F. L., 30, *41*
Mott, P. E., 20, 29, *41*

Murray, H., 98, *114*
Mussen, P. H., 174, *204,* 217, 219, 221, *232*
Myrdal, A., 28, *41*

N

Nadler, J. H., 304, 306, *313*
Naegele, K. D., 200, *202*
Nash, S. C., 5, *12,* 151, 154, *170,* 175, 177, 181, *202*
Nelson, D. D., 58, 59, *67,* 272, *287*
Nestel, G., *38*
Noble, H., 32, *39*
Norton, A. J., 6, 9, *11,* 45, 46, 48, 49, 62, *66,* 233, *286*
Nowicki, S., Jr., 176, *204*
Nuttal, J., 216, *232*
Nye, F. I., 13, 20, 26, 28, 29, 31, *39, 40, 41, 42,* 52, 56, 58, 59, *66, 67, 68,* 145, 165, *170*

O

Oakley, A., 24, 31, *41*
O'Connell, J., 102, *114*
O'Connor, P., 29, *43*
Office of Assistant for Planning and Evaluation, 76, 78, *114*
Ogles, R. H., 56, *68*
Oldham, J., 32, *39*
O'Leary, S., 131, *136*
Oppenheimer, V. K., 29, *41*
Orthner, D. K., 205, 218, *232,* 290, 291, *313*
Oshman, H. P., 272, *287,* 304, 305, *313*
Osmond, M., 33, *38*
O'Toole, J., 36, *41*
Owen, M. T., 52, 54, 55, 61, *67, 68,* 120, 121, 122, 123, 125, 126, *136,* 220, *231*

P

Palmer, F. H., 57, *68,* 272, *287*
Papanek, H., *41*
Papousek, H., 80, *114*
Parke, R. D., 5, *12,* 123, 130, 131, *136,* 148, *170,* 173, *204,* 205, *232*
Parnes, H. S., 24, *41*
Parsons, J., 60, *65*
Parsons, T., 4, *12,* 29, *41,* 206, *232*
Parten, M. B., 240, 264, *287*
Patterson, A., 79, *115*
Patterson, G. R., 238, 258, *287*

Payne, D. E., 174, *204,* 221, *232*
Pedersen, F. A., 84, 85, *115,* 337, *346*
Peirce, N. T., 336, *346*
Perry, J. B., 56, *68,* 74, 8ɔ, *113*
Perry, L., 176, *203*
Peters, D., 72, 104, 107, *114*
Peterson, E. T., 60, *68*
Phillis, D. E., 175, 181, *203*
Piaget, J., 264, *287*
Piotrkowski, Chaya S., 15, *41*
Pleck, J. H., 4, 7, *12,* 26, 27, 28, 29, 31, 36,
　　42, 46, 50, 51, 62, *68,* 150, *170,* 173, 175,
　　176, *204*
Plemons, J. K., 140, 156, *170*
Policave, H. J., 87, 95, *113*
Poloma, M. M., 16, 17, 26, *42*
Porter, A., 83, 84, *113, 116*
Portnoy, F., 89, 90, *114*
Powell, D. R., 100, 101, *114, 115*
Power, T. G., 130, *136*
Pratt, M., 17, 20, 27, *40*
Prescott, E., 79, 80, 81, 84, *113, 115*
Price-Bonham, S., 179, *204*
Propper, A. M., 31, *42,* 57, 58, *68*
Puncel, C., 81, *113*

Q

Quinn, R. P., 15, 20, *42*

R

Rabin, A. I., 57, 59, *68,* 225, *230*
Radin, N., 134, *136,* 144, 145, 147, 154, 164,
　　168, *170,* 174, 179, 180, 199, 200, 201, *204,*
　　208, 212, 215, *232*
Ragozin, A., 53, *68*
Rainwater, L., 24, *42*
Rallings, E. M., 31, *42*
Ramey, C. T., 53, *65,* 87, 93, 102, 103, *113*
Rapoport, R., 15, 16, 17, 18, 23, 27, 31, 33, *42*
Rau, L., 236, *288*
Ray, R. S., 238, *287*
Rees, A. H., 57, *68,* 272, *287*
Reid, J. B., 240, *287*
Reid, W. J., 173, *204*
Rendina, I., 130, *136*
Renshaw, J., 18, *42*
Reuter, M. W., 174, 179, *204*
Rhodes, S., 104, *116*
Ricciuti, H. N., *69,* 85, *115*

Richmond, J., 48, *68*
Robinson, J., 26, 31, *42*
Rocheford, E. B., 317, 330, *346*
Roff, M., 264, *287*
Rohe, W., 79, *115*
Romer, N., 57, 58, *68*
Roopnarine, J. L., 53, *68,* 86, *115*
Rosche, M., 98, *114*
Rosenbluth, L., 87, 95, *113*
Rosenkrantz, P. S., 60, *69*
Rosman, A., 242, *287*
Rotter, J. B., 236, *287*
Rouman, J., 57, *68*
Rosenmayer, L., 24, *40*
Roy, P., 58, 59, 60, *68*
Royce, J., 98, *114*
Rubenstein, J. L., 79, 80, 82, 84, 85, 87, 90,
　　96, *113, 115*
Rubin, K. H., 264, *287*
Ruble, D., 60, *65*
Ruderman, F., 73, *116*
Ruopp, R., 81, 95, 108, *116*
Russell, G., 123, 134, *136,* 139, 141, 142, 143,
　　144, 147, 150, 151, 152, 161, 162, 164, *170,*
　　171, 173, 175, 198, 199, *204,* 215, 218, 230,
　　232
Rustad, M., 4, 7, *12,* 46, 50, 51, 62, *68*
Rutherford, E., 174, *204*
Rutherford, E. E., 219, *232*
Rutter, M., 5, *11, 12,* 262, 279, *288*

S

Safilios-Rothschild, C., 24, *42*
St. Johns-Parsons, D., 23, 27, 32, *42*
Sale, J., 81, *113*
Santrock, J. W., 173, 178, *204,* 275, 284, *288,*
　　290, 293, 294, 295, 296, 298, 302, 304, 305,
　　313, 314, 318, *346*
Saunders, M., 83, *116*
Sawin, D. B., 5, *12,* 131, *136,* 173, *204,* 205,
　　232
Sawyer, J., 150, *170*
Scanzoni, J., 22, 29, *42*
Schaefer, E. S., 242, *288*
Schlesinger, B., 220, *232,* 290, *314*
Schooler, C., 24, *40,* 58, *68*
Schreiner, M., 57, 59, *68*
Schroeder, M. P., 51, *66*
Schubert, J. B., 216, *232*
Schudson, M., 17, 20, 27, *40*

Schwarz, J. C., 53, *67*, 93, *116*
Scott, P., 51, 57, 58, *69*
Sears, P. S., 174, *204*, 275, *288*, 289, *314*
Sears, R. R., 217, *232*, 236, *288*, 304, *314*
Seeman, M., 25, *42*
Seligman, B. B., 25, *42*
Sells, S. B., 264, *287*
Shapiro, D., 30, *41*
Sharp, D. W., 337, *345*
Shaw, D. A., 238, *287*
Shea, J. R., 24, *41*
Sheehan, A. M., 82, *116*
Shepard, L. J., 29, *43*
Shepher, J., 225, 226, 227, *232*
Sherman, D., 62, *65*
Shinn, M., 272, 273, *288*
Shipman, V. C., 272, *286*
Sibbison, V., 86, *116*
Simmons, C., 89, 90, *114*
Siegel, A. E., 52, 56, 60, *68*
Singer, D. G., 264, *288*
Singer, J. L., 264, *288*
Skelly, 22, *43*
Slocum, W. L., 26, *42*
Smith, A. D., 173, *204*
Smith, H. C., 32, *42*, 60, *68*
Smith, M., 279, *287*
Smith, R. E., 13, *42*
Smith-Lovin, S.,18, *42*
Smokler, C. S., 58, *68*
Sobol, M. G., 13, 24, *42*
Somers, K., 53, *65*, 88, *112*
Sonquist, H., 179, *204*
Spanier, G. B., 244, *288*
Speilberger, C. D., 236, *288*
Spitz, R. A., 88, *116*
Spitz, R. S., 24, *41*
Sroufe, L., 89, 92, *112, 114, 116*
Stafford, F. P., 27, *40, 42*, 56, *66*
Staines, G. L., 15, 20, 29, *42, 43*
Stallings, J., 83, 84, *116*
Steers, R., 104, *116*
Steinberg, J., 117, 120, 125, 131, 132, *136*, 205, *231*
Steinberg, L., 77, 78, 79, 83, 84, 85, 86, 87, 88, 89, 92, 100, 103, *112, 116*
Steiner, G., 73, 74, *116*
Stephens, M., 178, *204*
Stephenson, G. R., 120, *136*
Stern, P. N., 304, *314*
Stingle, K. G., 177, *203*

Stolz, L. M., 52, 56, *68*
Stolzenberg, R. M., 18, 31, *43*
Stott, D. H., 59, *68*
Strickland, R., 93, *116*
Sudia, C. E., 245, *286*, 337, *345*
Sullivan, K., 82, *112*
Sutton-Smith, B., 264, *288*
Sweet, J. A., 13, *43*
Symons, D., 5, *12*
Szolai, A., 51, *68*

T

Tangri, S. S., 32, *43*, 59, 60, *69*, 176, *204*
Taylor, C. M., 205, 220, *231*, 290, 291, *313*
Thomas, M., 59, *65*
Thomas, R., 17, 20, 27, *40*
Thompson, R. A., 56, *69*
Thurber, E., 57, 58, *67*, 318, *346*
Tickameyer, A. S., 18, *42*
Tiger, L., 225, 226, 227, *232*
Todres, R., 220, *232*, 290, *314*
Torgoff, I., 220, *232*
Travers, J., 81, 95, 108, *116*
Tronick, E., 130, *137*
Tucker, N., 139, *171*
Tucker, P., 175, *204*

U

U.S. Department of Labor, 13, 21, 31, *43*
Urban Institute, 76, *116*
Urberg, K., 61, *67*

V

Vaughn, B., 56, *69*, 88, 91, 92, 96, 98, *116*
Veroff, J., 25, 29, 38, *39, 40*, 48, 61, *65*
Vickery, C., 27, 31, *43*
Visher, E., 304, 306, *314*
Visher, J., 304, 306, *314*
Vogel, S. R., 60, *69*
Voydanoff, P., 16, *43*

W

Waite, L. J., 18, 31, *43*
Waldman, E., *43*
Walker, A., 97, *112*
Walker, K. E., 31, *43*, 51, 58, *69*
Wall, S., 55, *63*, 339, *344*

Wallerstein, J. S., 233, 234, 262, 285, *288*, 290, 306, 311, *314*
Wallston, B. S., 15, *39*
Warshak, P., 284, *288*
Warshak, R. A., 173, 178, *204*, 290, 293, 294, 295, 296, 298, 302, *313, 314*
Warwick, D. P., 20, 29, *41*
Waters, E., 55, *63*, 89, *116*, 339, *344*
Watson, C., 61, *64*, 145, *170*, 178, *202*
Weil, M. W., 51, *69*
Weiner, S., 83, *113*
Weinfeld, F. D., 200, *203*
Weingarten, K., 27, 29, *43*
Weinraub, M., 120, *136*
Weir, T., 55, *64*
Weisner, T. S., 174, *203*, 316, 319, 323, 332, 333, *345, 346*
Weiss, H., 17, 20, 27, *40*
Weiss, R., 233, *288*
West, M. M., 223, *232*
Westinghouse Learning Corporation and Westat Research, Inc., 82, *116*
White, I., 22, *43*
White, K., 60, *69*
Whitmarsh, R. E., 59, *69*
Wichern, F., 176, *204*
Wilcox, M., 83, *113*
Wilding, P., 244, *286*, 290, *313*
Wilensky, H. L., 31, 34, *43*
Willis, A., 53, *69*
Willmott, P., 20, 21, 26, 28, 31, *43*
Wilson, K., 304, 305, *314*

Wippman, J., 89, *116*
Wittig, B., 88, 89, *111*
Wolfe, D. M., 179, *202*
Woods, M., 31, *43*, 57, 58, *69*
Work in America, 20, 36, *43*
Working Family Project, 17, *43*
World of Work Report, *43*
Wu, T-S., 131, *135*
Wynn, R. L., 90, *116*

Y

Yankelovich, *43*
Yarrow, L. J., 84, 85, *115*
Yarrow, M. R., 51, 57, 58, *69*, 123, *137*
Yeats, K., 93, *115*
Yogman, M. W., 8, *12*, 130, *137*
York, R. L., 200, *203*
Young, M., 20, 21, 26, 28, 31, *43*
Yudkin, S., 52, *69*

Z

Zagorin, S. W., 272, *287*
Zajonc, R. B., 273, *288*
Zeiss, A., 178, *204*, 220, *232*
Zeiss, R., 178, *204*, 220, *232*
Zelazo, P., 53, *67*
Zeller, F. A., 24, *41*
Zimmerman, I., 303, *313*
Zissis, C., 60, *69*
Zurcher, L., 304, 305, *314*

Subject Index

A

Abortion, 335
Absenteeism, work related, 104
Academic curriculum, 81–82
Academic ability, 108–109, 342
Achievement, 24–25, 32, 32–33, 56, 59, 60, 63, 95, 98, 209, 217, 218, 219–221, 229, 241, 272, 276–277, 321–322, 330
Adoptive fathers, 205–206
Affection, parental (see also Warmth, Nurturance), 82, 121, 132–133, 205, 242, 246, 252, 265–256, 284, 304, 337
Age segregation, 82, 92
Aggression, 79–80, 92, 93, 101, 238, 239, 241, 242, 254–255, 257–258, 261, 267–268, 270–271, 271–272, 276, 277, 300–301, 343
Agricultural work, 225
Ambition, 32–33
Ambivalence, 97, 304
Androgyny, 150–156, 174, 179–180, 181, 197–198, 212, 221, 239–240, 275, 276–277, 301–302
Anger, 97, 240, 258–259, 265–266, 282, 292, 293, 294, 294, 299, 306, 307, 308, 309, 310
Antiauthority, parental, 317–318
Antimaterialism, parental, 317–318

Antisocial behavior, 83–84
Anxiety, 24, 90, 101, 240, 246, 259, 260, 263–264, 265–266, 271–272, 277, 281, 282, 292, 293, 294, 296, 297, 299, 306, 308, 309, 310, 338
Apathy, 240
Appearance, 297
Assertiveness, 200, 300–301, 337
Attachment, 97
Attachment, anxious, 88
Attachment, anxious-avoidant, 89, 90, 91–92, 95–96
Attachment, anxious resistant, 89
Attachment, secure, 88, 89
Attachment, child-mother, 53–54, 90–91
Attachment, preferential, 53, 88
Attentiveness, parental, 84, 267–268, 292, 301, 324, 335
Attitudes, parental, 24–25, 55, 97–98, 118–119, 122–123, 134, 236
Attitudes, prenatal, 126, 129
Australian families, 8, 139–171
Authoritarian parenting, 103, 292
Authoritative parenting, 93, 292
Authority, parental, 320–321, 332
Autonomy, 81–82, 107, 175–176, 252
Availability, parental, 143, 182, 186, 187, 189, 208, 209–211, 213, 214, 215, 227, 237, 301

B

Baby-sitters, 87–88, 89–90
Behavior, noxious, 238–239, 257–258, 259, 268
Behavior problems, child's, 248–249, 262, 263, 335–336
Behavioral responsiveness, 123
Belgian families, 57
Birth, 148, 313, 332, 335, 339, 342
  fathers presence, 166, 215
Birth control, 45–46
Birth order, 85
Black families, 45–46, 62, 81–82, 107
Bonding, 147, 159
Breastfeeding, 132, 147, 165–166, 323, 332

C

Career orientation, 14, 146, 218, 220
Career pressures (see also Work-family strains), 158–159
Caregivers, 129–130, 327, 328
Caregivers, training of, 106, 109, 110
Caregiving, 3–4, 55, 108, 121, 129, 132, 133, 141, 143–144, 144–145, 147, 156, 161, 164–165, 215, 244–245, 324, 325, 335, 339
Caregiving, extrafamilial, 4, 5–6, 71–111
Caregiving, primary, 129
Caregiving roles, 104, 140, 159, 163–164, 165
Center-reared children, 94
Child abuse, 62, 168
Child care (see also Caregiving), 20, 26–27, 27–28, 35, 50–51, 51, 55–56, 61–62, 72, 75, 102–103, 104, 106, 118, 122, 125–126, 135, 139–140, 144–145, 146, 148, 150, 155, 160–161, 162, 165, 168, 182, 184, 186, 187, 188, 190, 191, 208, 245, 334–335
Child care, commitment to, 20–21, 109, 162, 166
Child care, extrafamilial, 7–8, 71–111
Child care, federal support of, 73
Child rearing (see Child care, Caregiving), 4–5, 32, 30–33, 52, 122–123, 129–130, 132, 141–142, 181–184, 205–232, 250–251, 282, 283, 302–303
Child rearing, cost of, 198–199
Child rearing, pressure of, 195–196
Child rearing attitudes, 317–346
Childbearing, period of, 18

Childbirth (see also Birth), 323
  attitudes towards, 166
Childbirth, effect of, 119
Cognition (see also Achievement), 87, 175, 176, 192, 193, 201, 236, 264, 272–279
Cognitive development, 9, 86, 95, 98, 109, 199, 278
Cognitive-educational handicaps, 87
Cognitive stimulation, 79, 223
Communal living, 10, 174, 205, 315–316
Communication, parent-child, 110, 217, 218, 220, 237, 252, 283–284
Communication, parent-caregiver, 100, 101–102
Community Facilities Act, 74
Community organizations, 106
Community services, 33–34
Competence, 247, 249–250, 259, 264, 281–282
Competence, feelings of, 24–25
Competition, parental, 82, 282
Conflict, 159, 237, 262, 273–274
Conformity, 92, 309, 310
Consistency, parental, 96–97, 101, 102–103, 252, 283–284
Contact, parent-child, 90, 109, 120, 121, 131, 267–268, 335, 340
Control, parental, 25, 80–81, 103–103, 108, 175–176, 217, 223, 229, 237, 243, 252, 253, 260, 264, 278, 281–282, 292, 295–296, 302
Control, locus of, 209, 218, 219–221
Cooperation, 81, 88–89, 90, 92, 93–94, 94, 293, 294
Coping, parental, 234, 244–251
Creativity, 109, 337
Curiosity, child's, 101, 241
Custodial fathers, 244, 281–282, 285
Custodial mothers, 244, 284, 285
Custodial parents, 6, 262, 289, 290, 302–303, 312
Custodial parent, family structures, 297–298
Custodial parent, opposite-sex-child, 290, 297–298
Custodial parent, same-sex-child, 290

D

Day care, 71–116, 289–290, 290–291
  center-based, 177–178, 180–181, 225–226, 227–228
  cost of, 78
  ecology of, 99–108

effects of, 83, 85, 99
flexible hours, 83
full-time vs part-time, 80, 82
governmental support of, 107
licensed, 82
location, 83
nonprofit, 79
rate of use, 77-78
registration, 82
stability, 83
rearing, 87, 89
referrals, 82-83
training, 82-83
Decision making, parental, 29, 174, 179, 179-
    180, 181-182, 182, 183, 184, 185, 186,
    187, 188, 189, 190, 191, 208, 209-211,
    213, 214, 215, 276-277
Dependency, 217, 238, 258, 270, 271-272,
    275, 276, 321
Depression, 240, 245-246, 246, 249-250,
    258-259, 259, 265-266, 282, 306
Desertion, 337
Destructive behavior, 79-80, 277
Didactic style, parental, 191, 192, 193, 201,
    223, 325
Discipline, parental (see also Control), 81-82,
    109-110, 132-133, 178, 179-180, 181-
    182, 208, 236, 253-254, 279, 280, 324-
    325, 329, 332
Divorce, 5-6, 9-10, 48, 62, 96-97, 108, 175-
    176, 205-206, 223, 233-288, 305, 310-
    311, 319-320, 342
    economic conditions of, 234
    emotional conditions of, 234
    environmental conditions of, 234
    interpersonal problems, 248-250
    intimate relations after, 244, 248-250, 250-
        251
    visitation after, 250-251
Divorced fathers, 205, 244, 245
Druze families, 223-225, 207-208
    birthrate among, 223
Druze fathers, 225, 228-229
Dual career families, 16-17, 26-27
Dual earner families, 6-7, 16-17, 26-27

E

Economic security, 21-22
Economic stress, 236, 237, 244, 245
Economic support, 4-5, 139
Education, 56-57, 149, 224, 244-245, 319, 333

Educational goals, 332
Educational involvement, 92
Educational processes, 225-226
Educational qualifications, 49
Effectiveness, feelings of (see Control), 25
Emotional development, 86, 88, 88-92, 90, 98,
    261
Emotional relationships, 28, 236
Emotional security, 88, 96
Emotional support, 5-6, 50, 51, 139, 220, 237
Emotionally disturbed children, 263-264
Empathy, 177, 192, 209, 217, 218, 219, 229,
    229-230
Employed mothers (see Maternal employment)
Employment, 146, 147, 155, 161, 162
Employment, satisfaction with, 237
Employment roles, 164-165
Employment statistics, maternal, 45-46
Expectations, parental, 96, 192
Exploratory activity, childs, 90, 95-96
Expressiveness, 103, 217, 218, 220, 297

F

Families, blue-collar, 22-23, 32-33
Family, economic needs of, 13, 14, 18-26, 145,
    155, 103-104
Family, effect of church on, 34-35
Family, effect of economic system on, 34-35
Family, effect of political system on, 34-35
Family, effect of society on, 15, 34-37
Family, relationship to work, 14, 14-15
Family, size of, 18, 31-32, 48-49
Family, two provider, 13-43
Family conflicts, 20, 260-262, 306
Family day care, 77-85
Family disorganization, 236, 237, 244, 273-274
Family functioning, 18-19, 46, 105, 251-263
Family history, 317-346
Family milieu, current, 317-346
Family models, 315-316
Family organization, 3, 6, 142, 234, 278
Family relationships, 141, 158, 163, 265-266,
    285
Family stability, 53-54
Family structure (see Family organization), 292,
    293, 295-296, 297-298, 312
Family support system, 97-98
Fantasy, child's, 240, 242, 263-264, 266
Father absence, 83, 85, 91, 174, 235, 249-250,
    289, 305

Father-child relationships, 139, 155–156, 158, 159, 163, 167, 169, 209, 263, 295
Father custody (see Custody), 289–314
Father-son relationship, 57–58, 254–255
Fathers, child's perception of, 209, 221–223
  custody seeking, 174
  primary caregiving, 173–205
  role of (see Paternal role), 206, 218–219, 246–247
  perceptions of, 181–184
Female hormones, 4–5
Female roles, 2, 3, 7, 8, 9, 13 16, 36, 38, 45, 46, 47, 48, 50–51, 59–60, 61–62, 63
Female role, changing of, 7–8
Femininity (see also Female role), 150–156, 158, 175–176, 181, 184, 185, 193–194, 197–198, 199, 214, 215, 217, 229, 275, 276, 297, 300–301, 301–302
Fertility rate, 48–49
Financial status, 321, 323
Financial stress, 157, 282
Financial support, 250–251

G

Gender development, 209, 221–223
Gender differences (see Sex differences), 119, 130–131, 132
Gender identity, 4–5, 61, 176–177, 197–198
Gender role (see also Femininity, Masculinity), 217
Geographical mobility, 32, 33, 35
Grandparents, 180, 280, 319–320, 321, 322–323, 334
  dependency on, 321
  emotional support of, 280
Guilt, 24, 51, 52, 169, 195, 237, 240, 246, 251–252, 262, 265–266

H

Head Start, 73
Helplessness, 258–259, 259, 282
Heterosexual relationships, 4, 236, 247, 247–248, 249–250
High-risk environments, 91, 92
Home births, 323
Home care, 77–85
Home reared children, 87, 89
Homosexuality, 160–161, 168, 247–248
Hostility, interpersonal, 5–6, 93, 101, 103, 262, 265–266, 270, 343

Husband-wife conflict (see Marital conflict), 260, 261, 327–328
Husband-wife relationship (see Marital relationship), 104, 156–157, 169

I

Identification, filial, 6, 24–25, 174, 218, 221, 244, 247, 304–305, 321–322, 328
Illness, 323–324, 335–336, 342
Immaturity, 261, 270
Impulsivity, child's, 92, 264
Incest, 160–161, 168
Incompatibility, Marital (see Marital relationships, Marital conflict), 327–328
Independence, 32, 61, 158, 169, 209, 217, 218, 219–221, 229, 238, 276–277, 292, 294, 299, 308, 309, 310
Infant, resentment of, 121, 122, 123, 126–127
Infant-father attachment, 119, 123
Infant-mother attachment, 60, 91, 98, 119
Inhibition, child's, 239, 254–255, 277
Instructional interactions (see Didactic style), 95–96
Intellect (see Cognition)
Intellectual ability, 56, 81, 82, 88, 98, 188, 198, 220, 327, 331, 341
Intellectual development, 86–88, 199, 272–275
Intellectual risk, 338
Interaction, parent-child, 83–84, 90–91, 97, 102, 117, 119, 121, 122, 124–125, 125–126, 126, 129–130, 131, 132, 133, 134, 135, 143–144, 144, 154, 155, 159, 168, 245, 255–256, 258–259, 260
Interview measures, value of, 123–124
Intimacy, marital, 249–250
Intimate relationships, 244, 250–251
Involvement, parental, 133–134, 144–145, 209–211, 213, 215
Israeli families, 57, 205–230

J,K

Joint custody, 205
Kibbutz families, 207–208
Kibbutz fathers, 228–229
Kibbutzïm, 206, 223, 225–228

L

Labor, division of, 26, 26–28, 32, 120, 164
Language development, 95–96, 109

Loneliness, 59, 249, 281
Loss, sense of, 246
Love, 139, 175, 220, 222–223, 240, 249–250
Lower-class families, 28–29, 50, 57–58, 60, 73, 82, 87, 87–88, 200–201, 281–282

M

Male role (see also Masculinity), 2, 7, 8, 9, 13, 16, 36, 38, 46, 50, 59–60, 61–62, 63, 173
Male role, changing of, 7–8
Marital conflict, 233, 260–261, 261, 262, 263, 274, 278, 283, 306
Marital relationship (see Husband-wife relationship), 2, 5–6, 14–15, 26, 28–30, 52, 104, 140, 156, 159, 161, 276–277, 283, 305, 306
Marital roles, 20, 158
Marital satisfaction, 33–34, 283
Masculinity, 150–156, 158, 175–176, 176, 181, 184, 185, 186, 192, 193–194, 197–198, 199, 201–202, 211, 214, 215, 217, 218, 221, 222, 229, 275, 276–277, 277, 297, 300–301, 301–302
Mathematical ability (see also Achievement, Cognition, Intellect), 274, 275
Materialism, 320–321
Maternal adjustment, 258–259
Maternal attitudes, 126–127, 276–277
Maternal behavior, 8, 55, 102, 119, 130, 135
Maternal control (see also Control), 273–274
Maternal employment, 4, 5–6, 6, 7, 14, 24, 32, 32–33, 45–69, 145, 146–147, 167, 173, 177, 178, 180–181, 194, 196–197, 205, 206, 215–216, 216, 248–249, 276–277, 281–282, 321, 326, 331, 334
Maternal employment, economic necessity for, 47–48, 168
Maternal employment, effects on children, 52–60
Maternal employment, personal reasons for, 48–49
Maternal nurturance (see Nurturance, Warmth), 186–188, 276–277, 278
Maternal punitiveness, 188, 190
Maternal role, 10–11, 16, 86, 117, 144, 164, 165, 186–187, 218–219, 258–259, 259, 329
Maternal self esteem, 48
Maturity, 218, 237, 276–277, 278, 292, 293–294, 294, 299, 307, 308, 309, 310
Mental health, 24–25, 338

Middle-class, 28–29, 32–33, 48, 50, 56–57, 57–58, 59, 60, 76, 108, 119, 119–120, 142, 177, 196, 196–197, 198, 200–201, 208, 235, 281–282, 285, 291, 303, 307, 315–316, 331
Modeling (see also Identification), 10–11, 32, 57–58, 59–60, 145, 168, 174, 176, 177, 199, 199–200, 211, 212, 214, 215, 216–217, 220, 222–223, 224, 226–227, 229, 267–268, 272, 273, 276, 301, 302, 306, 316, 321, 323
Moral internalization, 219
Mothers, custodial, 233, 246, 289–314
    overprotective, 277
    role of (see Maternal role), 158–159, 218–219
    single and employed, 62
Mother-child interaction, 84, 102, 260, 280
Mother-child relationships, 88, 91, 95–96, 121–122, 134, 139, 147, 159, 163–164, 169, 237, 251, 262, 295
Mother-daughter relationships, 284
Mother-reared infants, 87–88, 89–90
Mother-son relationships, 245–246, 261

N

Noncustodial parents, 262, 294, 295
Nonintact families, 205–206
Nonfamilial child care (see Day care), 71–72
Nontraditional families, 45, 58, 72, 76, 106, 108, 117, 119, 119–120, 122–123, 125–132, 139–140, 141, 142, 145, 147, 148, 156–161, 161–169, 174–177, 200–201, 205, 209, 212, 215, 217, 218, 221, 337
Nontraditional lifestyles, 122, 122–123, 125, 129, 130–131, 131, 134, 163–164, 216, 319
Nursery school, 80, 236, 245, 332
Nurturance, parental (see also Warmth), 82, 139, 145, 150, 175, 179, 184, 205, 208, 209–211, 212, 213, 214, 215, 219, 220, 221, 221–222, 224, 225–226, 227, 228, 229–230, 237, 252, 260, 270, 278, 302, 337

P

Parent-caregiver communication, 100, 101–102
Parent-child conflict, 260–261, 262, 263, 278, 304
Parent-child interaction, 56–57, 140, 143–144, 144, 167, 168, 168–169, 235–236, 289–314, 292

Parent-child relationships, 14–15, 57–58, 103–104, 244, 251–260
Parental attitudes, 103, 122–129, 290–291
Parental availiability (see Availability)
Parental behavior (see Caregiving), 5, 118–119, 121, 122, 129–130, 131, 1–12, 132, 133, 145, 176–177, 196, 274, 298
Parental buffering, 262–263
Parental education, 85, 102–103
Parental employment, 140, 146–147, 318
Parental leave, 8, 118, 122, 126, 132
Parental responsibilities, 117, 119, 129, 143
Parental roles, 10–11, 32–33, 140, 141–142, 144, 146–147, 148–149, 150–156, 155, 158, 166, 169, 259, 283, 317, 318
Parental satisfaction, 33–34, 118–119
Parental sensitivity, 52, 122–123, 175–176, 177
Parental style, psychological origins, 134
Parental values, 32–33, 317–346
Parenthood, evaluation of, 120, 121, 122, 123, 125–128, 134
Parenthood, satisfaction with, 121, 126–127, 218
Parenting skills, 258–259, 280–281, 317
Parenting strategies, 292, 293–294, 296
Parenting styles, 293–294, 298–300
Parents Without Partners, 106, 291
Paternal availability (see also Availability), 179, 237, 273–274, 275, 276–277, 277, 278
Paternal behavior, 8, 119, 130, 135, 211, 218, 224, 227
Paternal caretaking (see also Caregiving), 124, 127–128, 190, 196
Paternal control (see also Control), 273–274
Paternal custody (see Custody, Father custody), 178, 205, 212
Paternal dominance, 276–277
Paternal hostility, 277
Paternal involvement, 8–9, 117–137, 181, 181–182, 182, 183, 186, 193, 196–197, 205–232
Paternal nurturance (see also Warmth, Nurturance), 186–188, 174, 190, 221, 273–274, 275, 276–277
Paternal punitiveness, 186–188, 189
Paternal responsibility, 8, 179–180
Paternal role (see also Father), 10–11, 108, 165, 186–187, 188, 218–219, 225
Paternal satisfaction, 122–123, 210, 218, 225
Peer relationships, 49, 79, 82, 83, 84, 88–89, 91–92, 92, 93, 94, 96, 108–109, 157, 161, 164, 167, 169, 176, 200, 236, 243, 260, 263–264, 264–265, 265, 266, 267–268, 269, 270, 270–271, 276, 319, 328, 329, 330
Peers, age-segregated, 82, 92
Permissiveness, parental, 237, 292, 295–296, 300, 343
Physical care (see also Caregiving), 179, 185, 209–211, 213, 214, 215, 224, 226–227, 227
Play, 87, 93, 95–96, 96, 102, 108–109, 120–121, 130, 132–133, 143–144, 144, 150, 160–161, 167, 238, 240, 244–245, 258, 261, 263–264, 268, 276, 284, 300–301, 302, 324, 337, 340, 343, 344
Poverty, 47
Pregnancy, 126–127, 162, 333
Pregnancy, motivation for, 333
Pregnancy, unwanted, 337
Preschool child care, 144–145
Preschool children, 9, 31–32, 52–57, 79–80, 165, 173, 176–177, 177, 179, 180, 196, 199–200, 200, 201, 233, 254–255, 270, 272, 275, 281–282, 285, 336
Primary caregiving, 139–140, 193, 193–194, 208–324
Problem-solving abilities, 88–89, 234
Professional families (see also Dual Career Families, Middle Class Families), 30, 142, 163
Prosocial behavior, 93, 94–95, 239, 241, 254–255
Psychoanalytic theory, 88, 302
Psychological adjustment, child's, 57–58, 58–59, 63
Psychological availability (see also Availability), 91–92
Punitiveness, parental, 193, 200, 221–222, 222–223

R

Rearing Environment, predictability of, 96–97, 100–101
Rejection, parental, 103, 220
Religion, 224, 325, 327, 329, 332
Remarriage, 281–285, 319–320
Resentment of child, 121, 250–251, 282, 302
Responsibility, parental, 26–27, 108–109, 122, 125–126, 132, 139–140, 141, 165, 199–200, 208, 243, 278, 281–282
Responsiveness, parental, 81, 119, 120–121, 131, 243, 324, 339

Restrictiveness, parental, 273–274, 276–277,
277
Role overload, 31, 32, 33, 61–62
Role sharing, 5, 173–205, 206
Role strain, 50, 51

S

School, child in (see also Achievement), 261,
263–272, 271–272, 278–279
Self-actualization, 216, 229–230
Self concept, 50, 140, 153–154, 155, 218, 244,
246
Self-control, 32–33, 218, 239, 254–255, 261,
264, 277–279
Self-doubt, 258–259
Self-esteem, 24–25, 32–33, 50, 51, 52, 58, 59,
158, 163–164, 167, 169, 217, 237, 247,
247–248, 249–250, 259, 260, 281, 292,
293, 294, 296, 297, 298, 299, 307, 308,
309, 310
Separation-reunion responses, 54, 89–90, 97,
233–288, 342
Sex differences, 32, 85, 131–132, 135, 140,
148, 160–161, 181, 192, 208–210, 218,
222, 225–226, 311, 340
Sex roles, 3–4, 4–5, 8, 10–11, 30, 50, 57,
57–58, 59–60, 60, 61, 99, 104–105, 117–
118, 112–123, 126, 131, 133–134, 134,
139, 140, 145, 150, 151–152, 152, 153,
154, 155, 158, 162–163, 165, 166, 168,
169, 174–175, 175, 176–177, 179, 184,
185–186, 186, 192–193, 197–198, 199,
212, 221, 223, 229, 236, 237, 239–240,
244, 270, 275–277, 277
Sexual dysfunction, 247
Sexual intercourse (see Heterosexuality,
Homosexuality), 249–250, 250
Sexuality, attitudes towards, 332
Sibling relationships, 109–110, 180–181, 291,
303, 311, 319–320
Single-earner families, 33–34
Single fathers, 205–206, 218
Single mothers, 10, 262, 315–316
Single parents, 9, 76, 93, 96–97, 99, 102–103,
105, 108, 244, 260, 262, 263, 264, 268,
272, 273, 275, 276, 289, 294, 303, 306,
310, 311, 312
Sociability, 292, 293–294, 299, 308, 309, 310
Social adjustment, 261–262, 285
Social class (see also Middle Class Families,
Lower Class Families), 30, 50, 181–182,
183, 198, 291, 303

Social competence, 94, 95–96, 296, 297
Social conformity, 292, 293–294, 299, 308, 309
Social contract families (see Unwed parents),
205, 315–316
Social Security Act, 74
Social structure, 99–100, 104
Social support, 16, 23–24, 122, 124–125, 160–
161, 169
Socialization, 32–34, 63, 92, 100, 130–131,
134, 140, 167, 168, 173, 174, 179, 181–
182, 186, 187, 188, 189, 190, 191, 208,
209–211, 213, 214, 215, 219, 225–226
Stepfather families, 29
Stepfathers, 283–284
Stepmother, folklore and the, 303–307
Stepmother families, 289–314
Stepparents, 245–250, 281–285
Stepsiblings, 311
Stress, 96–97, 104, 106, 234, 237, 244–251,
259, 260, 261, 263–264, 270, 271–272,
274, 278, 279, 280, 281, 282, 285, 319–
320, 336, 338, 342
Support systems, 103, 234, 279–281, 283–284,
294, 302–303
Swedish families, 8, 117–135

T

Teachers, 82, 83, 84, 94–95, 96–97, 191, 270–
271
Toilet-training, 101, 324
Traditional families, 2–6, 18–19, 45, 71, 75,
104–105, 118, 119–120, 122, 125–126,
129, 130, 131, 140, 143, 144, 147, 148,
151–152, 162, 163, 167, 168, 169, 174–
175, 176, 178, 200–201, 205, 209, 219,
221, 223, 224, 244
Traditional fathers, 122–123, 127–128, 129,
143–144, 167, 174, 177, 193–194, 197–
198, 205–206, 211, 212, 217, 220, 293
Traditional mothers, 99, 143–144, 167, 292
Traditional parents, 122, 123, 125, 131, 132,
134, 175, 199–200

U,V

Unemployed mothers, 48, 54–55
Unemployment, 146, 165, 330–331
Unwed parents (see Social contract families),
10, 174, 212, 333–334
Upper-class families (see also Social Class), 59,
60, 315–316

Verbal ability (see also Achievement), 189–190, 190–191, 201

W

Warmth, parental, 208, 222–223, 262–263, 292, 294, 299, 307, 308, 309, 310, 324
Welfare system, 72, 107, 321, 333, 334

Widowhood, 337
Women's Movement, 48, 107, 111, 118, 326
Work, evaluation of, 121, 122, 123, 126, 127–128, 129, 134
Work-family relationship, 15–18, 104–105
Work-family strains, 16–17, 29, 104–105
Working-class (see also Social Class, Lower Class Families), 16–17, 27, 30, 50, 163
Works Project Administration, 73–74

DATE DUE
